The Disfranchisement Myth

The Disfranchisement Myth

Poor Whites and Suffrage

Restriction in Alabama

GLENN FELDMAN

The University of Georgia Press • Athens and London

© 2004 by the University of Georgia Press
Athens, Georgia 30602
All rights reserved
Set in Minion by Bookcomp, Inc.
Printed and bound by Maple-Vail

The paper in this book meets the guidelines for
permanence and durability of the Committee on
Production Guidelines for Book Longevity of the
Council on Library Resources.

Printed in the United States of America
08   07   06   05   04   C   5   4   3   2   1

Library of Congress Cataloging-in-Publication Data

Feldman, Glenn.
The disfranchisement myth : poor whites and suffrage
restriction in Alabama / Glenn Feldman.
p.   cm.
Includes bibliographical references and index.
ISBN 0-8203-2615-1 (alk. paper)
1. Suffrage—Alabama—History. 2. Constitutional
history—Alabama. 3. African Americans—Suffrage—
Alabama—History. 4. Racism—Alabama—History.
5. Alabama—Race relations—History. 6. Alabama—
Politics and government—1865–1950. I. Title.
JQ4590.F45 2004
324.6'2'0976109041—dc22   2003022117

British Library Cataloging-in-Publication Data available

For my precious "Beka-Beka,"
who taught me what love was . . . all over again

The citizens of any society are very often the victims.
But in many ways, they are not only compliant,
they are complicitors.

It's important for us to remind ourselves that it's not just
the people at the top who are the enemies of the people,
but [often] the people themselves.

WOLE SOYINKA

CONTENTS

MAPS

ACKNOWLEDGMENTS

As with any project of this nature, I have a great number of people to thank. First, I would like to thank Derek Krissoff, history editor at the University of Georgia Press, for his intelligence and encouragement and for being an absolute delight with whom to work. Nicole Mitchell, Nancy Grayson, and Jon Davies have also been a pleasure to work with at the Press. I also thank the University of Georgia Press's two external readers for the manuscript and copyeditor Barb Wojhoski, who supplied excellent suggestions and comments that clearly strengthened the work. I owe Melody P. Izard a tremendous debt of gratitude for her technical expertise with the maps and graphics. A whole cadre of archivists and librarians lent their aid, in particular: Ken Tilley, John Hardin, Debbie Pendleton, Ed Bridges, and especially Norwood Kerr, at the Alabama Department of Archives and History; Jim Baggett at the Birmingham Public Library Archives; Liz Wells at the Special Collections Department at Samford University; Jean Spradlin-Miller at the University of Alabama at Birmingham's Sterne Library; Trudie Roy and Donnette Lurie at the Homewood Public Library; and a slew of others. For research support, my departmental colleagues, Ed Brown, Tracy Chang, and Judi King, and my dean at the School of Business, Robert E. Holmes, deserve thanks. Moral support from the following people also made the sometimes lonely task of research and writing a little less so: Richard Feldman, Daniel Feldman, Vicky F. Menke, Julia Garate Burgos Feldman, Brian Feldman, Jak and Judy Karn, Steve Martin, Chris Marston, Jim Reed, Diane McWhorter, Carol Ann Vaughn, Kari Frederickson, Ralph Johnson, Higdon Roberts, Dennis Dearing, Donny Bevis, and Frank Paige. Important intellectual influences from whom I have learned much, although I have not always concurred with their interpretations, are the late C. Vann Woodward, Sheldon Hackney, Wayne Flynt, William Warren Rogers Sr., Robert David Ward, Allen W. Jones, and the late Malcolm Cook McMillan. Other important formative influences are Natalie Davis, H. Irvin Penfield, Patrick J. Hawley, Lance Grahn, and Deborah Resha Madonia. Above all, I thank my talented, irreplaceable, and infinitely supportive wife, Jeannie, and the two angels I call my daughters, Hallie and Rebecca, the youngest of whom this book is dedicated to. For a five-year-old, she has been exceedingly patient, waiting "for Daddy to finish my book."

The author gratefully acknowledges the following material that was used with permission: Tables 22 and 23 are from tables 3 and 4, pages 203 and 204 of *From*

Demagogue to Dixiecrat, by Glenn Feldman, copyright 1995 by the University Press of America, Lanham, Maryland. The material on the Reconstruction syndrome and on the relationship between race, class, and politics is from pages 301–2 and 22–23 of *Reading Southern History,* edited by Glenn Feldman, copyright 2001 by the University of Alabama Press, Tuscaloosa, Alabama. The material on Tom Heflin and his sources of support is from pages 167–68 and 183 of *Politics, Society, and the Klan in Alabama,* by Glen Feldman, copyright 1999 by the University of Alabama Press, Tuscaloosa, Alabama.

The Disfranchisement Myth

INTRODUCTION

 Like those that surrounded the death of Samuel Clemens, rumors of plain-white resistance to disfranchisement have been greatly exaggerated. The myth that common whites opposed suffrage restriction is powerful, enduring, pervasive—even comforting in many ways. Although there is a definite element of veracity to the assertion, the historiographical myth that has grown up around it is more exaggerated than "true."

This is so for a number of reasons, not the least of which is because the myth received its historiographical baptism at the hands of southern history's highest priest, C. Vann Woodward. Woodward's eminence, derived from his status as the twentieth century's leading southern historian and one of the most important historians in America, was richly deserved and merited. But in this case, the magnitude of his authority has helped to perpetuate a legend that is, at the very least, greatly overdrawn and, at worst, seriously flawed. Woodward's interpretation of plain-white opposition to turn-of-the-century disfranchisement—like the few other instances in which his work has been revised—sprung from his deep sympathy for poor whites and the very real economic and political plights they faced. Suffice to say, this sympathy sometimes obscured Woodward's view of things and has been so thoroughly documented elsewhere that there is no need to say more about it here.[1] A second and important reason the myth has enjoyed a long life is that, like most myths, it is not completely wrong. As a matter of fact, it is absolutely "correct"—up to a point. There is no question that historians are quite right on two counts: (1) that, in general, Black Belt whites performed the greatest part in conceiving, crafting, and carrying out the disfranchisement schemes that swept across the South during the last decade of the nineteenth century and the first of the twentieth, and (2) that plain whites made up the lion's share of resistance to these suffrage restriction schemes.

It is on a third point that the myth runs into trouble: the more generic contention that plain whites rejected disfranchisement. It is one thing to say that the vast majority of the resistance was comprised of plain whites. It is quite another altogether to say that the vast majority of plain whites chose this path of resistance. The first is a demonstrable "fact." The second is a questionable supposition that logically, but not inevitably, flows from the first. Even more, it is one thing to say that plain whites sometimes rejected the specific disfranchising instruments crafted by elite-dominated constitutional conventions and state legislatures. It is quite another to argue that, in opposing these particular mechanisms, plain whites somehow rejected the general notion of "disfranchisement," especially the prospect of black disfranchisement.

Other factors have contributed to the myth's stubborn persistence. One not insignificant reason is that the idea behind the myth is actually quite logical. In fact, taking issue with the myth seems to fly in the face of common sense. On this point, historical hindsight is the culprit that clouds interpretation. Because we know now that things turned out rather badly for common whites in Alabama and elsewhere in the South, it is natural to suppose that the plain folk would not have contributed to suffrage restriction mechanisms that ended up limiting their own ability to vote. It does not make sense that plain whites would support something detrimental to their own interests. There is little question that the generic logic of the myth makes sense. People do not ordinarily do things that work to their disadvantage. More, though, questioning the myth exceeds illogic and enters into the realm of the disturbing, for there is something profoundly unsettling, even dark, about believing that people might actually contribute to their future misfortune by giving in to their present racism.

But assuming that people will act in a rational manner in their own best interest—a "best interest" apparent only in the long run—is to assume perfect human foresight or to argue that human action is uniformly governed by rational behavior. The first is to ask the impossible. The second is an assertion so prone to exception that it is essentially meaningless. Plain-white support for disfranchisement did work to the eventual detriment of plain whites, no argument there. In that sense, plain-white support for suffrage restriction was, indeed, "illogical," no argument there as well. Still, the question remains: Despite its disastrous consequences, to what degree did plain whites support suffrage restriction?

Some historians have dealt with this troubling question by simply assuming perfect human rationality and foresight. For example, one notable student of disfranchisement dismissed such theories because they allegedly "presuppose that the sole target of the restrictive movement was the black voter."[2] But this is not necessarily the case. In contrast, it might be pointed out that such an explanation itself presupposes perfect human rationality and foreknowledge among the electorate. In other words, if plain whites had feared that some of their own number might be caught up in the net of disfranchisement, they would never have voted for the measures. Apart from endowing the plain-white electorate with pure reason, this argument discounts the power of emotional issues such as white supremacy in political decisions, factors out the comforting power of suffrage-saving loopholes such as the grandfather and good-character clauses, and assumes that the Black Belt architects of disfranchisement would have been perfectly candid with the plain whites regarding all the repercussions and effects of the restrictive provisions they had crafted.

Various authors of the myth have propounded versions of it in a number of ways—not all of them compatible with one another. Anxious to demonstrate the essential nobility of plain and Populist whites in his path-breaking *Origins of the New South*, Vann Woodward offered an interpretation of suffrage restriction that became highly influential even though it was actually questionable on two points. Woodward reported that in Alabama, the white counties "turned down flatly" the 1901 disfranchisement constitution, while black counties carried it by "majorities often exceeding the white voting population."[3] While the second part of this sentence is correct, the first implies that plain whites overwhelmingly rejected the document. But in fact, many did not. More importantly, by giving such prominence in his disfranchisement discussion to the point that Alabama was the only state in which such a ratification vote was submitted to the people, Woodward left the reader with the strong impression that this dichotomy— plain-white "rejection" and privileged-white "acceptance"—was the predominant disfranchisement pattern across the region. This point was not lost on generations of future historians. Finally, Woodward cited V. O. Key Jr. only twice in his chapter on disfranchisement—once to specifically and rather dramatically dispute the political scientist's fait accompli thesis: that constitutional disfranchisement was merely the legal codification of a general and already extant de facto denial of black suffrage through extralegal means, conducted by privileged whites with the aid and abetment of defeated, disillusioned, and somewhat apathetic Populists.[4]

Interestingly, Woodward backed away from this interpretation a mere four years later in his well-known study of segregation, *The Strange Career of Jim Crow*. In that book, Woodward implied that poor whites bore a greater degree of responsibility for disfranchisement than he had previously assigned them. The success of demagogues who relied on racist rhetoric and imagery to target poor whites—Tom Watson of Georgia, James K. Vardaman of Mississippi, "Pitchfork" Ben Tillman and Cole Blease of South Carolina, and "Little Jeff" Davis of Arkansas—colored his analysis.[5] But by then, the damage had been done. For those determined to see the dichotomy of privileged "guilt" and poor "innocence," the original Woodward thesis was still comforting.

Other scholars have reinforced *the disfranchisement myth* in a variety of ways. The most seminal sustainment came from a student of Woodward's, J. Morgan Kousser. Kousser's immediate 1974 classic, *The Shaping of Southern Politics*, restated the original Woodward myth and rejected his teacher's subsequent refinement, but in a way so quantitatively sophisticated—replete with a regression analysis foreign to many historians—that for over a quarter of a century it discouraged detailed reexamination of the issue. In fact, as Michael Perman noted in 2001, his detailed *Struggle for Mastery* was the first exhaustive study of disfranchisement across the South attempted since Kousser's.[6] Yet, boiled down, Kousser's interpretation was substantially a restatement of Woodward's original presented in *Origins*—only made more directly. Kousser took specific pains to refute V. O. Key's fait accompli thesis in the most direct terms possible as a "mer[e] . . . tautology" that states "the obvious" but is not meaningful. Kousser then went on to make some fairly large claims: that his work would very clearly "disprove any notion that most Populists approved of disfranchisement" and that "the overall picture" is that "suffrage restriction in Alabama was a partisan issue."[7] Here, Kousser's belief as to the partisan and class nature of disfranchisement recalled Woodward's earlier Beardian claims that subsumed race in the disfranchisement struggle: "The Negro, supposedly the primary concern . . . was often forgotten in the struggle of white man for supremacy over white man." And again, that "[t]he real question was which whites should be supreme. . . . It was not Negro domination but white domination from the Black Belt that the white counties [this time of Mississippi] . . . sought to overthrow."[8]

Despite its many merits, fundamental aspects of the Kousser book warrant questioning and further inquiry. Kousser's ecological regression analysis provided *estimates* of vote patterns, not real or actual figures. His method focused on actual county returns, but only estimates of the mass of individuals' votes across a state.[9] Yet, despite the estimated nature of his numbers, Kousser's textual discussion betrays little hint of tentativeness or the absence of absolute certainty. Also, while the methodology effectively measured countywide support for candidates and referenda, it did not tell us whether a given county had been carried by one or one hundred thousand votes. Since the gubernatorial elections and state referenda were decided on the basis of aggregate votes of the masses of individuals, not the number of counties won or lost—or even, as in presidential elections, by the number of electoral votes associated with each unit (in this case, a county)—this omission is significant. By comparing the returns of counties that had gone Populist in the 1892, 1896, and 1898 gubernatorial elections and the countywide vote on the two Alabama constitutional referenda, calling and ratifying the convention, Kousser regressed to estimated results that he interpreted as little or no Populist support for "disfranchisement" or "suffrage restriction." In some cases his method actually produced *negative* Populist support for the 1901 referenda—a statistical, but not a logical, possibility. In order to accept Kousser's methodology and estimates on Populist voting uncritically, we would have to believe other uncertain results, for example, that a full 81 percent of the Alabamians who voted Democratic in 1892 chose not to vote at all in the 1901 referendum calling the new constitution.[10]

The difficulty lies in the nature of the question. Kousser was attempting to wrestle with the "ecological fallacy" of using aggregate data to infer individual behavior—ultimately an unknowable prospect. But in addition to a noticeable lack of qualification or the acknowledgment of speculation, assumption, and statistical and logical limits in his text, the Kousser method itself involved several questionable aspects. Kousser reports his findings with the utmost confidence in *The Shaping of Southern Politics.* In his brief "Note on Regression Estimation of Voting Behavior," the reader will find no hint of the swirling controversy over the accuracy of the statistical estimates provided by regression analysis. Nor does Kousser acknowledge the concern of some statisticians and political historians that scholars enamored of the then-novel application of statistical methods of political analysis to historical research might be overreaching, proceeding a bit too recklessly, or failing to cope adequately with the problems in using aggregate data to infer individual behavior. Allan J. Lichtman specifically warned fellow political historians about the "pitfalls [and] perils of naïve disaggregation," of failing to deal adequately with "aggregation bias" and the "ecological fallacy," and of "most historians" being "unaware" that the method "poses important methodological problems" in attempting to use aggregate data to make conclusions about individuals' behavior. Lichtman's cautionary essay, part of a journal series in which Kousser took part, contained numerous warnings that "the regression coefficient is not a panacea for the ecological fallacy," that historians "will rarely have perfect information" and should "beware" of the method's pitfalls and imperfections, and that the "estimates" derived by such analysis "may not even yield an accurate description of the political decisions of the entire population of individuals who share that attribute."[11]

Apart from the statistical assumptions and questions, there are more intuitive concerns such as the question of the definition of a "Populist"—a definition in flux during the time period under study. A Populist in 1892, 1896, or even 1898 was not the same as in 1901. Populism crested in Alabama in the early to mid-1890s. By 1901, the overall number of voters still clinging to the Populist label had shrunk. This was a period of frequent attempts at creating party harmony and the reentry of substantial numbers of former Populists and other anti-Democrats back into the regular fold—at least for a time. Free-silver Democracy, William Jennings Bryan's candidacy, and the Chicago Platform of 1896 on the national level, and the gubernatorial election of 1900 on the state level, were powerful catalysts for the resumption of party unity and the concurrent demise of Populism. Yet plenty of voters still regarded themselves as anti-Democrats, Independent Democrats, or as Democrats with only the most tenuous of connections to the dominant party. Kousser's method did not deal with the shifting and shrinking definition of Populist in Alabama—a critical part of the equation. Further, while Kousser may have effectively measured voting on the issue of calling a constitutional convention on suffrage or ratifying a constitution that limited suffrage, he made sweeping conclusions on the more general subjects of "disfranchisement" and "suffrage restriction"—not the calling of a constitution or the specific product of a convention's deliberations.[12] Kousser conflated two separate things: sentiment for or against disfranchisement with satisfaction on whether convention delegates had actually crafted a document that could perpetrate the deed on blacks while adequately protecting poor whites.

Michael Perman's work, detailed as it is, substantiated the disfranchisement myth in a way somewhat different than Woodward's, Kousser's, and others. Perman provided a number of insightful and compelling arguments in his book. He gave credence to Key's fait accompli thesis in a manner of speaking. He provided a clear interpretation that disfranchisement was aimed at and achieved reestablishing the post-Reconstruction dominance of the Democratic Party, eradicating two-party politics, and cementing white supremacy and the denial of suffrage for blacks. He also confirmed, contrary to other purveyors of the myth, that "[o]f course, white-county delegates tried to keep the prerequisites [for voting] as light as possible while still eliminating large numbers of black voters." Yet, Perman's recognition of this point was by design brief and fleeting. First, Perman gave credence to a stark dichotomy that exonerated most voters from any responsibility by calling disfranchisement a "coup d'etat . . . imposed from above against the wishes of the majority of the electorate." His larger point, though, was to consciously and purposefully eschew the "context" within which disfranchisement occurred while focusing instead on the "process" itself. Thus he ended up providing an interpretation that correctly applied responsibility to the Democratic Party leadership while, unfortunately, issuing a pass to the "rank and file . . . and the electorate at large" from bearing any appreciable responsibility.[13] As with V. O. Key's study, it is possible, perhaps likely, that those interested in perpetuating the disfranchisement myth will use this part of Perman's interpretation, while discounting the qualifiers, to buttress the old dichotomy.

Perhaps the largest problem with Perman's interpretation was that it—like Woodward's, Kousser's, and others'—understood disfranchisement as fundamentally a class issue between competing groups of white men. In his introduction, Perman explained that V. O. Key had actually furnished two differing interpretations for disfranchisement in his magisterial work. Key's first interpretation pinned responsibility for disfranchisement on Black Belt whites—a position Perman applauded.[14] But after noting that Populists had driven the disfranchisement effort in Georgia and South Carolina, Key backed off from his first interpretation and mused that perhaps the "sounder explanation was that whichever whites were on top at the moment" drove disfranchisement—an interpretation that Perman found less than satisfying.[15]

Yet both Key and Perman, as well as Woodward and Kousser, failed to see the forest for the trees. This forest was the fact that in each southern state the only truly consistent commonality was that—driven by the Black Belt or the Populists—disfranchisement was always driven by whites. In no southern state did black men disfranchise whites. An obvious point, certainly, but also one that steers us in a more productive direction than trying to see competition among white men of different classes. While class considerations certainly played an important role in disfranchisement, they did not play the deciding or fundamental role. First, last, and always disfranchisement was a racial thing. Whites disfranchised blacks in the southern states; blacks did not disfranchise whites. While class variables are unquestionably important, related, deserve significant attention, and should in no way be diminished, focusing on them primarily has helped to confuse more than to clarify. This focus has led Perman and Key, not to mention Woodward and Kousser, off into areas that are interesting and important but not defining. In fact, this distraction from the racial essence of disfranchisement has helped to fuel the myth of disfranchisement; historians have spent inordinate time trying to show Black Belt guilt and poor-white innocence, but they have not focused on the intrinsic character of disfranchisement. It was a pan-white movement that perhaps engendered various degrees of support among whites of different classes in all the states. But in the end, it was a movement aimed by whites at blacks, implemented by whites against blacks, and passed with enough white consensus on the overall goal of black disfranchisement to override white disagreement on specific means. And nowhere did white disagreement on methods translate into anything substantially more than poor-white concern about fellows of their own color and class being caught up in a net primarily designed to catch black voters—a net that virtually every white saw as desirable.[16]

In considering the myth's provisions, it is perhaps most surprising that, even for the "antis" (those poor whites opposed to calling a disfranchising convention and/or ratifying its constitution), white supremacy played a tremendously important role in their motivation. Far from being subordinate to, or even separate from, class concerns, race played an inordinately important role for the antis. This was also true, of course, for the plain folk who favored a disfranchising constitution. Much of Alabama's poor-white resistance to the constitution was actually a racially based dissatisfaction with the chosen method of the constitution—a suspicion that it would in some way perpetuate "black rule" and carpetbag conditions in which blacks would, voluntarily or not, have their votes counted while poor whites would be left out. Yet, because it is a poor fit within the parameters of the disfranchisement myth, this white supremacist aspect of poor-white opposition to disfranchising schemes has been given little, if any, attention by historians. Still, surprisingly, in Alabama it is there, it is plentiful, and it is very important. [17]

Some historians have been much less careful than Perman, even reckless with their various restatements of the myth. Perhaps the most overstated and thus most dramatically inaccurate distillation belongs to Samuel L. Webb in the 1997 publication of his revised dissertation on Alabama politics. While claiming that "[t]hese facts" of plain-white opposition to suffrage restriction "do not absolve them of racism," Webb tried, for all intents and purposes, to do precisely that— or worse yet, to argue that the racism meant nothing in real terms. "Hill Country anti-Democrats did not seek to exclude blacks from the political process," Webb argued in a sweeping and fancifully misleading statement. He compounded this large error by going on to claim that Hill Country whites "opposed all of the disfranchisement measures imposed on the state by white Democrats in 1901." In a separate essay, Webb restated the flawed myth even more clearly: "Alabama Populists and Republicans did not always agree on economic matters, but they agreed on the need for . . . opposition to disfranchisement. . . . Poor whites and blacks were disfranchised by men who publicly stated their desire to turn over control of the state to a privileged few." [18] Webb handled V. O. Key, the author of what many regard as the bible of southern politics, the way many handle evidence in a bible. [19] Consciously or not, he included those parts of *Southern Politics in State and Nation* that seemed to substantiate his view and did not include those that did not. In fact, Webb took specific pains to quote V. O. Key on each of the first four pages of his book, leaving readers with the impression that his book was substantiated by the weight of Key's authority, but he did not cite the esteemed political scientist even once in his discussion of the 1901 disfranchising constitution or the endnotes on the issue. [20] Webb also attempted a rather crude divorce of race from class—in fact a subordination of race to class considerations.

Yet Webb's and others' interpretive liberties are not, in and of themselves, novel. They are substantially the result of the normative conclusions of Morgan Kousser's quantitative work. In *The Shaping of Southern Politics,* Kousser was not at all shy about constructing stark and inflexible dichotomies between the racial attitudes and behavior of various classes of whites, based on numerical estimations. At one critical point in his Alabama discussion, Kousser presented an absolutely black-and-white contrast between racist Black Belt politicos and enlightened Populists, who, he claimed, defended the right of blacks to vote.

The Black Belt delegates, Kousser explained, believed suffrage was an "inherent right" for the white man and a transitory "privilege" granted to the blacks, while "[t]he Populists, on the other hand, kept to the older belief in universal manhood suffrage."[21] Despite the starkness of Kousser's conclusions, they were not based on infallible data or airtight quantitative methodology.[22] Nor were they based on indisputable logic. For instance, the exemplar of Black Belt racial exclusion that Kousser chose for this passage was not a representative of Black Belt interests at all. He was a spokesman for poor rural and textile-mill whites. More, Kousser's primary example of Populist enlightenment and racial inclusion was, unlike the implication, a profound rarity—even among the anti-Democrats.[23]

The disfranchising movement—as enshrined by the 1901 Constitution, the establishment of the 1902 all-white direct primary, and the lily-white movement among the Republicans—was the political expression of a broad whitening movement among virtually all white Alabamians and in all areas of life. To deny the broad consensus of the turn-of-the-century whitening movement among all classes of whites is to attempt to divorce race from class in the most artificial of ways. Yet this artificial separation is precisely what some historians would attempt. For example, Samuel Webb insisted in the strongest terms that racial considerations were divorced from and subordinate to economic motives for his plain-white anti-Democratic protagonists. He maintained that "race was rarely the dominant force in their political decision making," that their "motives . . . can be found" instead in their fear "of moneyed elites . . . [and] their 'plutocratic ideas,'" that the Jeffersonians were never "so obsessed with race that nothing else mattered," that regular "Democrats emphasized racial issues" while the politics of the Jacksonian and Jeffersonian Democrats "transcended race."[24] Yet, the construction of this simplistic and artificial dichotomy misses one of the most essential points of politics in the era: the vital and intertwined relationship between race, class, and politics.

Race and class have often been so closely bound in the region's history that to speak of them now as completely separate entities is to rip them apart with such force that one risks doing irreparable damage to both concepts—and thus speaking about what are basically artificial and incomplete constructs. As contemporary historians expand the scope of political inquiry to streets, stores, households, and train stations, they must continue to ask "Who gets what, when, and how?" and, perhaps most important, "Why?" Southern history—including the very recent past—is largely distinguished by the skillful, in fact, ingenious, manipulation of ingrained plain-white emotions (principally over race, but also over "God and country" issues: abortion, gun control, patriotism, school prayer, homosexual rights, display of the Ten Commandments, Confederate symbolism, traditional family values, and the morality and "character" of political candidates). We must keep sight of the fact that some southerners—elite white southerners—have proven especially adept at using the regional preoccupation with race, Reconstruction, and related emotional issues to preserve their privileged status in a rigidly stratified and hierarchical society. No one party has held a monopoly on this strategy. Long the province of the Conservative Democratic Party, more recently this has become the province of the newly ascendant—even dominant—southern GOP. In those junctures at which plain whites put race or other emotional considerations ahead of their economic interests, they made a conscious calculation of what was in their "real" interests—an estimation that might differ considerably from that of the historian. Painful as it may be, we must realize that in these instances (in which the bosses often profited more than anyone else), plain whites were more parties to their own demise than the mere victims of circumstance.[25]

White Democrats hardly unilaterally "imposed" suffrage restrictions on Alabama in 1901, as some have claimed, without considerable aid and comfort from Populists, former Populists, lily-white Republicans, Independents, and other plain whites devoted to a Jacksonian and Jeffersonian conception of government and only marginally attached to the Democratic Party.[26] Election returns and voting patterns in Alabama's white counties—not to mention support for black disfranchisement coming from anti-Democratic plain-white political leaders and newspaper editors—are simply too significant to make this argument credible. Rather, the regular Democrats were sufficiently skilled in the use of race as the quintessential emotional issue to manipulate plain whites into doing their bidding. V. O. Key alluded to this kind of skill, while not directly identifying its emotional nature, when he recorded begrudging admiration for the political skill of the outnumbered Black Belt whites in keeping the politics of the South revolving "around the position of the Negro." This skill, which Key defined as perhaps the "single theme" of southern politics, was their ability to turn "a shoestring" into "a decisive majority" at the most "critical junctures" of southern history.[27] In Alabama, 1901 was just such a critical moment. The Conservative Democratic Party made enough empty pledges and fashioned enough clever temporary suffrage loopholes to ease the fears of sufficient numbers of plain whites to allow, first, the calling of a constitutional convention to disfranchise blacks and, second, the ratification of a "flawed" document that obviously (in retrospect) contained hazards for poor-white voters. Like all Alabamians, plain whites made a choice at the turn of the century. The choice for them was whether or not to risk the disfranchisement of some of their own number—to place their future security in the hands of their privileged white brethren and seek the disfranchisement of blacks—or to forego the golden fleece of black disfranchisement and avoid the risk. Some plain whites, including Republicans,

Populists, and former Populists, took the risk. Some did not. In the end enough did so that it helped plain whites as a whole to lose out.

In recent years, the myth's rigid dichotomy of privileged-white "guilt" and plain-white "innocence" regarding the disfranchisement of blacks has gained increasing ascendancy in Southern history circles. The Woodward myth, backed by Kousser's quantification, has become so prevalent that many scholars simply repeat it as a given truth. Some do so with little investigation of their own into the matter. Samuel Webb, for example, makes huge and questionable declarations based on a mere four-and-a-half-page discussion of the 1901 disfranchisement movement.[28] Some articles and dissertations repeat the myth as gospel in only two-to-three-page descriptions.[29] Even Jimmie Frank Gross, who did substantial research into the issue—some of which indicated plain-white complicity—came away restating that part of the myth that blamed privileged whites while granting absolution to common whites.[30]

Yet, it is no disgrace to the plain whites' and anti-Democrats' reputation for economic liberalism to admit that their giving into their own racism played no small role in their undoing. To recognize this tragedy does not diminish the actual and considerable achievement of the anti-Democrats in taking a stand against Bourbonism and Conservative Democracy's reactionary and exclusionary economic policies. The economic progressivism of the anti-Democrats is not somehow erased or nullified by their racism and, more importantly, their indulging of it. But by the same token, the two cannot be held apart in separate spheres, as if they had no connection in the past, as if they have no connection in the present. Because race and class were profoundly, even intimately intertwined with the politics of the past, the two cannot be separated cleanly now— even for the sake of convenience, simplicity, or expiation on the racial score. The economically liberal accomplishment of the anti-Democrats is not nullified by their racial shortcomings. But because race and class worked together—because most blacks were poor, poor whites needed black votes, and white elites desired white solidarity to defeat potential biracial cooperation—we must at least recognize that the dissenters were less effective and ultimately less successful economically than they might have been, in part, because of their racial shortcomings.

The actual record of plain whites' reform accomplishment is still intact on the issue of economic liberalism. And no amount of their succumbing to the temptation of racist behavior can erase that. Yet some historians attempt to defend the indefensible parts of the poor-white record on race, or deny them altogether, or, worse still, to admit that they exist but argue that they had no importance.[31] It is not enough simply to admit that the Populists were racists. Aside from the inaccuracy of this oversimplification, such apologetic attempts miss one of the most central points of southern politics in the era. In addition to submersing any consideration of degree, such an observation conflates the Populist and Bourbon political programs and ideologies as if they had no distinction. If the Populists were no worse racists than their Bourbon adversaries, the political score was far from equal.[32] Although the privileged occasionally sought to recruit voluntary black votes, that strategy belonged principally to the various manifestations of poor-white anti-Democrats. The obvious racism of the privileged did not cost them significantly with respect to potential allies of color. Economic liberalism was not a hallmark of their program. The same cannot be said of the Populists, Republicans, and other Independent threats to entrenched Democracy. Their racism was a significant liability to their electoral chances. It risked the plain whites' credibility to attract and hold blacks to a standard of biracial class challenge and economic liberalism. Their racism risked their chances for electoral success. In fact, it risked their very chances for political survival. It was a luxury they could ill afford.

Apology, dismissal, and excuse-making for poor-white racism is sometimes done with a kind of misguided desperation that erroneously assumes all is lost unless the racism of the plain-white reformers can somehow be denied, mitigated, rationalized, apologized for, or forgotten altogether. But in trying to set the anti-Democrats apart from the regular Democrats on race, these historians have granted their protagonists an artificial and frankly deceptive enlightenment on racial matters. In some ways, Bibb Graves, the plain-white Alabama reformer who graced the governor's mansion in the 1920s and 1930s, is an exemplar of this type of treatment. Although very few Alabama enemies of entrenched economic conservatism can boast of being in the same league as Bibb Graves when it comes to economic reform, the Graves example is still informative. A member of the reform wing of the Democratic Party, Graves accomplished much in his economic battles with entrenched Conservative Democracy—and was himself a leading opponent of the 1901 Constitution. Still, Graves often stumbled on the issue of tolerance for blacks and other Alabamians of minority faiths and ethnicities. He achieved the governor's office with the backing of the huge and powerful Ku Klux Klan of the twenties. Once in office, Graves did little or nothing to curb a Klan that ran wild, sometimes even protecting that flank of his electoral support. Meanwhile the KKK trampled on the constitutional rights and liberties—and in many cases, the actual bodies—of blacks, Jews, Catholics, immigrants, moral nonconformists, "uppity" women, and others foreign to Alabama's prevailing status quo.[33] Still, Bibb Graves's lack of accomplishment in the area of civil liberties does not diminish his significant—one might even argue, towering—achievement in the economic realm of improvement for the state's poor-white working people. One must, nonetheless, recognize the reality that Graves did not demonstrate the same kind of concern for the state's blacks—poor or otherwise. Unlike Graves, some anti-Democrats, such as the Hill Country Populist and Republican leader Oliver Day Street, did not leave such a record of economic liberalism behind to balance a deep prejudice and woeful record on civil liberties.[34]

Curiously, the ascendance of the disfranchisement myth seems to be a relatively recent phenomenon. Between Woodward's monumental book in 1951 and Kousser's numerical restatement in 1974, wisdom that contradicted the myth had been available to historians from some of the most gifted scholars who have looked into the subject. Yet, strangely, it seems that their views on the matter have been all but forgotten in recent years. V. O. Key's work was decidedly mixed on the subject but was leagues away from the view that became the core of the myth's orthodoxy. Malcolm Cook McMillan, who in 1955 produced a superior and highly detailed study of constitution making in Alabama, concluded his classic book with the clear realization that plain whites had contributed much to their own undoing. McMillan concluded flatly that elite manipulation of poor-white racism worked well enough to convince many plain whites to vote for passage of the disfranchising Alabama Constitution of 1901—a conclusion based on mountains of research that historians have ignored and forgotten in recent years, instead hewing to the more popular and comforting disfranchisement myth. Black Belt elites "utilized the cry of 'white supremacy,' placed emphasis on Negro disfranchisement, and gave assurance that 'no white man would be disfranchised,'" McMillan wrote. "As a result, many whites of the hills, the wiregrass, and pine barrens voted for the new constitution in order to remove the Negro from politics and at the same time prepared the way for their own disfranchisement."[35] William Warren Rogers and Robert David Ward, leading scholars of Alabama history who did much of their work in the 1960s and 1970s, agreed with McMillan's view of the tragedy. They sadly reported that "[f]ar too many whites" aided the general movement for disfranchisement by "approv[ing] black disfranchisement" in the 1901 ratification vote.[36]

It is clear that Big Mule/Black Belt planters and industrialists were the movers and shapers of disfranchisement in Alabama. It is not the position of this book that this combination of privileged Conservative Democrats was not. Nor is it the position of this book that plain whites—as represented by anti-Democrats (Populists, former Populists, Independents, Republicans, and Jeffersonian Democrats) were not the people, along with blacks, who made up the overwhelming bulk of the opposition to the disfranchisement measures. They were. It is the position of this book that the disfranchisement myth has been too neatly drawn and that it is misleading. It is more accurate to conclude that the dichotomy of privileged white advocacy "for" and plain-white resistance "against" disfranchisement has been overstated, exaggerated, and even romanticized. In fact, a significant number of plain whites, including those opposed to the regular Democratic Party, did support disfranchisement efforts—only those aimed at disfranchising black voters. What is more, this poor-white support for black disfranchisement contributed in no small way to the misfortune eventually suffered by many poor whites who themselves lost the right to vote. In turn-of-the-century Alabama, plain whites were a lot more divided on the disfranchisement issue than statements claiming they "opposed all disfranchisement schemes," "turned down flatly" disfranchising mechanisms, and "kept to the older belief in universal manhood suffrage" suggest.[37] These kinds of overstatements, while accepted uncritically by many historians in recent years, have now passed into the realm of myth—a myth whose time has come to be reexamined.

CHAPTER ONE

Prelude to Disfranchisement

 At least four things make up the broad background in which Alabama's 1901 disfranchising constitution was written. First, it was constructed during an era of distinct national sympathy for white southerners and the race question they faced.[1] A federal retreat on reforming relations between the races broadly characterized the era. Second, it was part of a regional movement to whiten politics that found its origins in 1890 Mississippi.[2] Third, this movement reached its most advanced, extreme, and comprehensive form in Alabama.[3] If southerners were notorious for going to extremes, then Alabamians were among the most southern of them all. And finally, disfranchisement qualified as a "progressive reform" in keeping with much of the Progressive movement's innate character within Alabama and without. A large part of this character actually had precious little to do with "progress," "reform," or "liberalism" in any large sense of the words but much to do with purifying politics and controlling society's more "undesirable" elements. The disfranchisement reform effected by Alabama's 1901 Constitution, one historian has perceptively written, was "a bit like sweeping dirt under the rug in order to present a clean house . . . [like] closing banks to prevent bank robberies."[4]

"Skunks and Polecats": The White American's Black in 1900

Near the turn of the century, public opinion, North and South, was not very high where the African American was concerned. Race relations had, by 1900, sunk to deplorable depths in the country. The 1906 Atlanta race riot was matched only two years later in the northern town of Springfield, Illinois. Lynching was, after 1900, reserved almost exclusively for blacks and confined almost solely to the South.[5] This was a marked change. During the 1890s, for example, Alabama was the leading lynch state in the country, and whites comprised a full third of the state's lynch victims.[6] "Scientific racism," together with social Darwinism, was generally accepted as the prevailing wisdom. These intellectual creeds acted as a positivist buttress that both reinforced and engendered lowbrow racist attitudes and behavior. Given this national context, southern violence against black people, whom science considered to be something less than human anyway, was not surprising. Nor should it be considered all that surprising that whites in the region where most African Americans lived moved jointly toward disfranchisement and segregation, especially once it became clear that the federal government meant to provide no obstacle.[7] The 1901 Alabama Constitution and the cementing of Jim Crow took place in the warm and nurturing climate of sympathetic national opinion.

The "best" opinion in the country took an exceedingly dim view of the African American and, at least implicitly, approved of measures to restrict and control the race. *Century Magazine, Scribner's,* and *Harper's* routinely lampooned blacks in the most stereotypical ways. Leading intellectuals such as Henry Adams, Henry James, and John Fiske did not object morally to the rapidly deteriorating status of blacks in American law and society. James Ford Rhodes called blacks "innately inferior and incapable of citizenship." Harvard historian Alfred Bushnell Hart agreed that "[r]ace measured by race, the negro is inferior, and his past history [implies] . . . that he will remain inferior." Princeton University's William Starr Myers concluded that "[t]he negro must be . . . treated as a 'grown-up child'—with justice, but with authority." Lloyd McKim Garrison, grandson of the famed abolitionist William Lloyd Garrison, declared that "[t]he negro, beyond his sweet disposition and courtesy, has not the qualifications for a very useful citizen."[8] Alabamians were quick to pick up on the implications for disfranchisement and other forms of states' rights–sponsored control of blacks.[9]

Predominant opinion regarding blacks did not spring from thin air, though. The advent and ascendance of "scientific racism" (i.e., scientifically and medically "proven" conclusions regarding black biological inferiority) had much to do with the generally low opinion of black aptitudes held by America's best and brightest scientists, doctors, sociologists, and criminologists. Many of them subscribed to a view of irretrievable black inferiority, if not outright depravity. Numerous physicians and scientists wrote of blacks having "simple minds . . . smaller brain[s] . . . deficient judgment . . . [and a] lack of control in sexual matters." Dr. William Bevis's article in the *American Journal of Psychiatry* stressed the occurrence of a surge in black sexual passion and a simultaneous decline in "mental development" around the age of puberty. "[P]romiscuous sex relations, gambling, petty thievery, drinking . . . loafing" and all kinds of degradation and degeneracy consume their energies thereafter. "Without proper guidance," he concluded, the African American would make a "complete wreck of his physical and mental life." Dr. R. W. Shufeldt's 1907 book, *The Negro: A Menace to Civilization,* concluded that blacks were "almost wholly subservient to the sexual instinct. . . . In other words, negroes are purely animal." White females, Shufeldt wrote, were at particular risk because of the black male's "savage lust." Black rapists might even "increase the size of the genital fissure by an ugly outward rip of his knife." Such was "their nature," Shufeldt and other scientists felt, "and they cannot possibly rid themselves of that, any more than skunks and polecats can cast away their abominable scent glands and the outrageous odor they emit."[10]

Remarkably, though, northern sympathy and commiseration with the South would mark but a brief moment in the regional relationship. The time would not be long before national attention would again emphasize a rigid and simplistic dichotomy of southern white deviance and northern purity. But around the turn of the century, that day seemed a long way off. Oswald Garrison Villard, editor of the *Nation* and the *New York Post*, confessed in 1907 that "[i]t is our northern disgrace that a negro finds it harder to get work here than in the South." The *New York Age* agreed that blacks felt racial prejudice as intensely in the North as in Dixie. James Weldon Johnson, a black leader of national repute, said as much when he argued that any collection of white men in the South would find it impossible to congregate and speak for an hour without bringing up the "race question." "If a Northern white man happened to be in the group," he quipped, "the time could safely be cut to thirty minutes." Whites provided an even more intense commentary in 1911 when they seized a wounded black man from his hospital bed, dragged him through the streets of Coatesville, Pennsylvania, and burned him alive. When the victim tried to crawl out of the fire, the mob beat him back in with railings from a nearby fence.[11]

The "Best" White People: Race and Privilege

In Alabama, the legacies of the Reconstruction experience permeated many aspects of the age for all manner of whites. Chief among these was the painful memory of viable black suffrage and the consequences of real black political power. At the turn of the century, this question was resolved by removing blacks from active involvement in politics. In Alabama, this "reform" was codified in the new disfranchising state constitution of 1901 and consummated the following year in the adoption of an all-white direct primary for the Democratic Party. Victory in this primary was, of course, tantamount to election in a one-party state like those of the Deep South. Although the two have sometimes been considered apart, the 1902 primary was actually the consummation and logical encapsulation of the disfranchisement of African Americans so forcefully accomplished by the 1901 Constitution. It is not a coincidence that the drive for the direct primary came from those most closely associated with Alabama's plain and working-class whites. Nor is it a contradiction of the more elite-driven disfranchisement constitution of the previous year. The new constitution and the direct primary, to a large extent, represented the reconciliation of white political factions that had found expression in third-party challenges during the 1880s and 1890s from various Independent groups and, of course, the People's Party. While poor whites and their Big Mule/Black Belt adversaries still disagreed on many issues, especially the place of the poor whites in Alabama's political economy, they almost universally agreed that blacks should be eradicated from politics. And it was on this central point of agreement that white Democratic ascendancy was reestablished and rejuvenated at the dawn of the twentieth century.

Although the disfranchisement myth has underestimated plain-white involvement in disfranchisement, one point must be made clear at the outset: in Alabama, the move for disfranchisement was driven principally by the most privileged whites in society. That point cannot be—nor should it be—denied. Nowhere was this made more clear than at the epic 1900 Montgomery Race Conference, held in the cradle of the Confederacy under the auspices of the Southern Society for the Promotion of the Study of Race Conditions and Problems in the South. The society and its conference—both the brainchildren of Montgomery Episcopal rector Edgar Gardner Murphy—reflected his paternalistic outlook on the race question and his desire for "reform" of the racial status quo. Like most paternalists of his day, Murphy opposed lynching and the physical abuse of blacks. For that and his efforts on behalf of educational reform, he has been generously granted the label of "progressive." But Murphy was nevertheless convinced of the black race's biological inferiority. While favoring vocational and trade education for people of color as an effective method to teach citizenship, thrift, self-help, and productive work habits, Murphy and most of his confederates in the Southern Society stood firmly opposed to social equality, civil rights, and even black suffrage.[12] For Murphy, the difference was endemic. He felt that even illiterate whites should have the privilege of the franchise in the place of blacks because the white man "excels the negro voter by the genius of his race, by inherited capacity, and by a political training which has formed part of the tradition of his class."[13]

While the paternalists who dominated the Southern Society projected a view of the African American that, on the surface, appeared kindly, ultimately considerations of raw self-interest played a very important role in their thinking as well. Virtually all were devout apostles of the materialistic New South Creed and the profits associated with a dutiful, docile, and plentiful supply of black labor. Murphy himself, in fact, believed that slavery had exercised a positive civilizing influence on the African.[14] He also considered well-meaning northern enforcement of the Reconstruction amendments to be a form of baseless encroachment, harmful to southern whites as well as blacks, and he especially disliked "censorious and intemperate criticism from the North." The Yankee and the allied federal government—almost one and the same in the mind of white southerners—should, Murphy felt, demonstrate more patience and prudence in waiting for southern whites to improve conditions for the region's black population at a pace the ruling race deemed appropriate. "How long" should they wait, Murphy asked. "For seven years?—I say for seventy times seven years. We, in America, are dealing with no neighborhood quarrel. We are dealing with the historic forces of a whole civilization." [15]

Of particular concern to Murphy and his confederates in the Southern Society was the problem of poor-white antipathy and violence toward blacks, a worry echoed by black accommodationist, New South apostle, and Murphy friend Booker T. Washington. [16] The Tuskegee educator expressed delight at seeing "the best white people" come to Montgomery to articulate the "voice of the educated, cultivated white South [that] has been too long silent [while] we have heard the voice of the North . . . the Negro . . . the politician, and . . . the [white] mob." [17] Joining Murphy, who served as the society's secretary, were indeed the "best white people" from around Alabama and the South: the sitting president of the Southern Society, former U.S. Navy secretary and former U.S. congressman Hilary A. Herbert; education reformer and society vice-president J. L. M. Curry; former South Carolina governor William A. MacCorkle; North Carolina editor Walter Hines Page; Alabama railroad lawyers James Weatherly and Jeff Faulkner; and Birmingham's John Temple Graves. Francis G. Caffey of Lowndes County, a Harvard-educated soldier, lawyer, and professor, served as chair of the society's executive committee. [18]

Self-interest was central to the paternalists' rejection of what they saw as two extremes: the raw racism of poor and working-class whites and the aspirations of blacks for civil rights and political equality. The patricians who came to Montgomery, and their counterparts throughout the South, understood their task to be the reconciliation of contradictory white attitudes toward the former slaves, what Harvard historian Albert Bushnell Hart described as the tension inherent in the southern conception of blacks as "children of the soil." On one hand, property-owning whites generally viewed blacks as an absolutely necessary source of cheap labor. On the other hand, blacks were "distrusted by nearly all whites," poor and privileged, Hart wrote, "despised by more than half of them, and hated by a considerable and apparently increasing faction." [19] The solution to this dilemma for the paternalist boosters of New South materialism and Old South agriculture was a hybrid policy: support and encouragement for black education, thrift, and self-help and contemporaneous discouragement of social and political aspirations. For example, Murphy found it necessary to re-assure Alabama governor Joseph F. Johnston that no blacks would appear as speakers in Montgomery and that the Southern Society was not out to "champion the Negro at the expense of the white man." In fact, the paternalist boosters soothed the anxieties of average whites by telling them that the conference was being put on "more in the interest of the poorer whites than in the interest of the Negro."[20]

Paternalists played the central role in calling for the 1901 constitutional convention and afterward in pushing for the ratification of its disfranchising product. After ratification of the 1901 Constitution, paternalists continued to warn of the perils implicit in the pursuit of social and political equality for the African American. Hilary A. Herbert defended the worth of black life, labor, and vocational education but blamed political degeneracy and rising racial tensions on inappropriate African American aspirations for political power and the vote. Congressman Oscar W. Underwood reasoned that disfranchisement was really for the black's own good since it was certain to reduce racial bitterness and also political jealousy between various groups of whites. New South boosters such as *Atlanta Constitution* editor Henry W. Grady and historian George Fort Milton put forth similar views.[21]

At the heart of the paternalist position was economic self-interest: the availability of a cheap, docile, plentiful black labor force for the New South's factories and the Black Belt's large farms. Education, properly applied, would serve to train people of color in the pathways of good citizenship and obedience. Protection of blacks from poor-white mobs was not only a humanitarian impulse; it was an investment in human capital. Echoing Thomas Goode Jones, gold Democrat Bourke Cochran was open about the connection between paternalism and self-interest. "[G]overnment might be defined as an invention . . . for the protection of property. . . . The test of capacity for civilization is the capacity for voluntary labor," Cochran explained to a large white audience. "The Negro, occup[ied] almost exclusively in the field of labor, is the most important element. . . . Progress for the Negro is along the lines of industrial evolution . . . which the God of all races has prescribed as the sole pathway to civilization and liberty." Politics, on the other hand, would be the ruin of the black race.[22]

Leading planter-industrialist sources and Alabama's nascent reformers endowed the sentiments expressed at the Montgomery conference with enthusiasm and respectability.[23] Most of the old-style patricians as well as the new-style progressives realized that their industrial, economic, and political interests were best served by harboring a black population educated in the trades and vocations but discouraged from pursuit of social equality, political power, and civil rights. The program could be pitched in terms of providing material and economic improvement for the race through practical education, but the real profits would derive from docile, contented black workers who felt they were being taken care of by the paternalists. In Birmingham, one businessman advocated education for blacks to make them into more "efficient laborers" but warned the race against seeking social and political equality. Once blacks "begin to realize that their future lies along industrial rather than political lines," he reasoned, "no trouble will exist."[24] The *Birmingham News,* mouthpiece of New South industrialism, agreed that the African's mission was to elevate himself along a "parallel channel" of industry and material welfare, careful never to touch the white race's "social side" or to "dabble in politics for which he is no way fitted." To this end, Edgar Gardner Murphy criticized the common practice of white unionists excluding blacks from the skilled trades. Industrial exclusion, Murphy argued, would remove incentives for black self-help and lead to the race becoming a drain on society and the economy.[25]

Advocacy of a practical education for blacks was closely linked to privileged white self-interest. The *Birmingham Age-Herald,* another of the state's leading industrial exponents, espoused practical education for the race in order to prevent people of color from leaving the state for the greener pastures promised by northern labor agents. In a similar vein, Birmingham Board of Education president Samuel Ullman explained his advocacy of black education as something he did in the interest of white families who would benefit from well-educated domestic help. A prosperous Jewish merchant, Ullman perhaps wished to avoid bruising southern racial sensibilities and thus echoed the prevailing sentiments.[26]

The industrial and labor interests so apparent at the epic 1900 Montgomery Race Conference operated in conjunction with other privileged-white desires for black disfranchisement. Many Black Belt patricians had grown increasingly uneasy about their manipulation by force and fraud of the large black vote in their counties. So pervasive was the practice of "counting in" or "counting out," as the occasion demanded, that it had become recognized as a virtual art form—although a pursuit that for some jeopardized the very moral foundations of democracy. "Political morality demanded black disfranchisement," scholars of southern history have written. "Accepted by many whites, this assertion enunciated the curious thought that white dishonesty . . . could only be stopped by denying the black man one of his civil rights."[27] Indeed, the suffrage committee at the 1901 constitutional convention would adopt the poignant slogan, "White supremacy, suffrage reform, and purity in elections."[28]

Still, some in the conservative planters' machine stood by the practice for years. Patricians such as Thomas H. Watts, son of a Civil War Alabama governor, reasoned that the fraud was "less hurtful to the Negro [than shotguns] in the bodily sense,"[29] and a Perry County planter defended it as "a magnificent system that [unfortunately] cannot be . . . perpetuated. It is Christianity, but not orthodox. . . . It is wrong but right. . . . It is life instead of death."[30] Relying on religion to justify dishonesty that perpetuated racial prejudice was an interesting gymnastic, but not unusual in Alabama at the turn of the century or for decades following. Alabama governor William C. Oates had defended the practice of ballot-box stuffing as a necessity to keep whites from falling into the "awful gulf of despair which yawned before them" if black involvement in politics continued. The "recording angel will shed no tear," Oates assured some perhaps remorseful whites, "in blotting these acts from the record of the final account."[31]

Even as fraudulent manipulation of the black vote was giving way to legal eradication of it, more than one patrician leader stepped forward to defend the old practice as a necessary evil—if an evil at all. A leading mouthpiece for Alabama's burgeoning industry reminded voters that "the very best men," including ministers, had been involved in stealing black votes in their pursuit of the higher purpose of white supremacy.[32] The *Selma Times* defended the custom even more vigorously as a necessary antidote to Reconstruction-sponsored black enfranchisement and concomitant federal encroachment. We are "one of those papers that does not believe it is any harm to rob . . . the vote of an illiterate Negro. . . . [T]hey ought [n]ever to have had the privilege of voting." The ballot was forced on "them and the white people by the bayonet," the Black Belt newspaper argued, and the "first law of nature, self-preservation, gives us the right to do anything to keep our race and civilization from being wiped off the face of the earth."[33] "I have always deplored" the existence of conditions that made fraud a "necessary measure," Alabama's legendary U.S. senator John Tyler Morgan concurred. "But I count Negro domination of the white people . . . as an outrage that our people should not be compelled to submit to. . . . I have not censured any man for resorting to any means to prevent this wrong."[34]

More troubling to the oligarchy than the moral consequences of their fraud, though, was the threat a viable black vote posed in possible combination with poor and working-class whites. The biracial possibility, implicit in Reconstruction Republicanism, had grown steadily more visible through the Greenback-Labor movement and other Independent movements during the 1880s. In the Populist revolt of the nineties, it had become especially ominous. Despite their impressive rhetoric about cherishing the suffrage rights of plain whites, Alabama's powerful Big Mule/Black Belt coalition looked longingly at black disfranchisement as a net in which many poor whites could also become ensnared.[35]

Conflicting Allegiances: Populists, Plain Whites, and Race

But it must be said—and this is where the disfranchisement myth is at its weakest—poor whites were not simply the blameless victims of draconian patrician machinations. In fact, the willingness of poor whites to remove blacks from politics by statute contributed in no small way to their own eventual political demise. In Alabama, virtually all plain whites who opposed disfranchisement did so mainly because they suspected that their own voting rights might also be impaired, not because they viewed black disfranchisement as a distasteful prospect. Many common whites who eventually backed one or several methods of disfranchisement bought the privileged whites' promise that blacks could be disfranchised without touching the poor-white vote. Ultimately, both poor and privileged white postures toward black disfranchisement were determined by short-run estimations of how such a "reform" would affect their own narrow political, social, and economic self-interests.

Things got worse as they went along for the Populists in terms of paying the price for trying to mount a biracial challenge in the Deep South. But even during its heyday, the Populist commitment to biracial politics had often been incomplete, expedient, and ultimately ephemeral.[36] Although the Populists are due considerable credit for even attempting to organize a biracial challenge to entrenched power in the late-nineteenth-century South, this praise must be tempered by the realization that their coalition of poor whites and blacks was frequently uneasy, usually one-sided, and sometimes transparently self-serving.

However flawed and self-serving, though, being a Populist in the Deep South, at least during the 1890s, took courage and, eventually, a large toll on the psyches and esteem of the insurgents, a price that, for many, proved to be too much. The Populist attempt at biracialism involved serious risks. Often the insurgents faced the harshest of criticism for their politics—waves of social isolation and ridicule that eventually wore down even the most steadfast anti-Democrats and led some of them "down the gloomy road of bitterness, anxiety, and race hatred." In Marshall County, for example, Populist farmers taking their produce to market in Guntersville found themselves besieged by housewives denouncing them as "nigger lovers and nigger huggers."[37] During the 1890s, Populist candidates and their supporters heard themselves repudiated as advocates of "Negro and Republican rule" and voting "for the Negro," of constructing unnatural alliances between the "wooly-headed black-skinned negro" and "the blond blue-eyed" southerner. Their electoral efforts, especially fusion with the Republicans in 1896, implied the merging of "straight hair . . . with kinky hair" and "honest principles with dishonest principles," the formation of a "howling, fuming, stinking mob."[38] Even marrying a Populist in the South could lead to angry mobs of whites following the new couple, banging pots and pans and wondering how any "decent woman" could marry a Populist![39]

Yet the weakness of waging coalition reform based on pragmatism, even when it takes a real social and psychological toll on its adherents, is that it is inherently temporary. As external conditions change, no internal or, for that matter, eternal principle is present to hold in check the pragmatism that suggests ditching yesterday's friends for tomorrow's greener pastures.

In addition, all the Populists were not of one mind or even one pocketbook. Though they were generally in economic and political contradistinction to the Redeemers, there were degrees of separation between the privileged and the various types of individuals who became Populists and other kinds of anti-Democrats. Among the "plain" and "poor" whites loosely arrayed against the Redeemers was, of course, a collection of individuals whose interests did not always perfectly gel. On one end were the sharecroppers and day laborers, who looked at the world of the privileged across a gulf so wide that world must have appeared infinitely unattainable and foreign. But middling farmers and small tenants and even some small-town folks, who sometimes employed the croppers and laborers, also marched under the various insurgent banners at different times and places.[40]

Yet, ultimately, had the Populists been as serious about black voting as they trumpeted in 1892, their commitment to it would not have faded by 1900—but it did. Had they been as serious as they claimed about salvaging the black man's franchise, they might have lobbied for federal intervention and the monitoring of southern elections. But when confronted in 1890 with the possibility of federal voting registrars in the Lodge "force bill," the white Populists gathered at a national convention in Ocala, Florida, opposed the measure with wild hostility.[41] The southern Populists were white men first and political malcontents second. They were reformers, even genuine economic liberals, who must be given their due on that score. But their reform was laced with the arsenic of a self-interest and expedience that was all too apparent, especially to their potential black allies. It was an expedience that the insurgents could ill afford if they hoped to attract and hold allies of color. This racism exacted a higher toll on their movement—precisely because its only hope for success was biracial cooperation—than on that of their Bourbon counterparts, who made no bones about their taste for black political servitude. Populist reforms, as impressive as they sometimes were, were also conceived within the mainstream of southern conventions on race and social equality.

In fact, it was Populist opposition to two early Bourbon attempts at disfranchisement through literacy and property tests and a convention that has skewed much subsequent historical analysis.[42] Although Populists in the Alabama state legislature fought the two moves because they feared an ameliorated white vote, scholars have taken the two instances and extrapolated to imply permanent, unwavering, and unanimous Jeffersonian opposition to disfranchisement generally. Some have even extrapolated to the point of concluding that the insurgents were guardians of universal manhood suffrage—defenders of the black franchise.

Yet on a number of occasions, even before the moment of truth in 1901, a racial uneasiness spilled over into Populist support of outright white supremacy. For example, in 1894 a majority of the twenty-one Populists in the Alabama legislature actually voted against abolishing the convict-lease system, even though the practice combined the most abhorrent kind of race and class exploitation for the purpose of keeping taxes low and generating enormous profits for the state's burgeoning industries.[43] Populist leaders often carried racist baggage that was impossible to discard entirely once the farmers' movement picked up steam. Reuben F. Kolb, for example, commissioner of agriculture and two-time Populist candidate for governor in Alabama had by 1892 earned a reputation for severe enmity toward black political participation. In 1896, while still a Populist, Kolb publicly praised the Populists for preventing blacks from "infiltrating their ranks." After his Populist candidacies, Kolb would return to the Democratic fold and push for disfranchisement.[44]

Early on, many poor agrarians actually welcomed the prospect of a constitutional convention because it promised the removal of blacks from politics.[45] Alabama's Populists, sometimes termed Jeffersonian Democrats, actually got in on the ground floor of calling for the disfranchisement of black voters. In 1892 and again in 1893, the Alabama Populists called for the establishment of an all-white Democratic primary, which would, by its very nature, exclude blacks from politics. At the party's 1894 convention, which eventually nominated Reuben Kolb for a second gubernatorial run, the Populists called for a white party primary that would nominate a slate of candidates for state office and a new state executive committee. The *Montgomery Alliance Herald,* a Jeffersonian mouthpiece, frankly avowed the Populist purpose as wanting to "maintain white supremacy and to have a ticket selected where only white men will vote."[46] Populist leader William H. Skaggs offered his belief that "all agree" that, "rather than a blessing," the ballot had been a "curse" to the African American. For the 1894 election, white Populists implored blacks to "stay away from the polls" and "let the white voters settle the matter themselves." Some of the anti-Democrats even proposed a mass "disposal" of every black in Alabama to a separate, all-black state. After the election, a Hill Country Populist newspaper declared there was "little doubt now" that there would be, or should be, a constitutional convention to disfranchise blacks. The only question was "how to do it without disfranchising a large number of whites." If that could be done, then "[w]e would not object to a Constitutional Convention." The *Birmingham People's Weekly Tribune* agreed in late 1896 and early 1897 that the imminent convention should save the votes of "all whites," that the African American was now universally recognized as a "nuisance" to good government and, in fact, a "peril" to "civilization."[47] In 1898, the Populist version of biracialism was openly coercive. Populists declared that if African Americans did not support the ticket, they would allow Democrats to disfranchise all blacks. Only after their attempts to create a pure white electorate failed did the Populists begin to compete with the state's paternalists for the black vote.[48]

Plain whites disliked black voting because black votes allowed the Black Belt to dominate state politics and because many plain whites were devout adherents to the doctrine of white supremacy, which they thought should extend to a white-only electorate. Some favored black disfranchisement because Black Belt voting irregularity had proven to be an insurmountable advantage to their foes. Explained the Populist *Tuscaloosa American*, the day for "voting dead negroes and dogs in Alabama, has practically passed."[49]

Many Populists also welcomed disfranchisement because political alliance with blacks had been temporary, expedient, and distasteful to them; it grated against a persistent and powerful poor-white racism. William H. Denson, a congressman identified with the reform wing of the Democratic Party, the masses, Jeffersonian principles, and his friendship with Joseph F. Johnston, enjoyed the electoral support of Jeffersonian and Populist leaders such as Marshall County's Thomas Atkins Street. Denson eventually became a leading figure in the fight against ratification of the 1901 Constitution. But as late as 1899 Denson still favored a convention to draft a disfranchising constitution because, as he put it, the issue would "determine the question of whether or not the Anglo-Saxon race is to control Alabama . . . or shall it be a hybrid race hereafter?" "The plain English of it," Denson said, "is to eliminate the negro from the ballot box." "[And] in that step," he pledged, "I give my heart and my hand, and trust to the God that made us to preserve the supremacy of the white race. The rejection of the unfit is going on."[50] Only later, after Denson and other plain-white representatives realized that control of the movement for a convention had swung almost completely to the Black Belt, did he and his compatriots decide to oppose the convention, but not disfranchisement generally and certainly not the disfranchisement of black people. I. L. Brock, editor of the Populist *Cherokee Sentinel* and a Populist leader in the "Bloody Seventh" congressional district, was even more direct. At one point, he reminded Oliver Day Street, a former Populist and emerging Republican leader, "You know [as well as I that] the populists always were willing and ready for the negro to be disfranchised if it could be done without disfranchising the white man."[51] A Hill Country anti-Democrat echoed Brock's words almost verbatim: "We do not believe that one white man will be disfranchised . . . but undoubtedly a large number of negroes will. This should be a feature very agreeable to our friends the Populists, who were always in favor of getting rid of the negro vote."[52] "What do the white men of Cullman County think of being classed politically with the negroes?" another Populist editor from the Hill Country jeered bitterly. "Rather tough isn't it?"[53] Such commentary made it clear that for many insurgents their temporary alliances with blacks had been obnoxious, degrading, repellent—something they felt reduced to by adverse circumstances: "The white people . . . may be forced down on an equality with negroes," one allowed, "but they will hardly stay there."[54]

Most of the few "lily-white" Republicans left in Alabama favored the disfranchisement of blacks as a direct function of their racism and as the only hope for "respectability" for southern Republicanism. The racial division had already been much in evidence within the state GOP. In 1894, Alabama's lily-white Republicans had supported Reuben Kolb for governor, and the Populists, in turn, backed the Aldrich brothers, two lily-white Republicans running for congress. But at their state convention in Birmingham, the Populists refused to allow black Republicans to speak and physically drove "black and tan" Republicans from the hall. One Populist leader even threatened to shoot "every damned Negro who offered to vote." Infuriated, and already on mutually suspicious terms with the white Populists, black Republican leader William Stevens organized black-and-tan support for William Oates against Kolb. The lily-white *Huntsville Republican* chimed in by advocating the move toward a convention because "we . . . support white man's government. . . . [Presently] the illiterate Negro forms the basis of Republican strength in Alabama, men unfit to lead any party . . . the awkward, the uncouth, the unworthy . . . despicable to refined men." The Republican *Huntsville Tribune* promised that the overwhelming majority of north Alabama's white GOP would support a convention.[55]

Opposition to the calling of a constitutional convention—like the later resistance to ratification—was comprised almost solely of individuals such as Hill Country Populist Gilbert B. Deans, who feared that his poor-white constituents would be caught in the web of black disfranchisement. Deans and other Populists made certain to include specific denial of social equality for African Americans as an aim in their 1898 platform.[56] Fittingly, even Deans's opposition to Democratic electoral fraud was couched in the language of white supremacy. Such fraud was "negro rule under democratic supervision," the Shelby County Populist maintained. "Is that white supremacy?"[57] While Deans was acutely aware that privileged Democrats wanted to keep African Americans "in ignorance and vice" in order to "prey alike upon the poor, ignorant white man and black man," he was also painfully cognizant that patrician appeals to the "lowest prejudices of the white men"—his constituents—could, in fact, be quite effective. Interestingly, Deans's own reasons for opposing a convention included some that were overtly racial. He spared no denunciation of blacks who voted with the regular Democracy, damning them as "dangerous" and "evil," and reserved special opprobrium for their black leaders. As the "creature[s] of democracy and the social pet[s]" of the free-silver Democrats, Deans charged, they were "especially dangerous." Any danger of trouble between the races, Deans warned, will be "due solely to the evil work" of free-silver Democrats, who had erred in giving "prominence to the most dangerous class of negroes."[58] Indeed, there were some—not a great many, but some—African Americans who linked their fortunes voluntarily with the Bourbon Democrats instead of with whites they referred to as "poor-white trash," and this worried men like Gilbert Deans greatly.[59] David Williams Parker, editor of a black Tuscaloosa paper, praised the "decent white people" of the South, whom African Americans were "in a hurry to express words of love for," and denounced the "so-called white republicans and radical Negroes." Parker advised African Americans to look to Montgomery, not Washington, for help and assured them that the Democratic Party is "not so black and bloody as declared by some!"[60]

Still, Deans's and other Populists leaders' most oppressive recurring fears revolved around poor-white emotions and the power of white supremacy. In effect, they worried over the very real possibility that anti-Democrats could be distracted and dissuaded from class pursuits by the siren call of racial fidelity and racial solidarity—a doctrine so fundamental, so deep-seated, so emotional and ingrained that they themselves were unqualified adherents to its tenets. "[T]his beautiful theory" of white supremacy, worried Deans, could be manipulated to arouse intense emotions and "suspicion of a lurking danger and appeal to the most sensitive impulses of a people who are easily aroused . . . [by] racial prejudice and are ever ready to defend their state and their homes at any cost." Doubtless these concerns were valid and stemmed from the memory of Redemption from Reconstruction rule, when a politics of emotional white cooperation across class lines that muted economic dissent overwhelmed and ended foreign and "negro rule." It was no accident that the epic 1874 appeal for Redemption had been made from south Alabama to "the mountain counties" in language loaded with the emotion of chivalry and white supremacy, a language that resonated powerfully with deeply rooted plain-white emotions. A quarter century later the effects of these culturally engraved beliefs were still very much in evidence. Redemption, according to the editor of one Alabama Populist newspaper, marked the moment when the "spirit of the revolutionary movement" of black, Yankee, Republican, and federal rule "in Alabama [was] . . .

destroyed" by passion and pan-white solidarity on the racial issue. "The appeal to the whites for united race action," John Witherspoon DuBose wrote approvingly, "was heard with the ardor of earnest men thoroughly aroused to meet the menaces of fanaticism precipitated from without [and led to] . . . the fruits of [an] inestimable victory."[61]

Virtually all the other Alabama Populists and anti-Democrats who opposed a constitutional convention looked to protect members of their own caste and class.[62] They fought the movement because they were fearful a constitutional convention focused on disfranchisement, in its zeal to target blacks, would also hurt poor whites. The *Tuscaloosa American* took this line. So did the *Randolph Toiler.* So did the *Carrollton, Alabama Alliance News,* the *Cherokee Sentinel,* and a number of other anti-Democratic organs. The *Sentinel's* editor explained later that he and other Populists had no compunction about disfranchising blacks if they could only devise a way to do it without impinging on the poor-white vote.[63] The *Sheffield Reaper,* a mouthpiece for Shelby County's Independent Democrats, explained its opposition to the convention along racial and class lines: placing "unfortunate white men on an equality with negroes 'just down to the nigger' is not a principle of Americanism." An Independent Democratic editor in Tennessee warned his Alabama brethren that many common whites in his state had bought the privileged class's promise that the disfranchisement law applied "only to 'niggers' " and would not "disfranchise any white man. . . . But today," he sadly informed the Alabamians, "these same men are disfranchised and cannot vote."[64] The official Alabama Populist platform of 1898 made no mention of blacks being disfranchised or of opposition to the principle of disfranchisement generally. In fact, the platform did not mention blacks even once. It simply stipulated that the party was opposed to the calling of a state constitutional convention "under [the] present conditions" of elite Democratic control and against the goal of disfranchising the "poor and illiterate"—in other words, poor whites.[65] A dribble of additional opposition came from corporations anxious about higher taxes, railroads fearing regulation of their inflated freight rates, and even a few Black Belt leaders who worried about a loss of lopsided sectional power if a new constitution were to tamper with total population as the basis for apportionment.[66]

The issue split the Populists precisely because it was extraordinarily difficult. For insurgent whites the question pitted their unhappiness with a slanted economic playing field against their most deeply held prejudices and racial assumptions. A number of the Populists displayed an acute class consciousness and sense of racial justice: a realization that "[p]ast history" was replete with lessons of how the rule of the "so-called 'virtuous and intelligent' " had repeatedly been the rule of "the rich and the favored ones of the earth . . . the most tyrannical and despotic in character," a rule in which only "two classes exist, the master and the slave," and ambition was "crushed out of the toiling masses while the rich revel[ed] in vice and splendor."[67] Thus, the anti-Democrats were naturally suspicious of electoral reform that originated with their class adversaries.

Things also might have turned out differently for both the white anti-Democrats and African Americans if their early post-Reconstruction coalitions had experienced more success. There can be little question that electoral defeat hardened independent racial attitudes over time as despair and the natural tendency toward scapegoating set in. Studies of the early Redeemer movement suggest that cooperation between the have-nots and have-littles of both races perhaps ran more smoothly before the disappointments of the Populist 1890s.[68] Without question the difficulties confronting the Populists in trying to hold together a biracial alliance in the Deep South were large ones. And there can also be little doubt that the effect of repeated electoral defeats resulting from Redeemer fraud and violence must have been disheartening and demoralizing, especially since such tactics were utilized against the insurgents in a democracy whose founding rhetoric advertised itself as the world's most open form of government. Thus we are left to wonder what might have been if only the earlier independents had won more often.

Yet this acknowledgment, and the wistfulness and speculation that sometimes accompany it, should be tempered with considerable caution. We should be careful about leaping to the conclusion that all would have been well in the area of biracial cooperation if only earlier successes had been achieved. That is a possibility, but it is far from a foregone conclusion. Studies that chart early biracial cooperation in the anti-Redeemer movement also document that these same movements held within them explosive racial tensions—passions that festered just beneath the surface of the coalitions. Given the proper spark or scratched in such a way as to remove the thin covering of racial harmony, these relationships could combust. A Georgia anti-Redeemer who insisted that the black man be "let alone" in his legal, civil, and economic rights also acknowledged that he hailed from the white counties where "there is [much] prejudice against the negro." In fact, in his judgment, the prejudice of his white-county neighbors was worse than that of the whites of the black counties. "I have found," he told the state's 1877 constitutional convention, "that men who never owned a negro before the war, are usually [the] most intolerant towards him."[69] Another clue as to the fragile nature of the anti-Redeemer movement is found during the 1890s in Alabama, where growing cooperation with the Republican Party as "the party of Reconstruction" alienated white insurgents, especially in those places where the white dissidents' support for black rights "had been limited all along." An especially instructive example of the potential for problems is supplied by Lawrence County, perhaps the strongest seat of anti-Redeemer politics in Alabama from Reconstruction through Populism. A combination of conditions in Lawrence, including prewar free-labor ideology, strong wartime Unionism, growing soil exhaustion, and a depleted agricultural production that pushed more subsistence farmers into tenancy and the crop-lien system, made the county "the" hotbed of independent, Greenback-Labor politics and a militant biracial Agricultural Wheel. The county successfully and routinely returned majorities for the Greenback-Labor and Populist tickets in the 1880s and 1890s. Yet, confronted by an increasingly hysterical Redeemer press and emotion-laden charges that political insurgency meant socialism, communism, "animalism," immorality, and "fornicating with the Negroes," Lawrence voters supported both the call for a constitutional convention and ratification of its product.[70]

In Alabama, the overwhelming majority of the Jeffersonians desired the eradication of blacks from politics for a variety of reasons, ranging from pragmatic estimations of how the Populists might do in a white-only politics to religious and philosophical convictions against black political participation and black equality. Some of the Jeffersonians, who feared a constitutional convention precisely because they suspected the wealthy of plotting to purge their rolls along with African Americans, projected their rage against the oligarch onto the black. They were convinced that "the nigger in South Alabama," voting willingly or not, would be the instrument by which the call for a convention would be passed to their ruin. Other Populists explained that they had no objection to the calling of a convention or the abolition of the black ballot, only a very great fear of the "crowd that would . . . dominat[e] it . . . the old Palmer and Buckner fellows."[71]

The issue was so difficult—and so tempting—for anti-Democrats who wanted to get rid of black voters but protect themselves that some of them began to exhibit signs of schizophrenia resulting from the competing stresses. And always the memory and emotion of Reconstruction rule with its attendant "Negro supremacy" weighed heavy on their minds. One Hill Country Populist editor was so torn by the issue that he actually reversed himself in print within a month after he declared, "[W]e are opposed to the disfranchisement of any citizen, black or white, on account of illiteracy or poverty." Reconstruction and race, as usual in Alabama, were the reasons. "Little did many of us think when this negro vote was used to defeat us in the latter [18]60s and the early 70s that it would ever be used by our own people against us," he said in explaining his reversal. "But so it has been, and . . . it will always be . . . until the negro is eliminated from politics." Upon closer examination, though, even the original opposition to disfranchisement was colored by a concern that illustrated the interlocked nature of racial and class issues, a concern with methods that might entangle poor whites rather than blacks or elite whites. "[U]nder the plan that will be adopted," the Populist said in explaining his opposition, "every illiterate white man who will not vote for the machine will be deprived of his vote. . . . [W]e unhesitatingly and emphatically declare ourselves in favor of White Supremacy [because we] . . . believe that the peace and dignity of the whole South . . . can be made sure and permanent when all our offices are filled by men who secured their election by having . . . a majority of the white vote."[72] While the Bourbons might have felt they held a monopoly on race and Reconstruction memories in Alabama, the Populists did not agree. In fact, the Jeffersonians were almost as proficient as the Bourbons in resurrecting the emotional language and imagery of race, Reconstruction, and patriotism to combat their privileged opponents:

> Were the principles of populism right in 1892? If so, principles never change. . . . Is it an argument for you to desert your party today that the negroes were preferred . . . to you . . . [by] the democrats [who said] . . . they "would rather have the votes of the good democratic negroes than those of uncertain populists"? Sadly have those who control the destinies of the democratic party . . . today departed from their prayers in the [eighteen-] seventies—[Y]ou old men of the hills . . . well remember how State and county commissioners implored you to come to the aid of the black belt . . . and rescue them from negro rule and domination. You have not forgotten those days, nor those appeals to your patriotism, nor . . . in 1874 . . . a victory in Alabama, that you thought forever settled the question of negro supremacy in this state. Ah! Little did you then think that this same negro vote would one day be used to crush and annihilate you, first at the ballot box, and then be preferred to you. . . . It is a hateful sight.[73]

"Forces of Darkness": Convention Opposition and a Senate Contest

Opposition to calling a constitutional convention soon crystallized around former convention champion Alabama governor Joseph F. Johnston. An enigma to many of his contemporaries, in 1892 and 1896, Johnston had favored the idea of a convention that would constitutionally limit the franchise to, in his words, only "those with 'virtue and intelligence.'" In 1892 he had backed a Sayre-type of suffrage restriction.[74] The election of 1896, arguably Alabama's first in the Progressive Era, dramatized quite clearly the vitally important role race played in the state's politics. Johnston cleverly utilized a platform that, at once, gave assurances on the race issue to Alabama's Black Belt and to Hill Country whites and gave the Populists what they wanted on the currency question.[75] It was lily-white Populism and conciliatory Democracy—free-silver without the rhetoric or the baggage of black franchise. And it was amenable to the planter-industrialist clique. For the sop of free silver, the Conservative Democrats could reunite their party, maintain control, and avoid another fratricidal rift. It demonstrated that, given sufficient concessions on currency, many poor whites were ready and willing to forget their pledges about the importance of black voting and return to the Democratic Party. That is, things being equal between the Democrats and the Populists on currency, many rural whites were quite willing to let race dictate the way they voted.

To hedge his bet, Johnston campaigned against Reconstruction's "excessive" taxation and had surrogates, including T. G. Jones, denounce his opponent as a "nigger lover." Democratic newspapers such as the *Mobile Register* derided the Republican-Populist fusion ticket as "Repopnig." Accordingly, Johnston snowed under Albert T. Goodwyn, his 1896 Populist opponent, who did not begin to approach the massive totals that Reuben Kolb had generated for Jeffersonian Democracy in 1892 and 1894. In his inaugural address as governor, Johnston proposed a repeal of the Sayre Election Law in the countryside, but not in the cities, "an obvious attempt," in the words of one historian, "to strike at the Negro vote without harming the white vote."[76]

Reelected in 1898 on the free-silver platform and again with the support of many Populists and former Populists, Johnston (now called a "half-Populist" by some) increasingly understood that his base of support came from Alabama's plain folk.[77] In his 1898 biennial address to the legislature, Johnston suggested the disfranchisement of African Americans by constitutional amendment rather than by a convention to draft a new constitution, which carried a greater risk of poor whites being entangled in the net of suffrage restriction. White Populists warmly received "Red-headed Joe's" idea. Some, such as John W. Callahan, the Hill Country Populist editor of the *Randolph Toiler* who frequently lauded Johnston in the pages of his newspaper as "Our Populist Governor" and "a very good Populist," exhibited a sense of kinship, even ownership.[78] Following his 1898 triumph, Johnston grew increasingly anxious as he watched the movement for a convention fall under the spell of Alabama's most conservative elements—men like gold Democratic adversaries and patrician former governors William C. Oates and Thomas Goode Jones. To the "half-Populist" governor, the obvious threat was what a convention dominated by such men might mean for his plain-white base. For Johnston, who would repeatedly insist that he was just as good a white supremacist as his patrician foes, the goal was protecting plain-white votes, not black ones.[79] After polling the legislature to make sure that he had enough support, in "one of the boldest and most daring [moves] . . . ever attempted in the South," Johnston called a special session to repeal the 1898 enabling act that had called for a constitutional convention.[80]

The audacity of Johnston's move highlighted the importance the constitution was taking on for Alabama's powers-that-be and powers-that-would-be. Events accelerated in the wake of the Johnston-led repeal. In May 1899 the Democratic State Convention (DSC) met in Montgomery to issue a formal denunciation of the governor's actions and to set up an elite committee to overturn the repeal. The *Birmingham Age-Herald*, representative of industrial north Alabama, labeled Johnston's act "treason," while the Black Belt *Selma Times* was even harsher. "Joe Johnston hails from Dallas [County]," its editor wrote. "We speak of it with shame. . . . We call him Judas because he . . . bargains with the enemy for our undoing . . . [and] because the only thing left for him to do is to hang himself on the first tree." Other Black Belt editors raised the racial specter and preyed on primal white emotions by arguing that Johnston's act jeopardized "white supremacy and purer politics."[81]

The push of the privileged bore fruit. Six months later, the state legislature passed a second enabling act calling for a popular election on the issue of a convention; the measure provided for 155 delegates, most of them elected on the lower house's basis of apportionment. In January 1900 the DSC met in Montgomery to approve the new enabling act and in March reiterated its 1898 pledge to restrict the convention's power to increase taxes, change the basis of legislative apportionment, or, most importantly, disfranchise poor whites.[82] The DSC also included a plank that made black disfranchisement and the confirmation of Redemption from the dark days of Reconstruction crystal clear: "After an experience of thirty years . . . it has been demonstrated that as a race [blacks are] incapable of self-government."[83]

If anyone was still unclear that a constitutional convention meant to return the state to the ante-Reconstruction status quo, the Democrats' adoption of the campaign motto "White supremacy, suffrage reform, and purity in elections" should have erased any doubts. In Montgomery the DSC appointed a special committee to oversee the campaign for a referendum calling for a convention and chaired it with powerful Alabama Railroad Commission president John V. Smith. Again, Alabama's privileged Democracy invoked a stratagem of propagating and distributing the Great Lie: assuring plain whites that their interests could safely be left to the patricians while blacks were disfranchised. Any deviation from the Bourbon party line, of course, would qualify as heretical conduct that compromised white supremacy in the most serious way. Heavyweight patricians William C. Oates, Thomas Goode Jones, and U.S. senator Edmund L. Pettus lent their aid to the oligarchy's campaign committee. Congressman John H. Bankhead reassured suspicious poor whites that the disfranchisement of blacks would not harm them. On the contrary, he promised, black disfranchisement would allow a thriving two-party system of white voters to return to Alabama. John Tyler Morgan, Pettus's senior partner in the Senate, pounded the issue of racial treason by declaring that the only thing that really mattered to

him and the proconvention forces was the maintenance of "white supremacy."
Meanwhile, committee chair John V. Smith issued marching orders for the campaign that explicitly instructed his bureau of elite speakers to do everything they could to "quiet the fears of our [white] brethren in the hill counties and Wiregrass" on the matter of ancillary poor-white disfranchisement.[84] The privileged forces in control of the DSC knew full well that this fear was the only possible issue that could derail the disfranchisement train. Virtually all white Alabamians agreed on the goal of black disfranchisement. The only issue was calming the poor-white fear that they, too, would be, purposely or not, disfranchised by the measures designed to restrict black suffrage.

The convention issue was so important that Alabama's 1900 senatorial contest between incumbent John Tyler Morgan and his challenger, Governor Joseph F. Johnston, actually became a de facto referendum on the matter.[85] It is difficult to exaggerate the intensity of the animosity Johnston had engendered by his legislative maneuver to repeal the enabling act. Now, the governor's bid for the U.S. Senate seat of Morgan, a living institution, absolutely infuriated his former patrons. Always sensitive about matters of honor, the patricians damned Johnston as an unscrupulous traitor whose boundless and offensive ambition had transcended the level of mere crassness. The maneuver was more than just annoyance; now it imperiled the very foundations of white supremacy. In truth, the Johnston sacrilege brutalized their collective sense of propriety and integrity every bit as much as it violated their sense of racial security. But to the patricians, Johnston's action was not only obnoxious to their fundamental creed; it was also quite dangerous. Former governor and ally Rufus W. Cobb denounced the governor in near fighting words and lamented all "the work I have done for [him] . . . as I am fully convinced that he is a base ingrate [and a] political trickster with no political honesty in him."[86]

The senatorial race had all the makings of a family feud. The fifty-seven-year-old governor had gained his office largely through the good graces of men like Cobb, Morgan, and the others who now stood arrayed against him. A Civil War veteran, Johnston held impeccable credentials as the two-time chair of the State Democratic Executive Committee (SDEC), including having had the special honor of presiding over the Redemption election and restoration of 1874. An attorney from Dallas County, deep in the Black Belt, Johnston personified the "New Man" variant of the New South Redeemers.[87] In 1884 he had moved to Birmingham to assume the posts of president of the Alabama State Bank and member of the board of directors of the Jasper Land Company and the Sloss Iron and Steel Company. Yet despite his lofty pedigree, to many observers Johnston seemed Lilliputian next to Morgan, the unquestioned grand old man of Alabama Democracy. Morgan had won his spurs serving as a lieutenant to William

Lowndes Yancey in the secession movement and later served as a brigadier general in the War between the States. After the war he, too, returned to Selma and in 1876 gained election to the U.S. Senate, where he had safeguarded states' rights and white supremacy on behalf of white Alabamians for a quarter of a century.[88]

To add insult to injury, Morgan had invested his considerable stature vainly trying to stave off the legislative repeal of the first enabling act. During that struggle, as well as in his 1900 campaign for reelection, Morgan stressed that race—not free silver—was the central issue of any proposed constitutional convention. In effect, he argued, white Alabama was once again engaged in the sacred work of redeeming government from the Reconstruction apocalypse. Thus, to "recede or hesitate" in such a momentous affair as calling for a disfranchising constitution invites "disaster to the white voters." If Johnston would recommend such a course, then he would risk white supremacy for his own political ambition and was therefore "no Democrat."[89] Johnston responded with what was rapidly becoming a mantra. He insisted that he was just as good a white supremacist as Morgan, Oates, Pettus, Jones, Cobb, or any of the other patricians who now stood against him. He denied that he had any interest in preserving black suffrage. Moreover, he reasoned, since white supremacy was "complete and all-pervading," there was no reason for rushing into a constitutional convention.[90]

In the fall of 1900, the senatorial race took on added heat as three dramatic debates were scheduled between the two candidates, debates that would spend inordinate time and energy on race and the peril of Reconstruction revisited. For his part, Johnston denied any "personal" differences with his old "friend" and tried to confine the dialogue to Morgan's abandonment of William Jennings Bryan and free silver. But the old man would have none of it. At the start of the second debate, Morgan refused to shake Johnston's outstretched hand, an insult of serious proportions in the honor-conscious South. During one especially angry exchange during the third debate, Morgan marched across the dais with fists clenched and threatened, "governor or no governor," to hold the younger man "to account." Bystanders quickly restored order. At a Jackson County rally, a pro-Morgan speaker answered one heckler by throwing a drinking glass at him. The heckler responded with gunfire that narrowly missed its target.[91]

As the campaign progressed, race and a *Reconstruction syndrome* overshadowed all other issues. The syndrome—a psychological response to Dixie's traumatic experience of defeat, abolition, economic ruin, military occupation, and black suffrage—was a frequent reaction to politics and social issues manifested by a deep-seated negative or "anti" worldview. For much of the hundred years following the Civil War—especially during periods of crisis—Alabama, its politics, and much of the white South was chronically distinguished by the syndrome's most stubborn and ingrained components: antiblack, antifederal, antioutsider, anti-Yankee, antitax, and antiliberal impulses. While exceptions to each of these themes can occasionally be found, the frequency, intensity, scope, and degree of the negative feelings in the southern experience far outweigh their opposites.[92]

The syndrome was so powerful and pervasive in Alabama that it afflicted Populist and Democrat, poor and privileged, Black Belt and Upcountry, town and country, and city. In fact, perhaps no one articulated the syndrome with more passion and eloquence than John Witherspoon DuBose, editor of the Populist *Birmingham People's Weekly Tribune*. DuBose had not always been a political insurgent. Early in life he had been a scion of privilege and wealth. While still a young man, DuBose had inherited a large Marengo County plantation with many slaves, functioned as a stalwart member of Redeemer Democracy, and like other Black Belt planters, joined the Reconstruction Ku Klux Klan and the White Camellia. By 1894, though, DuBose had left the regular party behind and supported Reuben Kolb and the Populist ticket. By 1900, he was an intimate of Populists such as Philander Morgan and poor-white tribunes and "half-Populists" Joseph Johnston, Robert McKee, and Chappell Cory. Like others of his time and place, though, his growing economic liberalism did not correspond to racial progressivism. At the turn of the century, he replaced membership in the Klan and the Camellia with adherence to the White Shield.[93] For DuBose and other white Alabamians, the tenets of the syndrome played a central part in the crisis-drama over disfranchisement. Central to the ideology of the syndrome was revulsion for the existence of black suffrage—imposed at the point of federal bayonets, no less—a problem that demanded a solution. In fact, the subtitle of DuBose's *Forty Years of Alabama* put the issue squarely and simply: *A History of the Lapse and Recovery of Civil Government*. Completed in 1904, the manuscript made clear that the success of the disfranchisement movement was merely the final chapter in a recovery of civilization from the unnatural horrors of ignorant and corrupt black rule imposed on a noble and prostrate South by a vengeful foreign government in Washington. Before the war and Reconstruction, white rule represented civilization. After the war and Reconstruction, black involvement in politics was an abomination, a fatal pollutant; it marked the abject decline of civilization. Redemption in 1874 had marked the initial phase of recovery. The disfranchisement movement, embodied in the 1901 Constitution, was a culminating document marking the restoration of white rule and civilization, one and indistinguishable.

DuBose's history of Alabama read almost as a textbook guide for what would be called (and eventually discredited as) the Dunning School of historiography on Reconstruction. Evil "carpetbaggers" and dishonorable "scalawags," sometimes referred to as "the revolutionaries" or the "forces of darkness," dotted DuBose's pages as intermittent "battle[s] for white supremacy . . . [a] principle jealously guarded" by the state's whites, raged across the state. Slavery appeared as a gentle, civilizing period of tranquility when the "black toilers of the Alabama plantations . . . drew more of the fruit of their trial, for their own enjoyment, than the general agricultural population of Europe"—and when innate black proclivities toward immorality, sloth, sexual degeneracy, and crime were held in check by the religious/legal structure of the plantation regime. "The black belt negro . . . his morals, his religion, were of the master's daily care," DuBose wrote. "[H]e did not steal, . . . he did not swear nor drink strong drink because he was, in every moment of his life, under the moral restraint of plantation law founded on an abstract morality." Emancipation and enfranchisement of the freedmen had destroyed all of this. Black Belt counties, such as Dallas, had "been most afflicted" by runaway black rule. There the tax collector, the sheriff, and one commissioner were "white men." But the radicals had elected "a negro Judge of the Criminal Court and a negro Clerk of Beat Court, a negro clerk of the circuit Court, negro tax assessor, negro coroner and three negro commissioners, thus giving them entire control of the finances of the county in which they owned practically no accessible property [and] . . . [c]ontrol of the administration of justice was thus reposed in a class composed almost exclusively of negroes." "[M]alfeasance in office . . . stealing public money . . [and] [w]ild waste and reckless corruption seized . . . the forms of law," according to DuBose, as the "destruction of the public tranquility and the murder of the civil character of society" and the very "annihilation of the Republic" were celebrated by the "perpetrators in riotous delight." And always the federal government loomed as the ultimate force of evil—actually only the embodiment of Radical Yankee Republican rule "hostile" and "vengeful" toward the South. Restoration of states' rights and local control, therefore, was the only hope for salvation. The southern states were the

victims of Congress and . . . [t]he storm at Washington [that] gather[ed] in force. . . . [Reconstruction and black voting resulted in] degradation . . . catastrophe . . . evil . . . [and] in Alabama . . . the prolonged maintenance of the race line in politics. . . . Nullification and secession [were legitimate] . . . states' rights. . . . [Reconstruction had demonstrated] the geniuses of the role of the state . . . [and] the vindication of [secession and war]. [It had brought] military interference in civil affairs . . . [and] poverty [for] stricken farmers . . . disaster

[and] . . . an invasive enemy. . . . [M]anumission [resulted from] Congress legis-
lat[ing] upon the state monstrous schemes, radical and fanatical in which the approved customs of society and the laws of nature were alike condemned. . . . The
Southern States, with full governments of their own . . . [became] semi-military
provinces [leading to] perplexity and profound anxiety in the minds of careful
men who observed . . . Washington. . . . No orderly civil government could exist
in Alabama. Meantime . . . a Congress of the conquering states alone, busied itself . . . destroying the state. . . . [Wise men] . . . advise[d] . . . the freedmen . . .
"to let politics alone [and learn] . . . the utter absurdity of expecting or aspiring
to a condition of social equality with the white race" [and damned] the XIVth
Amendment as "inconsistent with the general theory of American free institutions." [Still, the Republican] party . . . vex[ed] Alabama from the seat of federal
power [and] . . . usurped the authority of . . . state governments. . . . [As a result,
t]he problem . . . which confronted Alabama . . . had never before been presented
for solution to any civilization. . . . [I]n this crisis . . . [f]riendly government from
within, and only from within, must be depended on to determine the methods
and civil procedures which might adjust the relations to each other of two unas-
similating races, in equal numbers, inhabiting the land. . . . [Thus, the] acts and
aspirations of the people of Alabama solemnly appeal[ed] to history, in their day
of trial and struggle, as acts and aspirations of the self-consecrated to the spirit
and forms of American liberty. They were punished by the Congress of a fraction
of the Union: their state government was extinguished [by] . . . the federal court
of supreme jurisdiction and despotic rule of the sword. . . . A masterful temper of
defiance where endurance had ceased to be a virtue, developed itself; a spirit never
abandoned.[94]

The DuBose history, written as a contemporary account of political events,
was a classic statement of Reconstruction syndrome language and theory. The
author, the editor of an anti-Democratic newspaper, hammered all the standard
Reconstruction themes—race, federal power, xenophobia, illiberalism—while
demonstrating almost perfect synchronization with privileged white political
foes on this defining subject. In Alabama, as in the South generally, the race
issue most often triggered the syndrome. During the 1900 election, John Tyler
Morgan vowed that he would look blacks square in the eye and tell them that
"I am in favor of taking away from you the right of suffrage." He challenged
Joseph Johnston to do the same. (See tables 1–3 in the appendix and maps 1
and 2.) The senator also branded Johnston's repeal of the enabling act as "patricide" against the Democratic Party, comparable to a cannibal devouring his
parents, and damned the governor for allowing a black Alabama militia company to enlist against the Spanish in 1898, for "stumbling on the race issue,"

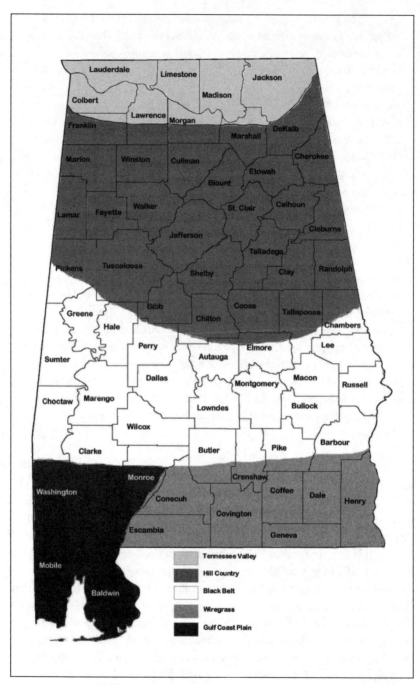

MAP 1 Alabama's Physiographical Regions

MAP 2 White Counties That Voted "for" John Tyler Morgan in 1900 Senatorial Race

and for repeatedly "evading the question of race." The *Birmingham Age-Herald* echoed Morgan's race baiting by condemning Governor Johnston for appointing a black as official chaplain and for addressing a black man as "Mister."[95]

Fully cognizant of the power of race in Alabama, the "half Populist" responded in kind. Johnston criticized Morgan's support for an imperialist foreign policy by asking Alabamians if they really wanted more "dark-skinned people in this country." The governor also repeated over and over that he was in favor of white supremacy, not black voting, and received aid on this score when Horace Hood and Chappell Cory's *Montgomery Journal* criticized Senator Morgan for voting to confirm Frederick Douglass's 1878 appointment as a federal marshal and for attending the wedding of a black senate colleague.[96]

In the end, though, Morgan's matchless pedigree, gold Democratic connections, superior political machine, and numerous Morgan Clubs throughout the state overwhelmed Johnston's shrewd use of state patronage as well as the endorsement of the senator's Populist brother, Philander Morgan.[97] Most importantly, it was Morgan's successful portrayal of Johnston as an unscrupulous individual who would somehow risk white supremacy that allowed him to sweep to an almost unanimous victory—sixty-two of the state's sixty-six counties— something that had not happened in Alabama in a very long time.[98]

What was perhaps most revealing of all was Johnston's failure to carry any significant portion of the old Populist vote. Close ties to north Alabama's poor whites and the insurgent plain folk of the hills and hollows had served "Captain Joe" well in 1896 and again in 1898. Yet, despite Johnston's best efforts to capture the Populist vote, including Reuben Kolb's stumping, J. T. Morgan swamped him among the Populists, former Populists, and assorted agrarian rebels—a foreshadowing of things to come in 1901, when the fundamental question, again, would be one of a disfranchising constitutional convention.[99]

CHAPTER TWO

Toward Disfranchisement

 The Morgan victory over Joseph Johnston was extraordinarily significant. For Alabama's white Democracy it represented the best chance for and evidence of unity that the party had experienced in over ten years. Alabama's Democracy had been buffeted and bruised by the Populist storms of the 1890s and even by the split between Palmer and Buckner gold Democracy and the Bryan free-silver variety. The infighting among white men had left deep scars and bitter feelings. It had caused the Democrats to resort to tactics they were not always proud of or even completely at ease with. As Alabama's regular Democrats watched the returns roll in for the "grand old man," however, they felt that at last they had cause for real celebration. They hoped that the scars were not beyond healing, the fractures not impossible to mend, their political souls not yet past the final point of redemption.

"The Most Glorious Victory": Hints of Political Unification

Political victory in sixty-two of a possible sixty-six counties was more than any fervent Democrat could have hoped for.[1] Populism had failed. The movement was basically over now. That much was clear. Counting in, counting out, ballot manipulation, superior organization, better financing, and, certainly not least, appeals to white solidarity had done in the insurgents. Defeated, disillusioned, and despairing of the prospects for a future biracial Independent movement, many of the anti-Democrats now turned on their erstwhile allies, the African Americans. The Morgan victory and its unparalleled degree made it clear, at least to the Democrats, that their fractured party was united again. More, it demonstrated that the unity hinged on the central concepts of white solidarity, white supremacy, antipathy to black suffrage, and a determination, once and for all, to rid the state of the Reconstruction blight of competing for inferior black votes. The time was ripe for a constitutional convention and a new, disfranchising constitution. In fact, the time had never been riper.

It was clear now that many of the old Populists had come back into the fold. And it was even clearer why they had done so. Raw emotion over white supremacy and Reconstruction had played as large a part as any other in making lions and lambs lie together again in Alabama. The Populists were white men, after all. The time had come for them, as it had previously for many Republicans and Independents, when they could not stand to hear once again how they had betrayed their race, how their unscrupulous political ambition was jeopardizing the very existence of their people. After two devastating Populist losses and the triumph of the free-silver faction in Alabama's fractured Democracy, race was now the foremost motivating issue.

As the Democrats worked out the political future of Alabama, they were self-consciously aware that they were engaged in a deadly serious enterprise, a project that would define and delimit politics for generations to come. They went about their work with the solemn realization that they were fashioning, not only a constitution that the state would live with for decades, but a whole way of doing politics. They were sanctifying the *politics of emotion* in Alabama, a politics based on the emotional appeals of race and Reconstruction to make sufficient numbers of the white majority forget their economic differences. It was a politics that salved wounded economic pride, sedated class tensions, and soothed the psyches of ordinary folks who wanted, somehow, to feel superior to other people. Sometime in the future, perhaps, race would be fortified with, or maybe even replaced by, other emotional fodder—religion, morality, patriotism, conventional sexuality.[2] But for now white supremacy was *the* emotional issue. And the patricians understood this reality very well.

Their celebration eulogized Morgan and defined the depths of their win. "You people of Alabama have won the most glorious victory in your history," Morgan's campaign manager informed his brethren. You have placed politics in Alabama on "a higher plane than they have been placed . . . for many a year. . . . You have done credit to yourselves, honor to your State [and] . . . filled the nation's heart with joy. . . . Your country will be better for it." Morgan himself was not only the "grandest living man in Alabama, but the grandest man that ever lived in Alabama." He was "Alabama's contribution . . . to the nation . . . the grand old man [who] . . . could win any fight on earth."[3] As unrepressed as Frank S. White's praise may seem now, he was not alone. J. Thomas Heflin, Chambers County representative of the plain people, concurred that Morgan was "the greatest Democrat Alabama has ever produced." "The greatness of some men, like objects seen through a mist, diminish with the distance," Heflin said, waxing poetic, "but Morgan, like a tower seen afar off and under a clear sky, rises in grandeur and sublimity at ever step. [He is t]he greatest son that Alabama has ever produced."[4]

Indeed, it was telling that the Democratic elite praised Morgan to the heights. Granted, Morgan had performed invaluable service as Alabama's senior senator in the country's upper chamber, safeguarding states' rights and home rule on race from the nation's capital. Still, the effusiveness of the praise signaled something deeper. John Tyler Morgan personified Conservative Democracy. The near completeness of his triumph represented to the privileged a kind of Redemption redux in which the effectiveness of the racial and emotional appeal had been decisively demonstrated. The future looked bright to Alabama's elite in 1900. In fact, they realized that, with the insurgent challenge all but buried, they stood a great chance of defining exactly what that future would be.

Unity, along with greatness, was the immediate watchword of the postelection celebration. Many of the old Populists and Jeffersonians, it was now clear, had come home. The question was why exactly, and what is more, what to do with them? and what to do with the newfound Democratic unity?[5] Actually, the Populists had been coming back into the party for several years before the election—1900 was more the dramatic culmination rather than a sudden occurrence. The trickle that began in 1896, prompted by personal attraction to Joseph F. Johnston and his free-silver sermons, picked up speed when the national Democratic Party coopted William Jennings Bryan and free silver in its Chicago Platform. Just two days after Bryan's nomination, Henry P. Burass, a schoolteacher and leading Populist organizer in Jefferson County, renounced Jeffersonian Democracy and came back into the Democratic fold. Robert A. McClellan of Limestone County followed suit. A Bibb County Populist did likewise, explaining that he would remain in the Democratic Party as long as it stood for "free silver and white supremacy." Even Philander Morgan returned for a short time. These defections and others led Joseph Johnston to chortle that the Populists are "coming back bodaciously" into the party.[6]

Over the next few years, other Populist leaders returned with a vengeance, some actually joining the right wing of the Alabama Democratic Party: former gubernatorial candidate Reuben Kolb, *Wetumpka Reform* editor Tyler Goodwyn, former congressman Milford W. Howard, Chilton County judge Samuel M. Adams, and I. L. Brock, the Cherokee County editor and probate judge. Other notable Populists followed the parade back into the party of their fathers, conversions that represented the return of thousands of prodigal insurgents: Birmingham attorneys John J. Altman and Peyton G. Bowman, state politico A. B. Brasswell, 1896 gubernatorial hopeful Albert T. Goodwyn, Limestone editor Hector D. Lane, and Sumter County's national Populist committeeman, Robert H. Seymour.[7]

There is no question that Alabama's Democrats felt more unified in 1900 than they had felt in a very long time. There is also no question that Alabama's leading political figures clearly realized that appeals to white solidarity had been an extremely powerful weapon in bringing back the white dissidents who had left the party under the Populist, Jeffersonian, and Independent banners—a development that was not lost on black observers. As H. C. Binford, Huntsville alderman, editor, and schoolteacher, lamented, "[T]here is nothing in politics for us" now. "It makes no difference which side" of the whites is involved. "[N]one of them want the Negro."[8]

The April 1900 Democratic State Convention in Montgomery became, then, a kind of homecoming celebration. One after another, leading Democrats extolled the "white man's convention . . . you assemble today, over 500 strong," and "the white people in a Democratic convention . . . men among whom there is no dissension . . . the faces of a permanently reunited Democracy."[9] "I love to look into your white faces, and to see your straight hair," silver Democratic congressman Henry De Lamar Clayton rejoiced. "I have wished for ten years to see the white people of Alabama united as they are to-day. I got tired of hearing of Alliances, tired of hearing about Populists. . . . But . . . the Populists and the Gold Bugs and the Platform Democrats, all have gotten together . . . we have buried our differences, we have united in a common cause . . . that the white civilization of Alabama is involved in the momentous proposition that the white men of Alabama must stand together now and forever."[10] Russell M. Cunningham, a silver Democrat, erstwhile ally of Joseph Johnston, and future lieutenant governor, agreed that a celebration was in order: "[T]his is a harmonious convention," the "gold men have come back and the populists have come back, and we are all together . . . the white people of Alabama to . . . maintain a white man's government—an honest government."[11] Thomas Heflin concurred: "The conservative populists of the State said to the regulars, you have been loyal to the faith, we will take down our flag and in the interest of harmony and white supremacy in Alabama we will meet you upon the Democratic altar. . . . I am powerful glad to see . . . the Democratic party of Alabama united under one flag. . . . [I]t is a reuniting of the white people of Alabama that means something in this commonwealth. . . . [T]he element that went out in 1892 have come back to stay," Heflin gushed, so now, "everything will be lovely."[12]

If the Populists and Jeffersonians could forget why they had buried their Independent movement to rejoin the Democratic Party, the regular Democrats were only too happy to remind them. The patricians never missed an opportunity to remind the late dissidents that they had done the right thing in putting race above all other concerns to rejoin the party of their fathers—the right thing not only for themselves but for their children, their children's children, and all of southern posterity. Such appeals, couched in the strong language of race and the Reconstruction memory, were, of course, emotional dynamite. They endowed the proceedings that would eventually culminate in a new constitution with a kind of self-conscious gravity and sense of importance reserved for only the most weighty and lasting of decisions. The homecoming also allowed the Jeffersonians to suppress the fact that their decision to rejoin had not been completely without coercion. It is true they had decided to put white supremacy above everything else. But they had done so only after succumbing to the most severe and relentless hammering by the patricians, who pointed out their racial treason, heresy, and sacrilege.[13]

"Stand Together": Race and Reconstruction as Unifiers

Alabama's most prominent political notables did the necessary work to drive the lesson home. A leader of the emerging progressive wing of the Democratic Party with strong connections to the old patrician wing, and a future U.S. senator himself, Frank White did much to nurture the powerful Reconstruction syndrome. No issue was more powerful. No issue was more emotional. Nothing else possessed the same capacity to make plain whites forget about, or at least subsume, their class interests. Knowing this, the Bourbons did much to feed and sustain the Reconstruction weapon. White tied the turn-of-the-century problem directly to Reconstruction and the problem of black rule, invoked religious authority in the process (another highly charged emotional weapon in the South), and set the stage for the logical result of a reunited white man's party, a disfranchising constitution. Perhaps most revealing was White's open advocacy of using race and Reconstruction to "arouse" the passions of the plain folk:

> God will bless you for what you have done. . . . [W]e set our race forward in a great movement that will make Alabama yet the greatest and grandest State of the Union. The great question of the elective franchise must be settled. The white line was formed in 1874, and swept the white men of Alabama into power. The white line has been reformed in 1900 to keep them in power forever. . . . We have disfranchised the African in the past by doubtful methods, but in the future we will disfranchise them by law. This cancer that has been eating upon the body politic, consuming the flesh, and poisoning the blood, must be taken away. This political vampire that is sucking the very life blood . . . of Alabama must be removed. . . . We have commenced the great work, we have commenced the agitation of the question, we will continue to agitate it, and . . . arouse the public mind until it becomes a permanent fixture there.[14]

One of the most emotional of all emotional issues in any time and place is, of course, posterity, the future, the world we leave to the children . . . our children. Fully aware of this power, the patricians combined race and responsibility to progeny to produce a wickedly potent concoction they did not hesitate to employ. The new white unity was "an unmistakable demand for a convention,"

Anniston's John B. Knox affirmed. "We will deal with this question" and deal with it in "no uncertain terms. We owe it to ourselves and to our children. Why, think of raising your children under a system like this."[15] One of Alabama's U.S. congressmen echoed Knox's reasoning and stressed that the emotional "for the children" issue could be used to blunt any inclination the old Populists might have to return to their economic insurgency. "[L]et us go to our brethren as we have in the past, and put our arms about their necks when they differ with us . . . on any economic question . . . and reason with them," H. D. L. Clayton recommended. "[L]et us tell them that the white civilization of Alabama is involved in the momentous proposition that the white men of Alabama must stand together now and forever. . . . Your wives, your little children, your school house, your churches—all that is good in our State, all that we hope to hand down as a blessed heritage to our children's children," he stressed, "is involved in that paramount question. . . . [L]et us not divide hereafter." And just for good measure, Clayton threw in the always-reliable war and Reconstruction reference. He was bearing this important message, he claimed, as a personal favor to the "grand old Third Division of Alabama."[16] Alabamians have "something in this fight for themselves, for their children, and for posterity," Frank White stated in the same vein. "[T]hirty years we have waited, thirty years have we stood chained by the despotism of ignorance placed around our hands by hate and jealousy. . . . What excuse can be given for enfranchising a race of slaves? Why was your sovereignty and mine taken from us and placed in the hands of . . . a race who had never ruled anything on earth?" It was "the political crime of the age . . . the folly of a nation," White answered. "We have borne it, we have tried it, we have experimented with it, but we have reached the last ditch, and now we must change or die," he explained. "Let no uncertain sound go out from this convention," a convention that "represents the white people of Alabama . . . pledged to white supremacy and a constitutional convention . . . harmonious and clear. . . . We can never vote so long as there is a black line drawn up against the white line, the white man . . . on one side and the black man on the other," he concluded. "I tell you, it cannot exist half white and half black."[17]

In Redeemer reality, fraud and ballot manipulation were, of course, the fault of blacks, who had refused to stay put in their place, and the federal government and Yankee meddlers, who had pushed them to get out of it in the first place. An important part of the black and Yankee crime had been the federal government's unwarranted usurpation of constitutionally guaranteed states' rights. In the Redeemer mind, this intrusion was a violation so great and fundamental that it justified any means necessary to restore sovereignty and order. As such, the corruption was understandable, even admirable. Yet its time and the time of African American political participation had to end. Ballot-box manipulation, John Knox explained, was "a revolutionary measure . . . justified upon that ground. . . . After the war the negro was placed in power throughout the State. . . . The South was prostrate, we could not resist by force of arms . . . because the negro had the federal government at his back. . . . [So] we did what we do. . . . We resorted to strategy . . . intellect . . . a greater intellect" than the blacks. The right of revolution, after all, Knox apologized, had long been recognized; "it is accorded to every people." During the hell of Reconstruction, southerners exercised that right, the north Alabama industrialist explained, but there must always "come a time when the right of revolution must cease, and we must return to constitutional government." The following year Knox would serve as the presiding officer for the all-important constitutional convention. His sentiments on black suffrage were exactly the medicine that reunited white Democracy ordered. For Knox and the overwhelming majority of white Alabamians, the connections between states' rights, home rule, black disfranchisement, and the hell of Reconstruction were all too clear when held up against the situation in 1901. Nefarious "outside influences" and the "ill-advised" meddling of "our Northern friends" and their "unwanted interest in our affairs" had led to three decades of muzzled states' rights for a once "free and sovereign people"—and the sad and unnatural consequence of inferior black involvement in politics. Alabama could only return to constitutional government, he stipulated, "by restricting . . . the right of suffrage, . . . by prohibiting *those people* from voting" [ital. mine].[18]

Still, not all regular Democrats were ready to forgive and forget quite yet. Even Henry Clayton recommended that the reunited white man's party "hug and kiss each other a while" and "hold love feasts" before going off to write a constitution together. "There is time enough for that," he argued. "[A]s a conservative democrat who loves his race above all else . . . I say . . . let us go slow . . . let us stay united and fraternize . . . a while . . . before we spring a new question. . . . We have not been overrun by negro domination since we expelled them in 1874, a few more years . . . can do no harm."[19]

But the mood of the age was such that counsels for caution and care were brushed aside with ease. For John Knox, the Morgan verdict made the call for a disfranchising constitutional convention very clear and immediate: "[C]alling a constitutional convention . . . was the great issue upon which the battle" had been "fought."[20] If the Morgan victory "means anything," Russell Cunningham told the unified convention, "it means that . . . [there is] nobody in Alabama . . . that objects to white man's government," the physician explained. The people of Alabama are "committed to white man's government by honest methods."[21]

The eradication of fraudulent methods—which, of course, the Redeemers themselves had perpetrated—endowed their crusade for a disfranchising constitution with a certain air of moral superiority. As foreign as the concept might seem today, the patricians felt they firmly occupied the moral high ground in the matter. And of course, this high station strengthened their argument—at least in their minds. But it was not all cynicism and expedience. Alabama's regular Democrats were sincere in their belief that they were engaged in something inherently good, a "reform"—even something sacred. White supremacy and honesty in elections were virtually indistinguishable, and seeking such sacrosanct goals was a kind of holy work. "Martin Luther's . . . reform in the Church . . . [and] every great reform movement" have met the "opposition of demagogues and opponents of every kind," John Knox noted to comfort his brethren. "But, gentlemen, . . . when we see the deadly miasma that rises from the swamp, and it is gradually stealing over this State . . . every part of it, . . . we should . . . rise to the full measure of responsibility and deal with it as honest men."[22]

Still, the religious and moral zeal had a definite edge of cynical self-interest to it. For three and a half decades the patricians had gotten away with fraud and ballot manipulation. There was growing evidence, though, that the poor whites were finally catching on. If they did so to any large extent, the Redeemers ran the risk of being hoisted on their own petards, or at least of becoming embroiled in a never-ending game of ballot manipulation against the poor whites, a kind of costly nuclear buildup of fraud that had no endpoint in sight. By 1900, the impetus to end these extralegal activities was certainly present. The fraud, however justified in the Redeemer mind, had gone on so long that it now permeated "practically every county" in the state. "We all know it," John Knox said alarmingly, but it has "gone on until it has reached [even] the white counties."[23]

One thing was patently clear to Alabama's Democracy. Emotion over race and Reconstruction had been the lifeblood for the reunification of white men. That kind of passion over the very same issues could be tapped again and again to cement the annulment of black voting. And it could be done in such a way as to shape the disfranchising constitution in a lasting and advantageous manner for those who would design it.

"Hammer Them, and Keep on Hammering Them": Dealing with Discord

The devil is in the details, though. Discord soon broke out among the regular Democrats over exactly how to proceed. Some—most clearly represented by figures such as John V. Smith, Sidney J. Bowie, Tom Heflin, and Bibb Graves—lobbied for a liberal, catholic view of allowing the old Populists to assume a real, participatory role in the new law making. Their attitude was one of forgiveness and inclusiveness. But more than that, it was a pragmatic approach to the new constitution that saw the participation of former dissidents as a sign of good faith and a relatively small bone to sacrifice for the big payoff of white solidarity—an enabling white solidarity that would allow the revised Democracy to have its way on virtually any political question. Others—most notably Francis L. Pettus, Robert J. Lowe, R. L. Seale, and W. A. Givhan—adopted a more dubious, less forgiving pose. They argued that the former dissidents should be held at arm's length, at least for a probationary period. While their position acknowledged the practical value of white solidarity, they took a more rigid approach that concerned itself with preserving privileged control of the party. For them, allowing the former Populists to participate fully, through county nominating committees for constitutional delegates, for example, was not a small bone. It was a major concession, one that risked the basic elite complexion of the Democratic and Conservative Party.[24]

These forces were not satisfied with mere caution and waiting. They wanted action on a disfranchising constitution, but they also wanted to punish the Jeffersonians for their infidelities in the past by cutting them out of the decision-making process in the present. While recognizing the value of white unity, they were not ready to trust again. In fact, they argued that granting blanket amnesty and trust to the old Populists was akin to throwing the baby out with the bath water: losing control of their own party to poorer, unpredictable white men in order to accomplish the legal disfranchisement of blacks. Frank Pettus, the Black Belt author of the initial attempt to disfranchise Alabama's black voters, in 1892, expressed this view well. "No man should be allowed to hold up the flag" of a reunified Democracy "as a dummy in front and shoot at it in the rear. . . . I don't trust any man to make a nomination for me . . . who has just dropped his gun from shooting at me. . . . [A] great many men . . . were in our conventions, and would go right straight back home and shoot at us. . . . [T]he time has not come, . . . please God, the time will never come in Alabama," Pettus pled to his fellows on the State Democratic Executive Committee, "when we call upon our enemies . . . populists and republicans and any sort of people . . . to make our platforms and put up our enemies." A two-time speaker of the state House of Representatives as well as president of the state Senate, the influential Pettus argued that the old Populists should be required to "show their faith by their works" before they were allowed full participation in nominating delegates to a constitutional convention, for example. After they "shall have gone into the canvass and made the fight side by side with us," the Selma Democrat stipulated, then maybe "the time shall have come . . . to forgive and forget." But "for the love of God, don't let us break down the democratic party in Alabama for the purpose of pandering to a few weak-kneed men," the Dallas County politician implored. The Democratic Party of Alabama is "above any other thing on earth to the white people of Alabama. . . . God forbid . . . that the bolter . . . the enemy of the party, no matter how repentant he may be, should come and . . . dictate to the great court of the party what its course of action should be." Like it or not, this was "the great moral sentiment of the people of Alabama crystallized," Pettus claimed, and "there is nothing between heaven or hell that is going to stop them in what they have undertaken to do."[25]

State railroad commission president John V. Smith, representing Russell County on the SDEC but then living in Opelika in Lee County, headed the opposition to Pettus's exclusionary view. White unity on the constitution question was the goal, Smith reminded the committee, and "where we can" get the "white people of Alabama united on this proposition" by making "such a small sacrifice . . . by making a little concession," the Democratic leaders would succeed in "harmoniz[ing] the white people of Alabama . . . strengthen[ing] the party" and achieving "a more nearly united front than if we stand flat footed . . . and say you cannot have any voice in this thing, but you may vote for our man, if you desire, after we put him in." Smith was in physical and thus perhaps closer sentimental proximity to the plain whites of his poor county and its neighbor than were some of his Bourbon adversaries on the SDEC. He stressed that the constitutional question was "a great question," one in which "every white man in Alabama feels a deep interest," and therefore, the convention should be composed of the broadest possible collection of "every trade and tribe in Alabama—except the colored tribe."[26]

Other SDEC members quickly jumped into the fray. State chairman Robert J. Lowe of Birmingham backed the Pettus position by calling Smith's proposal "absolutely the most radical resolution ever submitted" to the committee, one that tended "to disintegration." A Black Belt member from Greene County agreed that the party had suffered "untold evil . . . by inviting the enemy into our ranks. . . . [W]e find every four years the party disintegrating all the time."[27] The inclusive proposal found support, though, from several vocal members of the state committee. Sidney J. Bowie of Anniston countered by espousing the most inclusive view "that can be obtained." Thomas Heflin pointed out that it made little sense to "put the bars up" against the repentant prodigal Populists when the party had already forgiven men who openly rebelled in 1892 and "walked over this state with Democratic scalps hanging to their belts. . . . [We said to them,] "come back and help us carry on the fight for white supremacy in Alabama," Heflin recalled, "and a number came in, and the party has been built up wonderfully" as a result. The Chambers politico then proposed a milder substitute bill that required the former dissidents to take a loyalty oath and urged unity. "If we can pass a resolution that will tend to harmonize . . . [and]

unite . . . the white people of Alabama, . . . [then we should] bring them in and let us carry the fight to a glorious victory." John V. Smith endorsed Heflin's substitute resolution by citing the example of Populists in the Wiregrass who "want to help us" in writing a disfranchising constitution, but they "want a voice" in saying who the nominees to the convention should be, in saying "who shall represent them."[28]

For the hard-line Democrats, the issue was personal and, to a large extent, revolved around dissatisfaction with Lee County, which had gone Populist in the last election yet now wanted inclusion in the Democratic councils on disfranchisement. In fact, the debate was so personal for some of the executive committee members that it got downright ugly. The cry for inclusion, Robert J. Lowe pointed out, came "from Lee County crying to this committee, disturbing its deliberations at every meeting . . . since I have been a member. . . . I would not lay down the fortifications to invite the enemy in. . . . [D]on't let us depart from the time honored principles . . . of the party to satisfy . . . a county that is always in revolt," Lowe argued. If the "good people of Lee County . . . [differ from us, if they] seek to erect a tabernacle, let them dwell in it. . . . [Don't let us] destroy ours—open our doors and take down our walls, in order that they come in easy." That was all the encouragement Francis Pettus needed. "Who shall make the constitution for you and I to live under, and for our children to live under, for the next 100 years?" Pettus asked in a prescient prediction about the document's eventual longevity. "Populites . . . [have] no more right to talk about writing a constitution for me and for my children than the blackest negro that lives on the soil of the State of Alabama. . . . I would rather . . . an old family of negroes [that lives] on my place should write my constitution" than the white dissenters who now had returned to the party. It would be a great deal better for the State of Alabama for Lee County to "move across the line and go to Georgia . . . rather than we should allow the populists and republicans" to write the constitution, Pettus suggested bitterly. "[B]y the eternal Gods," he vowed, "Lee County stands in a damn bad odor. . . . [W]e had better let Lee County go to the damnation bow wows and [instead] uphold the integrity of the Democratic party."[29]

The opposition's response to Pettus played up the practical usefulness of white unity bought with such small coin as participation in county nominating committees for constitutional delegates. Both sides agreed that appeals to white supremacy and the Reconstruction memory were indispensable in reunifying white men. But the argument over how race and Reconstruction emotion should be used to achieve white solidarity pointed up the differences in approach and style. The inclusive wing sought white solidarity through a policy of openness and participation. The hard-liners did not dispute the value of white solidarity in Alabama politics. Instead, they thought that Holy Grail could be better won through force and ostracism, not the olive branch of inclusion. Sidney J. Bowie reasoned that Morgan's "glorious victory" in August 1900, "the most complete and perfect victory we have had in the State of Alabama," had been accomplished using the same methods that had achieved the victories of 1896 and 1898, under a broad and inclusive "resolution which invited every white man in the State of Alabama to come in." "Now," Bowie told his fellow Democratic notables, "I don't see how the party can benefit itself by closing its doors." The policy of leniency would "strengthen us in the white counties" of Alabama.[30] John V. Smith agreed; "it will bring white men back into the Democratic party [and] . . . line them up in favor of a constitutional convention, it will make it easy . . . to carry . . . and go with us in this matter. . . . It is a bigger question" than just Lee County, Smith explained. "It don't do to keep out any white man—it will strengthen us in the wire grass section." "My gracious alive," he maintained, allowing the former dissidents to participate in selecting convention delegates was not so great a sacrifice as to be a do-or-die issue. It was a bone to throw the Jeffersonians, not the main course.[31]

Still, the hard-liners were not convinced, largely because they believed that white solidarity should be compelled rather than bargained for. Hot social discomfort through the charge of racial treason, rather than successful entreaties about the comfort of racial solidarity, was the true route to electoral success. The dispute centered on methods, not goals. White solidarity and prioritizing white supremacy—achieved by carrot or by stick—was still the central goal of the Democrats. In reality, pressure through ostracism and pressure through the inclusive attractions of conformity both worked their magic on the poor-white Jeffersonians. Yet, Democrats like Francis Pettus were sure their hard road was the best one to follow—a route the SDEC decided to take, in the end, by a single vote. "[W]e have made it extremely [difficult] in the State of Alabama, for a man wearing a white skin to vote against the democratic nominees—that was our purpose," Pettus admitted in perhaps the most direct possible explanation of the race-baiting strategy. "The only way to conciliate the enemies of Democracy is to hammer them and keep on hammering them," he exhorted. "[T]he only way to stop Independentism is to make it infamous." That is how the Populists had been defeated, "[b]y hammering them, by making it so hot for them they could not stand it any longer." The same strategy had worked with Republicanism. "[T]he time was a gentleman could not speak to a Republican" in Alabama, Pettus recalled fondly, and consequently "Republicanism died among the white people." In the present circumstances with Independent holdovers and prodigal Populists returning to the Democratic fold, "the only way to treat this matter is to make it absolutely infamous. . . . If you make Independentism in Alabama absolutely infamous, there will be the end of it."[32] The advice was a clear admission of what kind of politics had worked in Alabama in the past, what would work in the present, and what would continue to work in the state for a century after the 1901 Constitution was put on the books. The turn-of-the-century disfranchising era was an absolutely critical time in Alabama politics for its legal codification of the disfranchisement mechanisms. But it was also critical in that it saw the lasting establishment of political methods of racial and moral distraction that would work so well in the state for decades.

Central to the success of this kind of distraction was offering the plain whites a sense of inclusion and sedative membership in something superior. Hot pressure might move the Jeffersonians to forswear their sacrilege, but comfortable acceptance would make their transition back to the Democratic Party that much easier. To this end, the SDEC passed, on 26 April 1900, the formal Democratic pledge that many poor whites would subsequently rely on as an insurance policy for their decision to support a convention and a new constitution. In the spring of 1900 they did not know this policy would eventually turn out to be virtually worthless:

> Resolved, That it is hereby understood and declared that no white man in Alabama shall be disfranchised for want of property, education, or for any other cause, except the commission of a crime.[33]

"A Wicked Generation": Breaks in the Ranks of Plain Whites

Significant evidence, which, frankly, has been underestimated by many scholars, suggests that the push-pull strategy of the privileged was effective. The Reconstruction-based appeals and pressure to conform espoused by Frank White and the "hammering" ostracism advocated by Frank Pettus resulted in substantial poor-white support for the disfranchisement movement. Even in Populist strongholds such as Chilton County, which historians have long used as a leading exculpatory example to buttress their arguments for poor-white blamelessness and an alleged Jacksonian and Jeffersonian "transcendence of race," the debate over disfranchisement was much more divided than has traditionally been portrayed.[34] It is true that Chilton County's representative at the 1901 constitutional convention, Lewis H. Reynolds, opposed the calling of a disfranchisement convention and its product early and consistently. But he did not oppose all forms of disfranchisement.[35] And his defense of poor-white voting cannot, by any mental gymnastic, be construed as a defense of the black right to vote. Nor by any means did all his brother Populists—even in the heart of the Hill Country, in places like Chilton County—share his opposition to a convention and a disfranchising constitution.[36]

The Chilton County example, far from showing Populist unanimity on the disfranchisement question, actually demonstrates deep division. The Populists, such as they remained in 1901, *were* in fact united with one another—and with their Bourbon adversaries—on one question: the desirability of blacks losing the vote. The Populists disagreed among themselves whether this universal white goal could be accomplished without poor whites also losing the right to vote. L. H. Reynolds certainly recognized the magnitude of the problem and the upcoming referendum on whether to call a constitutional convention, "the most important election ever held in Alabama—a direct stroke at the hearts of the common people."[37] A number of other Chilton County Populists agreed with Reynolds. "[A]ny man who is simple enough to believe that they are only after the 'negro in the wood pile,' " jeered one, "ought to have a free pass to heaven for being [a] fool."[38] Another Populist warned that "the party that conceived this measure [was] working quietly in the ambush," using influential speakers to travel the whole state "to influence the plain people" to vote for a convention. He denounced the "wily scheme" to garner votes from the common folk by promising that "no white men will be disfranchised," thus "making the negro a foot log to get across on." "The fact is," he cautioned, "they want to make a jim dandy, cracker-jack constitution for themselves and their kind."[39]

Unfortunately such warnings were not uniformly heeded, even in the Populist strongholds of Alabama's Hill Country. Race and the recurrent Reconstruction syndrome were too powerful. "Are we as true, Southern patriotic citizens, going to vote down the convention?" one exercised Chilton Populist asked incredulously. "May the Almighty God forbid that we should forget what the old Confederates fought so bravely for in the days of [18]60–65 . . . to keep the infernal negro out of politics." "Why then," he asked, "should we not as sons of the Confederates disfranchise the negro? . . . Can we not disfranchise the negro and not the white man, certainly we can. . . . [V]ote in the interest of our wives and children, get the brute out of politics."[40] "[T]he new constitution is principally to disfranchise the negro. Now, how you are going to do it is the question," another Chilton Populist wrote. "The proper thing to do with the negro," he recommended, "is to colonize him and send him to his African home. He has been a curse ever since he was introduced here."[41] Increasingly, as the Populists wrestled with the problem of how to disfranchise blacks while protecting poor-white votes, their rhetoric and reasoning took on almost every imaginable manifestation of race prejudice and religious proscription against race mixing, including stock stereotypes about black immorality, predisposition to crime, laziness and sloth, savagery, aberrance, sexual degeneracy, and generally inferior human worth. Calling on all these arguments as ammunition, another Chilton Populist recognized the obstacle that the Reconstruction amendments presented to disfranchising African Americans yet held out hope:

> What to do with the negro is a problem that is puzzling the ablest statesmen of to-day. The negro today enjoys every privilege the white man does, notwithstanding it is against nature. God intended the white man should rule. The white man trampled under foot God's command. . . . Thou shalt not mix with . . . a wicked generation . . . lest you be cut off and assigned your portion in the regions of hell with those who forget God. . . . Federal appointments where [the Negro] dominates the white man . . . prominent positions where he can live off the fat of the land while the poor white man with superior intelligence and qualifications makes his living by the sweat of the brow. . . . Does not every intelligent man know that the negro is in principle a brute? He has no remorse of conscience. Every day [brings news] . . . of some diabolical crime he has committed on some woman. . . . Any crime that is comprehensible to his mind is practical with him, and still we invite him to aid us in our progressive government. Not long can a nation prosper practicing a social equality with such a dissipated and damnable race. The negro . . . was the indirect cause of the Civil war. . . . [N]ow it is possible . . . after the dawn of 36 years, . . . are we going to deny [the vote to poor whites] . . . just in order to eliminate the negro vote . . . ? I do not favor the embarrassment of the poor, unfortunate white man on account of the negro. . . . The problem can be solved. . . . Remove the negro into the humiliated station of life that nature intended for him. . . . Here is luck to all who are opposed to trusts and incorporations and negro domination, but favor white supremacy.[42]

The division in Chilton County, even among the Populists, found strong echoes across Alabama, even in other parts of the Hill Country that historians have long portrayed as solidly against disfranchisement. Some anti-Democrats clearly recognized the patrician deception for what it was—yet not all by a long shot. A good example of sophisticated comprehension of the planned bait-and-switch tactic of the privileged was supplied by I. L. Brock, editor of the Populist *Cherokee Sentinel.* "We have known democratic politicians long enough to know that they keep up a sham battle over the race question while they are practicing some diabolical crime upon the people," he wrote. "Let the people beware when they [the regular Democrats] raise the race question. [It] is an old scare crow . . . to arouse hatred and prejudice." Still, even the savvy Brock recommended that the best way to "obtain the desired reform" of black disfranchisement without harming poor-white votes was to target the "intelligent negroes." They were "the ones to disfranchise," the Populist editor explained, because the intelligent blacks exercised a large influence on the "[ignorant] pur-chasable Negro vote." Without the learned blacks telling their illiterate brothers how to vote, "[t]he ignorant ones [would] divide or stay home."[43]

It gets worse. The Pickens County *Alabama Alliance News,* a Populist news-paper in a county with substantial Hill Country characteristics, congratulated itself for opposing a disfranchisement convention because it recognized the Re-deemer Democracy was planning to use the carrot of black disfranchisement to lure poor whites to participate in crafting a document that would also hurt them politically. "The democratic party organization looked upon the body politic as suffering [from] . . . a severe sickness" of black voting, the newspaper explained in metaphoric fashion, "but when it attempted to administer the remedy" of a Democratic-controlled constitutional convention, "the people" recognized their thirst for control, "and the democratic party is today a mighty sick nigger." In fact, the Populist newspaper breezily referred to blacks as "darkeys" and "nig-gers," a policy that likely did not do much to encourage biracial cooperation.[44] The same newspaper reported that the State Democratic Executive Commit-tee had summarily and rudely turned down a proposal presented by Populist spokesman Zell Gaston. In return for having the Democratic-controlled SDEC give seven state-at-large delegate seats to them, the Populists had offered to link arms with the Democrats in calling for and shaping a constitutional convention for the disfranchisement of blacks. A similar rebuff occurred at the local level. After these rejections, editor Emmet R. Calhoun concluded that perhaps the best way to solve the problem was to rejuvenate the Populist idea of instituting an all-white Democratic primary to freeze out black voters, in effect, and "settle the differences" among white men within the party.[45]

Vacillation, indecision, and equivocation continued among the poor whites. Some Hill Country Populists even believed the constitutional movement was an elaborate Bourbon plot to disfranchise poor whites while leaving black suf-frage alone—a Democratic ruse to accomplish the disfranchisement of poor whites, while actually protecting the right of blacks to vote. Manipulating and influencing the black vote was "the life and mainstay of the democratic party," Emmet Calhoun argued, "the goose that lays the golded eggs." There was no way the Bourbons would actually harm the African American vote. Confident that in his county white Populists could defeat the few white Democrats in a standup fight among white men, the editor accused a county representa-tive to the state legislature of being a race traitor for favoring a constitutional convention: "[H]e prefers negro supremacy and democratic success to white supremacy and democratic defeat." The privileged plot to trick poor whites into disfranchising themselves while actually preserving black suffrage should be patently clear to anyone, the Populist editor felt, "even if his skull was as thick as that of the negroes."[46] During the midst of the controversy over calling a convention, the same Populist editor of the *Alabama Alliance News* reprinted a Robert McKee editorial on "the Negro" to make very clear the Populist position on blacks voting. McKee, the well-known editor of the *Montgomery Southern Argus,* was thought of as an outspoken partisan very close to the Jeffersonians and Joseph Johnston and even considered a "crypto-Populist" by some contemporaries. In 1892, he did vote the Populist ticket. Some historians have described McKee as "an archetypal Jeffersonian" and a "Jacksonian Democrat." One has gone so far as to claim that the influential McKee was an insurgent who "emphasized money and finance instead of race . . . [who] did not merely contribute to Alabama's political discourse. He set the terms of the discourse and made sure that it transcended race. . . . Many Democrats [individuals like McKee] became Populists because of ideas unrelated to race."[47]

In light of this final, large claim, it is instructive to consider McKee's influential opinion of "the Negro," expressed at the height of the disfranchisement controversy and reprinted enthusiastically by Hill Country Populist editors:

> The [*Montgomery Southern*] *Argus* is a white man's paper—conducted by white men for white men. It treats the negro as an inferior dangerously misplaced in his relations with men of a superior race, and refers to him only as necessary for the information or edification of those who must work out the salvation of whites and black, if this can be done, in spite of him. He is the white man's problem, in the solution of which he cannot help. In his place, he deserves no protection. His place is not in the schoolhouse, which draws him from all useful employment; nor in politics which he debauches and degrades; nor in the army which inspires him with presumption and qualifies him for leadership in lawlessness. He should be paid fair wages for his labor, protected in good behavior against violence, given justice in the courts, punished leniently for all minor offenses, and restrained from brutality threatening the home by summary execution. What else can be done for him or with him, is the problem of civilization in conflict with barbarism.[48]

Other poor-white opinion makers and representatives supported disfranchisement openly or opposed the calling of a disfranchising constitutional convention with logic that made very clear the anti-Democrats' desire to have their cake and eat it too: to help disfranchise blacks while retaining the vote for poor whites. The *Marshall Banner* supplies an interesting example in this respect. Regarded by contemporaries and peer journalists as a Populist newspaper and sometimes referred to as the *Albertville Banner* because of the Hill Country seat of its publication, it is probably most fairly described as a "half-Populist" mouthpiece. Its editorial policies in the spring of 1901 were thoroughly supportive of free silver, Joseph F. Johnston, William Jennings Bryan, and Jesse F.

Stallings. The newspaper routinely and favorably reprinted editorial copy from Hill Country Populist and insurgent papers such as the *Cherokee Sentinel,* the *Cherokee Harmonizer,* the *Ashville Southern Alliance,* and the *Attalla Mirror,* while damning former Populists who returned to the Democratic fold as hypocrites and crass opportunists who had only used the Populist label for selfish reasons. An ardent foe of calling a constitutional convention, by the end of the convention's proceedings, the *Marshall Banner* had changed its editorial tune to endorse ratification and denounce anyone—even poor-white tribunes such as Johnston, Shelley, and Stallings—who would stand in the way of ratification and blacks losing the vote.[49]

"Leave It to the White Skins": Plain-White Views on Politics

Contrary to some historians' claims of its minor importance, race was a major factor in the thinking of poor Hill Country whites who supported a convention and of those who opposed a convention; in fact, it figured in the thinking of these whites on virtually every political question. In fact, it is impossible to separate completely the racial reasoning from its intertwined class logic. The example of Emmet Calhoun of the *Alabama Alliance News* is instructive, but there are plenty of others. One poor white in Etowah County, weighing the calling of a convention, explained it this way: "Now I can tell you that the white folks up here want to see the negro disfranchised, but they don't intend that two-thirds of the white men in the white counties shall . . . be disfranchised." This Upcountry native could see no logical reason why Black Belt whites should resist unified white action on politics in 1901 because white solidarity had redeemed the state from "the perils of negro suffrage" during Reconstruction. "We saved them from negro domination [in 1874]. Can't we . . . the white men in North Alabama and the Wiregrass . . . be trusted?" he asked.[50] "Not a vote cast by the Populists and reformers in the white counties in the past six years has amounted to anything," another dispirited Populist explained in damning "negro supremacy"; they were "killed by the negro vote."[51] The *Marshall Banner* explained its opposition to the calling of a constitutional convention in terms very similar to those of the *Alabama Alliance News,* terms that can only be described as racial. Disfranchisement, through the constitutional convention, was a Democratic scheme to "defraud white men, honest white men, with blue eyes and straight hair. God forbid [this] disgrace . . . and . . . reproach and shame." North Alabama's Hill Country was where the "atmosphere [is] as pure as ever enjoyed by God's creatures, here where nothing but white supremacy has always and ever will exist."[52] The *Marshall Banner* repeatedly explained its opposition to a constitutional convention in terms that showed an oppressive fear of poor-white men—not blacks—being disfranchised. W. H. Bartlett, a Republican also supported by Populists who served as Marshall County's delegate to the 1901 convention, did the same: "I am opposed to the disfranchisement of any white man . . . and will vote and work to maintain the right of suffrage to all white men."[53]

Such logic—informed and imbued by the racial consideration—found echoes even in south Alabama. Since the vast majority of the anti-Democrats were concentrated in Alabama's Hill Country, the Wiregrass, and the Tennessee Valley, Populists were among the rarest of commodities in planter country. Outnumbered as they were, their strain of dissent tended to run even stronger in the heart of the Black Belt monster, the belly of the Bourbon beast. The *Choctaw Alliance,* for example, supported a disfranchising constitution fervently. Feuds between Bourbons and white Populists over which way African Americans would voluntarily vote ran to blood in Clarke County.[54] But it was the intense opposition to a constitutional convention furnished by the Wiregrass Populist *Geneva Reaper* that offered the most intriguing window into the racial thought and motivations of even those anti-Democrats who *opposed* a convention—an aspect of the disfranchisement question that has not been adequately studied. Published by a group of local Populists, the *Reaper* thought of itself as the "index to Geneva's liberal and progressive" residents, which it most certainly was *if* the subject at hand happened to be economics or even some social policies. Race, though—the question of disfranchisement, to be precise—was a different story. The *Reaper*'s Populist editors felt intensely alone in their opposition—an interesting point considering the supposed unanimity of Jeffersonian sentiment against the constitution.[55] Their opposition was couched partially in class terms, of course, but also contained a very strong element of intertwined race reasoning. "Why not leave it to the white skins . . . leave the question to the white folks?" the Populists asked. "The white skins don't need any nigger votes. . . . [T]he white people of Alabama are getting devilish tired of nigger domination," said the exasperated editors in explaining their opposition to a new constitution that they thought would merely perpetuate black voting while ruling out poor whites. "The negro has held the balance of power in this state about long enough."[56]

As should be very clear by now, despite historians' claims to the contrary, Hill Country anti-Democratic sentiment in favor of disfranchisement is not hard to come by in the primary sources—only in the secondary ones. Captain A. McHan, Confederate veteran, Populist candidate for Congress, and the publisher of Populist newspapers the *Sand Mountain Signal* and the *Boaz Signal,* came out openly in his new newspaper, the *Gadsden Tribune,* for the calling of a disfranchising convention.[57] The *Marshall Banner,* which opposed the calling of a convention, ended up shifting gears and enthusiastically endorsing ratification of its disfranchising product.[58] The *Clanton Banner*—despite the historiographical exaltation of Chilton County as a hotbed of antidisfranchisement sentiment—did the same.[59] The Jeffersonian *Attalla Mirror*, in the heart of Alabama's Hill Country, supported the calling of a convention and advised blacks to satisfy themselves with remaining only a " 'hewer of wood and a drawer of water' for . . . the white man . . . the most favored brother of all races." This quite satisfactory arrangement had worked well "since time immemorial," and tampering with it now could only bring about "no good"; such tampering "stirs up strife and discord." Educated blacks such as Booker T. Washington were the exception rather than the rule and, owing to their small number, could in no way justify continued enfranchisement of the whole race. Washington was "not the only black-berry on the vine," the *Mirror* reasoned, and " 'when you educate a negro you spoil a good field hand'. . . . God intended the negro for a servant and that is what he should be."[60] The only really important question for the Etowah newspaper, a question eventually answered to its satisfaction, centered on race: "The question is: Will the Constitutional Convention disfranchise the negro?"[61]

Other Hill Country anti-Democratic sentiment in favor of disfranchisement is abundant. The *People's Protest*, a Populist newspaper published in Cullman, repeatedly expressed support for the notion and prospect of black disfranchisement. It praised various disfranchisement methods, calling one the "shrewdest scheme" and another a "very good" safeguard. If the proper methods could be worked out in a new constitution, the Cullman Populists reasoned, "by all means, let us have it."[62] A number of Populists in Pickens County, much to the chagrin of one local editor, did the same because they believed Bourbon promises that "the only object" of the convention was to "disfranchise the negroes."[63] Some Marshall County Independents followed suit.[64] White Republican newspapers across the state lined up to support disfranchisement. In Alabama's Hill Country, lily-white Republican organs such as the *Coosa River News*, the *Jacksonville Republican*, and the *Anniston Republican* backed black disfranchisement.[65]

In other poor-white areas, the Tennessee Valley and the Wiregrass, anti-Democratic support for disfranchisement found expression in a variety of venues. The *Huntsville Tribune* and the *Huntsville Republican*, as well as white Republican rank and file, articulated GOP support for disfranchisement.[66] A Populist from Dale County placed his trust in the "sincere . . . promises" of the regular Democrats and their "good faith" to come through on their promises to the people that no white would "ever be disfranchised," a pledge that had been greeted with "a whoop and the wildest enthusiasm." The Wiregrass Jeffersonian almost held his breath as he hoped that the convention would "act aright" and treat disfranchisement as a racial issue, so that "no man in whose veins the Caucasian blood flows, [would] be disfranchised."[67] A leading Populist newspaper in the Wiregrass held that whites could settle their political differences "without an appeal to the negroes vote" and argued bluntly that "disfranchisement of the negroes is a consummation which every white man ought earnestly to wish for. . . . The negroes are incapacitated for self-government . . . and are in no way fitted for the duties of citizenship."[68]

Privileged Strategy: "Show Them What Is Right and They Will Vote for It"

By the eve of the convention referendum, Alabama's Democrats were fairly confident that they were making progress among their poorer white brethren. The best intelligence indicated that some white counties were still against calling a convention, but others were coming along rapidly. News from some of the white counties, even those in the Hill Country, was encouraging to the Democrats. Critical for all white counties was the issue of the pledge made by the Democratic Party in Montgomery that no white man, regardless of birth, poverty, or illiteracy, would find himself without a vote. Put simply, in places where poor whites believed the pledge or at least talked themselves into believing it, they prepared to vote for a convention. In others, where the pledge was not believed, the prospects among the white dissidents were much dimmer.

The shrewdest patricians realized that they needed, at the very least, to keep up the appearance of being sincere about the pledges. Otherwise, the referendum incline would be too steep to scale. Russell County's John V. Smith, elected state chairman of the Democratic campaign committee to pass the referendum, emphasized the need for every Bourbon speaker who took the stump to "lay particular stress upon this one fact": that the pledge would be kept and the document submitted back to the people for ratification as a safeguard. This was essential. "We must quiet the fears of our brethren in the hill counties and in the wire grass," Smith explained. "We must by absolute assurances of good faith let them know that these pledges" would be kept, so that when the time came, "every white man in Alabama [would] be willing to vote for and ratify" the constitution. Emphasizing the pledge, the state railroad commission president iterated, endowed the Redeemer program with a moral superiority that enmeshed itself with racial purity: the "high moral plane of right and justice [so] that our battle cry shall be: White Supremacy, Suffrage Reform, and Purity in Elections." Young Gessner Williams of the Black Belt agreed that "the people have to be satisfied" that the vote of no white man was to be touched, or all bets were off. John B. Knox concurred that, for the time being, the party had to stand by the various pledges, even if they found the idea of protecting the franchise of poor-white dissenters abhorrent. Appearances had to be kept up, no matter how repulsive some elites felt it was to pander to the masses—even if "we . . . as individuals . . . approve of these restrictions or not."[69] Once the convention had been safely called and had done its work, differences could be addressed. "After it is framed and submitted to the people for a vote," Judge Thomas W. Coleman of Greene County explained, "then comes the time for the fight . . . then let the tug of war come. . . . [L]et us have the convention first."[70]

Regular Democratic notables were encouraged by preliminary canvasses of the various counties that reported numbers of Populists, Republicans, and Independents supporting the Democratic push for a constitutional convention. Of course, the outlook in some counties was grim, pledge or no pledge. Blount, Butler, Chilton, and Dale still looked as though they would go against the convention.[71] But other white counties, even in the Hill Country, exhibited Populist and Republican support for a disfranchising convention. In Etowah County, poor whites lined up to support a new constitution because the Morgan-Johnston campaign had been waged expressly on the "straight issue" of a convention and "white supremacy."[72] Fayette County Populists and Republicans were "as much in favor of" a disfranchising constitution "as the Democrats." "Wherever I talked to a white man," a leading politico reported, "everybody speaks in favor of it. . . . [A]ll the people are in favor of disfranchising the negro." At a Russell Cunningham speech in Fayette, a large audience made up equally of "Populites" and Democrats expressed "unanimous" support for a disfranchising constitution.[73] Charles P. Beddow, a Birmingham labor lawyer close to the Populists, reported that he himself was for the convention, and that Jefferson County was fairly split on the issue, with allegiance to the Montgomery platform absolutely essential "in order to allay the feelings of the people" that they might lose their votes.[74] Observers on the ground expressed confidence that Calhoun and Lamar Counties' various classes of whites solidly backed the convention. Lily-white Republicans in Morgan County were "almost solidly in favor of a constitutional convention to disfranchise the negro." In Saint Clair County, several leading Populists assured their Democratic counterparts that they would curry "hearty support" for the constitutional convention among their insurgent brethren. Talladega's "white people were solid" for the constitutional convention, "Populites and all." A number of local Populist leaders, with their party in the midst of disintegration, openly preached to their flocks in favor of the constitutional convention. The situation in Tallapoosa was very much the same, with white insurgents "in favor of disfranchising the darkey, but . . . afraid in doing that, that some white man will accidentally be disfranchised."[75]

A number of anti-Democrats outside of the Hill Country were also unquestionably supporting a disfranchising constitution. White Republicans in Lauderdale and Lawrence Counties in the Tennessee Valley lined up to support the convention. The situation in Madison County was similar, a local politico reported, and there should be "no trouble" in carrying the county.[76] Some of the Black Belt counties also brought good news on this front. The "lion and the lamb," Populist and Democrat, "have laid down together" in Lee County, on the issue of calling a convention, John V. Smith happily reported. In Marengo County, Gessner Williams checked in: "[T]he Populists are all in favor of the convention," while, ironically, the gold Democrats and the "sound money men" were leery because they feared an increase in taxation. In Montgomery, a Republican ticket offered in opposition to the Democratic slate actually helped the regulars in their efforts to win over the county's insurgent farmers. "[N]ow, you know it is not constitutional in Montgomery county for a Radical to be elected to any office," joked one optimistic Democrat. A Perry County Republican admitted that "frankly . . . the best element of his party" was in favor of the convention.[77]

Evidence appeared indicating that the labor element of the Populist coalition of farmers and workers was preparing to back a call for a disfranchising constitution. Populists such as John Witherspoon DuBose praised the white solidarity that cut across class lines that they witnessed at the turn-of-the-century. The white laboring classes in Birmingham, DuBose noted approvingly, "are separated from the Negroes, working all day side by side with them, by an innate consciousness of race superiority. This sentiment dignifies the character of white labor. It excites a sentiment of sympathy and equality on their part with the classes above them, and in this way becomes a wholesome social leaven."[78] On the very day of the statewide referendum on whether to call a disfranchising convention, Hill Country poor-white tribune J. Thomas Heflin introduced two members of the Legislative Committee for the Birmingham Trades Council to the State Democratic Executive Committee meeting in Birmingham. White union workers, Heflin told the SDEC, were "heartily in favor" of the disfranchising movement and wished only to have the Democratic Party's assurance that a new constitution would not tamper with protective employee liability acts.[79] D. H. S. Moseley and Frank Arrico presented a letter on behalf of between fourteen thousand and sixteen thousand of their voting members that pledged white unionist support for the constitutional convention if employee liability were left untouched.[80] Such support would continue after the actual convention was held. The *Birmingham Labor Advocate*, official organ for organized labor in Alabama, encouraged its readership to ratify the new constitution and not to let themselves be frightened by the "bugaboo that white men will be disfranchised."[81] The United Labor League, closely tied to District 20 of the United Mine Workers (UMW), also advised white union workers to ratify the document that disfranchised blacks and not to be scared into opposing it by fears that white men would also lose the vote. Even the Knights of Labor—generally noted for their willingness to embrace biracial labor activism and acutely class conscious in places like the Wiregrass—followed a different course when it came to disfranchisement. The Escambia K of L endorsed ratification as "a very wise and judicious thing" because the new constitution promised to restrict the "reckless voting of a debased and foreign element."[82]

Still, even in places where Populists and Republicans backed the convention, there was a genuine and persistent fear that "somebody will be disfranchised."[83] In other places, where the opposition typically ran higher, some poor whites realized that "one of the chief objects" of the whole movement was to "disfranchise the poor white man." The idea was "having a wonderful influence" against calling a convention in some of the white counties.[84] The fear was oppressive for the poor whites of the hills and the Wiregrass. For many of them, it was the only obstacle to their full-throated support for a disfranchisement convention. This self-interested fear along with strong sentiment against increased taxation present among various whites since Reconstruction, some disillusionment and apathy, and the demands of the planting season were the biggest impediments to carrying the plain-white vote for the convention.[85] Concern for black voting was, for all intents and purposes, nil among the whites.

Accordingly, much attention was paid to the question of methods. What methods could be utilized to at once calm poor-white fears over their own suffrage and fire their simmering desire to see blacks disfranchised? As so often in Alabama's history, white supremacy, white solidarity, and the on-going psychological redemption from Reconstruction supplied the compelling answer. Thomas L. Long, representing the predominantly Republican Upcountry county of Walker, described the strategy:

> The way to win this fight is on white supremacy. [That is what] the battle cry should be through[out] Alabama. On one side is the negro, and on the other is the white man. . . . God Almighty intended that the white people should rule this county. . . . [T]he way to win this fight is to go into the mountain counties and talk white supremacy, and that the platform means what it reads . . . that we will have a fair election among the white people of Alabama. . . . [O]n that line is the way to make this fight. . . . I don't believe it is a good policy to go up in the hills and tell them that Booker Washington is allowed to vote or . . . anybody else because they are educated. [T]he minute you do that every white man who is not educated is disfranchised. . . . [W]e should go to them and tell them . . . we will adopt the

Louisiana Grand daddy clause, the Mississippi clause—both combined . . . if necessary. . . . [T]hat is the way and the only way to win this fight. . . . I am not afraid
of the white people of Alabama. The very minute you trust the ballot to the[m] . . .
it will go Democratic like it did before the war, and we will have [only] two parties. . . . Walker furnished two regiments to the Confederate army . . . they are patriots there. . . . [A]ll the negroes, as quickly as they understand it will disfranchise nobody but themselves, they will fight it. . . . [W]e can . . . overcome that
only by arraying the white people of Alabama. . . . [I]t is going to take work. . . .
[W]e need it on the line of white supremacy and fair elections, with annulment . . .
of the 14th and 15th Amendments that was never legally ratified in the State of
Alabama. . . . We need speakers . . . to draw the line and say "which side will you
take?" . . . [T]his is the way to win this fight. . . . We have won since 1874, and the
white people will win, . . . but we must win it on white supremacy, like George
Houston won it in 1874.[86]

An essential element of waging such emotional politics was keeping things
simple, even vague and blandly general. To this end, the patricians designed
and capitalized on a tactic that can be termed *the distracting power of vagueness.*
The policy sedated poor-white fears while offering comforting yet fairly vacu-
ous pronouncements of goals and platform. It was implemented with a cold,
calculated, and frighteningly successful efficiency. Detail and specificity risked
probing and additional study. Study risked actual knowledge of the issues. And
that risked the patrician position. The elites banked on the fact that most poor
and working people did not have the time or educational background to make
an extensive study of the issues, hence their reliance on more emotional considerations. "You cannot expect men of ordinary vocations to have studied constitutions," W. C. Oates explained, but "whenever you show them what is right,
they will vote for it." A former Alabama governor, Oates advised his peers that
"it is better not to enter upon an argument" or even "a suggestion . . . of the
difficulties" involved. "There are grave questions" to be answered, he explained,
and "the more discussed, the graver they are."[87] It was much better and easier
to let the poor whites be governed by their emotions rather than engage in discussions on rational and specific issues. Such discussions just tended to muddy
the water and make success that much more difficult to achieve.

There was no reason to discuss constitutional issues or disfranchisement
methods in detail, Thomas W. Coleman agreed. In fact, doing so could only
place a sure thing at risk. "Go before the people" upon a "broad . . . platform,"
the Black Belt jurist counseled his fellow Democratic speakers. The pitch should
be broad enough so that it says simply, "[T]his State should be governed by the
white race of Alabama." Then, Coleman advised, no one "can successfully attack

it." "Why raise" other issues, Coleman asked, when doing so might "drive off votes" by leading the plain white to "begin to doubt whether or not he will be permitted to vote."[88] Anniston industrialist John B. Knox likewise "cautioned" the Democratic bureau of stump speakers preparing to go into the hills and pine barrens "against going into details" or discussing any "particular form of relief." The best strategy was to keep things simple and vague to avoid being pinned down or raising suspicions and fear. Getting too specific might risk the support of plain whites who, "while they favored a Constitutional convention," might be "opposed to a particular form of relief." Merely state, Knox instructed, that "we do not propose to take any backward step" on the great "question of the ignorant negro vote." He counseled his colleagues to play to the weakness of the plain whites, to assure Alabama's plain folk that white people "throughout the South" were "united" in seeking "a remedy for the intolerable situation" of black voting. They should persuade plain whites that white solidarity on the issue would be an act of sectional patriotism and tell them that the Democrats were "honorably pledged" to submit the constitution back to the people for ratification.[89]

Of course, the beauty of a general sword of vagueness was that it was double-edged and often impossible to prove or disprove. It could be wielded with good effect to both inflame and soothe emotions—sometimes at the same time—depending on the type and utility of the emotion. Vague charges of race treason and visions of radical revolution could be used to arouse plain-white passions as readily as fuzzy promises of perpetuating white supremacy could be used to calm them. Emmett O'Neal, the son of a former governor, a future governor himself, and a rising star in state politics, entered the 1901 discussion over methods of persuasion with his usual force and eloquence. As a spokesman for north Alabama's burgeoning industrial interests, O'Neal was an economic and, of course, racial conservative who was quite sympathetic and responsive to the concerns of business. He was an elite of the new sort, an industrial elite, tied to the Black Belt planters by a shared economic conservatism and political alliance. Yet, as a native son of Lauderdale County, O'Neal was also intimately familiar with the plain whites of north Alabama—their hopes and fears, their dreams and insecurities. He knew what moved the plain folk. He also knew what kinds of emotion—fear, pride, jealousy, lust, anger, grief, hatred, insecurity—could move them to rash action or frighten them into paralysis. His strategic and tactical advice to the economically and racially conservative Big Mule/Black Belt elite hit on all the most compelling themes that could persuade Alabama's poor whites to lay aside their class differences and sedate their fears (at least momentarily) in order to support the Redeemer project: states' rights philosophy as a cover for raw racial power, nostalgia for the Old South and the Confederacy, resentment over the Reconstruction "nightmare," hostility toward the federal power that had enabled black rule to happen, obsessive pride in white supremacy and white solidarity, an extreme and unhealthy suspicion of outsiders, and a righteous indignation that justified a forceful and lasting remedy.

[W]e ought to present to the people . . . but one issue . . . that the paramount purpose of the constitutional convention is to lay deep and strong and permanent in the fundamental law of the State . . . white supremacy for ever in Alabama. . . . [W]e ought to go before the people on that issue, and not suggest other questions on which we differ. . . . Let us say to the people of Alabama that this is a race issue, that the white race, whenever it has come in contact with an inferior race, with Mongolian or negro—must and will dominate. Let us say to the colored people . . . we guarantee to them equal and exact justice [but] . . . we will never consent to share with them the responsibilities of government in Alabama. That is the position. Let us not go and say how we are going to do it. Let us just say to the people of Alabama that the right of each sovereign State in this Union to control its suffrage was a right ante-dating the [U.S.] Constitution . . . before the Federal compact. . . . [W]hen the victorious North, in a moment of passion and hate, not [to] . . . benefit the negro, but . . . [to] humiliate the . . . South, struck down the great safeguard of local self-government, the right of each State to regulate and control its own suffrage, we were forced to submit by dire necessity, but . . . we will never lay down our honor, and never cease to combat, that iniquitous measure— the 15th Amendment. . . . [T]he enfranchisement of the negro race . . . is . . . simply monstrous. . . . [I]f there is any way by which we can restore the rights of the people of Alabama as a sovereign State to regulate and control its own suffrage . . . we intend to find it and adopt it in Alabama. . . . [T]hat is the position on which we can win . . . with the people of the white counties in North Alabama. . . . [I]n the dark days of the past, when the foot of the carpet bagger and scalawag was on your neck, you appealed to us . . . the white counties . . . for relief. . . . [T]he white counties of North Alabama will again come to your aid and see that the . . . convention is successful. . . . [W]e ought not to go before the people and discuss too many issues . . . except the paramount question of suffrage. Present it to the people forcibly and without equivocation . . . that we, the people of Alabama, propose to settle this question . . . so as to eliminate the entire negro race as a voter in Alabama.[90]

While certainly resonant in 1901, O'Neal's advice to the conservative elite was also remarkably enduring. It provided a race and Reconstruction blueprint for tapping plain-white emotions to serve elite purposes that, unfortunately, would remain relevant in Alabama for generations to come. Tweaked and kneaded with the newer yet still vague emotional issues of religion, morality, and traditional family values, the strategy would persist and even flourish into the present in Alabama—long serving the master of economic conservatism under several different party labels.[91]

April 1901: "A Majority of the White Men Are Opposed"

Eight months after John Tyler Morgan's benchmark victory over Joseph Johnston, Alabamians voted to call a constitutional convention. Forty-one of the state's counties voted "for" the calling of a convention; most of the twenty-five "against" counties were white counties in north Alabama and the Wiregrass. The measure passed statewide by a majority of 24,800 votes (70,305 "for" and 45,505 "against"), with the largest majorities clearly coming from the Black Belt. Dallas County, for example, which was home to 45,372 blacks among its total population of 54,657, returned an astronomical 97 percent vote for the convention: 5,668 "for" to only 200 "against." Similar results occurred in Greene County, where 19 votes (or only 1 percent) out of 1,498 were registered "against" calling a convention; Hale County, which logged 97 percent "for"; Lowndes, which logged 3,226 "for" and only 338 "against"; Marengo, which reported only 241 votes "against"; Perry and Sumter, which combined had 112 votes "against" as opposed to 3,735 votes "for"; and Wilcox, which reported only 25 votes "against" (or 1 percent) out of a total 1,714 votes cast. Such results led two scholars to note accurately that "[i]t seemed as if blacks had voted for their own disfranchisement" and another to conclude that "even on an issue so vital to the Negro as his franchise, the Black Belt leaders could still manipulate the Negro vote."[92]

The disfranchisement myth, repeated by many scholars since, probably began with claims such as that of Chilton County Populist Lewis H. Reynolds. Consoling himself after the referendum loss, Reynolds claimed (albeit inaccurately) that at least "*one fact* has been clearly demonstrated" by the referendum: "that *a majority of the white men* of Alabama are opposed to the *whole movement*" [ital. mine].[93] Other Populists made similar erroneous claims that have since been accepted as truisms. "When this call was submitted to the white people of Alabama," the *Geneva Reaper* claimed, "less than 20 per cent of the democratic voters upheld it. . . . The call for a convention carried . . . through P & B [Palmer and Buckner, gold Democratic] influence, and against the wishes of the white people."[94]

The mistake was understandable (see table 4 in the appendix). That almost 90 percent of the Black Belt voted "for" calling the disfranchisement convention is usually the first point of focus for scholars examining this issue. That over 90 percent of the opposition to calling the convention came from the white counties is usually the second point of focus for scholars. The two points taken together have led scholars to the mythical dichotomy of Black Belt support for disfranchisement and white-county resistance to it. But a third, and often unnoticed, point is that the white counties, while they did supply the bulk of opposition to calling the convention, did not do so in anything like a consensus manner. Far from it: on a percentage basis, the vote was split in half in the white counties—with an actual numerical majority voting "for" calling the disfranchisement convention: 42,247 "for" to 41,829 "against" (see tables 5 and 6 in the appendix and map 3).

These returns indicate that the racial appeal of the constitution's effectiveness in disfranchising blacks won over many white voters in the white counties—just over half of them, given the figures. In addition, since blacks still voted relatively freely outside the Black Belt, and we can safely infer that most blacks in the white counties voted against calling a convention advertised as seeking their own disfranchisement, this further detracts from the split white decision in the white counties. That is, if the vote were split in the white counties among all voters, factoring out the black vote in the white counties as "against" calling the convention leads to the conclusion that, in fact, an even clearer and larger majority of white voters in the white counties voted "for" calling the disfranchisement convention (see tables 1 and 2 in the appendix). Statewide, the picture is even more decisive when we add white "for" votes from the Black Belt to the white total. It becomes clear that the majority of whites, both in the white counties and statewide, voted "for" the calling of a disfranchisement constitution. Finally, even if Reynolds and later historians had correctly interpreted the figures, the justification for concluding that a majority of white Alabamians were "opposed to the whole movement" of disfranchisement or "against suffrage restrictions" in general would still be questionable.[95] A sounder conclusion would have been that a majority of white voters rejected a particular disfranchisement instrument—or suspected elitist skullduggery in crafting an instrument that could be used to ensnare poor whites along with blacks—to such an extent that they voted against it.

Looking at the state by section makes the point even clearer (see table 7 in the appendix and map 1). Much of north Alabama actually went "for" calling a constitutional convention. Contrary to C. Vann Woodward's claim, Alabama's white counties did not "turn down flatly" the movement toward disfranchisement through a constitutional convention.[96] All nineteen of the Black Belt counties went against the convention. But five of the seven Tennessee Valley counties actually voted "for" the convention: Colbert, Lawrence, Limestone, Madison, and Morgan. Even the two that did not (Jackson and Lauderdale) only narrowly voted "against" calling the convention (44 and 46 percent "for"

MAP 3 White Counties Voting "for" April 1901 Referendum

it, respectively). The ten Wiregrass counties split down the middle, with Escambia and Covington registering over 60 percent "for" it. Again, the Wiregrass counties that voted "against" the convention did not do so by overwhelming odds. Butler and Coffee Counties, for example, logged a full 46 percent "for" the convention. Two of the three Gulf Coast Plain counties went "for" the convention; Washington County registered a whopping 82 percent "for" it. Even the vaunted Hill Country split on the issue. Eleven of the twenty-seven hill counties returned votes "for" the convention, including 87 percent in Randolph and Chambers counties, 75 percent in Talladega County, and at least 60 percent in Lamar, Tallapoosa, and Tuscaloosa counties. Bibb, Calhoun, Cleburne, Jefferson, and Walker also went "for" the convention. While Cherokee, Chilton, Marshall, and Saint Clair are usually cited as evidence of overwhelming Hill Country opposition to a constitution, six Upcountry counties that voted against the convention actually logged at least 40 percent "for" it: Blount, Clay, Coosa, Elmore, Etowah, and Marion. Almost half of Alabama's white counties (twenty-three of forty-seven) actually voted to call the constitutional convention in the April 1901 referendum—a stunning reality.

A deeper look at the racial makeup of white counties and their votes on the referendum indicates that many whites in the white counties voted "for" the convention (see table 8 in the appendix). Bibb County, for example, was 66 percent white. Combined with its 34 percent black population, Bibb should have returned an overwhelming percentage "against" the convention—if the myth of blanket poor-white opposition to disfranchisement were true. But Bibb returned a 56 percent majority "for" the convention. Clay was in a similar situation—only more so at almost 90 percent white. A full 42 percent of Clay County went "for" the convention. Cleburne was even more dramatic. It returned a 53 percent majority "for" the convention even though the county was 94 percent white. Calhoun, Chambers, Colbert, Covington, Crenshaw, Escambia, Henry, Jefferson, Lamar, Lawrence, Limestone, Madison, Mobile, Morgan, Pike, Randolph, Talladega, Tallapoosa, Tuscaloosa, Walker, and Washington did the same—some of these counties with 80 percent white populations.

Striking, yet not traditionally mentioned, is the fact that a great number of poor whites in Alabama obviously voted to call a convention. Despite the years of warnings, for many, the chance to eliminate the African American from politics was just too attractive a prize to resist.

CHAPTER THREE

Disfranchisement

 Collaboration between common and elite whites allowed white people to maintain their racial dominance of Alabama. But the co-operation many plain whites granted the elites for use in the emotional race issue was also used by the privileged to help them retain political and economic dominance of the state. To be sure, the privileged did not seek plain-white permission before using their compliance against them. And while this by-product may not have been the primary motivator or even an anticipated outcome for Alabama's plain whites, that circumstance did nothing to make it less lethal. Plain-white cooperation in 1901, as in other critical junctures in southern history, had—despite the single-minded racial intention—profound and intermingled social and class implications as well.

The organization, framework, and opening ceremonies of the constitutional convention made it clear that Black Belt whites and their privileged industrial allies were firmly in control of the historic summit. All but 14 of the 155 delegates (all white) to the convention were regular Democrats. Seven Populists, six Republicans, and one Independent Democrat rounded out the assembly.[1] The critical selection of a convention president also illustrated just how firm was the oligarchy's control of the convention's direction. Tennent Lomax, a Montgomery County prosecutor, stood opposed to William C. Oates. The former governor, of course, had plenty of experience and fine credentials but was not amenable to the north Alabama whites who would eventually have an important hand in ratifying whatever document the convention produced. Oates had previously called the "grandfather clause" loophole that safeguarded poor-white voting "absurd." He was a confirmed paternalist on racial matters who opposed the universal disfranchisement of every black person in Alabama as "unwise and unjust." The compromise that was worked out illustrated again that the 1900 gubernatorial result signaled, to a very large extent, the reconciliation and unification of white Alabama Democracy around the central issue of race. Regular Democrats agreed that Anniston's John B. Knox, a representative of north Alabama industry, former chair of the State Democratic Executive Committee (SDEC), and, perhaps most importantly, Joseph F. Johnston's

74

1896 campaign manager, should serve as president. Oates and Lomax gracefully withdrew, and Knox was in.[2]

The next order of business concerned the vitally important appointment of committee chairs and members, and in these decisions Knox showed himself to be the trustworthy representative of Alabama privilege. He tapped former congressman George P. Harrison, a well-known corporation lawyer, to chair the committee on corporations. He packed the committee on taxation with Harrison and another former congressman, William A. Handley, probably the most prominent railroad, mine, and bank booster in the state, and included admonitions against high taxes in his plenary speech. Knox appointed Louisville and Nashville Railroad attorney Gregory L. Smith to head the judiciary committee, William C. Oates to chair the legislative committee, Thomas Goode Jones for the executive committee, north Alabama's Emmett O'Neal as chair of local legislation, and, most importantly, Judge Thomas L. Coleman for the committee on suffrage and elections. To assist Coleman, a Black Belt graduate of Princeton, former slave owner, Confederate veteran, legislator, state supreme court justice, and delegate to the 1865 constitutional convention, Knox placed twenty-one attorneys on the committee of twenty-five.[3]

Knox's opening presidential address set the tone for the convention by reiterating the now-numerous Democratic State Convention and SDEC pledges not to disfranchise poor whites while effecting the universal white goal of black disfranchisement. He directly announced the purpose of the meeting as the establishment of white supremacy "by law" as a replacement for methods of "force and fraud." Knox took explicit pains to ease poor-white fears by praising the grandfather clause and making a clear distinction between poor whites and blacks. "[T]he Negro is not discriminated against on account of his race," Knox initially claimed, "but on account of his intellectual and moral condition." But then he went on to explain that, really, race was the main factor—an inherent distinction that promised to protect the franchise of plain whites. "There is a difference . . . between the uneducated white man and the ignorant Negro," Knox stressed. "There is in the white man an inherited capacity for government, which is totally wanting in the Negro. Before the art of reading and writing was known, the ancestors of the Anglo-Saxon had established an orderly system of government. . . . The Negro, on the other hand, is descended from a race lowest in intelligence and moral perceptions of all the races of men." To those who listened carefully, though, near the very end of his inaugural remarks Knox set the groundwork for a loophole that would, in the long run, favor the privileged over the plain. Just before he closed his address, Knox added that poor-white suffrage would be protected—but only temporarily. The no-white disfranchisement pledge of the Democratic Party, he stipulated, would be honored but would not extend "beyond the right of the voters now living."[4]

A Cancer on the Body Politic: The Disfranchisement Question

Convention delegates made no bones about addressing the central issue before them: the disfranchisement of blacks. Patricians of both the planter and the industrialist type clearly led the movement as they had for several years. Captain Frank S. White, a critically important bridge figure between the old conservative Democracy of Morgan and the emerging progressive wing of the party, openly stated in calling for the convention: "We have disfranchised the African in the past by doubtful methods, but in the future we will disfranchise [him] by law. The cancer that has been eating upon the body politic . . . must be taken away." Emmett O'Neal, son of a governor, a future governor himself, and spokesman for north Alabama and industry, was, along with Frank White, an emerging powerhouse in state politics. O'Neal encouraged the convention to move decisively in disfranchising blacks and assured delegates that, because of the country's imperialist foreign policy, white southerners now enjoyed the sympathy rather than the hostility of the North in regulating their domestic racial conditions.[5]

The critical question before the convention was not whether blacks should be disfranchised.[6] Rather, the real question was, How exactly should this be accomplished? Paternalists such as W. C. Oates felt strongly that qualified blacks should be protected in their franchise, lest the whole race lose hope and become a massive burden to society. "They constitute a large minority of our state's population—over 800,000," Oates reminded his fellow delegates. "Among them are many honest, industrious, and good citizens capable of fairly understanding the issues." The Little Mule mouthpiece, the *Mobile Register*, was even more direct about the economic value of reliable, educated, contented black labor. The African American was as much a part of the South as "cotton, corn, iron ore, or coal," its editor wrote. "Being here always he must be recognized as a stable component entering into the welfare or harm of the state [and] . . . must be so treated that he will count for the good of the state and its progress." Toward this end, the black man must not be deprived of the ballot by "subterfuge when he meets the requirements of the suffrage laws."[7] In fact, Judge Coleman's suffrage committee kept in constant touch with, and was greatly influenced by, leading paternalists both in Alabama and throughout the South. Through a running series of correspondence, the suffrage committee sought and received counsel from U.S. senators Morgan and Pettus, former Navy secretary and U.S. congressman Hilary Herbert, and notable representatives of the plain whites such as the former Populist governor of South Carolina, Benjamin "Pitchfork Ben" Tillman.[8]

Younger delegates generally took a more restrictive stand regarding blacks than did the paternalists. "We of the younger generation," Gessner Williams declared, "have known but one slavery, and that—slaves to the negro vote." No black, for Williams, no matter how educated or refined, could ever be the equal of the "least, poorest, lowest-down white man [he] ever knew."[9] While Williams hailed from the Black Belt county of Marengo, this type of sentiment was most commonly expressed at the convention by individuals such as J. Thomas Heflin, a delegate representing the poor-white, Hill Country textile county of Chambers, who also enjoyed strong support from a number of Populists. "I believe as truly as I believe that I am standing here," Heflin informed the convention, "that God almighty intended the negro to be the servant of the white man."[10] Important for both Williams and Heflin was the emotional imagery of a coming race war. Would they not want the "lowliest white man that plows the cotton row in South Alabama or the corn row in North Alabama . . . to shoulder the musket . . . against the black," Williams asked his fellow delegates. Heflin agreed. "Some day the clash will come," the aspiring demagogue warned, plucking the chords of poor-white racial fear, "and I do not believe it is incumbent upon us to lift [the black man] up and educate him and put him on an equal footing that he may be armed and equipped when the combat comes."[11] Newman H. Freeman, a lily-white Hill Country Republican delegate from Winston County, assured the assembly that he would cheerfully disfranchise as many blacks as any regular Democrat. Thomas L. Long, representing the Upcountry whites of Walker County, where many miners had supported Populist candidates in the past, spoke against black suffrage of any kind, even that of "Booker T. Washington or any one else."[12]

Noted historian C. Vann Woodward commented on such utterings by arguing that the new twentieth century in Alabama and the South "belonged neither to the fallen Populists nor to the old Jones-Oates type of patrician—but to the Heflins."[13] But what Woodward failed to say here was that Heflin and other demagogues such as Georgia's Tom Watson and South Carolina's Cole Blease, who also appealed to poor and working-class whites, were largely the logical outcome of the Populist loss. Shorn of a realistic chance at electoral victory, many of the old Populists—personified most viscerally by Watson of Georgia, Tillman of South Carolina, and in Alabama by men like Reuben "Run Forever" Kolb and the Hill Country's Oliver Day Street, Frank Crichton, and Captain A. McHan—jettisoned the heavy and uncomfortable baggage of tolerance and alliance with blacks and were guided by self-interest only. For most of them, this self-interest did not include a place for racial enlightenment. Further, while Woodward and other historians have almost uniformly interpreted Heflin's comments as representative of a "radical" racist position, the commentary was actually the more vulgar and less polished expression of a basic and very common sentiment about the fundamental worth of blacks shared by many at the convention—including paternalist whites. Despite his plain speaking, Heflin viewed himself as the friend of blacks "in their proper place." In actuality, convention president John Knox's opening speech had differed from the plain-white representatives more in tone than in content.[14]

O. D. Street's odyssey was especially enlightening. A leading Hill Country Populist and son of the Hill Country Farmer's Alliance and Populist leader Thomas Atkins Street, the younger Street never relinquished his faith in the poll tax as an effective disfranchising mechanism to get rid of black voters.[15] Street, who left the fading Populists to become the state's leading Republican and patronage dispenser for much of the first half of the twentieth century, was a devout opponent of federal activism and a racial, ethnic, and religious bigot who set new lows for intolerance during the heated 1928 presidential election in Alabama.[16] As late as 1943 the Marshall County Republican was still giving aid and comfort to the white supremacist efforts of Democratic governors such as Chauncey Sparks, usually couched in the Reconstruction syndrome language of hostility toward "foreigners" and meddling "outsiders." "The Negro must do his part," Street announced. "As a member of the . . . Republican National Committee from 1916 to 1936 . . . I have made a study of this question and I believe I know more about it than do many of the outsiders who wish to decide this question for us." Street complained that for many years "I have had to listen to the same claptrap from these same political Negroes, . . . [who want] not what they *deserve* despite the fact that they are Negroes, but what they want *because* of the fact that they are Negroes. . . . I am opposed to the repeal of the poll tax law." For decades after the 1901 constitutional crisis, Street would color his politics by referring to the "awful condition prior to 1901" and lament the period from Reconstruction to 1901 when "outsiders (high officials of the United States) . . . set the Negro astride the necks of the white people of the South." Even in the midst of the Great Depression, Street's Republican opposition to the New Deal fondly recalled the critical turning point of 1901 as a moment of white reinforcement of Redemption. "I am old enough to remember what went on in Alabama before payment of a poll tax was required for voting," Street would ritualistically warn.[17]

As it had since the Civil War and would continue to do long after the 1901 Constitution, the Reconstruction syndrome played a large part in the disfranchisement question for Alabama whites of all classes. The Redeemers and the anti-Democrats often expressed their desires for a disfranchising constitution—

and even their worry over poor whites losing the vote in the general push to disfranchise blacks—in the clearest terms of Reconstruction legacy: white supremacy, antifederalism, sectionalism, xenophobia, and a morbid fear of taxation. Witness one exasperated Jeffersonian's explanation of his support for a new constitution: "If Yankeedom will let us alone, we'll manage the negro. It is not the negro problem down South, it's the Yankee problem."[18] A Jeffersonian from the Hill Country who favored ratification concurred by utilizing the prevailing and enduring fiction that southern whites knew best how to maintain peaceful and "mutually harmonious" race relations. This legend, so strong at the turn of the century, would long provide a comforting and insulating fable for white southerners engaged in the twentieth-century battle to resist changes in race relations imposed by northern and federal forces from without and by "outsiders" and those not accepted as true southerners from within. Southern whites had done "a good part by the negro" in providing adequate jobs and public schooling. "This is all he can expect," this Jeffersonian reasoned in tying the franchise to education and employment. The southern white man has been the "negroes best friend, and if . . . the northern fanatics will let the negro alone it will prove much better for both races."[19]

Varieties of Black Thought on the Constitutional Convention

Formal black response to white plans for disfranchisement was predominantly of the accommodationist variety—and as much, or more, concerned with the designs of poor-white anti-Democrats against African Americans as with those of the patricians. Four black groups sent formal petitions to the convention, the most influential signed by Tuskegee Institute principal Booker T. Washington, Huntsville Normal and Industrial School president William H. Councill, and thirteen other leading African American teachers, bankers, businessmen, and physicians.[20] Their petition betrayed a sense of inevitability about black disfranchisement as they asked for "some humble share" for the black man "in choosing those who shall rule over him." But their plea also made it clear that black elites felt educated, literate, and industrious blacks like themselves should be allowed to keep the franchise.[21] Washington himself expressed support for a property qualification while opposing the grandfather clause and the registration plan, both of which could work to safeguard the poor-white ballot.[22] While the Washington-Councill petition has been criticized as timid and accommodationist by a number of historians, it paled in comparison to that of a black Decatur physician who praised the "Southern white man" as the "best friend" of a "weak race" and opined that American slavery, "though wrong," was "a blessing to us."[23]

A few souls even saw the new constitution as perhaps an opportunity to get *more* of the race voting. Ad Wimbs, a black Republican leader, privately hoped that black political leaders could get at least sixty thousand blacks registered by appealing directly to the county registration boards on a local, one-on-one basis. Thus, by extending "the olive branch" to the whites who would invariably control the boards, Wimbs hoped to "beat them at their own game" by holding out the fruit of black votes to the "professional ballot-box thief," who would be unable to resist the temptation, especially in the Black Belt. But as Wimbs confessed to Booker T. Washington, "I may be dreaming."[24]

Black elites were perhaps most worried about a plain-white movement at the convention to tie state educational funds to the amount of taxes paid by each race. The movement, led by Erle Pettus of Limestone County, was clearly identified with the state's poor whites, who increasingly realized that their future political influence was closely tied to their ability to read and write. Their future racial "superiority" vis-à-vis blacks likewise depended on keeping people of color as uneducated as possible.[25] "When you educate a negro you spoil a good field hand," a Jeffersonian from Alabama's Hill Country quoted a regional proverb in explaining his opposition to black education. The African American did not have a "sufficient mind" to master complex subjects such as mathematics or science, he explained, except in cases where he "has white blood in his veins." The average black had no more idea about the classical subjects, even after being schooled, than "a hog knows about Sunday."[26] A Wiregrass Populist newspaper added its dismay that the new constitution provided for school monies to be distributed equally between the races. What Black Belt county in Alabama, the anti-Democrat editor asked, would "ten years from now, or even five years . . . not be under negro domination, if this educational clause is allowed to stand and is honestly administered?"[27]

Obviously, the measure would have proven disastrous to the cause of black education—and black suffrage—while enhancing poor-white prospects for retaining the franchise. Of course, this was precisely the point. Erle Pettus, the white-county author of the discriminating education provision, was also the sponsor of other legislation designed to deepen the legal, social, and political divide between his poor-white constituents and black people. In fact, the legislation was crafted to preserve for plain folk the material rewards of being classed as "white" in a society dominated by whites. At the 1901 convention, Pettus proposed a law making miscegenation illegal that became part of the constitution and would not be stricken from the Alabama books until November 2000. He also put forward the suffrage restriction that perhaps most directly challenged the Fifteenth Amendment. It suggested limiting the franchise solely on the basis of race, color, and previous condition of servitude, not poll taxes;

literacy tests; property, educational, and character qualifications; or any such subtle mechanisms. Exercising some measure of discretion, the convention declined to pass a measure in language that constituted so direct a challenge to the federal compact.[28]

Blacks vehemently resisted the education schemes of the poor whites and addressed most of their arguments to the patricians who valued their labor. If the African American should conclude that no matter how "intelligent or useful he makes himself" to white society, there is "no hope of reward held out before him," the black leaders argued to the paternalists; he will "become a beast, reveling in crime and a body of death about the neck of the State. . . . In a thousand ways," they warned in striking the familiar chords of New South materialism, "the ignorant, shiftless, criminal Negro will retard the progress of the white race."[29]

Indeed, despair had already set in for many blacks, partially owing to a feeling among African Americans that they were beset by all classes of whites in Alabama—legally and economically by the "better whites" and physically by the poor whites. They had no idea of the "insults and hardships" that blacks in Alabama had to endure daily, William H. Councill lectured the Bourbons. All over the state, in every form of commerce and activity, "the Negro stands muzzled and manacled" while "unkind white men belabor our backs with impunity," the educator complained. He did not request absolution from the law for African Americans, only simple justice. "Punish the Negro—whip him until the blood runs in streams when he is wrong," Councill asked the patricians, "but let justice be done to him though the heavens fall." Others despaired of even appealing to the "better whites." Black people had gotten "so used to being slighted" that they had "ceased to kick," one Huntsville black concluded. "What's the use?"[30]

Some black entreaties also sought to appeal to white paternalists as the potential guardians of the elite-black franchise and to divide whites along class lines. Each of the three black petitions in addition to that of Washington and Councill focused on education for blacks and black worth to the state in the form of labor. One of these, a petition by W. H. T. Holtzalaw, principal of an African American school in the Black Belt, explicitly contrasted the image of a docile black labor supply with poor-white work habits and the inclination to join labor unions. "[I]f you of the dominant race will be generous in your dealings with us, generous in the matter of education," Holtzalaw promised, "you will ever have at your door a people who will not trouble your sleep with dynamite nor your waking hours with strikes."[31]

On both the issue of black education and that of limited suffrage for worthy African Americans, the position of the black accommodationist was actually quite close to that of the white patrician. Economic self-interest was an integral part of this Wade Hampton–style paternalism. William C. Oates, for example, objected strongly to the blanket disfranchisement of every single African American in Alabama—a position that did little to endear him to Alabama's plain whites. Fellow former governor Thomas Goode Jones agreed. "The negro is under us," he lectured the convention. "He is in our power. We are his custodians. . . . We should extend to him, as far as possible, all the civil rights that will fit him to be a decent and self-respecting, law-abiding and intelligent citizen of this state. . . . He is part of our economic system. . . . If we do not lift him up, they will drag us down." The state's leading reformers supported the Oates-Jones version of paternalism. Edgar Gardner Murphy, Episcopal rector of Saint John's Church in Montgomery, reinforced the paternalist suffrage position with an open letter to the convention. Prominent education reformer J. L. M. Curry followed suit.[32]

Some blacks of more modest socioeconomic status agreed with the controversial assertion by later historians that the elite and middle-class black accommodationist approach had, in fact, facilitated the onset of disfranchisement. The *Mobile Southern Watchman*'s vocal black editor, a man who represented black folk and working-class opinion, risked a great deal by lampooning Booker T. Washington as "the white man's ideal Negro" and advised the Tuskegee educator not to "show us how to be men and then blame us for being men." *Mobile Weekly Press* editor A. N. Johnson lashed out against the convention's alleged conscience wrestling over the issue of disfranchising worthy blacks. "What have the white men of Alabama ever cared about opposition to any political rascality they wanted to carry through," he wrote. All of this talk about the popular vote became "farcical in the last degree." Thomas Goode Jones responded by tongue-lashing the African American editor as one of those "fools with pens" who construct "double obstacles in getting a wise solution to our troubles." Still, a group of rural blacks who responded by meeting at Camp Hill to form the Afro-American Exodus Union evidently agreed with Johnson.[33]

Other types of black protest over disfranchisement occurred. Two black ministers spoke out strongly against the prospect of black disfranchisement, denying emphatically that "the negro is . . . satisfied" with white rule and explaining that what passed for acquiescence was actually only temporary submission because African Americans were "powerless to help themselves." The submission was only "by force and with discontent." Still, the preachers foreboded trouble if unfair treatment such as disfranchisement continued. In that case, they promised, blacks would seek whatever opportunity they could to "weaken . . . this system of semi-barbaric slavery." The country was only "making trouble for itself in the distant future," they lectured. Disfranchisement was "a cancerous sore" that would eventually rise to the surface in a dramatic "eruption." Scandalized whites, including Jeffersonians, reacted with shock and anger, but other blacks took comfort in the resistance. J. L. Giles, a Montgomery black, sued the local board of registrars in federal court for violating his Fifteenth Amendment rights by denying him the vote under the new constitution. In a move consistent with the federal government's general retreat on regulating state race relations, Justice Oliver Wendell Holmes wrote the majority opinion for the Supreme Court that denied Giles's cause of action.[34]

"All Coons Look Alike": Plain-White Opinion on Black Disfranchisement

Open defenses of black suffrage by whites were exceedingly rare, even exotic, in 1901, at the convention and throughout Alabama. The fact that it was a Populist-Republican who defended the right of black suffrage at the convention has done much to obscure the equally important fact that the vast bulk of other plain whites were not interested in preserving the black vote. A great many, in fact, were actively interested in doing away with it. Saint Clair County delegate N. B. Spears has gained much attention from historians—and rightfully so—because he violated state sensibilities in the worst way by praising Abraham Lincoln, abolitionist William Lloyd Garrison, and the Reconstruction amendments as the greatest ever "pinned to the beautiful Goddess of Liberty." A glaring lack of like-minded support for black suffrage among the anti-Democrats has not, however, received its due attention from historians. "I do not believe it is right to disfranchise any man simply because he is a Negro," the Tennessee native and son of a former Union general said, scandalizing the convention. Spears also advanced the prophecy that legal disfranchisement would "make the negro look to Washington and not Montgomery for protection," damned voting rights restrictions as "tyranny," and asked that blacks be treated as citizens, not slaves.[35]

Still, the most notable thing about Spears's heresy was that it *was* so notable. The importance of Spears's racially liberal stand was its novelty and absolute uniqueness—not the fact that it was uttered by a Populist. To put it simply, Spears's view of black voting was shared by virtually no other white person in Alabama, Populists included. For all intents and purposes, other Alabama Populists just did not feel the same way about black suffrage that Spears did. A considerable number of the anti-Democrats actually backed disfranchisement. Even those who opposed the movement did so on the grounds of protecting white suffrage, not black. Projecting Spears's sacrilegious opposition to black disfranchisement onto "the Populists" or "the anti-Democrats" as a whole is, like all projections, an illusion. It is a comforting illusion, a romantic and long-standing one, to be sure, but an illusion just the same. Some anti-Democrats openly applauded passage of the April 1901 referendum as the sign that blacks were on the verge of being disfranchised. "Mr. Ethiopian," rejoiced one Hill Country Jeffersonian, "fare ye well. Thou has cast thy last ballot."[36] Even in the most extreme and exceptional case of Jeffersonian opposition to blacks being disfranchised that we can find, the devil is in the details; the reasoning behind the position makes all the difference. The *Geneva Reaper,* a Wiregrass Populist newspaper, actually came out against blacks being disfranchised because its editors believed such a move would not survive federal constitutional muster—a position it saw as so rare that it felt nakedly alone. Still, the *Reaper* denounced white competition over the black vote as "hav[ing] made a fool of the negro— led him to believe that he holds the balance of power. . . . [T]his great negro blubber . . . has a tendency to debauch the negro." Instead of seeking formal constitutional disfranchisement and thereby risking a setback in federal court, the Populists proposed a safer way to achieve the pan-white goal of getting rid of the black vote. "[W]hy not disfranchise . . . the negro, . . . virtually, by unanimous consent" among all white men, "by ignoring him at the ballot box?" the *Reaper* suggested to its Populist readership. "In plain words, the negro stands today in Alabama totally disfranchised if the white people would allow him to remain so." That way, "the white men of Alabama [could] settle their political differences between themselves," in the best of all possible worlds. "The negro has long since learned that he cannot hope to rule this state."[37]

The most frequently repeated reason for the disfranchisement of black voters was that most of them were ignorant. In fact, the issue of an illiterate and ignorant black electorate was a real one in 1900. And as such, it deserves serious consideration by scholars today. Recent political and historical orthodoxy has made even consideration of the possibility that some black voters were "ignorant" to be a virtual anathema, as if such a possibility is the same as suggesting native and indigenous black inferiority (which it is not). It should be recalled, though, that earlier in the twentieth century political orthodoxy associated with the Dunning School had worked in the opposite racial direction—yet still stifled rather than fostered scholarship that sought the truth rather than conformity. For much of the twentieth century, consideration of the possibility that blacks might have deserved the vote was tantamount to scholarly excommunication or at least exile to the periphery of the profession. But the fact is there *were* illiterate blacks voting in 1901 Alabama, and the sentiment behind some of the disfranchising effort was the widely perceived "ignorance" of black voters. For these reasons, the issue must be engaged, as far as possible, removed from the emotional constraints of present-day, or yesterday's, political orthodoxy.

It is on this point of black ignorance that early southern historians were most sympathetic to the white architects of disfranchisement. Prominent among the apologists was John Witherspoon DuBose, historian and former editor of a Populist newspaper, closely identified with Jeffersonian politics, the white masses, Joseph F. Johnston, and Robert McKee.[38] But it is also precisely on this point that the disfranchisers, and their historiographical defenders, were at their most inconsistent. In the first place, if there were a large number of illiterate blacks in 1901 Alabama, whites had only themselves to blame. What more was to be expected of a race that was involuntarily pressed into chattel servitude, kept there for three centuries, and denied even the most rudimentary schooling as something that would "spoil a good field hand" and result in a "ruin't nigger?"[39] Second, it is quite a leap to accept the suggestion that formal education should have been the primary criterion for the most basic exercise of political rights, voting. If that were truly the case, much of the state in 1901—black and white alike—would have been disfranchised.[40] Truth be told, much of the black populace was in fact "ignorant"—*if* illiteracy is used as the defining measure.[41] But the percentage of illiterate whites was also abysmal. In fact, because whites outnumbered blacks in the general population, the number of illiterate white voters was nearly half that of illiterate blacks. Yet if the claims of the patricians were to be believed, these whites had no reason to fear that they would also lose their votes in the dragnet of black disfranchisement. What is more, it is not at all clear that illiteracy meant "ignorance" in terms of politics. It did not take much book reading for a poor black—or a poor white, for that matter—to discern that the whites of the Black Belt did not have their ultimate interests at heart. In fact, Alabama's regular Democrats spent much time in their councils chalking up the black vote in the white counties as being in the bag against a constitutional convention or ratification of its work—regardless of these black voters' formal degree of literacy.[42] Perhaps the most effective argument against equating formal literacy with political literacy was made by the disfranchisement architects themselves in their high estimation of black bloc-voting against the 1901 Constitution.

Then there is the problem of the U.S. Constitution under which Alabama and the rest of the nation were living. The Fifteenth Amendment had specifically enfranchised people of color in 1870. Alabama disfranchisers were seeking to circumvent that provision and were not bashful about acknowledging their goal. The fact that the Supreme Court put its stamp of approval on southern laws meant to accomplish the evasion of this very part of the federal compact was a clear measure of the national and pervasive character of racism at the turn of the century—not the ratification of a southern desire to act in accord with the U.S. Constitution.[43]

Educated blacks must also be considered. While the disfranchisers allowed a literacy loophole that in theory could permit educated blacks to continue to vote, the whole raison d'être of the 1901 Constitution was to disfranchise blacks—all blacks, one way or another. We need only recall convention president John Knox's opening assertion that all whites, no matter what their wealth, education, or social station, had "an inherited capacity for government, which is totally wanting in the Negro."[44]

But the patricians were hardly alone in their determination to see even educated blacks deprived of the right to vote. In general, poor whites felt even more strongly about this issue than the paternalists. This was true even of the poor-white *opponents* of a disfranchising convention because they feared a loss of white votes, not black ones. It can be acknowledged that educated and literate African Americans were rare in turn-of-the-century Alabama, that the reality of 1901 was not the reality of today in this regard. Many whites in Alabama and the other southern states rarely encountered literate blacks. At least that much can be gleaned from the official literacy statistics.[45] Yet plain whites knew enough to know that they did not want wholesale education of the race; they sensed that such a development would in some way threaten the fragile social, political, and economic advantage they held over blacks. Paternalists, for their part, wanted blacks educated only within the strictly circumscribed parameters of vocation. The postures of these different classes of whites both spoke more clearly than their own voluminous rhetoric on the nature of black inferiority. Conscious or not, their stances on education belied their published conviction that black "inferiority" was endemic—that it could not be abolished by the application of education and classic cultural attainment.

Just two days after the referendum on calling a convention had been held, a Marshall County Jeffersonian newspaper (which had resisted the referendum) raised a fury over a violation of the color line that it viewed as particularly objectionable because of its implied threat to established gender relations, "pure" blood lines, and racial distinction: Booker T. Washington's commencement address at Converse College, a women's college in South Carolina. "That don't sound so much like 'white supremacy,' which you here in Alabama howled so much" about to pass the referendum, the *Marshall Banner* lectured its proconvention opponents. " 'All coons look alike' to us, educated or uneducated," the Hill Country Jeffersonians explained, "and . . . when we stoop to invite [Washington] or any other negro to address the schools of the fair young women of our Southland, it is a reflection upon us and shows that we have lost proper respect for our female institutions." Any "man who has a daughter in such a school," the editorial argued, relying on the weight of social conformity and a narrow conception of bona fide southern "patriotism," is not "a true Southerner nor has he proper respect for his daughter or she would be called home immediately." As if the connection to disfranchisement were not clear enough, the newspaper spelled it out for its plain-white readers: "[S]ome people in Alabama . . . will yell themselves hoarse over a constitutional convention for white supremacy. If you want white supremacy don't 'slobber' over one class of negroes and cuss the others, for . . . 'all coons look alike' to us and have the same smell whether his name be Booker Washington [or not]. . . . [H]e is still a negro and should understand that he must remain in the proper place."[46] As strong and frankly obscene as such sentiment was, it found support from Jeffersonian Democrats around the state, including those who differed with the Marshall County citizens over (and had supported) the call for a disfranchising convention.[47]

Microcosm: The Battle of the Suffrage Committee

Virtually everyone in Alabama knew that the 1901 constitutional convention had been called, far and away, to decide the momentous issue of suffrage.[48] Consequently, the proceedings in the suffrage committee over exactly how to achieve this end became the main event of the convention. While some students of suffrage restriction have focused on the clash between Democrats and anti-Democrats, actually by 1901 that conflict was largely passé. The real story of the 1901 convention was the struggle, not between regular Democracy and insurgent challenges, but within the newly comprised regular Democracy itself. It should be recalled that 1901 was not 1892 or even 1896, and the same political lines and labels did not apply as well. By 1901, a great deal of the old Populist rank-and-file had marched back into the Democratic fold. The Democratic State Convention of 1900 had been, to a marked degree, a celebration of this very fact. Moreover, now that the economic panics of the 1890s had passed, Alabama politics returned from the class storms that had figured so prominently in the decade to its more regular pattern of race and class in which white over black was the fundamental reality. It was on this point that the old white insurgents had laid down their weapons and returned to the party of white supremacy. Despite the revelry, though, the reality was more an uneasy truce and careful alliance than a wholesale lovefest. Plain whites were, to a large extent, back under the umbrella of Alabama Democracy, but they still required some proof that their reentry had not been in vain.

Thus, the struggle between the Black Belt, with its industrialist allies, versus the white counties was one of the main stories of the 1901 convention. Left to their own devices, the Big Mule/Black Belt coalition, despite a hundred solemn pledges and resolutions, would have liked to effect the immediate and complete disfranchisement of their erstwhile white foes. Protections from the white-county delegates, no matter how incomplete or fleeting, were a central point of conflict at the 1901 convention.

What was not so apparent before the convention was that this debate—specifically the argument over the adoption of a minority or majority report in the suffrage committee—would encapsulate not only the convention but also the most pressing issues involved in the towering political question of the period. Black disfranchisement as the ultimate and (with a single exception) unanimous goal was not in question. What *was* still very much in question was how exactly to accomplish this end. Certain forces at the convention, very powerful forces, viewed the meeting as an untold opportunity not only to rid the state of the albatross of black voting but also to kill two birds with one stone: to abridge the poor-white vote, along with the black, to the greatest degree possible. Predominantly older, of the Black Belt and industrialist variety, this traditional Bourbon force was small in number but large in influence. Others realized that the convention had been called only with the significant assistance of many plain whites who would, once the meeting adjourned, have to ratify or reject the convention's work. It was largely a generational conflict, to be sure. But it was more than that. Typically the leading spokesmen for the majority faction were younger than those backing the minority report, but they also were predominantly of the white counties and thus had much more in common with, and greater knowledge of, the plain whites of the agricultural hill counties, the pine barrens, and the Wiregrass.[49] White *unity*—as the indispensable bridge to ensure white *supremacy* and white government and civilization—was uppermost in their minds. They were not about to sit still and watch while the planter-industrialist elite jeopardized this plain-white support and the success of disfranchising blacks by statute simply because the old guard was ready to forget their pledges and seize an opportunistic partisan advantage. Sensitive to this charge, some majority-report adherents sought to short-circuit the objection by explicitly declaring that it was not a partisan question.[50]

In a real way, the competing factions within the reorganized Democratic Party were operating in two distinct political worlds. The authors of the minority report were stuck in a kind of Black Belt time warp, still fighting the old Populist wars out of habit and unextinguished conviction. Witness their demand for the immediate and unqualified retraction of the Democratic pledge and the instant disfranchisement of as many poor whites as possible. Their desire recalled the knee-jerk reaction of the old warrior who knows only to lash out against his ancient opponent, whenever and wherever the opportunity presents itself. Their up-and-coming adversaries in the majority, for the most part, were not committed to everlasting plain-white political participation or parity for the folk with the forces of white Democratic privilege. That point should not be misunderstood. Their rival plan, after all, guaranteed poor-white voting through loopholes for a mere year after ratification of the constitution.

Still the majority, led mostly by those of the white counties, realized that by 1901 most of the old insurgents had already come back into the Democratic fold and were fundamentally compelled by notions of white unity. With this white unity intact, based on racial solidarity and conformity, the possibilities for unimpeded governance were endless. The majority Democrats believed the politics of the 1890s, temporarily rent by economic panic and uncertainty, had been eclipsed by the unifying crisis of racial opportunity. These newer Democrats were not about to see this recent and enabling racial harmony ripped asunder for partisan reasons that no longer held the same relevance they once had—especially for a nakedly partisan plan whose end could be accomplished in a more palatable manner twelve months after plain white votes would help ratify the constitution leading to their own eventual exclusion.

Language and rhetoric was an indispensable part of the debate—and very telling. Advocates of the minority report clothed their objections to blanket black disfranchisement in the language of paternalism and, more importantly, concern over the threat that the supremacy clause and the Fifteenth Amendment of the U. S. Constitution presented. While both sentiments were undoubtedly genuine, an overriding end was—if not stated as often or as clearly—the ensnarement of as many "ignorant and vicious" whites in the net of black disfranchisement as possible. To this end, the minority adherents adroitly summoned the nightmarish specters of Reconstruction to bolster their cause and serve as a fearful warning of what might happen to Alabama again if it proceeded headlong and recklessly to disfranchise every African American in the state on the simple basis of race, color, or previous condition of servitude.[51] No one wanted to revisit that horror and ignominy. The old guard knew well that fear and loathing of the Reconstruction era could work in their favor. Curiously, though, the majority conjured the Reconstruction imagery as skillfully as the Black Belt minority—rendering the memory of Reconstruction hotly contested terrain for both factions of Democrats. The majority employed the potent imagery of the Reconstruction legend in a slightly, yet significantly, different way. They stressed the strong and emotional reminder of the sacrifices that the South's plain whites had made for the Lost Cause. For Alabama to turn its collective back on them now, the white-county delegates argued passionately, constituted more than just a lack of gratitude or a weak memory; it was dishonorable and disrespectful to the memory of Confederate heroism and, by extension, everything for which the Confederacy had fought.

The debate over which report to adopt hit on the most important issues involved in the meeting. More than that, it made clear just how important plain-white support for the disfranchisement movement was—for, in essence, that is what the majority and the minority of the suffrage committee were fighting over. Had the minority report prevailed, the issue would have been more essentially partisan than racial. It is possible, even likely, that if the minority report's adherents had been successful in their push for the almost instant disfranchisement of poor whites, the convention's handiwork might never have been ratified by the masses, voting irregularities or no. As it was, the more patient and subtle, yet still essentially exclusive, posture adopted by those in the majority proved to be the cleverer and surer course to both ratification and the eventual purification of the electorate on, most importantly, racial grounds, but class distinction as well. In this way, the battle over the minority and majority reports was the titanic confrontation, the deciding moment of the convention and, in fact, the disfranchisement movement in Alabama. Its favorable settlement along the soothing lines of the majority report did much to calm poor-white fears and set the stage for a more positive reception by the masses during the ratification process.

As the central issue of the convention, suffrage naturally garnered the most intense emotion, energy, and debate by far of any topic before the assembly. The suffrage committee's report to the convention only promised more. The committee's majority report proposed the most elaborate, exhaustive, and intricate scheme of disfranchisement ever concocted by any southern state.[52] Its authors divided their report into a "temporary plan" and a "permanent plan," which was to take effect on 1 January 1903. The temporary plan called for voting to be restricted to males over the age of twenty-one who owned forty acres of land or property worth at least $300, could read and write, and paid a cumulative annual poll tax of $1.50. Thus, voting was to be restricted by literacy and property tests as well as by a cumulative poll tax. Under the temporary plan, though, an "understanding clause," a "good character clause," and a "soldier and fighting grandfather clause" promised to protect the vote of poor whites, including Confederate soldiers and their descendants, at least until the first day of 1903. Somewhat puzzling to many onlookers was the temporary plan's inclusion of a "registration plan," which called for a board of three county registrars made up of "reputable and suitable persons" to administer the temporary plan. Obviously, the beauty of the registration boards was in their dexterity. Delegates could argue for them as a sheltering mechanism for protecting the voting rights of poor whites who were propertyless and illiterate, much like the good character clause. Yet, once in operation, the boards would be free to work their magic in reverse if they were so disposed: to bar plain whites who had managed to scratch together a poll tax, property, or sufficient literacy. The permanent, post–1 January 1903 plan was clearer. It provided for five disfranchising mechanisms with no corresponding loopholes for poor whites: property, education, employment, crime, and the poll tax. All five could be equally applicable to blacks and poor whites.[53]

Here the proceedings in the suffrage committee got sticky. An extremely influential minority of the committee formally opposed the idea of a temporary plan with loopholes that would protect poor-white suffrage—even for as little as a year. Seeing the chance to rid the state of their old poor-white antagonists, the highest-powered Bourbons thrust forth an alternative plan under cover of noblesse oblige and concern about the Fifteenth Amendment. In reality, they recommended what amounted to an open retraction of their pledge to protect poor-white voting: the immediate implementation of a permanent plan that would disfranchise both blacks and poor whites. Of course, this was exactly the nightmare that suspicious white folk had feared in early 1901—that the privileged would use plain-white votes to call for a constitutional convention, make reassuring pledges, then feel free enough once in convention to renege.[54] When tested this way, survival and gain won out over pledges and honor, despite the volumes written and spoken by the genteel about that abstract notion. Not surprisingly, it was the most privileged members of the suffrage committee who spearheaded this move—all of them leading representatives of the planter-industrialist alliance, most of them from the Black Belt: W. C. Oates, gold Democrats Stanley H. Dent and George P. Harrison, and the "progressive" campaign manager of John Tyler Morgan's 1900 election run, Frank S. White. Morgan, the "grand old man" himself, fellow U.S. senator Edmund L. Pettus, former governor Thomas Goode Jones, SDEC chairman Robert J. Lowe, and paternalist education reformers Edgar Gardner Murphy and J. L. M. Curry vocally supported this minority position to renege on the pledge immediately both inside and outside the walls of the convention. The members of the supporting cast were almost one and the same as the most vocal proponents of suffrage retention for deserving blacks—a posture that suggested privileged Democracy, while certainly interested in disfranchisement through the legal vehicle of a constitution, was not yet ready to turn its back completely on fraudulent manipulation of black votes in the Black Belt.[55]

The minority position for reneging and jettisoning the grandfather clause picked up considerable steam (now that the convention was actually underway) from the most notable forces of Black Belt privilege. Former governor Oates declared that he was for eliminating "all those who are unfit and unqualified." And what if the rule should strike the vote of a white man as well as a black? "[L]et him go," Oates answered. "There are some white men who have no more right . . . to vote than a negro and not as much as some of them." A fellow delegate concurred, admitting that "[s]ome of the sorriest men I ever knew wore the grey." The state's major newspapers, located in planter and industrialist country, exhibited remarkably little patience or reverence for solemn pledges by joining in the chorus. The *Birmingham News, Birmingham Age-Herald, Mobile Register,* and *Montgomery Advertiser*—all leading mouthpieces for the most privileged planters and industrialists in the state—in a seeming fit of amnesia about the preconvention pledges to protect poor-white suffrage, spoke out against the temporary plan because of its inclusion of the grandfather clause. One Black Belt proponent of the minority report argued that the inconsistency involved in retaining a grandfather clause for poor whites was too much to bear. It would result in the black-county delegates, who were asking relief from political fraud, to go home and "perpetrate the most outrageous fraud in all the history of fraud." The industrialist *Birmingham Ledger* reasoned that if Alabama had some Confederate soldiers and their sons who did not have enough pride to learn to read yet would "march up to the polls" to vote anyway, they should be "laughed back to the woods."[56]

For the majority-plan Democrats who viewed recent white solidarity as a good thing, an enabling thing, the minority's clarity of purpose was chilling. "I do not stop at the exclusion of the negro, but [want to] exclude the . . . vicious and notoriously corrupt white man," Oates, the spiritual leader of the patrician minority stated. In fact, he went on, if it were up to him alone, he would not trust a poor white with the ballot "as quickly as [he] would a negro of intelligence and good character." After all, he explained, "all white men that were soldiers [were] not angels, nor [were] the descendants of them."[57] Only a one-armed Confederate hero, which Oates was, could have gotten away with this last sacrilege. The former governor's attitude toward the inclusion of a few deserving black voters was certainly not enough to come close to threatening white supremacy, because they were, as he stipulated, after all "of an inferior race." Yet it was tied to his realization of the worth of retaining industrial and agricultural black labor, a sense of paternalistic religious duty toward the inferior (because "God and the Bible teaches . . . the strong . . . to do kindly to those who are in his power"), and "a sense of attachment" and noblesse oblige between slave owners and especially the older freedmen.[58] Despite the obviously self-serving elements of Oates's paternalistic ideology, especially as regards subservient and docile labor, he believed himself to be a protector of African American interests—even in the fraudulent manipulation of their vote.[59] Perhaps emboldened by the ancient war hero's almost reckless honesty, Tennent Lomax, Oates's principal rival for the convention's presidency, blurted out the Black Belt goal as he spoke in favor of the nebulous three-member registration boards: "Now, gentlemen, I am not here, and we are not here, to disfranchise the negro race alone, we are here for a higher purpose."[60]

More common than such lucid moments of brutal honesty, though, was employment of the most powerful levers of emotional politics in service to the cause. Oates provided an almost classic example of bloody-shirt waving to argue for the elite's minority report: "I am not ashamed of my associates who signed the minority report, Men of civic renown and large experience . . . one of them at the age of 16 followed the immortal Forrest through scenes of blood, another, the youngest and among the bravest Brigadier-Generals of the Lost Cause, while the third sat on his horse as complacently in the smoke of battle as in his pew at church while guns hurled torrents of destruction into the ranks of an invading foe." Oates regretted that the prominent men of the minority report had failed to sway many minds, other than a few of the most prominent among the remaining delegates, yet defended his comrades as men of impeccable southern white patriotic and martial credentials. One of the concurring delegates, he was proud to recall, rode with John Brown Gordon "through the jaws of death, even in the last wild charge he made, not the least dismayed though the world wondered." Acknowledging that the convention faced a difficult task in trying to tread gingerly between the Fifteenth Amendment and outright black exclusion, the raison d'être of the summit, Oates reasoned that the Alabama convention could accomplish what many thought was impossible because they were, indeed, without peer in the annals of world history. "Are we not Southerners who fought for four immortal years against four and a half times our number, and carried the flag of the Storm-Cradled Nation to victory on a hundred fields?" Oates asked with a full throat. "Is it not possible for us to do what no other people have done? . . . [I]t is."[61]

While such emotional outbursts are almost shocking to read today, patricians like those of the minority position regarded their fight as a life-and-death struggle, not unlike their experience in war. Handled incorrectly, the consequences of a flawed constitution and judicial rejection by a federal court meant, in their minds, the possibility of a return to the intolerable conditions that followed Appomattox. Free people were never placed in "a more narrow or more tortuous channel through which to guide the ship of State," Frank White worried in referring to the provisions of the Fifteenth Amendment. The consequences of fashioning protections for poor whites, undeserving whites at that, could mean the unconstitutionality of the whole document and a return to the darkness of Reconstruction. "I saw Reconstruction with all its horrors," a sober Frank White recalled. "I saw the white men of my State placed under the domination and the heel of the black race."[62] Other patricians of this stripe expressed repeated concerns about having a new constitution declared unconstitutional if it included loopholes to safeguard poor-white suffrage while disqualifying blacks, basically, because of race, color, and previous condition of servitude.[63] "Why endanger the whole plan?" George Harrison pled. "I . . . warn you against any step that is likely to produce another reconstruction . . . when we went through what was worse than four years of war. . . . It was awful."[64] Black Belt members outside the committee who voted for the minority position likewise viewed the convention's purpose as a movement to do away with the possibility of Reconstruction. Since the dark era, one these delegates described, "the negro problem is still the malignant, fretting, running sore on the body politic and . . . every fiber of her [Alabama's] political organization is suffering from the poison of this plague spot."[65]

The stakes were extraordinarily high, the minority stressed, not just for themselves but for posterity itself. I never spoke with "a profounder sense of . . . responsibility," Thomas Goode Jones admitted. "We are speaking here of questions . . . which may return to vex our children, and our children's children, for a hundred years to come."[66] Oates concurred that the convention was considering a constitution "for the people hereafter, people who have to succeed us after my heirs have gone down to the grave and after you and I sleep in Mother Earth."[67] In the minds of the patrician minority's members, there was no limit and no precedent to the seriousness of the task before them. The race question, according to one Black Belt member of the minority camp, was "one of the great world questions" that still remained to be settled: "What are the dominant races to do with the inferior races?"[68]

Still, by no account should patrician rejection of the poor-white loopholes and their opposition to complete black disfranchisement on the basis of race and color be construed as a fledgling form of civil rights. The patricians were under no illusions. They sought the preservation of white supremacy as much as any white in Alabama and were not worried in the least about a few scattered blacks voting, especially when the old methods of fraud were still available to them. "The . . . gap is mighty narrow and the mote is mighty near closed on the road" that would allow any African American to vote, Oates explained comfortingly. Such instances would be very few and far between, the former governor assured the convention, "like angel's visits." In light of the predominating impediments to black voting, "is it good to be radical in anything," he asked, "or is it not best to be reasonable?"[69] Robert J. Lowe, the state Democratic Party chairman, also expressed the sentiment that "obnoxious" safeguards of poor-white voting, such as the grandfather clause, were superfluous because "white supremacy [was] safe in Alabama, absolutely safe." There would "never come a time when there [would] be danger of negro domination in Alabama."[70]

Opposition to the minority report consisted essentially of two elements. One faction included those white-county delegates who, although not technically anti-Democrats, were still in closer physical and perhaps ideological proximity to the plain folk of the hills, the hollows, and the pine barrens. The other type of opponent was also a regular Democrat who placed value on retaining white consensus that crossed class lines, at least for a year, as a pragmatic necessity to aid in the ratification process. Neither part of the majority represented anti-Democracy per se, although some members of the first group did enjoy Populist support and certainly realized that their political futures depended on retaining their credibility and amity among the plain whites.[71] Both groups, though, keenly realized the importance of keeping pacified recently converted insurgents and other Jeffersonians who might bolt the cause of black disfranchisement if the convention's restrictions against poor whites became too onerous or too transparent. Unlike the more impatient and more blatantly partisan Black Belt minority, both elements of the majority realized the need for some sedation of poor-white fears, at least for a while. Thus the "temporary" section of the majority plan.

Delegates from counties with many poor whites knew all too well that the transparent ill will in the minority report would alienate a large part of their own constituencies. Increasingly nervous, these delegates began to realize that, in their constituents' zeal to cooperate in disfranchising blacks, they had once again blindly entrusted their welfare to the oligarchy. Shaken thus, they themselves fell back on the tried and true logic of race and Reconstruction. Hailing from one of "the Piney Woods" counties, which were largely white and agricultural, J. O. Sentell of Crenshaw County informed the convention that his people were "intensely interested" in the great question of suffrage and elections because the black man had become "a menace to good government." While the majority report contained "some features" that the Crenshaw representative did "not entirely agree with," Sentell conveyed his belief that "in the main . . . it [was] the very best solution of this problem that could be gotten up." It would give them what they "want[ed] in the white counties . . . to disfranchise the negro . . . because they are not fit to vote," the Wiregrass delegate explained. The grandfather, character, and understanding clauses were sufficient to offset the threat presented by the property and educational qualifications. "So that lets in every white man," Sentell noted, breathing a sigh of relief. This was only logical after all. The matter had little to do with education or property, the white-county delegate argued; it had to do with "the laws of nature" that demonstrated "the fact that the white man is the superior and . . . is the only race that has ever shown the capacity to govern himself and . . . others. . . . [T]he negro has his place and the white man has his . . . and . . . the white man is destined to rule . . . the inferior race."[72] Mike Sollie, also of the Wiregrass, agreed with his fellow delegate that black voting "contravened the laws of nature." Asking whites, "the proudest and best example of the world's greatest race," to consort with blacks, even at the polls, was like asking the proud eagle to consort with the snipe or the lion with the hedgehog. How could "the sons of Caucasian fathers, of Saxon . . . lineage" enjoy the full measure of liberty and freedom, Sollie asked, when the same freedoms were accorded to "the ebon sons of dark and benighted Africa?"[73] J. T. Martin, a Hill Country delegate from Calhoun County, stressed that he spoke for neither Democrats, Populists, nor Republicans, but "to patriots everywhere" to join hands and make one great and determined effort to "preserve in its purity this sacred inheritance transmitted to us by our fathers." The plain people, "from hill-top to hill-top," Martin explained, had relied on the repeated pledges of the Democratic Party not to disfranchise a single white man. He himself had lobbied for a convention based on that very pledge. "We did it, and the people believed it," Martin reminded the delegates, "they voted for this Constitutional Convention and honored us with their confidence. . . . [And] never, no, never, so help me God, will I deliberately ignore the pledge I made my people."[74]

Committed above all to political survival, J. Thomas Heflin of Chambers County also valued the pledge. "[I]f I am untrue to my promises made to my people on the stump," Heflin vowed, "when I come to the judgment, may God forget me."[75] Mistakenly identified by some historians as a representative of the Black Belt, Heflin was actually a darling of plain whites: the textile workers of Chambers County, small dirt farmers, and other rural folk, including a number of Populists, across the state. More than just a routine error of identification, this mistake, which both J. Morgan Kousser and Michael Perman made, is actually a rather large one that can easily contribute to misinterpretation. Grouping someone as notable as Heflin in the Black Belt camp misses some of the very important infighting among the regular Democrats at the turn-of-the-century and the critical role that competing for, or dismissing, plain-white political support played in these fratricidal struggles.[76] No one exceeded Heflin in the color of his oratory or his ability to prey on the most sensitive and interwound heartstrings of race, religion, patriotism, and morality that moved white southerners so deeply. Stressing the absolute need to keep the pledge, Heflin waxed biblical: "I say to the white people of Alabama, as Ruth said to Naomi, I will not leave you . . . for whither thou goest, I will go . . . where thou diest, I will die, for the white people are my people and their God is my God."[77] Religion was a useful tool for Heflin, but nothing worked like the perfect mixture of race, religion, and patriotism to whip up a strong batch of the politics of emotion:

> [T]he Caucasian hewed out a Republic. . . . [T]he proudest race that ever lived established a government that will never fall. . . . [T]he white man drove the red man from his home . . . and took possession of this land as we find in the Bible that

God gave His servants command, to go up and possess the land. I verily believe
he reserved America . . . for the permanent settlement of the Caucasian race . . .
[for] the negro . . . to be the servant of his superior, the white man in this country. . . . [I]n Africa . . . [t]he negro wander[ed] through the woods like a beast of
the field. . . . I know he is inferior to the white man. . . . He knows it himself. . . .
Scripture will sustain my position on that. . . . [S]triking from him the title slave,
and placing in his hand the ballot was the most diabolical piece of tyranny ever. . . .
The white people who love the ballot [and] . . . the sanctity of their fireside . . .
want to exercise that great weapon in the defense of things that are right and sacred. . . . I am not an enemy to the negro. I am a friend to him in his place. . . . I
love the old-time Southern negro . . . in his place as a slave, and happy and contented . . . the old black mammy . . . [and] the lullabies she has sung. . . . Why, . . .
I saw this morning a little fellow coming down the street . . . as happy as could be,
with a piece of watermelon in one hand and a set of cane quills . . . in the other,
blowing "Boogoo Eyes." . . . [But] I tell you that the old negroes are passing out
and the young bucks that are coming on have got to be attended to. . . . The white
man bought this country with his blood, and the blood of his descendants inherited it, and the negro has no right to help make the laws. . . . [T]here are racial
distinctions and prejudices implanted by God himself that cannot be wiped out
by any human law. . . . This is our country by virtue of inheritance, and it is right
that we should rule it. . . . Now, let us move along [and] . . . settle this question of
the suffrage and perpetuate white supremacy for all time to come. If you do it . . .
Alabama will prosper as she has never prospered before . . . contented, happy and
[with] . . . the great cause of morality, temperance, industrial development, education and religion . . . prosper[ing]. [A]nd the grand old ship of state will sail on
and on, and will finally land in the sunny harbor of peace and happiness and bask
in the smiles of an approving God.[78]

Delegates from counties with many poor whites also relied on Reconstruction sentiment and the powerful memories of the Lost Cause to bolster their
cause. While the Black Belt authors of the minority plan had used Reconstruction as a warning against testing the Fifteenth Amendment by including loopholes to safeguard poor-white suffrage, the white-county delegates in the majority employed Reconstruction to the opposite effect. They called on the deep
emotions conjured by the Reconstruction memory and the valorous Confederate sacrifice to endow their cause of protecting poor-white suffrage with the
strength of those associated and enduring passions. Far from viewing measures
protecting the poor-white vote as a threat to the document's constitutionality and a harbinger of another period of Reconstruction, these representatives
of the plain folk cast them as, in fact, an insurance policy *against* the return

of Reconstruction. The broadest possible white suffrage, and the least black, meant the best and most patriotic government. The Fifteenth Amendment was "an abominable crime . . . a crime against the civilization of the age and against the white people of the South," according to a delegate from the Wiregrass. It had been "organized in prejudice, the sole purpose . . . to humiliate our beloved Southern people who were already crushed beneath the iron heel of war. . . . I shall never respect such an amendment," J. O. Sentell vowed in the finest tradition of southern recalcitrance, although the South might be forced to obey it. There was no need for conflict or confusion, the Crenshaw delegate hastily added, for "the white man is destined to rule, and he will rule . . . the inferior race as well."[79] A Hill Country delegate struck the central note by depicting the work of the 1901 convention as the long-awaited remedy for the "darkness" of Reconstruction that had been forced on the white South by "unwise, unstatesmanlike, and vicious legislation."[80] Mike Sollie, of the Wiregrass, damned the Reconstruction amendments as the most "radical wrong" in all of human history; a "continuing menace and blight . . . a cup of bitterness . . . a bitter and nauseous pill . . . an aching and deadly pain" that had placed the white South on "an artificial, enforced, and unnatural political level . . . with the slave of all the ages past, the negro." For Sollie and his common-white constituents, the blight had to be removed by a disfranchising constitution. "Nothing short of the most intense hatred" could have led to the Reconstruction amendments, Sollie concluded. "It was as if the victor should stoop above his prostrate foe and inject into his veins a virulent poison that would corrode and stagnate his blood and infest him with corrupting sores all the days of his life." The emotion associated with the Reconstruction political memory, which Sollie could not have experienced firsthand, was, even three decades later, almost too much for him to bear. "I do not remember the bitterest of the experiences or the gloomiest of the days that followed, as the older delegates here do, but the spirit of my father, who gave first his fortune and then his life to the Lost Cause, lives in me, and swells my bosom almost to bursting when I remember our wrongs." Truly, the Wiregrass native concluded in connecting the dots between sectional loyalty, racial order, and family fealty: "I am a son of the South."[81] Though they largely stood apart from the majority report, because of concerns about the partisan three-member registration boards, anti-Democratic delegates shared this camp's concern about the unconstitutionality of the document bringing on another Reconstruction. "I fear for more reconstruction," Coosa County Republican John Porter declared. "Are we willing to risk the chances of reconstruction again? . . . Are we so forgetful as to be carried off by sentiment again? . . . I hope not."[82]

Related yet somewhat distinct from the Reconstruction memory, patriotism and war remembrances were also pressed into service to save the poor-white

vote and provide the requisite reassurances to nervous plain folk. Thomas L.
Bulger, a Tallapoosa County delegate speaking for the poor whites, argued forcefully to persuade the Redeemers to include a grandfather clause. The South's
poor-white farmers "laid down the plow and the hoe . . . went to the battle
front . . . [and] poured out their blood like water," he reminded the convention. These brave men followed Lee and Jackson "from Sumter's coast . . . to
the famous apple tree where Lee surrendered. Those are the men I would exempt from the understanding clause."[83] The old Confederate soldier, another
Hill Country delegate flatly explained, had "been fried in the fiery furnace and
came forth pure gold. Are you afraid to risk the affairs of the State of Alabama"
to such men?[84] Of course, Tom Heflin got himself into the act in the most hyperbolic way. The men who wore the gray were "the bravest that ever drew a battle
blade[, t]he bravest that ever crossed the field of carnage," he claimed. The "historian will record the fact that the Confederate soldier was the bravest that ever
lived in the annals of time," the one who comes closest to the "world's highest
idea of a soldier." Yet, Heflin drove the point home, the authors of the minority
report would "undertake to put . . . the negro . . . upon the same level" with
this hero. "If you want to make a foot race," the Chambers delegate sardonically
suggested, "let us make it with the descendants of our own tribe." For representatives of the plain people, the disfranchising constitution was the restoration
of a "glad time" and an "old condition" of "self-government" and "home rule,"
when "[no]body but the proud Caucasian" was able to cast a vote.[85] A number
of the plain-white delegates pled the case for suffrage protection as payment
for past debts and hardships endured for the Lost Cause and warned that there
would be hell to pay if this patriotism was somehow blasphemed. But perhaps
none argued as eloquently as J. T. Martin of Jacksonville in the Hill Country:

[T]he rank and file of the Confederate Army was made up of poor men . . . [who]
owned no property . . . [and] never owned a negro in their lives, but they fought
for principle and for conscience sake. . . . [W]hen those men were called to arms
from their homes, they left the plow standing in an unfinished furrow upon the
hillside farm. He left there a wife and a group of little children, the oldest, perhaps,
not more than 10 or 12 years of age. The father gone, that boy, under the guiding
hand of a loving mother, stepped between those plow handles and year's end to
year's end worked and labored in order to supply his mother and little sisters and
brothers with the necessities of life. Did he go to school? No, . . . for he never had
time to go to school. He stood in front of that cabin door, and with all the strength
and energy of his young life, drove back the wolf of want and hunger from the sacred confines of that home. Then, when the war was over, his father came back, perhaps on one leg or with an empty sleeve by his side, broken in health and wounded

in body, a hero without success, a disabled soldier without a pension. His country could not help him and therefore that boy continued to labor between those plow handles not only to support that mother but to enable that decrepit and broken-down Confederate soldier to live, literally growing from childhood to manhood between those plow handles. Now, . . . I put the question to you before God and man, will Alabama today, like a cruel and unnatural mother, lay the heavy hand of oppression upon him? Almighty God forbid it. [B]ut . . . Gentlemen . . . if you . . . do, beware that you do not sound the death knell of your Constitution.[86]

White-county representatives were especially suspicious of the temporary plan's inclusion of a registration plan. This measure provided for the governor, state auditor, and commissioner of agriculture and industries to appoint three "reputable and suitable persons" in each county to act as a registration board to administer the plan. Anti-Democrats uniformly opposed it and, for principally that reason, voted against the majority report. Yet their opposition to the plan, sometimes taken as evidence of good faith toward black voters, actually revealed a strong concern about protecting the votes of poor whites, not blacks. Hill Country anti-Democrat Newman H. Freeman—who had previously indicated his willingness to disfranchise as many blacks as any regular Democrat—opposed the plan as a slick way for the Bourbons to disfranchise poor whites under the "good character" clause, even during the temporary phase of the constitutional plan. With this new development at the constitutional convention, poor whites "might just as well say, 'Oh King, where is thy crown?' " the Winston County Republican lamented, "for it will be equal to monarchial government and we will be subjects." Freeman's concern, still, was clearly poor-white suffrage, not black. The Winston Republican vowed never to register his vote for "anything that will have the tendency to disfranchise any white man in Alabama," for the "poor man's freedom is all he enjoys in this world," and I would never "deprive him of that God-given right. . . . I never will disgrace my father's grey hairs by depriving him of the only free right this Government granted him after he has fought for his country and his people." Besides, Freeman argued, the registration boards as embodied in the Mississippi Plan, although fine in theory as a mechanism that disfranchised blacks, had been an abject "failure" in practice because "still there are negro voters in Mississippi. . . . [S]o you see, it is a failure."[87]

Lewis H. Reynolds echoed Freeman's concern about the registration boards using the character clause to disfranchise plain folk, if left unchecked by a Populist or Republican member. Reynolds regarded the all-Democratic makeup of the boards as a major impediment, a deal breaker. If the Democrats abandoned it, though, there was room to talk: "We in the opposition are not demanding perfection. We do demand that the power of the kings be curtailed. We prefer a limited to an absolute monarchy." Like Freeman, L. H. Reynolds exhibited a willingness to disfranchise some blacks as long as white votes were held sacrosanct. He threatened the convention with the wrath of the plain folk at ratification time if adequate protections for the poor-white vote were not included. "I . . . warn you," the Chilton County Populist told the convention, "there must be some provision adopted whereby . . . the electorate will be fairly and impartially made up . . . that . . . by the eternal gods, the white men of this country will vote." When pressed on the issue by Tom Heflin, who no doubt wanted to recruit as many anti-Democrats to the majority report as he could, the Chilton County Populist stipulated that, "yes, sir," he would be in favor of disfranchising some blacks and apologized if he had given the impression that he was opposed to a document that would disfranchise blacks. "I am as broad as you are" on the question of disfranchising blacks, Reynolds assured Heflin.[88] While the spokesmen for the few remaining insurgents labored vigorously to persuade their class betters to protect their concerns, blacks such as the editor of the *Huntsville Journal* were literate enough to read the broader handwriting on the wall: "It is good by with poor white folks and niggers now."[89]

Regular Democrats on the majority side who were not quite as connected to the common people as Heflin, Sollie, Bulger, and company still shared their practical interest in retaining plain-white support for the disfranchisement effort. A good example of this type of pragmatic regular Democrat was the young Gessner Williams, an exception as a Black Belt member of this group. We should "put ourselves in the position," he advised his peers, so that "when we go out to secure ratification . . . all we will have to do is set up on the stump and kindly and pleasantly begin every speech by saying . . . white men of Alabama, we have carried out every pledge that we made you." Can you disfranchise "a single white man" and still carry out the pledge, he challenged his Black Belt counterparts on the minority side. "Can you disfranchise the mining vote of Jefferson County?" Gregory L. Smith, a wealthy railroad attorney, called the temporary plan strictly a "child of necessity." Without such reassurances to the plain whites, he recognized, it would be "almost impossible" to ratify the constitution.[90]

Perhaps the two best representatives of this type of sentiment were Emmett O'Neal of Lauderdale County and Dr. Russell M. Cunningham of Jefferson, both of whom had firsthand knowledge of the plain whites of north Alabama.[91] Like their counterparts on the minority side, and even their poor-white cohorts on the majority, these delegates were highly skilled in stoking the chords of a *race-based conformist citizenship* that used mainstream conceptions of morality, patriotism, and religious orthodoxy in service to its cause. It was an ideology that equated good citizenship with individual fidelity to a status quo notion of white supremacy buttressed by prevailing ideas of what constituted good religion, wholesome morality, and civic virtue. And it was very, very powerful— especially in the emotional and religious-conscious South. In other words, to qualify as a good citizen in such a society and certainly as a good person, one had to hew to orthodox views on white supremacy, which were supported by and, in turn, bolstered conservative, status quo notions of religion and morality and a vague but powerful notion of patriotism.

The doctrine was decidedly patrician in origin, for it served the purposes of the most privileged members of southern society in preserving a status quo with them at the top of the social and economic pyramid. Yet once crafted by the elite, this consensus of good southern citizenship was adopted by all but the most radical and alienated in the white South. Only the rarest of characters deviated from the pervasive creed. Though founded with white supremacy as its cornerstone, the doctrine and its ethos extended to proper "conservative" behavior on a myriad of social, economic, gender, and political questions. From time to time, usually during the most severe financial downturns, significant numbers of poor whites revolted against the most conservative economic elements of the doctrine. Yet this insurgency was usually temporary, short lived, and unsuccessful. Even when it persisted, the overwhelming majority of the economic rebels were so infused with the prevailing ethos of the society in which they had been raised that they were able to wage their economic warfare without radically or permanently altering their own conservative views on race, religion, low taxation, "meddling Yankees," or an invasive federal government. None but the most radical, rare, and disaffected whites stood against this tide of consensus mores, thereby consigning themselves to the utter fringes of southern society, ostracism, and eventual irrelevance within the Deep South. Economic revolt meant economic revolt in Alabama—not social, racial, or even, most times, political revolt with regard to the most basic assumptions about the role of the federal government in doing anything more than handing out emergency relief or economic aid to business. Thus it was that white Populists in Alabama could wage heated economic insurgency against the Bourbons, yet still adopt— with an equal or greater fervor—native southern hostility to Reconstruction, black suffrage, and northern/federal liberal intervention on social and political issues.[92]

Accordingly, Russell Cunningham pressed God into service on behalf of Aryan supremacy, arguing long and loud that the protections to plain-white suffrage embodied in the majority report were the preferred route to disfranchisement because they were based on primordial distinctions. The safeguards were based on a constitution that existed "before there was a written Constitution or a recorded fact." The Jefferson County physician invoked the "laws of the Almighty" and the "laws of nature" as sanctifying the supremacy of the "Arian race." Due only to the most strenuous efforts of his white brother, the organized "benefactor" of the race lowest in potential, the African had been converted from "a savage into a fairly civilized people." Left on his own without benefit of white assistance, the African would still be "a slave today" and would stay "a slave forever." He would still be in "Darkest Africa," a country as dark then as it was when the black was taken into slavery, a place that was as "unillumined by the sunlight of Caucasian enterprise . . . as it was at the time of the Christian era" and would be, Cunningham predicted, "as dark four thousand years from now as it was four thousand years ago if unimproved by Caucasian intelligence and enterprise."[93]

Believing the poor-white vote would be integral to their future success—personal as well as regarding constitutional ratification—some Progressive-wing Democrats such as Cunningham supplemented their racial arguments for protecting poor whites by invoking the Reconstruction nightmare lick for lick. Conceived in "hate, executed in malice, and maintained by force," the Fifteenth Amendment was "the great mistake, . . . the great crime" of human history. Its federal bayonets, marshals, prisons, gallows, and the confiscation of property were the culmination of prejudice, bias, and "hatred," according to the doctor. Still, the white man had survived. Redemption had been the initial white effort to right the "organic laws of the universe" and the "eternal law of nature," but the disfranchising constitution of 1901—replete with its protections of the suffrage of the state's plainest white citizens—was the "supreme and final effort to throw off these forces." "[It is why] we are here today," Cunningham explained.[94]

Emmett O'Neal was, first and foremost, a guardian of north Alabama industry. Yet, hailing from Lauderdale County in the Tennessee Valley, O'Neal knew what worried plain whites and, if placated, how useful their support could be. As the convention wore on, O'Neal threw the weight of his growing influence behind the majority report because he believed, perhaps from contact with the poor whites back home, that sufficient safeguards or at least lip service would have to be offered in order to compete for a considerable portion of the plain-white ratification vote. Very few delegates were able to match O'Neal in eloquence or in his ability to tie together logically every element enunciated by the majority camp to fashion an argument that would at once convince the convention's delegates to back the majority report and sufficiently reassure the poor-white insurgents hanging on the convention's proceedings. O'Neal began by tipping his hat to the purpose of the convention and the graveness of the problem before them: the "most momentous ever submitted to a free people," on whose wise solution "depended . . . the very life of the State." He next moved quickly to a justification for limiting black suffrage based on the inherent and obvious racial inferiority of the black man. Such restriction had to be accomplished for "the sake of our civilization." What "we have here," O'Neal explained, are "two distinct races, one two thousand years in advance of the other." Africans had, of late, been "naked savages living on the banks of the Congo or Niger." Invoking the social Darwinistic arguments of the age, O'Neal claimed that for these two millennia, the white race had been progressing to the top of the species' order, while the black had stood still, "as uncivilized today as he was before the birth of Christ."[95] Like some of the other delegates and Populists outside the convention hall's walls, O'Neal argued that white rule was actually in the best interest of blacks, whether they knew it now or not. The white race had to dominate because "it is the superior race," O'Neal told the convention, "and in that domination the negro will find the safest pledge and guarantee of just and impartial administration." The Fifteenth Amendment was, in the first place, not simply "a political blunder, but a crime . . . against the white people of the South [and] . . . against the black people of the South . . . a costly and ghastly failure . . . against us as well as the negro."[96]

Having established the seriousness of the task that lay before them and its racial rationale, O'Neal next turned to plucking the sentimental heartstrings of Reconstruction and connecting the dots between its return and the danger of sexual and racial amalgamation. The Fifteenth Amendment was "the colossal crime of the nineteenth century," the north Alabama politico declared, thrust on the "hopelessly unfit . . . negro" by the Yankees in "hot and vengeful haste." Moreover, this act was perpetrated for the most ignoble of reasons: "not to elevate or protect [the Negro], but to humiliate and degrade us." What ensued was misery and ruin, "a carnival of crime . . . without parallel in history . . . corruption, misrule . . . intensified racial prejudice . . . repressed freedom . . . debauched suffrage . . . demoralized labor . . . retarded growth," the forcing of whites to resort to desperate measures, and the adoption of fraudulent methods that "debased and lowered [their] moral tone."[97] O'Neal tantalized his audiences with the notion that the underlying threat was not merely political. It was sexual too—and in that respect, jeopardized the continued existence and, therefore, political and economic supremacy of the white race and of the white male. "Not satisfied" with the humiliation of the white South through emancipation and enfranchisement, "the North" set its sights on "regulat[ing] the social relations" of the races for the purpose of "forcing an assimilation of the negro, and destroying Southern civilization." Redemption from this nightmare—and this was the principal lesson for 1901—had been only partial; it had occurred only through "the Grace of God" and by as many white men as possible forming a "solid phalanx" against the northern/federal/black threat, submerging "all differences of opinion on . . . governmental questions," and exercising perfect solidarity in the interest of "white supremacy and good government."⁹⁸

The lesson for the 1901 completion of the redemptive work of 1874 was unity among white men of all classes. Here was the message to the poor whites listening beyond the walls of the convention hall in Montgomery as well as the delegates within who wanted to frame the strongest constitution possible. "Division amongst them meant ruin," O'Neal plainly reminded everyone. Whenever the whites divide, the "negroes . . . hold the balance of power and we have failed to accomplish our mission," he explained. "Cannot we, brothers, kinsmen, inheritors of the glorious past . . . forego our petty bickerings and unite to accomplish this glorious mission . . . to guarantee to future generations the blessings of Anglo-Saxon civilization and liberty?" he asked plaintively. And then came the line so many plain folk around the state had been waiting to hear: "We cannot afford to disfranchise the ignorant or illiterate white. It was the illiterate and uneducated white man that fought the battle of the Confederacy." To provide just the cap that was needed to the extremely powerful argument he had constructed, the Tennessee Valley delegate called down on the plan the blessings of God. In so doing, O'Neal made passage of the majority report and ratification of the larger document a holy duty. Wherever the white man "has come into contact with an inferior race," O'Neal said, reminding the convention's northern observers of their own racial stance, the "race instinct will assert itself, and the white will dominate and control." This reality was not to be tampered with. It was not to be "decried, derided, or denied," he explained, because it was a "divine ordination" that preserved the "integrity and purity" of the races. More, anyone who would stand in the way of this natural state of things was a sinner and a heretic of the highest order. The logic was pure social Darwinism, linking nature to God and providing a religious bulwark against social change. "The races of men are the creations of God, the markers of his will," O'Neal preached. Anyone who dared attempt to contradict "this race instinct is defying a power which is higher and wiser than that of man." And so the argument was sealed—a powerful argument indeed.⁹⁹

Right in the Sight of God: Plain Whites during the Convention

The fatal flaw in the position of poor whites sprung from the racism and the racial self-interest they held in common with their privileged foes. The opportunity to see blacks disfranchised was so attractive to them that many were willing to place their own welfare in the hands of the Bourbons in order to accomplish the deed. A great many plain as well as privileged whites felt that any white man, no matter how poor or uneducated, was inherently superior to any black man, no matter how wealthy or cultured—and that the franchise should hinge on this conception of an intrinsic and immutable white supremacy. That common whites were disinterested in the disfranchisement of blacks, much less *against* measures to disfranchise blacks, is simply not the case—at least not in Alabama.[100] For poor whites, not only was white superiority the way it *was*. It was the *way things had to be.* Feeling innately superior to blacks was psychological salve for common whites, who knew they were the economic equals and competitors of African Americans.

Evidence of this fatal flaw abounds in the Alabama case. A Hill Country Populist, for example, expressed the desire of many in his county for a document to be crafted that "will knock the negro out and leave the white man."[101] Others throughout the Hill Country repeated the concern about white men losing the vote.[102] L. H. Reynolds himself told the home folks in Chilton County that he had "many . . . objections" to the "vicious" constitution that had been proposed, largely because it discriminated against poor whites in favor of blacks. If the new constitution were adopted, Reynolds warned his constituents in hyperbolic fashion, "every man in Alabama will be disfranchised," even those who thought the "soldier clause" would protect them. Then the "old soldier" who had neither education nor property, Reynolds said in stoking the racial flame, would have to "stand aside and see the negro that comes up . . . take his ballot and vote."[103] Upcountry delegate Thomas Bulger of Tallapoosa preferred to put his trust in the grandfather clause "because it is a white man's clause . . . because it practically permits all white men to vote, and practically denies all negroes to vote." A Hill Country Jeffersonian paper concurred because "most white men can vote under it and the Negro cannot. . . . [It] alone repays the [whole] expense of the convention. It is worth a million dollars to Alabama." A Wiregrass delegate agreed that it was the "intransic *[sic]* force and intelligence" within the white man that qualified him to vote, for he is "the ripened product of thousands of years of good breeding. . . . The meanest white man in the State is within the saving clause," because, unlike the African American, "at one time, he had a worthy sire."[104] A Hill Country Jeffersonian who opposed the call for a constitutional convention only to wind up later supporting ratification stated the case as simply, if crudely, as it can be put: "A negro is a negro, after all, and has the same smell whether he is 'larned or unlearned.' "[105]

Such explications of immanent white superiority and, consequently, the right of franchise for poor whites, struck a responsive chord with emerging north Alabama powers like Emmett O'Neal and convention president John Knox of Anniston. In the heat of the convention's debates, it was sometimes difficult to gauge the difference between sincerity and lip service, but even Knox spoke at least the rhetoric of pacification. Whether these regular Democrats intended that qualifying measures such as the grandfather clause should be installed in perpetuity is another question. The evidence of their own majority report, replete with its temporary clause, suggests otherwise. Still, the realization among these pragmatic delegates that the grandfather clause was needed to secure the white-unity vote set them apart from their more principled and extreme Black Belt adversaries. The poor white and his descendants were educated "not in books but in traditions," O'Neal reasoned. The freed slave and his descendants, on the other hand, had "no traditions of liberty, no pride of ancestry, no environment which fit him to intelligently discharge the duties of good citizenship." In other words, the circular argument went, blacks were to be punished by a loss of suffrage in perpetuity because they did not have experience with liberty because they had been slaves, and rightfully so because their endemic makeup had suited them for such. This immutable distinction between the races, John Knox argued, constituted an indigenous and inerasable "difference . . . between the uneducated white man and the ignorant Negro."[106]

Even those convention delegates customarily relied on by historians devoted to the disfranchisement myth as the staunchest, most clear-cut opponents of suffrage restriction behaved in ways grayer than the black-and-white depiction usually supplied.[107] It simply cannot be said that even Populists and Republicans spoke against all suffrage restrictions at the 1901 constitutional convention. They did not. Winston County Republican Newman H. Freeman and Coosa County Republican John H. Porter both favored adopting a poll tax—the restrictive measure that probably ended up doing more mischief to poor-white voting prospects than any other.[108] Chilton County Populist Lewis H. Reynolds spoke in favor of a character clause that could be used to disfranchise blacks but stressed his opposition to any whites being disfranchised. Further, Reynolds told the assembly that if the constitution could be crafted in a satisfactory way that would protect plain-white voting, he was "ready to help . . . ratify it, and [would] do all in [his] part of the State to ratify it."[109] In answer to a direct question of whether he would disfranchise blacks or not, Freeman replied: "I will sir. I am willing to sacrifice anything on that line, but the white man, and the man of my own color, I shall never agree to sacrifice."[110] In explaining his opposition to adopting a whole raft of disfranchisement measures, John Porter stipulated: "[T]his is a white man's country. . . . The white man is ruling, the white man is going to rule it. . . . White supremacy is as complete in Alabama as it is possible for it to be. The negro is satisfied with this." Still, Porter reminded the convention, "[w]e met here to disfranchise somebody. No white man is to be disfranchised. . . . [T]he poll tax . . . is the only solution. . . . [I]f any are to be disfranchised, let them disfranchise themselves."[111] Lewis Reynolds voiced a similar mixed position:

We are here . . . to . . . do 'what is right in God's sight.' . . . [N]o one will be heard to say that there is no intention to restrict the suffrage. The suffrage then, is to be restricted—limited. . . . We are told however that the discrimination is to be confined to the negro—that no white man is to be disfranchised. . . . Mr. President, I am opposed to disfranchising white men, but Mr. President, I favor disfranchising those not of good character. The vicious should not be permitted to vote, and if one cannot qualify under a good character clause, I am here to assert that he should be disqualified. . . . [Also], I say that I am in favor of disfranchising every negro in Alabama that is vicious, that will sell his vote or barter his vote in an election." [112]

Debate over the other provisions of the majority report also pitted Bourbon against plain folk. Blacks were already considered nonfactors. Suffrage committee chair Thomas Coleman addressed poor-white concerns about the use of property and educational qualifications by raising the tried-and-true race issue. As Alabama's privileged Democrats understood well, race was the most emotional subject that could possibly be injected into any political issue. Injected properly, race held the potential—as had been demonstrated repeatedly since 1874—of winning plain-white votes over to the standard of Conservative Democracy. The fight over the 1901 Constitution was no exception. Rather, it was perhaps the most dramatic example of race being used to drive a *politics of emotion* over a *politics of reason.* No one party held a monopoly on this strategy. Rather, it was a lesson that the Democratic and Conservative Party mastered first and other conservative ideological causes such as the Hoovercrats, the Dixiecrats, and George Wallace's Independents would later use. Still later in the twentieth century, the South's ascendant GOP would master it, using first race and the backlash against civil rights and later the new racism of religion, patriotism, "character," and traditional morality. [113] "Strike out" the property and educational qualifications section of the plan, Thomas Coleman assured the convention, "and there is not a negro in Alabama that will not vote." Besides, he went on, in what was certainly alarming language for the state's common folk, the whole purpose of the restrictions were "to enable those who should exercise the franchise to exercise it." Privileged whites increasingly lobbied for inclusion of a poll tax as a measure that would guarantee the disfranchisement of all but the "conservative and intelligent." One Machiavellian delegate went so far as to suggest that the poll tax be purposely allowed to accumulate—that the measure not be accompanied by any adequate mechanism for collection. That way, he explained, the tax could "pile up so high that . . . the vicious voter [poor whites] will never be able to vote again." Literacy provisions had to be supplemented by a poll tax, other Redeemers pointed out. Otherwise fraud would necessarily be involved in those Black Belt counties where the literate black population outstripped the white. A black-county spokesman explained the importance of the poll tax as a protection "by which the Black Belt [would] live or die." "We cannot surrender ourselves to the negroes," he iterated, just "for the purpose of allowing a few thriftless men in North Alabama to vote."[114]

The prejudice against African Americans in virtually unanimous evidence among the 155 white delegates to the 1901 convention was so deep, so ingrained, so all-encompassing that it exercised an extraordinarily powerful influence on everyone at the convention, both friends and foes to the various methods of suffrage restriction discussed. Many whites sincerely believed that disfranchising black voters was to be done, not just for the good of whites, but for the good of blacks as well. Others argued that blacks had no interest in voting or participating in the political life of the country. As difficult as such a mindset is to understand today, it is an index of the almost universal acceptance of black inferiority at the turn of the century—not just among the Democrats, Republicans, and Populists in Alabama, but across the nation as well. Electoral cleansing, as a Black Belt delegate intoned, was a necessary part of the "high standards of citizenship" that should "appeal strongly to every friend of both races . . . to those who feel that white supremacy is necessary to the good of the state."[115]

Some white anti-Democrats at the convention, such as the Hill Country Republican John Porter, were steadfast in their belief that black Alabamians were happy with white supremacy and white political domination. In the Alabama countryside, this comfortable plain-white mindset found strong echoes as well. The Populist *Choctaw Alliance,* for example, dubbed a letter from one of its readers as "full of truth" when it described the "typical negroes of the State" as the "men behind the plows . . . the happiest men that live." The "cares of government are not for them," the reader contended. They are "content to govern a mule down a long cotton row, and leave to the white men the government of the people." Perhaps these "negroes" might, from time to time, become inclined to interest themselves in politics, but "just then a hound jumps a rabbit in a blackberry patch and the 'votin' ' is left to settle itself." Such is the bent of their "excitable natures. . . . 'The negro question' has never worried the negroes of the farm." The majority of them do not even "know that they are the subject of any question. They are happy and content to let the white man govern them." The bond that existed "between the slave-holder . . . and his slaves [still] exists today." And it is a "kindly feeling." "The negro looks to the planter for everything," the letter read. " 'Cap'n' or 'Boss' they consider their guardian. No matter what the press of the North may say about the negro's condition in the South . . . the white man and the negro understand one another." "No matter what" the constitutional convention may decide, the "negro will not care." So long as he can "get something to eat, go rabbit huntin' occasionally, coon huntin' often, and church every night, he will be content to let others do the voting."[116]

Alabama's convention delegates knew full well that they were acting with the strong sympathy of whites in the North as well as the South. White Alabamians, no matter their varied opinions on economic issues, agreed on the question of disfranchisement for blacks. In large part, it was precisely this plain-white desire for some suffrage restriction that the skilled privileged were counting on to also effect the ruin of their plain-white political opponents.

When the dust finally settled, the convention voted to table the dissenting minority report by a count of 109 to 23. The delegates also voted 104 to 14 in favor of the temporary plan, including its grandfather clause, and 93 to 19 to accept the whole majority report. Only nine of the convention's fourteen Populists and Republicans voted against adoption of the majority report. Only eight actually voted against adopting the whole constitutional document.[117] Charles B. Beddow, Birmingham labor lawyer, spokesman for working-class whites, and law partner of the fiery Populist Peyton G. Bowman, initially voted against the constitution because several of his suggestions had gone unheeded. Before the convention adjourned, though, Beddow formally reversed himself and changed his vote to one of approval.[118]

But perhaps the most sobering aspect of the vote is the realization that voting against the constitution as drafted did not amount to opposition to disfranchisement generally and was certainly not the same as opposition to black disfranchisement. Eight of the fourteen delegates who voted against adoption of the convention's suffrage plans were Populists and Republicans. A point not usually juxtaposed with this one but nevertheless of great leavening importance is that six of the most prominent regular Democrats also voted "nay" to the convention's suffrage restrictions: former governor William C. Oates, SDEC chair Robert S. Lowe, George P. Harrison, Stanley H. Dent, William H. Banks, and Frank S. White. None of the six, of course, by any stretch of the imagination could be called an opponent of disfranchisement. Yet all found fault with the particular suffrage scheme drawn up by the 1901 convention and recorded their votes against it.[119]

CHAPTER FOUR

Ratification

Alabama governor W. D. Jelks set 11 November 1901 as the date for the state referendum on ratification of the new constitution. Once the date was set, Redeemer Democracy moved at lightning speed to set up an elite committee of fourteen to work for ratification, headed by U.S. congressman Oscar W. Underwood, a Birmingham representative of Alabama industry. Aided by such luminaries as Eufaula's U.S. congressman Henry De Lamar Clayton, Tuscaloosa's future governor William W. Brandon, U.S. senator John Tyler Morgan, and Jelks himself, Underwood set up headquarters in Birmingham largely because Jefferson County was seen as a crucial area to carry. The county with the largest population in the state, it had returned a mere twenty-vote majority in the enabling election that called the constitutional convention and was the home of former governor Joseph F. Johnston, leader of the antiratification forces. Virtually all the spokesmen for privilege—planters and industrialists—supported Underwood's committee, even nascent business "progressives" the stripe of Braxton Bragg Comer, Frank S. White, and Hugh S. D. Mallory. From the start, race was to be used as the big stick with which to compel obedience from plain whites who might view the constitution as a potential threat to their vote. Toward that end, Underwood's committee adopted the prescient slogan, "White Supremacy! Honest Elections! and the New Constitution! One and inseparable!"[1]

"I Am Speaking for the White Man": Opposition to Ratification

In contradistinction to the myth that has grown up around disfranchisement, plain whites were torn by the issue—even after it had become clear that privileged Democracy meant to renege on its many pledges of protection. The opposition to ratification was led unquestionably by plain-white spokesmen such as Joseph F. Johnston, the "half Populist" who was still backed by Populists, former Populists, and anti-Democrats of all stripes. But just as certainly, these men opposed the constitution and disfranchisement because they saw it as detrimental to poor-white voting—not because they felt badly about blacks losing their votes. On the contrary, black disfranchisement was a welcome goal for virtually all plain whites and their spokesmen. But this black disfranchisement also had to be accomplished without risking the emasculation of poor whites. In their view Alabama's 1901 Constitution did not, contrary to earlier pledges, offer adequate protection to poor-white suffrage. Former congressman Charles M. Shelley chaired the committee against ratification. Former congressmen William H. "Billy" Denson and Jesse F. "Piney Woods Jess" Stallings, as well as future governor Bibb Graves, also became leading figures in the fight against ratification. Acknowledging that Jefferson County—the spot where north Alabama industrial interests collided with north Alabama poor-white interests—was critically important, the antiratificationists also set up shop in Birmingham.[2]

If anyone in 1901 labored under the impression that reform-wing Democrats and plain-white tribunes such as William Denson fought ratification because they stood opposed to disfranchisement generally or black disfranchisement in particular, all he or she had to do was recall Denson's preconvention support for black disfranchisement, support that he unabashedly articulated as late as 1899. Although Billy Denson never formally became a Populist, he was closely associated with free silver, the Farmer's Alliance, Populists, and Jeffersonian Democracy and enjoyed the support of leading Jeffersonians such as Thomas Atkins Street and James H. Meigs of Marshall County.[3] Anyone who harbored the illusion that plain-white opposition to the constitution in some way approximated plain-white opposition to disfranchisement needed only to consider the detailed nature of Denson's view of blacks in politics, an animus that incorporated narrow notions of religion, morality, patriotism, and sectionalism to form a potent witch's brew of exclusion and illiberalism. Denson deplored black participation in politics, especially black and federal identification with the Republican Party, which was out to

> hob nob with niggers. . . . They want to repeal our laws against the inter-marriage of the races [and] . . . force our children and the negro children into the same school room. . . . The white people of the South do not want any such. We have not the time to trade horses crossing the stream, all the white voters must unite. We must not have any fussing and quarreling. . . . No matter what organization you belong to, you owe an allegiance to the Democracy of the South. [The Republicans] against us are traitors to our institutions and our religion. [They] . . . and the niggers are traitors to our wives and daughters. The man who votes for [a Republican] is a traitor, a scoundrel and an outlaw against . . . our society and against . . . God . . . [and] in favor of pulling down our society and our religion. . . . We must be united. . . . If you split at this time you make way for [the Republican] and his niggers. . . . We must maintain white supremacy in the South. No compromise will

be permitted. Our very religion is at stake. This is no child's play. . . . We are doing all right in the South. All we want is to be let alone.[4]

Of course, black opposition to ratification existed. At a 25 September mass meeting in Birmingham, *Mobile Press* editor A. N. Johnson issued a prescient warning to the plain folk that the "unfortunate white classes" were unwittingly being "used as instruments to effect their own destruction." Black antiratification leaders also stressed that their fight against the constitution was in no way to be confused with the plain-white efforts of the Johnston-Denson-Shelley dissident Democrats or white Republicans—both variants of disaffected plain whites in which they had no faith. Instead, the African American leaders proposed a mass exodus to the northern states, where, it was naively supposed, "the rights of manhood will be respected."[5]

The lack of African American confidence in the plain-white leadership of the antiratification forces had deep roots. Many blacks preferred to hitch their wagon to that of the Big Mules and Black Belt planters in preference to the plain folk, a choice they considered the lesser of two evils. Some of them had been making these kinds of choices for a long time. In the 1896 Democratic gubernatorial contest between Richard Henry Clarke and Joseph Johnston, blacks organized to vote for the more conservative Democrat so effectively that "Captain Joe's" lieutenants wrote off Marengo, Clarke, and even the Populist county of Choctaw well before the balloting began.[6] Patricians such as T. G. Jones believed that most blacks voted willingly for the Redeemers throughout the 1890s; white Populist backlash against blacks postelection commonly cited such alliances. Indeed, patricians such as Jones argued that the black response was only sensible. The plain-white representatives who opposed ratification were also insisting that the qualifications be made "more stringent" against blacks, Jones claimed, an attempt he was committed to blocking as a paternalist who thought himself "considerably ahead" of his lawmaking associates on the race issue. If the plain folk succeeded in turning down the document, it would "only be to have a sharper instrument."[7] In 1901, as blacks watched white Alabama Republicans desert them en masse, they wrote off the anti-Democrats and reform-wing Democrats as any kind of buttress between themselves and political oblivion. Black mass meetings resulted in no confidence in either Johnston's antiratification group or the GOP, and they thus resolved to fight the issue in court. A black Mobile editor sardonically recorded his lack of faith in plain-white opposition to the constitution. Such whites were not to be trusted. They were merely like "lizards who changed color from time to time."[8]

As the battle over ratification raged, it became increasingly apparent that the black suspicions were well founded: the antiratificationists had no qualms about African Americans losing the ballot.[9] Unfortunately, some later historians have conflated plain-white opposition to the 1901 Constitution with plain-white opposition to disfranchisement generally, including black suffrage.[10] The two positions, however, were poles apart. Joseph Johnston, the "half Populist," explicitly told a Montgomery crowd that he was "not speaking for the Negro in this campaign. I am speaking for the white man, who can vote now . . . but next year only the Lord and three registrars will know what he can do." The real reason for rejecting the constitution as written, according to Mars Joe, was the inclusion of the registration boards, which, in his view, would cancel out the grandfather clause safeguard of poor-white suffrage. "Other devices are infant abortions," Johnston propounded, "compared with this leviathan of irresponsible and unregulated power." In a Lee County debate with convention president John Knox, ratification opponent and poor-white tribune Jesse Stallings became visibly irritated when blacks in the crowd began applauding his statements—obviously confusing Piney Woods Jess's opposition to the constitution's proposed methods of disfranchisement for opposition to the actual disfranchisement of blacks.[11] For his part, William H. Denson stipulated that he opposed ratification precisely because the question involved was "whether or not the Anglo-Saxon race [was] to control Alabama, or [should] it be a hybrid race hereafter?" Denson specifically advocated "elimination [of] the negro from the ballot box," but not at the cost of poor-white disfranchisement.[12]

Actually, at the time it was occurring, the Jeffersonians were very open about their racial double standard on suffrage, that is, their desire to abolish black suffrage while preserving their own vote. One Hill Country Jeffersonian reported that a poll of poor whites in his county found "in nearly every instance," that the only objection they lodged against the proposed constitution was "the suffrage clause—*nay not even the suffrage clause itself,* but to their own fear that under its provisions *they* were to be deprived of *their right* to vote" [ital. mine]. His reply was aimed at convincing his independent brethren that they would be better served by the constitution's passage: "That fear is groundless. . . . [There is n]ot a white man who votes in the coming election, but who will also be able to vote in all future elections."[13] A fellow Hill Country anti-Democrat reassured his friends and neighbors that they, the "poor and unlettered," should not fear losing their right to vote under the new constitution.[14] Despite such assurances, even from fellow anti-Democrats, some Populists remained steadfast in their opposition to ratification because they could not overcome the fear of losing their vote. For some of these anti-Democratic opponents of the constitution, a preoccupation with the race issue played a large role as well. "The fight is now on to determine whether the white skins of Alabama shall hereafter rule or whether the state is to still remain under negro domination," explained one

Populist opponent of ratification. The constitution issue was simple: "Which will rule, the negroes or the whites?"[15]

"The Niggerest Sort of Nigger": Poor Whites and Ratification

While historical accounts traditionally portray solidarity against ratification among poor whites in north Alabama and the Hill Country, the reality was actually much more mixed. It simply cannot be said with any degree of accuracy that poor whites and anti-Democrats in Alabama's hills, hollows, and pine barrens lined up as a phalanx against the constitution. Many influential plain-white leaders went beyond differentiating between plain-white suffrage safeguards and black disfranchisement to favor outright ratification of the flawed disfranchising constitution—even with the obvious risks it posed to continued plain-white voting. Three highly influential Alabama Populists—Reuben Kolb, William Skaggs, and Joseph Manning—came out in support of ratification. The staunch Populist newspapers, the *Choctaw Alliance* and the *Ozark Free Press,* did the same. So did the Hill Country's Jeffersonian Democratic *Clanton Banner, Marshall Banner,* and *Attalla Mirror,* and its Republican *Coosa River News.* From the Tennessee Valley, the *Huntsville Republican* as well as many of its lily-white readers joined in the endorsement pool. At times, the *Cherokee Harmonizer* endorsed a new constitution, and the *Alabama Alliance News* claimed that disfranchisement would work to the advantage of the Populist Party. Reuben Kolb canvassed the state in support of the disfranchising constitution. Thomas Heflin, self-appointed tribune of Alabama's plain whites and himself supported by a number of Populists, fervently supported ratification.[16] For many ordinary whites—Upcountry farmers and other plain folk sometimes disparaged as "hillbillies," "rednecks," and "crackers"—the single overwhelming attribute of the constitution was that it did, in fact, disfranchise black people. North Alabama representative Erle Pettus, it should be remembered, had led a poor-white movement within the convention not only to disfranchise blacks but also to guarantee that their disfranchisement would be permanent—that their exile to political oblivion would be for life, and the lives of their children, and their children's children—by denying blacks equitable state funding for education.[17] "What we would like to do in this county more than any other two things," a Hill Country spokesman for Tallapoosa County's plain whites had explained at the convention, is "to disfranchise the darkeys, and educate the white children."[18]

For some Jeffersonians, the process consisted of carefully weighing the risk to poor-white voting against the goal and likelihood of black disfranchisement. In the final analysis, some simply preferred to believe the Redeemer pledges—even after seeing a draft of the constitution with its specific provisions. The fear of poor whites losing the vote, wrote one former Populist, was "groundless." "Disabuse yourselves of that false idea, gentlemen," he urged, "and vote for the ratification of the new Constitution. . . . If we had the slightest fear that one solitary white man . . . would be deprived of his right to vote," the Jeffersonian explained, "we would oppose ratification as strongly as we knew how, but as it is we earnestly urge every man to . . . vote . . . for its ratification."[19] "[T]he new instrument says that . . . if you be a white man . . . [you] can register and vote," reasoned another. "If you doubt that, read the instrument for yourself."[20] "Friends, get the new constitution and read it," an enthusiastic Jeffersonian organ urged its poor-white readership. "[I]t will not disfranchise a single white man in this state."[21]

For advocates of the new constitution, it was Booker T. Washington who again, unwittingly and partially, rode to their rescue. While the Tuskegee educator's April commencement address to young white women at Converse College had raised blood pressures across the South, that breech of the color line was nothing next to his October 1901 dinner at the White House with Theodore Roosevelt—a mere month before Alabamians went to the polls to decide the question of ratifying a new constitution. Like the speech to young women, Washington's dinner with Roosevelt and his family was seen by white southerners as an especially potent racial offense because it concerned domestic life and the invisible but very real barriers that had been preserved between the races as concerned gender and family roles. To Alabama whites, the dinner was an act that challenged their interlocked status quo in a way so fundamental and so repugnant that it called forth the most primal of emotions. For some poor whites still straddling the fence on ratification because they worried about a potential loss of white votes, the episode was so emotional and so contrary to the most basic tenets of their "way of life" that they granted it the power to push them over the edge onto the side of outright approval. The *Marshall Banner,* for example, a "half-Populist" Jeffersonian journal in the Upcountry that had fervently opposed the call for a constitutional convention because it feared poor whites would lose suffrage, abruptly reversed course and issued a full-throated endorsement "for" ratification.[22] The offense was so great, the implication so large, for Alabama whites, regardless of their particular social or economic standing, that some reacted with an almost irrational passion. The *Geneva Reaper,* a Populist newspaper in the Wiregrass, damned Washington as "the negro freak" and Roosevelt as well in a style so emotional that it recalled a scorned lover denouncing an unfaithful suitor caught in an act of infidelity. "Poor Roosevelt! He was the hero of the South but for a day," the Populists lamented. "He might now just as well sleep with Booker Washington, for the scent of that coon will follow him to his grave."[23] Democratic mouthpieces in the Upcountry knew their neighbors in the hills well enough to know that the dinner would become a factor in the debate over ratification. The *Lafayette Sun* rejoiced that the dinner had "planted more cussedness in the race than can be gotten out except by disfranchisement."[24] But no one outdid the editors at the Hill Country Jeffersonian Democratic weekly the *Attalla Mirror*. The intensity of their outburst over the White House dinner made it obvious that the emotionalism of race had much to do with the Jeffersonians' support for disfranchisement. Witness the newspaper's diatribe against "Booker Washington":

> This coon looks like all others to the Southern white man. He doesn't dine at our tables and he cuts no ice with us. . . . Booker Washington . . . has been dined by President Roosevelt at his table with his wife and children in the White House. Just think of it! A negro dining with the president of these United States! Can any decent white man, regardless of politics, . . . endorse this action . . . ? If you do you are meaner and lower down than the measliest nigger that ever purloined a chicken or served a sentence in the chain gang. . . . [T]he dignity of our highest office been lowered. . . . Where is Roosevelt's boasted impetuous Southern blood? . . . Roosevelt has a perfect right to dine the blackest and measliest nigger out of the chain gang at his private table, but . . . not . . . in the White House. . . . It is our Holy of Holies. . . . Theodore Roosevelt is not sufficiently decent to be president of a North Georgia horse wrapper's convention. . . . [Nothing can] take away the odor of that black and tan dinner party. . . . May no Southern man . . . ever forgive or forget. . . . [The dinner] will have the savorily influence upon the white men of Alabama to ratify the New Constitution. . . . Roosevelt and his bur-headed guest [gave us] . . . the grossest insult ever handed down to the American people . . . There are places we know of, thank God, down here in our own Southland that . . . [if] the "bur-head" . . . dare attempt[s] to think [of] such a thing—he will take the rope line route—which means the nearest tree. . . . Think of your posterity, your children and children's children—before you make up your mind to vote against the new constitution. . . . Booker has . . . show[n] himself to be the niggerest sort of nigger, and . . . he, like his color and his kind, only bathes on special occasions, such as Xmas and Fourth of July. Remember th[is] . . . slap in the face with an Ethiopian by one who holds our customs and traditions in contempt, and . . . cast one ballot with the end . . . of relegating the African to a respectable distance in the rear. The new constitution offers you the accepted opportunity.[25]

Not only Populists, former Populists, Jeffersonian Democrats, and Independent Democrats joined the Bourbons' ratification movement. White Republicans also lined up to favor outright ratification of the flawed document because it promised to disfranchise black people. Former Greenbacker, Allianceman, and now lily-white Republican Charles P. Lane of Huntsville favored approval of the document because "only the Negro [stands] in the way of respectability" for the Alabama GOP. For Republicans, the issue was not simply one of "respectability," of course, it was *racial* respectability, the most fundamental prerequisite for political success in Alabama. The editor of north Alabama's *Huntsville Republican* explained that any imperfections in the new document should not stand in the way of ratification. "When we came into the world it was a white man's government," he wrote, "when we go out we want to leave the conditions . . . as near as possible as we found them. . . . [W]ithout qualifications, apologies, excuses, explanations, criticisms, or 'buts' we are for it."[26]

The Great Lie: Gullibility and Privileged Tactics

Integral to the plain-white support of ratification was an acceptance by many of the Great Lie. And integral to the sirenlike appeal of the Great Lie was the patrician emphasis on the one thing that virtually all whites, privileged and poor, held in common: race and the memory, still relatively fresh, of the Reconstruction nightmare. Frank White, John Tyler Morgan's campaign manager and a future senator himself, personified what would soon be somewhat charitably designated as an emerging "reform-wing" of the Democratic Party. But White made it clear that neither old-style patrician Democracy nor new-style progressivism had any interest in blacks voting or genuine black advancement in the realms of civil or political rights. The Reconstruction experiment, White reported, had only "demonstrated that the negro has no capacity to rule, but a great capacity to ruin."[27] Any action that risked spoiling the accomplishment of black disfranchisement was tantamount to racial treason, White argued, pressing sensitive poor-white buttons, especially selfish worries about their own loss of suffrage. In October, John B. Knox delivered an epic speech in Birmingham in favor of ratification. In it, the convention president repeatedly drove home the point that "the great object" of the 1901 Constitution had been, and was, to "maintain white supremacy." Every other consideration should be sacrificed to achieve the paramount goal of whitening politics. U.S. senator Edmund Pettus simply announced that every white man in Alabama who believed in white supremacy should vote for the new constitution. The *Montgomery Advertiser* and the *New Decatur Advertiser* agreed that "white supremacy" was the heart of the ratification issue. They issued a clear and powerful message that the opponents of ratification—no matter the reasons for their fears—were engaged in the disgraceful business of spreading racial heresy.[28]

Key also to common whites' acceptance of the Great Lie was the lie itself: the repeated assurance and pledge that the interests of all whites, plain folk included, could be safely left to the patricians. More than that, spokesmen for the oligarchy, one after the next, tied obedience on the racial issue of disfranchisement to prosperity and benefit for plain whites and specifically promised to safeguard poor-white suffrage.[29] One Black Belt delegate even went so far as to argue that even if Black Belt boards registered and voted African Americans, it would still be done "in the best interest of the [whole] State," including common whites. "White men have nothing to fear from the Black Belt," he promised.[30] During the battle over ratification, propagation of the Great Lie became more important than ever. Bourbon spokesmen flooded north Alabama, the Hill Country, and the Wiregrass—traditional centers of resistance to the oligarchy—in order to persuade suspicious plain folk to ratify the document: to go for the carrot of black disfranchisement without thinking too much about the stick of poll taxes, property qualifications, literacy tests, character clauses, education requirements, employment restrictions, and registration boards. Senator Pettus reassured north Alabama's hill folk that the fighting grandfather clause had been specifically included in the new constitution to protect their right to vote. Hilary Herbert promised that ratification of the new constitution would, in fact, reinvigorate two-party politics, which would actually work to the advantage of whites from the hills, the hollows, and the pine barrens. Redeemer spokesmen repeatedly pointed to white supremacy as the most important reason to vote for ratification—as a form of patriotism, fidelity to race, and solidarity in a great, solemn, and selfless undertaking that would advance civilization for posterity. More than a few Bourbons pledged that ratification and the privileged role in government would serve "the interest[s] of all the people," including Alabama's yeomen, poor, and working-class whites.[31]

"Keep the Infernal Negro Out of Politics": The Ratification Debate

While some have tried to make the case that plain whites put race aside to oppose disfranchisement, unfortunately it is all too clear that in Alabama many did not.[32] For many plain whites, race ruled the debate over ratification, just as race had ruled the debate over the calling of a constitutional convention. Overall, it was at least as important, if not more so, than class concerns. Of course, race and class worked together in the past and should be evaluated that way in the present. Race was profoundly and intimately tied to—not separate from and certainly not subordinate to—class concerns. White supremacy was the ultimate emotional weapon of the Bourbons because, to put it simply, it worked well and it worked often. One reason the belief in white supremacy was so strong among the plain folk in Alabama's hills and hollows was because it possessed the emotional capacity to ease a stark economic reality: poor-white competition with blacks. Giving in to their racial fears and insecurities enabled elite whites to get the better of the plain folk, an upper hand they used to perpetuate caste preferment over blacks and economic privilege over plain whites. Race and class were irretrievably bound. They still are. It makes little sense to try to divorce them today.

Perhaps it is the ultimate measure of the race issue's enormous power that anti-Democrats who both favored *and* opposed ratification conceived of the problem in similar terms of the racial obsession. In Chilton County, a Populist explained his rejection of the new constitution because, as crafted, it had failed to "free the State from the negro." On "the contrary," the distressed anti-Democrat explained, "every young negro that can read and write . . . the most vicious class of the negro . . . can register and vote. . . . God forbid."[33] In the same county, a Populist stronghold, other Jeffersonians recommended approval of the new constitution precisely because of racial concerns. Frank Crichton, the former-Populist editor of the *Clanton Banner,* urged ratification of the new document because he did "not believe that one white man [would] be disfranchised under the new Constitution, but undoubtedly a large number of negroes" would. The number of African Americans who would still be able to vote, Crichton assured his poor-white readers, would be "comparatively small." "[A]nd with all white men registered, what influence can that small number have?" he asked. "That is the safeguard of this suffrage proposition."[34] Crichton ran numerous editorials and editorial letters to back up his position. The "most important" reason to ratify the constitution was because "white supremacy [would be] forever assured, and the negro equality imbedded in the old instrument [would be] eliminated, and . . . no worthy white man . . . disfranchised."[35] Crichton's editorial the next week, calling for ratification, repeated some of this editorial's ideas and phrases almost verbatim.[36] And again: "The registrars will be white men and they will register their white neighbors. . . . [P]lainly speaking, they will register all white men and white supremacy will be fully . . . [and] forever . . . established. This is what the new constitution means."[37] To bolster the case for ratification, Crichton summoned the period's prevailing moral and sexual stereotypes surrounding blacks:

> For a third of a century the negro has voted in Alabama, and always votes solidly against the interest and welfare of the state. His racial instincts and low moral status, prompt him to ally himself against everything that is elevating. . . . [In many counties] he holds the balance of power and may become a potent factor for evil. . . . Restrain him and treat him kindly, and he becomes a useful citizen. Remove restraint, and he reverts to barbarism and lust. The adoption of the

new constitution insure[s] peace and order, under . . . law, reject it, and white supremacy can only be maintained by continuing those method[s], which are repugnant to our feeling, and justified only by the intolerable alternative of fatal submission to the rule [of an] . . . inferior and servile race.[38]

The choice was simple: white supremacy by law or white supremacy by rope—but white supremacy all the same.

Reconstruction—with its syndrome of prohibitions against racial equality, federal activism, Yankee and alien intruders, and liberal spending and taxation, especially for programs that included blacks—was a major part of the racial obsession. The powerful concern with race and Reconstruction was more than just an issue or even a major issue. It was a preoccupation, a fixation, an overwhelming and intrusive concern that demanded attention. And it was quite telling about the power of this fixation that, for the anti-Democrats, it held the capacity to define both support for and opposition to the constitution. Redeemers such as Sidney J. Bowie went into the white counties to encourage plain whites to think of ratification along the lines of Reconstruction: the document meant the "elimination of the great bulk of the incompetent, vicious and ignorant negro vote, without the disfranchisement of any white man, . . . [the guarantee of] white supremacy . . . by law, . . . [and] the limit . . . [and] reduc[tion] . . . of taxation."[39] Of course, appeals such as these from the Redeemers were consciously calculated to press the buttons of poor whites who might, under other circumstances, oppose ratification. To be sure, some anti-Democrats still opposed the constitution, even in the face of such appeals. But many of them did so precisely because of the same concerns raised by Bowie and the Redeemers—emotional race and Reconstruction concerns.[40]

Yet, in this same Hill Country Populist stronghold of Chilton County, some poor whites responded to the Reconstruction rhetoric in the way the Redeemers had hoped. One Chilton County Populist pled passionately for disfranchisement because he saw it in perfect keeping with southern patriotism, "what the old Confederates fought so bravely for in the days of [18]60–65 . . . to keep the infernal negro out of politics."[41] Another said he supported ratification because, in the new constitution, "[s]tate taxation ha[d] been reduced" and because "in days past the cloud that threaten[ed] our horizon from . . . the menace to the white people growing out of the negro vote . . . was dark and ominous." Because " 'history repeats itself,' " leaving the old constitution in place left intact the peril of blacks again coming "under the leadership of vicious white men," as they had during Reconstruction.[42] Former Populist Frank Crichton relied on and ran editorials that used such reasoning to argue for ratification of the new constitution: "Vote for ratification and you will always be proud of having done so."[43] His *Clanton Banner*'s reasoning for backing ratification was explicitly colored by race and the issues of Reconstruction:

> The principle of negro equality is firmly imbedded in the old constitution. This is stricken down by the new constitution and in its place white supremacy is written in the fundamental law. No white man is disfranchised except for crime and the vote of the vicious, incompetent and corrupt negro is stricken down now, and forever more. . . . The old constitution makes force or fraud in many localities essential to the proposition of white supremacy. In others, where the negro holds the balance of power, bribery and corruption have been resorted to. . . . The new constitution . . . provides a plain and sure path to honest elections in the future. . . . The old constitution was written in haste with federal soldiers surrounding our ballot boxes and a hostile Republican administration in Washington. The new constitution was written after full reflection. Adequate debate was had. . . . No federal troops were near us, and in our efforts to secure the supremacy of our race and write it in the fundamental law, it had the full sympathy of all good citizens throughout the civilized world.[44]

Battles such as these between poor whites—compelled by race and Reconstruction, and yet arriving at different results—went on throughout Alabama. Jeffersonian advocates of ratification commonly cast the question as one transcendent of party lines and old partisan feelings. For them, the issue was one that went to the very core question of survival of the white race—or, perhaps more accurately, the survival of race privilege associated with racial distinction. Moreover, they hoped that, by convincing their poor-white brethren of the essential racial nature of the issue, they could sway voters to their side. To this end, they employed the emotional fodder of patriotism, family, and religious duty to fortify common racial orthodoxy. "This should not be a party election or fight," one plain-folk adherent of ratification recommended.[45] "This is not a question of party politics," another proratificationist agreed in invoking the emotional ammunition of children, legacy, and posterity. "[IT IS] NOT A PARTY QUESTION," still another insisted. "We cannot for the life of us imagine even how its adoption or rejection can be made a party threat."[46] "[I]t is a question that deeply concerns you now and as long as you live," one explained, "and . . . your children and grandchildren." In backing the constitution, the Populist *Choctaw Alliance* provided an advanced statement on duty to posterity over partisanship, which it described as "a duty you owe to your State, your country, yourself, wife, children, grandchildren, great-grandchildren, and all ages to come." A Populist newspaper in Etowah County relied on what it termed "a duty you owe to your God, your family and your country" to argue against ratifying a new constitution. A Butler County Jeffersonian organ split the difference and summoned fear of "scalawag republicanism" to arrive at a murky result that neither recommended nor rejected clearly the prospect of a new constitution.[47]

Racial solidarity aimed at racial advantage (and, of course, an intertwined class advantage for poor whites) is what these Jeffersonian advocates of ratification preached. Regardless of its warts and potential hazards, ultimately the new constitution provided for the disfranchisement of blacks. That alone should be enough to garner the support of all whites. "[T]he white people have met and formed a constitution that virtually disfranchises all the negroes and gives to all white people the right to vote," a Marshall County Jeffersonian reasoned. "The negroes have been a great barrier in politics . . . and every white man should want to get him out of politics entirely. . . . [D]o you blame the white people of Alabama for wanting a new constitution? . . . Arouse yourselfs white men, and do your duty. . . . Go to the polls and vote for the new constitution," came the battle cry, "then in the future there will be only a white man's party in Alabama."[48]

At this time and in this place, race and Reconstruction were accepted as deathly serious and intertwined issues in the eyes of white southerners, regardless of class. Some Jeffersonians understood their support for ratification almost as a sacred reenactment of Redemption. The prohibitions of the Reconstruction syndrome were never so powerful as in the most critical moments of southern history, years such as 1874, 1928, 1948, 1954, 1964, and 1968. Fall 1901 was just such a moment in Alabama—perhaps the most critical of all. As such, the concerns of Reconstruction again, at least temporarily, took center stage. "The new constitution means lower taxation . . . and the permanent disfranchisement of the African," a Jeffersonian in Etowah County stated bluntly. "Will you go on record as opposing these things?" A Wiregrass Populist echoed the argument about taxes for blacks.[49] The sectionalism and racism that were part-and-parcel of the Reconstruction ethos were alive and well in Alabama's Hill Country. Much of the rhetoric there was quite blunt—even vulgar. Yet its very crudeness rings of sincerity. "America, like ancient Gaul," a Hill Country Jeffersonian mouthpiece proposed in discussing ratification, should be divided into three parts, "one to be inhabited by the Eastern Yankees, one by the Southerners and Westerners, and the third by the Africans, known in our tongue as niggers." More, these divisions should be separated by "impregnable, insurmountable and impassable walls." Along with fiscal retrenchment, sectionalism, and a strong aversion to taxation, the bitterness of military defeat and occupation was never far from the minds of white southerners, including those Populists who advocated constitutional disfranchisement. One Hill Country Populist publication raised the prospect of white landowners using "monkies [sic] to pick cotton" as a replacement for black slave labor. The newspaper then paralleled the "problem" of freed blacks to that of monkeys, conjecturing that such an idea might spur the Republican Party of the north to "organize another war," overpower the South "again," and "set the monkeys free."[50]

For some Jeffersonians, the constitution's imperfections did not mean that Alabama's poor whites should oppose it. The document's singular achievement was its disfranchisement of blacks. Because of that, "[i]t is . . . the duty of every[one] . . . in this commonwealth to vote for the ratification of the new constitution. . . . [And] if the constitution does not suit you in every particular that should not keep you from accepting the instrument as a whole."[51] The *Attalla Mirror* wrapped its arguments for ratification in an explicit Reconstruction logic:

> Day by day it is more fully demonstrated that the United States is divided into two separate and distinct sections, a North and a South . . . despite the teaching of the effervescing press . . . that there is no North, no South, but one grand, magnificent, loving . . . unified country, [and] that the civil war has been forgotten. . . . We know the New England Yankee abhors us, and the feeling is fully reciprocated by the Southerner. . . . When a lynching occurs . . . the North rises up . . . and calls us "the crude, barbarous, uncivilized South." . . . The Mason & Dixon Line will exist so long as the Chinese Wall stands. The pyramids of Egypt run a greater risk of toppling and falling to earth. . . . Time, that grim iconoclast of the ages, shall never break our idols, shall never wipe out sectionalism in America. A Southerner is born with hatred in his heart for those men who invaded and devastated the beautiful and prosperous Southland of his fathers. [T]he first tale his mother tells him is about Sherman's shameless, hellish, devil-inspired and devil-directed march to the sea. And . . . a recital of that never-to-be-forgotten and God-forsaken incident . . . is . . . sufficient to stamp malice and hatred of the immortal kind in one's mind and heart. A Northerner is born . . . with jealousy and envy in his heart for those people who wore themselves out licking his ancestors, and the first nursery yarn his mother pours into his eager ears is about the Old South's cruel (?) treatment of the darling negro—in our language nigger—and the first book he reads is "Uncle Tom's Cabin," written by a miserable hag. . . . Thus it is we are born and raised and thus it will ever remain.[52]

Yet race was such an important factor for the Jeffersonians that it also figured centrally in the thinking of those who opposed the actual disfranchising measures that had been worked out in the convention. This angle of the disfranchisement question has not been given due attention by historians. Not only did a good number of Jeffersonians see and define their opposition to disfranchisement in terms of race, they also accused the proratification forces of exactly the same charge with which they themselves had been tarred: racial treason. Like their poor-white counterparts, antiratificationist Jeffersonians accused white ratificationists of putting partisan and class considerations above those of race. For example, the *Newton Harmonizer,* a Wiregrass Populist mouthpiece, denounced Oscar Underwood and the Redeemer ratification forces as being "so partisan" they had subordinated the all-important issue of race and were "ready and willing to ignore all the white people in the State of Alabama" who were not members of "what they [were] pleased to call the Democratic Party."[53]

Other Populists who opposed ratification did so largely on the basis of how they viewed the racial aspects of the proposed constitution. Some looked at the literacy, property, and character clauses and decided that blacks stood to gain something that poor whites did not if the constitution were ratified; hence they opposed it. "[L]et's see what it all amounts to," complained one anti-Democrat. "This convention was going to disfranchise the negro, but instead it has enfranchised him—appropriated money to educate him. . . . [This] will cause many a white man to shudder at the enormity of its deadly work. . . . [W]hen the constitution is ratified," the Populist predicted, "the hands of the white people are bound, maybe, for all time to come."[54] "For 35 years the negro in Alabama has held the balance of power in politics," grieved the *Geneva Reaper,* "and now it is worse. . . . [The] constitution . . . is obnoxious to the whites." One Populist shaper of Hill Country opinion, the *People's Voice* of Etowah County, consistently fought a disfranchising constitution because of its fear that thousands of "poor and illiterate white men" would lose the vote. But on judging the tide for a constitution to be too strong, the Populist newspaper asserted that "disfranchisement may check things slightly" but could not do enough to restrain "lawless negroes" from their customary rampages. In the opinion of the Etowah Jeffersonians, "the only practical solution" was to move beyond even disfranchisement to a complete "separation of the races." Another Hill Country Jeffersonian journal, this one edited by a former Republican, interspersed its frequently vocalized fears of a new constitution with reviews of new books such as *The Negro Beast,* "a most wonderful book" that "will open the eyes of any 'nigger lover.' "[55]

November 1901

In the end, privileged Democracy had its way again. Without question, Alabama's Black Belt led the way to ratification of the new constitution. On this point, there is no discussion. Alabama's voters ratified the constitution by a vote of 108,613 to 81,734. Most of the 26,879-vote majority came from twelve of the Black Belt counties, which returned a tally of 36,224 "for" votes to only

5,471 "against." In fact, most of the 26,879 margin of victory actually came from black votes (17,021), beyond a probable certainty, stolen votes. In Dallas, Hale, and Wilcox Counties the combined tally was a fantastic 17,475 "for" the constitution and only 508 "against." The total "for" vote in these counties included 12,360 more votes than the total number of eligible white voters. Fourteen other Alabama counties, all but one in the Black Belt, also cast more total votes for the constitution than their total number of eligible white voters. Ten counties, in the Black Belt or on its periphery, returned more votes in the election than their total number of males over the age of twenty-one.[56]

The Black Belt totals were so extreme that they screamed fraud and manipulation (see table 9 in the appendix). Hale County, for example, reported 98 percent "for" ratification—a measly 95 votes countywide against ratification in contrast to almost 4,700 in favor. Dallas and Perry were just behind, with 97 percent of their ballots counted for ratification, a combined 11,334 "for" to 323 "against." Greene, Sumter, and Wilcox came in at over 90 percent "for," while Macon and Marengo both registered 85 percent "for. The nineteen Alabama counties that can be described as Black Belt, the heart of Bourbon Democracy, recorded almost 80 percent of their vote in favor of constitutional ratification.

Concluding from these data that the tenets of the disfranchisement myth were valid, as in the April referendum, was again understandable, even alluringly obvious. Almost 80 percent of the Black Belt voted "for" ratification, usually the first point of focus for scholars examining the issue and a reality very difficult not to fixate on. That the white counties made up a whopping 85 percent of the opposition to ratification is usually the second point of focus (see table 11 in the appendix). Taken together, these points have led scholars, quite understandably, to interpret the referendum results in terms of an obvious, yet still mythical, dichotomy: Black Belt support for disfranchisement and white-county resistance against it.

But as with the April vote calling the convention, the November referendum also contained a crucial, yet mostly obscured, pattern. While the white counties supplied the bulk of opposition to ratification, they did not do so in anything approaching consensus (see tables 10 and 11 in the appendix and map 4). Once again, anti-Democratic and historiographical depiction to the contrary, the actual split in the white counties was a deep one, almost half and half. The divide indicates that, in the final analysis, the racial appeal of the constitution's effectiveness in disfranchising blacks still won over many white voters in the white counties—virtually half of them, given the actual figures. Moreover, since African Americans still voted relatively freely outside the Black Belt, and we have evidence to suggest that the overwhelming majority of blacks voted against ratification, the split in the white counties against ratification could not have been an even split among whites. This becomes obvious once the black vote in the white counties is factored out of the "against" totals. The inescapable conclusion is that the half-and-half white vote in the white counties was actually considerably less than half against ratification. Or stated another way, as with the April 1901 vote to call the convention, a majority of whites in the white counties actually voted for ratification. Once white votes from the Black Belt are added to this white total, it becomes even clearer that most whites in Alabama, regardless of social station, voted for ratification and constitutional disfranchisement.

It is apparent that anticonstitution warnings did have some salutary effect in the November election. Yet it is difficult not to make use of the proverbial conclusion that it was "too little, too late." It is also possible that the April-to-November drops, where they occurred, signified a dissatisfaction with the proposed particulars of the constitution's protections for poor whites, in contrast to an earlier, more general enthusiasm for black disfranchisement. In the Black Belt, three counties (Choctaw, Lee, and Lowndes) actually defected from the proconstitution fold and returned majorities against ratification (see table 12 in the appendix). This slight shift from the April election, when all nineteen Black Belt counties showed perfect discipline, indicates that the warnings of the anticonstitution forces had some effect. Even more enticing, this anomaly suggests that patterns of ballot fraud and manipulation were not absolute or uniform, that control over election machinery could vary over time and place—even in the seemingly immutable Black Belt. At least one of the rogue Black Belt counties (Lee) had been considered problematic in the high Democratic councils for some time.[57] Although Lee returned a 73 percent majority for the calling of the convention, the county could only muster 33 percent for ratification. Two other Black Belt counties recorded precipitous drops in support of the disfranchisement agenda at the polls, although these counties did not technically qualify as "unredeemed" in November 1901 (Autauga 89 percent in April to 50 percent in November, and Russell 92 to 58). Yet, table 12 also makes clear that the Black Belt trend toward a lower "for" vote in November than in April did not hold across the section. Four counties (Clarke, Hale, Macon, and Pickens) actually increased the size of their "for" vote between the two referenda—suggesting in reverse that the level of county control over election machinery was variable. And Dallas, Monroe, and Perry Counties stayed the same, or virtually the same, between the two elections.

In the white counties a measure of variability also existed but again not a decisive level (see table 13 in the appendix). As one might expect, there was more movement in the white counties away from the constitution's specific disfranchising provisions than in the Black Belt. Thirty-one of the white counties showed some increase in opposition to a constitution between the April ref-

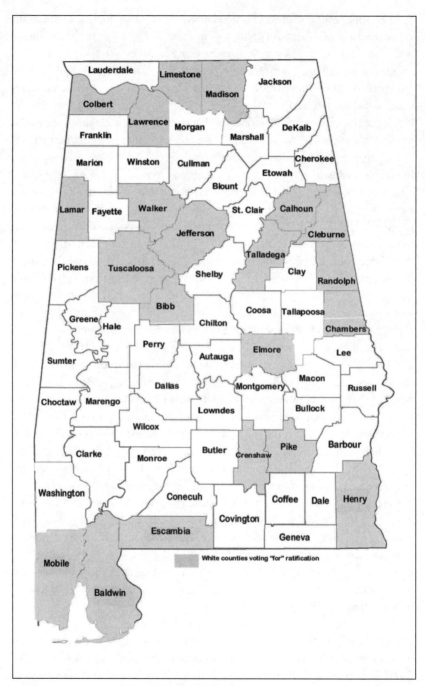

White counties voting "for" ratification

MAP 4 White Counties Voting "for" November 1901 Ratification

erendum and the one in November. A few showed large-scale movement. In Covington and Marion, the "for" vote fell twenty points between elections. In Jackson and Tallapoosa, it fell twenty-six and twenty-seven, respectively. Morgan, Randolph, and Washington Counties' totals were truly dramatic—more than thirty percentage points. But even in the white counties, things worked the opposite way as well. Sixteen white counties actually increased their "for" votes between April and November. Baldwin ratcheted its support up by twenty points, Limestone by twenty-six, and Elmore by a remarkable thirty-two percentage points.

An examination by section makes the split in the white counties very clear (see table 14 in the appendix and map 1). The Tennessee Valley again ruptured, this time with four of the section's seven counties voting "for" ratification. Both Limestone and Colbert returned over 70 percent for the new constitution; Madison recorded almost two-thirds in favor. Even "the" hotbed of post-Reconstruction anti-Redeemer politics, Lawrence County, came in at almost 60 percent "for." The cleavage in the Wiregrass was similar. Four out of the ten counties voted outright for ratification. Another third notched over 40 percent for the new constitution, indicating a jagged division in the region. The Hill Country vote was eleven counties "for" and sixteen "against," as it had been on the referendum on calling the convention. Tom Heflin's home county of Chambers led the way with almost 90 percent in favor of ratification, but Cleburne and Talladega also came in with two-thirds or more for the new constitution. Elsewhere in the Upcountry, Bibb, Calhoun, Elmore, Jefferson, Lamar, Randolph, Tuscaloosa, and Walker recorded proratification countywide votes. What is more, eight of the sixteen Hill Country counties that went against ratification still returned over 30 percent in favor of the new constitution. The Gulf Coast Plain barely lost the "for" support of Washington County, which defected with 48 percent in favor of ratification. But the section still returned a majority of its counties, Baldwin and Mobile, in favor. All told the vote among the state's white counties was twenty-one "for" and twenty-six "against"—hardly a flat rejection of the document.

These surprising results hold when we reexamine the question of how Populist counties voted in 1901. Traditional estimations point out that, viewed as units, Populist counties went overwhelmingly against the 1901 constitutional movement—more evidence to suggest a clear dichotomy between privileged support and plain rejection of the disfranchising movement. Yet, as with the 1901 referenda votes, the reality is actually much more mixed, even deeply split. Of the thirty-seven Alabama counties that went Populist in 1892, their vote on the 1901 referendum on calling the convention was virtually even: eighteen "for" and nineteen "against" (see table 15 in the appendix and map 5). On the

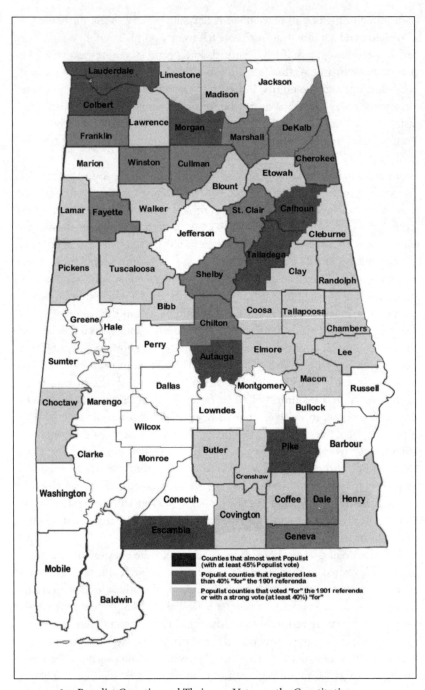

Counties that almost went Populist
(with at least 45% Populist vote)

Populist counties that registered less
than 40% "for" the 1901 referenda

Populist counties that voted "for" the 1901 referenda
or with a strong vote (at least 40%) "for"

MAP 5   1892 Populist Counties and Their 1901 Votes on the Constitution

November 1901 ratification referendum, the counties went fifteen "for" and twenty-two "against." When we add those Populist counties that did not technically vote "for" the referenda but still had strong votes within the county (at least 40 percent) for them, the split is even more obvious: twenty-five "for" and twelve "against" on the April 1901 referendum and nineteen "for" and eighteen "against" on the November vote. Looked at another way, the split is still present. If we factor in the eight counties that had strong Populist votes in 1892 (at least 45 percent), yet still did not technically "go" Populist, we get a total of forty-five Populist and strongly Populist counties to weigh. Of these, twenty-five were "for" as opposed to twenty "against" on the April 1901 referendum, with twenty-two "for" and twenty-three "against" on the November vote.

The results are very similar for those counties that went Populist in the 1894 and 1896 elections as well (see tables 16 and 17 in the appendix and map 6). Of the thirty-six Alabama counties that went Populist in 1894, their vote on the 1901 referendum on calling the convention was fifteen "for" and twenty-one "against" (see table 16 in the appendix and map 6). On the November 1901 ratification referendum, twelve counties went "for" and twenty-four "against." When we add those Populist counties that did not technically "go" for the referenda but still had strong votes within the county (at least 40 percent) for the them, the split is clearer: twenty-three "for" and thirteen "against" on the April 1901 referendum, and seventeen "for" and nineteen "against" on the November vote. Looked at another way, the split is still present. If we factor in the nine counties that had strong Populist votes in 1894 (at least 45 percent), yet still did not technically "go" Populist, we get a total of forty-five Populist and strongly Populist counties to weigh. Of these, twenty-three voted "for" as opposed to twenty-two "against" on the April 1901 referendum, with nineteen "for" and twenty-six "against" on the November referendum.

For several reasons, this trend tapers off slightly as we go to the 1896 election (see table 17 in the appendix). First, we must remember that Populism peaked in Alabama in 1892 and 1894. Thus, looking at how Populist counties, as measured by the 1892 and 1894 elections, voted in the 1901 referenda makes much more sense than looking at how the few remaining Populist counties from the 1898 election voted. Populism was in its death throes by then, with many of the old anti-Democrats making tentative and sometimes temporary reentry back into the Democratic Party. Second, the 1896 gubernatorial election itself is a suspect yardstick of Alabama Populism since the election featured a Populist candidate, Albert T. Goodwyn, against a "half-Populist," Joseph F. Johnston, who supported free silver and had coopted a large number of plain-white voters to his standard. Ten of the historically Populist counties that went Populist in both the 1892 and the 1894 election went for Johnston in 1896 and thus were not

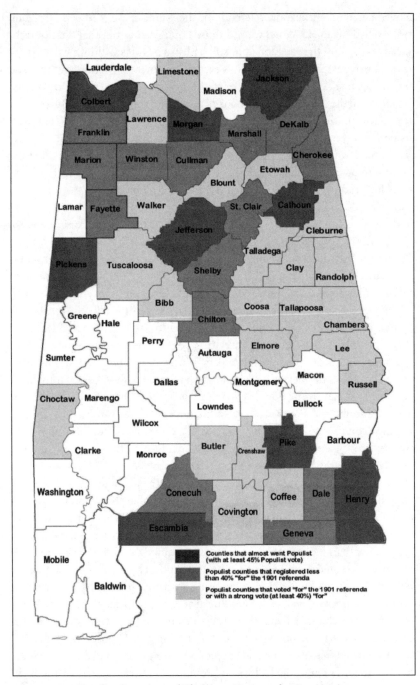

MAP 6   1894 Populist Counties and Their 1901 Votes on the Constitution

counted as Populist counties in subsequent analysis of 1901 referenda voting: Blount, Chambers, Clay, DeKalb, Lee, Limestone, Randolph, Tuscaloosa, Winston, and Walker counties (see table 18 in the appendix and map 7). A strong case can be made that the 1892 and 1894 gubernatorial elections give a truer measure of Alabama Populism than do later elections. Seventeen counties that went Populist in either the 1892 or the 1894 election or in both did not in 1896. Eleven of these seventeen voted "for" the April 1901 constitutional referendum. The count in November 1901 was ten counties "for" and seven counties "against." If we weigh in strong proreferendum votes in these counties, the results are fourteen "for" and three "against" on the April referendum and eleven "for" and six "against" in the November vote.

It cannot be asserted, of course, that plain whites in Alabama voted overwhelmingly for ratification. It is not being presently so argued. But it *has* been argued that plain whites in Alabama voted overwhelmingly against the constitution—that plain whites flatly opposed disfranchisement itself, the very idea of disfranchisement, and the disfranchisement of blacks, no less. It has been claimed that a simple dichotomy suffices to explain disfranchisement in this southern state and, by extension, in the South: that poor whites opposed the constitution while the Democrats shoved it through by hook and crook; that the white counties turned the proposition down while the black counties carried it through alone; that poor whites opposed disfranchisement while the privileged were solely responsible; that poor whites put their class and social interests ahead of all else and resisted the siren call of racial solidarity and patriotism.[58] Clearly, the picture is more complex than that. At the very least serious divisions were at work—even among the plain whites, even in the white counties. The most conservative estimation of these referenda should acknowledge that, at the barest minimum, many plain whites in Alabama voted for disfranchisement— even the particular type of disfranchisement mechanism framed by their class "betters"—and, in doing so, did little to help their own political and economic prospects.

Mythology, Political Defeat, and Its Consequences

As in virtually every Alabama election between 1874 and 1901, the ratification vote was remarkably close outside the Black Belt. Historians have customarily dealt with this circumstance by making the point that Black Belt control of African American votes by force and fraud was responsible for these patrician triumphs. And this is certainly a point worth making.[59] But it is only one side of the disfranchisement coin.

Populist counties in 1892 and/or 1894 but not
in 1896 that voted "for" the 1901 referenda

Populist counties in 1892 and/or 1894 but not
in 1896 that voted "against" the 1901 referenda

MAP 7   Populist Counties in 1892 or 1894 and Their Votes on the 1901 Constitution

Contemporary political commentators contributed significantly to the myth that exonerates plain whites in Alabama from having had a hand in the dirty business of disfranchisement. And since then, many historians have been far too willing to accept such claims. Contemporary overstatement of the divide between Bourbon and anti-Democrat on the issue constructed a stark, rigid, and malformed dichotomy. Part of the effort was apparently a defensive impulse to deal with a very bitter defeat. "It is a satisfaction . . . that every white county in the state went against ratification," one north Alabama newspaper inexplicably claimed in evaluating the results of the November election. The interpreter consoled the antiratificationists that "[t]his show[ed] clearly which side had the endorsement of the white people of Alabama." A Populist organ was not quite as dramatic yet made the same point. It claimed a mere "25,000 clear majority" among the "whites in the white counties." Another way of dealing with the unpleasantness of reality was to assert that fraudulent Black Belt tactics had, in effect, been responsible for adverse election results regardless of which county in the state was being discussed. The implication: plain whites were not responsible for the constitution or its ratification. The constitution's opponents enlisted the reality of massive fraud in the Black Belt to explain away adverse election returns across the whole state. The effect of the commentators' reflexive defense was twofold: it exonerated their poor-white fellows who had ignored the ample warnings and, as soon became apparent, contributed to their own rapidly accruing misfortune; and it soothed their own egos. Otherwise the constitution's opponents would have had to confront the fact that they were not as persuasive, even among their own, as they had supposed. For later historians, the fact of Black Belt fraud supplied an escape hatch for plain whites, who could exit the disfranchisement debacle with their nobility and a comforting reputation for racial "enlightenment" intact. Hence the election was "one of the most gigantic steals"; it was "carried and counted in over the heads of the white people of Alabama" and was "the most disgraceful episode in" any given county's history.[60]

But another point, very much obscured by the disfranchisement myth, is that the closeness of the vote outside the Black Belt also demonstrates that poor whites were, in large measure, the contributing authors of their own demise. The non–Black Belt vote was excruciatingly close, almost even in 1901.[61] It was so close, in fact, that it narrowed the gap between actual political reality and the oligarchy's desired version of reality. Put another way, had plain whites around the state voted en masse against the constitution—had they really, in C. Vann Woodward's words, "turned it down flat"—the constitution probably would not have passed. The resulting gap would have been impossible for the Black Belt to bridge, voting irregularities or no. But because so many plain-white folk defined their self-interest as keeping blacks below them instead of raising themselves up to the level of the bosses, they swallowed the Great Lie. The gap was spannable, and Alabama's privileged coalition had its way yet again.

Alabama's 1901 Constitution was devastatingly successful in shrinking the state's electorate to a more privileged white voter. Blacks lost the vote in droves. In 1900, for example, fourteen Black Belt counties had a combined total of 79,311 voters on their rolls. By 1 January 1903, this figure had dropped to just 1,081. Dallas and Lowndes Counties, both 75 percent black, showed only 103 registered black voters between them. Statewide the story was much the same. In 1900, Alabama was home to 181,315 blacks who were eligible to vote. By the first day of 1903, the state had only 2,980 registered black voters, although at least 73,674 literate blacks were living in Alabama. Thus, there were fewer than 3,000 black voters in 1903 Alabama, compared with 140,000 in 1890 and over 100,000 in 1900.[62] Moreover, the effect was enduring. At the end of World War II, the black Collegeville community in Birmingham, home to over 8,000 blacks, had just 11 qualified voters.[63]

But plain whites—due in no small part to their own efforts to deny African Americans the franchise—lost the vote as well. By the first day of 1903, the expiration date of the constitution's temporary plan, 3,350 Black Belt whites, in a small area of the region most populated by poor whites, had been disfranchised. Statewide, the total number of white registered voters fell by 41,329— from 232,821 in 1900 to just 191,492 in 1903—despite a generally growing population and the efforts of many poor whites to register under the permanent plan. In 1904, the novelist Thomas Nelson Page estimated that fully 50,000 white Alabamians had been disfranchised by the constitution's poll tax and the illiteracy and vagrancy clauses. Over time, the constitution continued to have a devastating effect on poor whites. Because white population outstripped black, by 1941 more poor whites than blacks had been disfranchised by the provisions of the 1901 Alabama Constitution, primarily by the cumulative poll tax: 600,000 whites to 520,000 blacks. Yet the disingenuousness of the patricians persisted beyond 1901. Five years later, after the poll tax had worked incredible hardship on poor-white voting, convention president John Knox actually blamed poor whites, not "the Constitution itself," for the massive loss of suffrage. According to the industrialist, the culprit was an insufficiently developed sense of personal responsibility. In other words, "it should always be remembered" that they had "made good on [their] pledge . . . that no worthy white man should be disfranchised." According to Knox, poor whites who could not afford the cumulative poll tax were losing the vote in droves because of their own sloth, character flaws, and shiftlessness, not the constitution's provisions, but "simply because they refuse[d] or omit[ted] to comply with its terms." Further straining to make his point, Knox maintained that the new constitution had "lightened . . . the burdens of the people" by making a heretofore compulsory tax voluntary.[64]

Knox's alibi notwithstanding, Bourbon use of the race issue had clearly done in Alabama's plain-white folk. "[R]acism has never imposed sufficient unity on the white majority," an eminent historian has argued, "to override for long the fundamental pattern of group conflict." Perhaps not—especially when things got back to "normal." But race, racism, and racial conditions—often fortified with other powerful emotional concepts such as patriotism, religion, and memories of the Lost Cause and Reconstruction—did so at the most critical junctures in Alabama's history.[65] The 1901 experience bequeathed Alabama with yet another in a long line of examples—Redemption, the Greenbackers, organized labor, Populism—of race and emotion being used as effective weapons to overcome economic issues. The legacy was powerful and would continue to be discernible in Alabama through the rest of the twentieth century and into the twenty-first.[66]

The Great Lie—the assurance that poor whites could best serve themselves by allying with their class betters in the Black Belt and their industrial allies—proved its worth yet again in 1901. Privileged Alabama whites told the Great Lie, early and often, from 1865 on. Ratification in 1901 was merely another chapter in this long and familiar story.[67] All white folk had to do, according to the lie, was to help privileged whites maintain white unity and refuse to succumb to the chimera of allying with poor blacks against the oligarchy's interests. The Bourbons, of course, could be relied on to look after the general and economic interests of their common-white brethren.[68] There were different strains of the Great Lie, variations on a theme suited for different times and places in the state's history. But central to all variants was the logic of white unity, the memory of Reconstruction, and the consequent peril to white civilization if poor whites attempted to forge a biracial class coalition with poor and working-class blacks.

The Great Lie contained all the elements of most lies. It was self-serving, not particularly noble, and, of course, untrue. Plain whites faired miserably by forsaking biracial class politics for white solidarity and what they hoped would be status, power, and respectability. But more than that, the Great Lie proved the wisdom behind the old adage: "Fool me once, shame on you. Fool me twice, shame on me." Plain whites believed the lie because they *wanted* to believe it. If the shame of propagating a self-serving tale belongs to the Redeemers, the tragedy of believing it, repeatedly to their own detriment, belongs to many of Alabama's plain whites. Alabama's bosses can be blamed for appealing to race and exploiting the ugliest of racial prejudices, but ultimately, some portion of the responsibility for the force with which those appeals resonated lies with the white folk who wanted to hear them. Some plain whites clearly recognized the patrician deception for what it was. But far too many wanted to have their cake and eat it too: to feel socially, economically, morally, and politically "superior" to blacks, yet unharmed vis-à-vis Alabama's patricians.[69]

The privileged class's post-1901 forgetfulness of its pledges to protect poor-white suffrage should not have come as any great surprise. No less than twice during the convention, Bourbons had beaten back attempts to extend the temporary suffrage protections beyond the 1 January 1903 deadline. Some Redeemer spokesmen supplied the polite reasoning that they did "not want to put a premium of ignorance in [their] own blood" and added that no guarantees of the ballot had been held out to Alabama's "unborn ages." But Charles H. Greer of Perry County had been more direct. He admitted that Black Belt whites did not know "which is worst, to have the heel of the White Belt upon [their] necks, or have the negroes upon [their] right arm."[70] Other patricians justified abandonment of the plain whites because the promises of protection had allegedly been made "hurriedly and unwisely"—even though the promise had been made repeatedly for years leading up to the constitutional convention.[71] The normally mild-mannered suffrage committee chair, Thomas L. Coleman, had betrayed much in his angry response to N. B. Spears's scandalous suggestion that black voting be preserved. Coleman announced that "if there were no other reason for calling [the] convention, . . . it would be sufficient . . . in order that so many of [his] constituents might be eliminated from the suffrage plank as to retire that gentleman from entertaining those sentiments."[72] At a midconvention meeting of the Alabama Press Association, nineteen of the group's thirty member newspapers voted to renege on the pledge. These admissions—accompanied by almost constant references to the need to prevent voting by the "ignorant and vicious . . . the mean . . . [and] the weak and vicious" and to reserve it only for "the intelligent and virtuous"—provided ample handwriting on the wall.[73] In 1905, four years after the deed, convention president John B. Knox admitted that, despite all the pledges and promises, the "true philosophy of the movement" all along had been, in fact, to target blacks and poor whites: "to . . . place the power of government in the hands of the intelligent and virtuous."[74]

"Poor Honest White People": Calibrating Political Self-Interest

In the end, the tendency for many poor whites to behave in ways that were ultimately detrimental to their political self-interest was largely the function of an exceedingly narrow conception of what constituted that self-interest. Far too many poor whites in Alabama focused primarily, singularly—even obsessively—on the plight of the poor-white man, however considerable and precarious it may have been in reality. The exclusive nature of the focus, though, subsumed the fact that, at least in a class sense, poor whites were joined at the hip with poor blacks (in other words, with most blacks). By focusing too specifically on their own interest, defined according to class and race yet completely cut off from people of color who shared a similar social and class situation, many poor whites made their position more vulnerable vis-à-vis the state's privileged whites. For these poor whites, the first, last, and only question was, How will a new constitution affect poor whites? To the answer, they tied an automatic response. If they could convince themselves that the answer to that question was positive, their posture toward the constitution (and its disfranchising purpose) would be positive. If the answer to that question was negative, they assumed a negative posture. By defining the issue in such narrow terms, they did not concern themselves with the question of disfranchisement in principle, only in practice—only whether they and their kind were to escape the dragnet once it was in place. This was an extraordinarily risky proposition. If they talked themselves into believing enough safeguards were present to exempt people of their color and class, many poor whites were willing to go along with the constitution and disfranchisement because they had no fundamental aversion to disfranchisement. In fact, a great many relished the prospect of African Americans being disfranchised. Once the law was written, though, poor whites had to rely on the effectiveness of the constitutional safeguards and loopholes and the prospect of planters and industrialists keeping their word, a very risky proposition indeed.

This narrow conception of the question was all too apparent in the frequent and confusing vacillation on the constitutional issue by anti-Democratic newspapers as they shifted in their estimation of whether or not poor whites would be harmed by a new document. In May 1901, as the constitutional convention was set to get underway, the Jeffersonian *Cherokee Harmonizer* dismissed northern objections that blacks were about to be disfranchised as the bitter carpings of "South-haters." "Don't fret about your brother in black," the *Harmonizer* advised its insurgent readership, "the time has come when he must and will have to go to the rear. The sooner the better for the Southern people." Yet, within the month, as it watched the convention proceedings unfold, especially the maneuverings of gold Democrats such as W. C. Oates, the *Harmonizer* became increasingly alarmed by Black Belt machinations to control the summit's direction and warned poor whites to "[k]eep [their] eye on this gang." Just before the November ratification vote, the *Harmonizer* was convinced that the all-important grandfather clause safeguard was to be "expunged" from the new constitution, and it pled for its readers to vote against ratification. Under the new constitution, the newspaper warned, three in ten poor whites would lose the vote, but, worse yet, "a great many negroes [would] be allowed to vote."[75] Trying to keep up with the Populist *Choctaw Alliance* on the issue was like trying to watch a tennis match from midcourt. The newspaper's position changed so frequently that an observer trying to keep up was likely to get whiplash. The only constant was the Populists' concern for the future of poor-white—and only poor-white—voters. For most of 1898 through 1900, the editorial policy of the newspaper consistently opposed the prospect of a constitution, expressing fear that the illiterate white voter would be left behind. In early 1901, assuaged by suitable assurances and the promise that the work of the convention would be submitted back to the people, the *Alliance* came out in support of a convention. But the clarion call to "duty" in supporting the convention applied only to "every white citizen in Choctaw County," not to blacks. By July, though, growing unease over the patricians' intent to honor their protective pledges to the white folk was increasingly apparent in the pages of the Populist newspaper. The next month was devoted to singing the praises of the grandfather clause as an ennobling feature of the prospective law that would uplift politics by securing a future role for plain folk in the life of the polity. The Populists invoked romantic parallels with the vibrant political life of the hills of east Tennessee and western North Carolina and the deeds of plain-folk heroes such as Andy Jackson, Zeb Vance, and "Parson" Brownlow. "Charles Lamb has spoken of the wisdom in the face of a man who could not read and write," the Populists reasoned. "Daniel Boone could not read, but what a mark he made!" The "illiterate whites of the South," the *Alliance* argued, possessed a discernment and political judgment that at least equaled "their educated neighbors," but blacks were "quite different." "Their dense ignorance of all political questions is relieved by no gleam of tradition." In the end, the assurances of poor-white suffrage retention—and the promise of black disfranchisement—were enough for the Populist paper to support the new constitution.[76] A host of other anti-Democratic and Populist newspapers set their course on the constitutional issue exclusively by their estimation of how legal disfranchisement would affect only poor-white fortunes.[77]

Perhaps the best example of the effect the Populist fixation on the poor-white plight could have was supplied by the *Ozark Free Press*. Written and edited by a committee of leading Populists in Dale County, the *Free Press* functioned as one of the leading mouthpieces for Populist thought, not only in the Wiregrass but in the entire state as well. Its editorials were remarkably savvy, demonstrated an acute and well-developed class consciousness, and showed a mature sense of the South's regional personality by presenting its class arguments in explicitly religious terms. In 1899, on the prospect of a constitutional convention, for instance, the *Free Press* wrote: "God help the honest poor men of Alabama. They are about to be doomed to eternal serfdom. . . . The common poor man . . .

the poor wool hat boys . . . will be outlawed by that convention of rich lawyers and corporation plutocrats. . . . After[wards] you had better be a rich man's dog than an honest poor man in Alabama. . . . How can any self-respecting farmer vote for the convention? . . . [S]ave your neck from the halter. . . . Christ was a poor man and the rich officials crucified him. The same class is trying to crucify God's poor and unlettered today in Alabama."[78] Over the next years, as the editorial committee watched their insurgent fellows in Dale and the surrounding Wiregrass counties trade in their rebel clothing for the raiment of regular Democracy and party harmony, they shouted warning after warning. "No populist," no "self-respecting man can afford" to go back to the Democratic Party of Alabama unless he wanted to wear the "gold yoke . . . the 'yaller' livery" of the *Montgomery Advertiser* and other leading forces of privilege and wealth.[79] Through the 1900 primary, the *Free Press* stayed its hand but did not hold its tongue. In that election, one the newspaper adroitly equated with the call for constitutional change and disfranchisement, the Wiregrass committee saw its best efforts go for naught as fellow Populists marched into the polls and voted for, in effect, a constitutional convention—a development the *Free Press* saw as nothing less than tragic. "The saddest part of all to us is that some of the populists went into the democratic primaries and voted for the Constitutional Convention," the newspaper grieved. "If this is their last year to vote, they have [only] themselves to thank." William J. Samford could "never have carried" the county over Jesse Stallings "but for the support given him by the populists." "It is bad enough to have our democratic brethren force a Constitutional Convention on us, but unspeakably worse when they do it with populist aid and indorsement." Seeing the handwriting on the wall for a constitutional convention, the Populist newspaper quickly turned its attentions to trying to win "safeguards" and suitable loopholes and assurances once the summit was called.[80]

The last straw came just three months later. Seeing Populists all around them shed their insurgency to return to the Democratic Party and support the call for a new constitution, the editorial committee of the *Ozark Free Press* finally decided to come clean with its county readership and admit that, actually, they had "favored the disfranchisement of the negroes for two years" now but had "held [their] convictions in abeyance" in order to prevent even more confusion and disorder "in the populist ranks." As always, the *Free Press*'s posture was determined ultimately by estimations of how such-and-such a measure would impact poor-white people—not black people—fifteen hundred Populists alone in Dale County, it estimated. Declaring that it was clear and undisputed now— "The Populist party is dead"—the insurgent newspaper saw no option other than to go "back to the democratic party" and join the chorus for black disfranchisement through a new constitution. Once the admission had been made, the effect was somewhat liberating as the Populists approached the idea of black disfranchisement with relish. The "disfranchisement of the negroes" was "best for the plain poor honest white people." Making sure that "no negro be allowed to vote in Alabama," the Populist committee reasoned, would "lift this black cloud from our state; hanging here as a portent; looming up menacing. . . . The white people can settle their differences without an appeal to the negroes vote." The disfranchisement of blacks was actually a democratic measure, merely the function of the popular will, they reasoned. "Nine-tenths of the populists and nine-tenths of the democrats," the *Free Press* wrote, "are in favor of disfranchising the negroes." And to be absolutely honest, black disfranchisement was really the fault of the blacks themselves. "The negroes have brought disfranchisement upon themselves by selling out their votes. For years the editor of this paper has warned them that such conduct would sooner or later . . . provoke their disfranchisement. Our warnings have now ripened into . . . disgust. . . . [T]he negroes have themselves to thank—themselves only!"[81]

With their honest feelings now on record, their conviction that disfranchisement of the African American would now lead to "purer politics" and was "better for him and for us," the *Free Press* turned its attention to the larger task of reforming and democratizing the new, largely harmonious Democratic Party from within. A key element of such a reform effort was a provision for which the Populist newspaper had already been lobbying hard: a white primary.[82]

Disfranchisement Cemented

 Time would eventually make the price that many poor whites had paid for black disfranchisement all too clear. But that time was not the direct aftermath of the ratification referendum. Contemporary and later rhetoric to the contrary, Alabama's white voters had, at best, split on the issue of disfranchisement. For those thousands of plain whites who had voted for a convention and ratification, many of whom were anti-Democrats of one sort or another, in November 1901 the immediate glow of victory felt very warm. "The latest coon song is entitled: 'Will they miss me at the polls?' " a Jeffersonian headline from the Hill Country gloated. "The coon is now voteless, yes even as much so as a rabbit, in Alabama," read another. "WANTED—A coon what can exercise an electoral franchise," a third mocked. "On account of the scarcity of the commodity; will pay handsomely for same." And always, the race and Reconstruction rationale loomed large. "The ratification of the new constitution has removed those . . . galling . . . conditions, under whose . . . weight the state has struggled so long, but *uncomplainingly* [ital. mine]," a proratification Jeffersonian celebrated. "[T]oday she stands free and unhampered from any condition thrust upon her by aliens . . . [and] carpetbaggerism . . . during the days of reconstruction. . . . [W]e have just got rid of the average coon in politics." In the giddy atmosphere surrounding the celebration of the general white achievement, their revelry sometimes reached the obscene:

THE COON

The vote has been cast,

As we count she gets bigger:

But we ask you now

Where's the nigger?[1]

A Liberalizing Reform: The All-White, Direct Democratic Primary

If race and Reconstruction produced distortions in health, education, and agricultural reform, politics was certainly not immune to its effects. In fact, it might be argued that the political realm was the most direct and perfect product of Alabama's ongoing race and Reconstruction obsession. For example, a number of historians have lauded the establishment of the direct primary system as a monumental achievement in the march toward greater and more inclusive democracy. But at heart, the primary was also a delimiting all-white, racially exclusionary mechanism that served to buttress—in fact, to solidify—the legal disfranchisement effected by the 1901 Constitution. Touted by many as a liberalizing, democratizing "reform" because it benefited poor-white political prospects, the primary also fundamentally cemented black exclusion from politics because it was an all-white system as well a direct system.[2] V. O. Key actually viewed the all-white primary as a more delimiting disfranchisement measure than the poll tax.[3]

Momentum for the primary came mainly from a group of poor whites and "reform-wing" Democrats who had opposed the 1901 Constitution because they believed it represented a danger to poor-white voting. Leading representatives of the plain folk, figures such as Joseph F. Johnston, Charles M. Shelley, Jesse F. Stallings, and P. C. Steagall, unabashedly described their goal in seeking a direct primary in much the same racial terms as they had described their opposition to a new constitution, as first and foremost "good government, white supremacy, and honest elections . . . white supremacy in fact."[4] These tribunes of the plain folk laced their speeches calling for a primary with racial imagery and argument—and connected very closely the idea of reform with racial purity and a cleansing of the ballot. A primary would consolidate the influence of the white counties of north Alabama, Johnston explained, and secure to the revised Democratic Party that "harmony . . . that can only be had amongst Anglo Saxons when they know they have had a fair chance."[5] The former governor was so confident about the prospects of a primary being passed to improve poor-white political prospects that he privately joked that this time the bosses had to give in to the popular white will: "Heads we win, tails they lose."[6]

He was right. This time it was the privileged who went along with a plain-white-driven movement. Throughout the 1890s, privileged Democracy had opposed moves for a direct primary. With the 1901 Constitution firmly in place, though, many oligarchs felt that it was now safe for white men to disagree on politics since so many plain whites had been disfranchised along with blacks, and because the malapportioned legislature still rested safely in the hands of the planter and industrialist cabal.[7] They also saw the direct primary quite clearly as part of the movement for legal disfranchisement and "whitening" effected by the new constitution. As former Governor William C. Oates explained, the gentry went along with the direct primary reform because it meant "a white primary . . . economy, wise government, [and] elimination of the negro."[8] The

Big Mule–dominated *Birmingham Age-Herald* agreed that the primary was "the answer to Negro suffrage" and should work hand-in-hand with the new constitution to ensure a white electorate. The combination would allow white men to disagree in the primary and still present a united front in the general election so that "the Negro vote," such as it was, "would not count."[9] In this way, white supremacy was to be encrypted. In the August 1902 Democratic primary, the first all-white direct primary held in Alabama, patrician sentiments were justified as gubernatorial candidate W. D. Jelks rolled to an easy victory over plain-white tribune Joseph F. Johnston.[10] The Jelks win, convincing by any standard, was generally appreciated as confirmation of widespread acceptance of white unity and the 1901 Constitution, a document, explained a white Republican, that was now clearly "accepted by a great majority" in Alabama.[11]

Even more than "populism," the terms "progressivism" and "reform" have been used so often and so differently that they are now of limited utility. Particularly in a southern sense, because of race, both terms can now mean little, nothing—or worse yet, everything. Various scholars have defined, stretched, shortened, and gerrymandered the terms in ways that are so convoluted and confusing that now even many historians are uncertain exactly what they or their colleagues mean by the labels.

The central reason for this uncertainty is that a confusing question lies at the heart of the matter: Is it enough that a "change" occurred during the years generally accepted as the Progressive Era for it to qualify as a "reform"? For some, the answer is obviously yes. If that is so, it begs the further question of whether the terms, used in this specific way, actually bear any intrinsic relevance to the words as they are understood in a more general sense.[12]

In point of fact, the direct primary originated as a delimiting mechanism and an instrument of self-interest rather than as a democracy-widening tool. During the 1870s, proponents of the primary had pushed the measure as one for securing white unity against "Radical and Negro rule." Twenty years later, Alabama's Populists favored it as a way to gain some control over the political process dominated by Bourbon-led party conventions at the state and county levels.[13] Around 1898, the Johnston reform-wing of the Democratic Party resurrected it as a possible way to unseat John Tyler Morgan.[14] Once it was implemented in 1902, as historian Wayne Flynt accurately observed, aspiring demagogues and politicians used the primary "to inflame the white masses over some grievance, real or imagined . . . from corporation control of state government to fear of Negro rapists."[15] But in all of its various manifestations, the direct primary represented racial control and factional self-interest.[16]

The idea of an all-white primary held special allure for poor-white Jeffersonians around the time of the fight over the 1901 Constitution. Anti-Democrats expressed wide and varied support for the idea that such a primary would work hand-in-hand with the new constitution to eliminate African Americans from politics. Some even recommended that the referendum over ratification be restricted to a white-only "primary" vote that would put the constitutional question, as well as future political decisions, in the hands of only whites. Lewis H. Reynolds, the Chilton County Populist, favored the idea of an all-white primary—in fact, he proposed it at the 1901 convention.[17] The Hill Country *Marshall Banner* endorsed the white primary as the hope for "unity once more [for] the white people" of the state; the *Clanton Banner* as "the fairest way" to settle political questions.[18] Populists around the state clamored for it as well.[19] One People's Party mouthpiece admitted that it "pray[ed] for a white primary" that would "leave the [political] question to the white folks."[20] The *Gadsden Tribune* and the *Alabama Alliance News,* Hill Country Populist papers, and the *Ozark Free Press* from the Wiregrass backed the provision editorially.[21] Lily-white Republicans also liked the idea. The Upcountry's *Jacksonville Republican* and the *Anniston Republican* followed suit with endorsements.[22]

Yet the all-white, direct, Democratic primary was not a done deal simply because Alabama's plain whites wanted it to be. Significant Big Mule and Black Belt opposition to the primary first had to be overcome where it was most firmly entrenched: in the party councils of the Democratic and Conservative Party. Many plain whites—who by 1902 had reentered the temple of regular Democracy or stayed without but lent a hand on disfranchisement—expected to exact the price of a primary and greater say in political matters in return for their aid on suffrage restriction and the tantalizing possibility of their permanent reentry into the party. The problem for plain whites came in the form of those privileged planters and industrialists who now had what they wanted in the new constitution and might not see the need or benefit of continuing to make common cause with plain folk. A good example was supplied by John V. Smith, the influential president of the Alabama Railroad Commission. In early 1901, Smith had spoken forcefully and effectively in the highest Democratic councils, calling for moderation, toleration, and inclusiveness where the poor whites were concerned—many of them former anti-Redeemers. But by 1902, Smith had changed his tune. With the convention safely called, and the constitution passed and ratified, Smith spoke vigorously against continuing to hold out an olive branch toward the plain folk.[23]

Perhaps the most effective spokesmen for the primary were regular Democrats from the white counties. Long used to Black Belt domination on the state executive committee, in state offices, and in the legislature, these representatives of the white counties viewed 1902 as the time for the white counties to finally get their due, their just desserts for having furnished so many votes for the cause of a new constitution. These regular Democrats, who had long stood on the front lines against the political insurgents in their own counties, desperately desired peace and unity—as much out of a sense of exhaustion as of opportunity glimpsed for their plain constituents. As such, they stressed party harmony in their reasoning, arguing, sometimes not very subtly, that the new-found Democratic unity based on the concept of white solidarity among different classes of whites would be jeopardized if the drive for a primary were thwarted by the privileged members of the SDEC. While praising harmony and unity as a good thing, these white-county delegates—sometimes expressing resentment at having to work so hard to keep their plain-white constituents in the party—communicated the "dangerous" and potentially rebellious effects that might accrue if the mass-white desire for a primary were rebuffed.[24] Likewise, representatives of the white counties stressed the "graveness" of the primary question and the overwhelming popular support that was massed behind it—two additional rhetorical means to suggest revolt if the planters and industrialists did not step aside on the issue.[25] A further appeal to simple fairness and equal legislative representation, as well as much talk about "conditions" having changed from white imperilment to solidified white supremacy after 1901, also endowed their logic with the implied threat: either the Big Mule–Black Belt coalition accede to the primary demand, or the party would face division and perhaps even renewed anti-Democratic revolt.

Once a white-county delegate made the actual motion in committee, others from the white counties rushed to support the measure.[26] Party unity and harmony based on white solidarity and supremacy were perhaps the most frequently recurring themes in their logic. "[H]armony above all things harmony" in the Democratic Party was the rationale behind the push for a primary, a Talladega County member explained—a harmony founded on white togetherness and unity in a "white man's party."[27] At times the debate in the SDEC got rocky, as patrician challenged white-county plebeian on why the party should allow former anti-Democrats to vote in a direct primary. Under intense questioning by the planters and industrialists, William J. Samford of Pike County argued that "it does not signify at all" if a voter had been a Populist or a Republican in prior elections. If he had now, as a "white man in Alabama," come into the Democratic Party in good faith and shown "his good faith by his works," then that voter was "just as good a Democrat as any man." Bibb Graves, a plain-white representative with a long and illustrious career still ahead of him, argued forcefully along the same lines. He made it explicit that "all the white men in Alabama" should be wooed into the Democratic Party because the chief goal of the epoch was "to get the white people together."[28]

Calls for unity were supplemented by emphasis on the "seriousness" of the situation around a primary, a constant reminder that the "conditions" that had, since 1874, justified Black Belt domination of the state and party had now changed. Like the stress on unity, both arguments, flipped on their backs, were thinly veiled threats of political revolt. Political unity and harmony was valuable and enabling for the Democratic Party. Without the primary, that unity was in jeopardy. The situation was "serious," so serious, in fact, that short of a suitable settlement of the primary issue, there might be revolt. "Conditions" had changed. That was good. But "change" inherently meant that conditions were not immutable. Without a favorable adjudication of the primary issue, there could be a relapse into chaotic political insurgency and the ever-present possibility of biracial political challenge. The Democratic Party stood proudly in 1902 as "a white man's party," without any "fear of dominion because we have eliminated the negro vote," as one Hill Country SDEC member noted, celebrating the new conditions. "It is a consummation" that the white men of Alabama had "worked and labored . . . and devoutly prayed for." It was true that the new constitution had "purified" the electorate by "eliminat[ing] the negro as a political factor," an SDEC member from the Tennessee Valley concurred. The old conditions, in which "the negro" was a "menace to our peace and prosperity . . . no longer exis[ted]"—nor did any rationale for continued Black Belt domination.[29]

The white-county delegation on the state executive committee fortified its argument with what amounted to two other veiled threats: a reminder of majority rule and an appeal to simple fairness. A number of committee members claimed that the state and the press were overwhelmingly in support of the primary. Defy this groundswell of support at your own risk, they warned the oligarchy. Under the old conditions, simple fairness had necessitated bowing to Black Belt preeminence, because the black counties had provided, through force and fraud, thousands of votes. New conditions, though, dictated a new conception of what constituted simple fairness: the proposition that one white vote in the Black Belt should count no more than one white vote in the white counties.[30] The threat came in the realization that the old conditions and demands for party unity in the face of the black threat were no longer relevant. With so few blacks voting after 1901, the iron bands of white solidarity that had long tied the white counties to the Democratic Party were slipping off. To emphasize the point, primary advocates invoked the national treasure of majority rule. W. J. Samford of Pike County conveyed his belief that press "education" of the white masses had been so extensive that even the most eloquent and beautiful arguments for retention of the convention system of nomination were doomed. Now any argument along that line, no matter how elegant, would "never get it out of their minds the idea that one democrat is as good in one part of that State as in the other." Thomas Heflin described that majority who wanted a white primary, with his usual color and hyperbole, claiming that nine-tenths of the state was behind the idea. But a Jackson County member of the SDEC probably put it best. "They want a primary, I tell you," he said about his plain-white Hill Country constituency. "I live with them, and I know them, I am one of them, and I know what they want," he told the committee, "they want a primary and they are not going to be satisfied" without it.[31]

Lest the veiled threats not work, plain whites around the state and in the party councils communicated a more explicit version. One marched up to the chairman of the state Democratic committee and told him flat out: "If you don't give us a primary, you are digging your graves." At the SDEC, Emmett O'Neal echoed the admonition. "I tell you gentlemen . . . I speak plainly," O'Neal warned. If the party decided to recommend against an all-white primary, it "invite[d] revolt" and perhaps even "disaster." In "all candor," an Upcountry committee member concurred, "you [just] cannot" go to places like Talladega, Tallapoosa, and Lauderdale counties and try to sell a package of goods against the primary. The argument of those hill folk is "unanswerable." They were "all brethren" there, Tom Heflin reminded his fellows on the SDEC, and none of them wanted another revolt against Democracy and defeat at the polls. But, he advised, there were "those upon whose back the harness of the party [did] not weigh heavily," and it would "not take very much" for them to "step aside now and then." While not countenancing revolt himself, W. J. Samford relayed the overt and imminent threat. "We have heard the roll of the thunder, and seen the flash of the lightning," he warned the committee, and if the SDEC defied the will of the majority, they would "rebuke" the party at the very first opportunity.[32]

For their part, a number of the patricians fought the white-county movement, which was beginning to seem increasingly ineluctable. Their methods varied. Some raised legal technicalities and issues of parliamentary procedure. Others questioned the authority of the SDEC to call for a primary, since the popular vote would replace the convention system that had created the executive committee in the first place—a kind of legal patricide. Still others suggested that a direct primary would only give the plain whites too much power and result in "irreconcilable" men controlling the party and electing demagogues like Ben Tillman as opposed to true "statesmen" such as Edmund Pettus and John Tyler Morgan.[33] Some Black Belt spokesmen took the setback particularly hard. A Sumter County pol, for instance, was virtually despondent. "[W]e are done for. . . . We are in for it," he lamented. There "[is] no way out of it, we have done fixed ourselves . . . and there is nothing to do but stand down. . . . A black belt county was big a few days ago, but now is a little fellow."[34]

Robert J. Lowe made several arguments before going back to the well of race and Reconstruction one too many times. Easily conversant with the winning formula of Alabama politics, the party chairman tried to cast privileged opposition to the primary as a function of tradition, loyalty, racial fealty, conservatism, and proper religion. Support for the primary, then, was the opposite: the equivalent of Republicanism, race treason, and actual political and religious sacrilege. In making the case, Lowe provided one of the clearest explanations possible of how white supremacy and social and political conservatism were connected, and would long be connected, in Alabama. It was not merely a "Democratic" Party, Lowe intoned, nor even a national Democratic Party. It was the "Democratic and Conservative Party of Alabama." That meant something. Lowe instructed his committee that "conservative" meant that the party was born to "conserve the liberties, the property, and the lives of the white people of Alabama who were exposed to the dangers incident to Reconstruction." It meant the party would "conserve the interests of the white people of Alabama for the preservation of a white man's government in Alabama." Anyone who would "impugn the system" of Democratic state conventions, then, impugned the whole system underlying white supremacy and conservatism and was essentially a "vicious" human being and disrespectful as well. "I shall vote to stay in the beaten paths of my fathers," Lowe vowed melodramatically. They "walked in a straight enough [line for me]," their methods were "honest enough for me," and "[I do not think myself] better than they were," the chairman said. Moreover, the "Good Book says 'Remove not the ancient marks,'" and any heretic who would come now and "throw slime and mud" on the "good old ways of the fathers [is not] as good" a person "as I am."[35]

This time, though, the Black Belt machine was somewhat split against itself on what to do. A number of the regular Democrats adopted a more pragmatic approach, one that better compensated the white counties for their assistance in the constitution making of 1901. Alfred M. Tunstall of Hale County, the state-at-large replacement on the SDEC for the late Francis L. Pettus, who had been one of the most vehement opponents of the white counties, showed a far more developed sense of white reconciliation and solidarity than his predecessor by casting his vote for the primary. Other Black Belt members of the committee encountered pressure and ridicule from their sectional peers because they too voted to support the primary. Still others from the Black Belt grudgingly acquiesced in the primary movement but insisted that only regular Democrats from the white counties, voters who had "shown their faith by their works," be allowed to vote. After all, B. M. Miller of Wilcox County explained, "we don't want to be killed by Populites, do we?"[36]

In the main, though, the split on the SDEC between the various white factions over the primary was regional and economic. Its racially exclusionary nature was a given. Black Belt Democracy, now that it had used the banner of white solidarity to achieve a new constitution that cemented its inordinate power, saw no need to actually raise the white counties up to its level, regardless of the assistance it had received. For the white counties, though, parity was the price of their racial cooperation in 1901. The white counties, cognizant of the role they had played in helping to pass and ratify the new constitution, believed, in the absence of continued large-scale black voting, that the time was right to equalize sectional representation. When it came, the vote on the measure was very close. It passed 16–13 in the state executive committee, with the white counties winning just enough Black Belt support to carry the measure (see table 19 in the appendix).[37] Probably more common than enduring enmity between the sections was a kind of grudging acceptance that the primary, while inconvenient, was not the death knell of planter-industrialist power and was, in fact, the price that had to be paid for the enabling rhetoric of white solidarity. Black Belt figures such as H. S. D. Mallory seemed to realize this. Mallory exhibited a half-hearted, almost invariable type of opposition to the primary. He voted against the primary in committee, but once it passed, recommended that it be put into effect without delay. Mallory's behavior seemed to bear out the astute observation made by one historian that the primary was "a sop to the masses" that resulted in "no loss of power" to the oligarchy.[38]

That conclusion was additionally borne out by the first all-white direct Democratic primary, held in September 1902. In that gubernatorial contest, which pitted the "half-Populist" Joseph F. Johnston against William D. Jelks as the standard-bearer for regular Democracy, it was clear that the Populist moment was truly over. Jelks won sixty-two of sixty-six counties, taking two-thirds of the vote in both the Black Belt and the white counties (see tables 20 and 21 in the appendix and map 8). By 1902, white solidarity and black exclusion were indeed intact.

"Every White Man Will Show How He Stands": Lily-White Republicanism

In fact, the disfranchising constitution, the all-white direct primary, and lily-white Republicanism were intertwined as part-and-parcel of a general whitening occurring in Alabama at this time. Nor was the whitening movement native only to Alabama. It stretched across the South at precisely the same moment, making the racially exclusionary changes of disfranchisement and all-white primaries kindred and temporal spirits with lily-white Republicanism. In North Carolina, historian Glenda Gilmore documented the trend, writing that

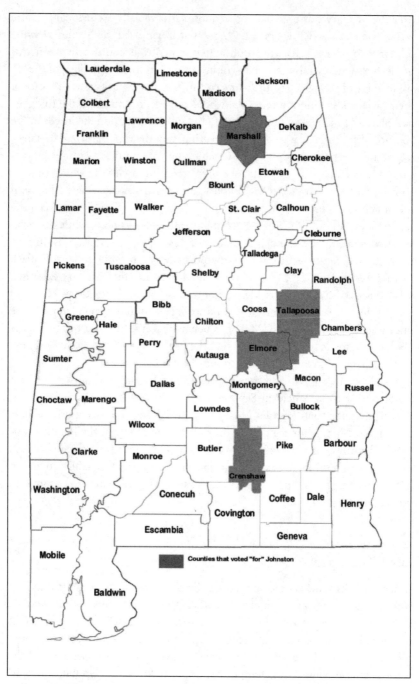

Counties that voted "for" Johnston

MAP 8   Vote by County in 1902 Democratic Gubernatorial Primary

"[w]hen black leaders looked to the Republican party, it looked away." Jane Dailey's study of Virginia similarly noted that the Old Dominion's GOP "deserted black voters just at the moment they needed [it] most."[39]

Not all anti-Democrats were Populists, former Populists, Jeffersonians, and Independents, of course. Republicans made up a small but important part of the opposition to regular Democracy that could be found in Alabama. Lily-white Republicanism was strong, basically, where Populism and Independentism were strong: in those poor-white counties of north Alabama, the Hill Country, the Tennessee Valley, and the Wiregrass.[40] While the Republicans, like the Populists and Independents, still had serious differences with regular Alabama Democracy, the one thing virtually every white Alabamian could and did agree on was the desirability of removing blacks from the political process. White Republicans had, by and large, backed disfranchisement openly and vocally. Some students of the period have speculated that in Alabama perhaps a majority of the Populists joined the ranks of the lily-white GOP after 1896. This seems uncertain simply because of the math involved. If most of the Populists had joined the Republican Party, the GOP would have been huge in Alabama, much larger than it actually was. Still, it seems reasonable to conclude that many of the Populists did join the GOP.

Republicans had also provided support for the notion of an all-white direct primary that would purify politics and make political questions, by definition, white questions. In Republican thought, these developments built one upon the other and provided reason for optimism and the impetus for renewed efforts to make the Republican Party more exclusively white. William Vaughn, chairman of the state GOP, had always "contended that the republican party was inherently strong among the white people of Alabama." Now that disfranchisement had been legalized and codified, the GOP, Vaughn and other lily-whites thought, was "to have its great opportunity." "Every white man [would] show how he stands," and the lily whites were hopeful that, in a sanitized white political arena, their traditional strength in north Alabama and the piney woods could be built upon and extended.[41]

To this end, Alabama's lily whites inaugurated a purge movement contemporaneously with the disfranchisement and direct primary movements, designed to compound the racial purification of their party. The state party expelled A. J. Warner, W. J. Stevens, and T. J. Ellis, three "politically irresponsible colored men," for daring to run black candidates for the 1898 state GOP ticket.[42] Just as the Democratic-led disfranchisement movement found ample support from anti-Democrats and Republicans—and the poor-white and anti-Democrat-led white primary movement enjoyed backing from the regular Democrats and the Republicans—the lily-white movement perfected the triangular relationship of cooperation among whites of different parties to oust the black man from politics. Democrats and Jeffersonians cheered on the lily-whites' expulsion efforts against African Americans. "Here is our only wish," one Jeffersonian told the Republicans. "Put the negro out! That is our motto, yesterday, today and forever! Put them out, and once out, keep them out! This is a white man's country; let no black man presume to be officious."[43]

Lily-white leaders like William Vaughn had not always been such avid proponents of the racial cleansing of their party. Both Vaughn and another leading lily-white, Julius Bingham, had begun their political lives as "black and tan" Republican adversaries of Robert A. Moseley, Alabama's white Republican leader until 1896. Capitalizing on William McKinley and Mark Hanna's signal that they had no problem with the racial purification of the GOP in the South, Vaughn and Bingham renounced "black and tan" politics, took patronage positions as a U.S. district federal attorney and chief internal revenue collector for Alabama, respectively, and seized control of the Alabama GOP. Vaughn, aided by Hanna and McKinley, became state chairman of the Republican Party in 1896.[44]

Though Vaughn and Bingham did not agree on everything, they were of one mind on the fate of the African American. Soon after they seized control of the party machinery, they launched a formal movement to expel blacks from the Alabama Republican Party. In April 1902, they got a resolution passed that piggybacked on the 1901 Constitution to specify that only those citizens allowed by the new constitution to vote would be allowed to participate in Republican Party proceedings—a move that cut black Republicans out of the party councils in one fell swoop. And the lily-white leadership enforced their resolution by posting armed guards at the doors of its 1902 state convention, prompting black Republicans to file protests in Washington, D. C., and for some to threaten violence. Ad Wimbs, the only black member of the state executive committee, protested vigorously and vowed to appeal to the national party, while the *Huntsville Journal*'s black editor wrote that the white Republicans were more eager to expel blacks from politics than the Democrats had been. William Vaughn confirmed such dire predictions by bragging publicly that the Alabama GOP was no longer the "Negro party."[45]

Retribution was swift and sudden, and like most forms of liberal counterattack against the state's deeply rooted white supremacist tendencies, it came from Yankee "outsiders" and the federal government. Black appeals to the national Republican leadership did not fall on deaf ears, since McKinley's untimely assassination had left Theodore Roosevelt and his brand of progressive Republicanism in the White House. Roosevelt and General James Sullivan Clarkson, one of his chief aides, heard the appeals of black Alabama Republicans such as

Ad Wimbs, Bill Stevens, and Booker T. Washington and responded immediately with no-nonsense directives to the Alabama lily-whites to cease their expulsion efforts.[46]

The lily-whites may have been Republicans, but they were also white Alabamians, and they reacted in the way that has been synonymous with white Alabama for decades: defiance. One of the Republican's three state patronage referees, William Aldrich, began denying Roosevelt's recommendations and siding with Vaughn and Bingham in his appointments. The lily-white faction rewarded Aldrich by running him for the state house from Shelby County, while his brother, Truman, supplied editorial support and curried former-Populist support from the pages of his *Birmingham Times.* The *Huntsville Republican* weighed in by informing Teddy Roosevelt that, no matter how badly he wanted to, he could not stop "the white movement" in Alabama's GOP. Prominent industrialist, biblical scholar, and Republican leader James Bowron publicly advocated a white-only party in Alabama and proclaimed Roosevelt's biracial policy a "mistake." For his part, Julius Bingham packed his bags to travel to Washington to confront General Clarkson directly.[47]

The national forces won out convincingly, though. Clarkson rebuffed Bingham in person. The president axed William Vaughn as federal district attorney and Bingham as state revenue collector and forced the state party to rescind its resolution barring black participation. And at the 1904 National Republican Convention, Roosevelt's forces refused to seat the lily-white delegation from Alabama, forcing the southern Republicans to reopen their doors to black people.[48]

The Broader "Whitening" of Alabama

Disfranchisement in Alabama was the political expression of a larger contemporaneous movement that undertook to "whiten" life in the state in a whole inventory of areas. Denial of the right of blacks to vote occurred at roughly the same time that race relations were hardening in a variety of sectors. Jim Crow segregation, long practiced in a de facto sense, was becoming a reality in a de jure way as well.[49] Lynching, which in Alabama had customarily included whites as about a third of its victims, became increasingly reserved for African Americans only—a "black punishment" deemed inappropriate for whites as a crass transgression of the color line.[50] Progressivism itself, as a variety of scholars have demonstrated, was principally "for whites only."[51] Alabama's version furnished little exception to this rule. Reforms in health care, education, public welfare, and the like were remarkably skewed to benefit whites and usually to exclude blacks or to include them at only the most meager levels.

Disfranchisement, the direct primary, and lily-white Republicanism were the political expression of this broader whitening movement among virtually all white Alabamians. To deny the kinship of the turn-of-the-century whitening movement among the various classes of Alabama whites is to fail to appreciate a critical relationship between race, class, and politics. Elite white southerners have usually proven more adept at using the regional obsession with race, Reconstruction, and related emotional issues to protect their privileged status in a rigidly stratified and hierarchical society. This artifice has been the monopoly of no single party, but rather an all-purpose multiplier of plain-white votes for conservative purposes. At those times that plain whites put race or other emotional considerations ahead of their rational economic interests, allowing elite whites to benefit, plain whites bore a significant portion of responsibility for their own subsequent misfortune.

This relationship between race and class was perhaps the most fundamental point of southern politics in this period, as well as in most others. Conservative Democrats mastered the art of using an emotional brand of politics based on race to distract many plain whites from focusing on their economic interests. For a century, race and Reconstruction slights and "injustices" that focused on home rule and hostility and repugnance for federal government were the fodder for this type of Conservative Democratic politics.[52] Confronted by the modern Civil Rights movement, though, one-party Democratic strength gave way to rump, independent, and eventually Republican challenges. Often these elite challenges have succeeded by adding considerations of religion and morality to the racial staple—in essentially the same way that race was once used alone—to wage a politics that has been effective in distracting many plain whites from economic issues and instead garnering their support for elite issues. The underlying goal, for these modern conservatives as well as their Conservative Democratic forbears, has been the preservation of a *status quo society*—sharply divided, hierarchical in nature, and founded on the most traditional understanding of relations in the areas of race, gender, class, ethnicity, and religion.

Suffrage restriction in Alabama, as in other southern states, took place at about the same time that the color line was being drawn more definitively across a host of places. But aside from disfranchisement, probably the other single most notable "reform" of the Progressive Era in the South was segregation. Throughout the latter part of the nineteenth century, division of the races had been gaining increased currency in Dixie. Around the turn of the century, Jim Crow became even more standardized and concrete.[53] The hardening of Jim Crow occurred in Alabama as elsewhere throughout the South. In 1892, Alabama passed a segregation ordinance for railroads, street railways, and public education. Plain whites, such as Samuel M. Adams of Chilton County, took an active role in the development of Jim Crow. Adams, a Baptist minister, floor leader of the Farmer's Alliance in the Alabama House of Representatives, and later a Hill Country Populist leader, formally objected even to the word "equal" being included in the "separate but equal" bill. Adams withdrew his motion only after it was explained to him that the Jim Crow law had a better chance of passing court muster if the word "equal" were left in.[54] Upcountry Jeffersonians backed Jim Crow by recommending that America be divided into three distinct regions: one each for Yankees, southerners, and "niggers."[55]

Racial intolerance was also dramatically demonstrated in Alabama's continued use of mob rule. Lynching was "reformed" during the Progressive period, but its reforms were as curious as those in other sectors of social and political life. After 1900, the frequency of lynching declined dramatically. But at the same time, it became a practice reserved almost exclusively for blacks. During the 1890s, the decade when Alabama lynched more people than any other state, a full one-third of the mob's victims had been white. After 1900, though, blacks made up nearly all of Alabama's lynch victims (see tables 22 and 23 in the appendix).

Extralegal violence had long held a central place in southern society as a blunt instrument designed to hold back a host of black aspirations, both economic and political. After 1865 violence kept blacks tied to the farm, away from the polls, and even away from towns. Some scholars have stressed that extralegal violence and intimidation were even more important than the institution of the poll tax and other legal disfranchising mechanisms in keeping blacks away from the polls after the turn of the century.[56]

Despite the protests of some paternalists, the increased racialization of Alabama lynching was part of the general turn-of-the-century deterioration in race relations that actually nourished segregation and disfranchisement. Demagogues, appealing mostly to poor whites, combined anticommercial appeals in their most vulgar form with a blatant Negrophobia to help fan the flames of racial prejudice. Their efforts found fertile ground among poor whites, according to one historian, especially when blacks threatened the fragile economic status of poor whites by becoming strikebreakers in the mines, tenants in depressed farming counties, candidates for public office; were perceived as "uppity" in other ways; or, worst of all, posed some sort of sexual threat—real or perceived.[57] The sexual peril very clearly demonstrates the interrelated nature of various conceptual themes in the minds of poor whites. The sexual threat was serious because it was sexual, no doubt. But what made this gender threat lethal was its allied racial and economic aspects. Poor whites feared interracial sex like the plague, not simply because they had some philosophical aversion to the idea of miscegenation, or because they didn't like the idea of blacks and whites sleeping together. Interracial sex and—more to the point—interracial offspring, threatened the survival of the white race as a distinguishable race, replete with the economic and social privileges and preferences that even poor whites enjoyed because of their societal classification as "white."[58] In this way, poor whites, because of their precarious economic state, had at least as immediate a stake as their privileged white brethren in the maintenance and preservation of white supremacy.

Accordingly, Thomas Heflin's defense of lynching was not unusual among poor whites and those who represented them. The severity of the race/class/ sexual threat that was interracial sex ran to blood. For example, two Hill Country Jeffersonian newspapers that had supported the movement for disfranchisement reacted to a Saint Clair County incident in which authorities had prevented a lynching and, in the process, killed several members of the mob. It was "a pity" for authorities to kill "several white men in order to save the life of a brute" who was obviously "guilty of so heinous a crime" as raping and murdering "white women."[59] Plain-white insurgents mocked industrialist calls to end the reign of Judge Lynch by recommending that newspapers such as the *Birmingham Age-Herald* be given a dose "of calomel" and denounced such editorials as "soft, sticky, maudlin, poppy-rottish essays."[60] Reacting to Booker T. Washington's infamous White House dinner with Theodore Roosevelt, one anti-Redeemer declared that, should Washington ever violate white Alabama sensibilities in so brazen a manner, for "such a thing—he [would] take the rope-line route—which [meant] the nearest tree." Another newspaper, the Populist *Greenville Living Truth*, took a sectional posture. The Populists warned Yankees to stop their "intermeddling" in southern racial affairs because they understood "as much about the Southern negro . . . as they [did] the inhabitants of Mars" and were offering only "cheap and useless advice." The "worthy darky" had nothing to fear from his friend, the southern white man, the Populists explained. If a black lived down South and "behave[d] himself" then "he [would] be taken care of." If not, white southerners would deal with "bad negroes" in their "own way . . . in a swift and inexpensive way."[61]

This general whitening impulse dominated the political age in Alabama. But the era's other movements also intimately involved race and considerations of black suffrage. Prohibition, the age's most obvious moral reform, was no exception. Alcohol was thought to be especially dangerous as a passion inflamer. Dry forces often overtly advertised their efforts as necessary ones in order to protect "the white man and white woman from the violence of the liquor-crazed black." Others favored prohibition because they believed the law would provide Alabama with a population of "sober and industrious blacks." In 1907 the state legislature made local option the law, and forty-five counties went dry, but the issue continued to be prominent in state and local politics.[62]

As a rule, temperance advocates viewed disfranchisement as a positive reform because it removed the presence of the "wet" black vote. It also erased the more general distraction of black suffrage and freed whites to concentrate on the "real problem" at hand, alcohol. Prohibitionists attacked black "dives" as "Deep, Dark, Damnable Dens of Degradation" where blacks and whites rubbed elbows in easy familiarity, where black men visited white prostitutes—casting into jeopardy the purity and survival of the white race.[63] In this way, temperance forces successfully tapped into the deepest, darkest racial fears of the white Alabamian by tying together liquor, crime, and interracial sex. They particularly objected to the selling of liquor bottles with pictures of naked white women on them as an especially dangerous enticement, one that threatened to subvert the very foundations on which southern society rested.

The contemporaneous move for women's suffrage was intimately connected with the race issue as well. In fact, one historian of the subject has argued that in Alabama the women's suffrage issue actually "turned" on the race question. While a fruitful, vigorous, and diverse discussion of white supremacy's relevance to the cause of women's suffrage has taken place among scholars, it is clear that in Alabama, as with most political questions, the issue of white supremacy was extraordinarily important.[64]

Most southern proponents of women's suffrage favored a states'-rights approach to the problem as opposed to a federal law. According to their logic, state control was essential because it was the only guarantee that the extension of suffrage to women would not also result in the extension of the vote to *black* women or the return of suffrage to the black males who had just been removed from the voter rolls. Alabama suffragists Patti Ruffner Jacobs and Julia S. Tutwiler repeatedly assured state lawmakers that white women could be enfranchised without risking the enfranchisement of black women—or the reenfranchisement of black men—because the constitutional safeguards of 1901 would still work to block black voting of any kind.[65]

The forces aligned against ratification of the Nineteenth Amendment were formidable. Most daunting of all perhaps was the opponents' appropriation of the race issue and the language and symbolism that rested on the familiar and always malleable terrain of Reconstruction. Reliving the period was, of course, anathema to all but the rarest of whites. Even recalling the epoch conjured a primeval loathing of the African American that had been seared into the recesses of the region's mind by the racial "hell" of Reconstruction, when evil northern whites misled docile and ignorant blacks into rebelling against their natural white superiors. The Selma-based Alabama Association Opposed to Woman Suffrage asserted darkly that the proposed law was "the most dangerous blow aimed at . . . white supremacy since the Civil War" and adopted an official battle cry in keeping with other simple yet successful appeals to political emotion: "Home Rule, States' Rights, and White Supremacy."[66] The Woman's Anti-Ratification League, headquartered in Montgomery and led by Marie Bankhead Owen, declared itself "unalterably opposed to all interference by the federal government" and deemed it essential for the conservation of "social order and the maintenance of white supremacy" that states' rights be preserved forever.[67] A Montgomery judge branded the Nineteenth Amendment the "[b]lood brother of the Fourteenth and Fifteenth Amendments . . . conceived in inequity and born in sin based on . . . carpetbag scalawaggery, dominated by the most depraved considerations for racial equality." A state lawmaker opposed this "device of northern abolitionists," which would eradicate the wall "between the Anglo-Saxons and those who mongrelize and corrupt them" and would undo the noble work of the "wise and patriotic men who [had just] purified the ballot box from the contamination of negro votes." Do not "surrender our great state's control of her own electorate," he urged his peers, "into hands that may be regardless of our welfare, our happiness, . . . and our great traditions."[68] Such arguments—steeped in the blood and mythology of race and Reconstruction—resonated powerfully in early-twentieth-century Alabama, just as they had in 1901. The state failed to ratify the amendment.

Cognizant of the risks they had taken in helping to approve the new constitution, many poor whites approached education after 1901 as a kind of leverage they wanted reserved for themselves, not extended to their black economic competitors. In fact, many plain whites saw education as the key to their continued enfranchisement under the constitution's literacy provision—a tangible political, social, and economic advantage they held over blacks. During the convention, one Hill Country white representative had even declared that, above anything else, the white counties wanted to "disfranchise the darkeys and educate the white children." Organized labor had traditionally provided a beacon of light for at least the possibility of attempted biracial cooperation in the dark and inhospitable landscape that was the Deep South.[69] Granted, biracial labor activism was the imperfect function of a mixed bag of pragmatic and principled motives. Yet it was a far sight more progressive than the naked exploitation of racial tensions offered by industry and the chamber of commerce. But on the education issue, important elements of unionism stumbled. Around Alabama, working-class white spokesmen agitated for increased educational expenditures from the state, while lobbying to deny blacks the same funds. "The negro is a parasite," explained J. B. Wood, former president and secretary of the Birmingham Trades Council. "[H]e pays no taxes, no school taxes."[70] White urban workers joined rural white folk—dirt farmers, part-time artisans, and small to middling farmers—once the heart and soul of Alabama's Populist party, to continue to support the idea raised at the 1901 convention by plain-white delegates to tie state educational expenditures to the amount of taxes paid by each race.[71] Under the plan, white folk would profit from the taxes paid by privileged whites, while black education would suffer.

On the point of education for blacks, the interests of white organized labor and rural white folk often dovetailed. Plain whites proved adept at using the now obsolete arguments of older patricians that black education would open the door to social and political ambition and to racial conflict.[72] "This is a white man's country," organized labor spokesman Henry C. West declared. "I am opposed to negro education because it is an established fact that an 'educated negro' is as a rule a worthless imp." The first vice-president of the state federation of labor agreed: "[S]uch negroes are insolent, overbearing, contemptuous of white men, not amenable to discipline, and with a lurking disregard for law." The *Birmingham Labor Advocate*, official organ of the state branch of the American Federation of Labor, warned that schooling blacks would only inculcate a strong desire for political and social equality. If frustrated, conflict would ensue; if fulfilled, chaos would result. Such sentiments paralleled those of demagogues who appealed to poor whites throughout the South. According to the "White Chief," James K. Vardaman of Mississippi, blacks were "lazy, lying, lustful animal[s] [whose conduct] resemble[d] the hog's." Education would only "spoil a good field hand and make an insolent cook."[73]

In Alabama, the anti-Democrats' outlook on education for blacks, even vocational education, was dim. Education, now more than ever after passage of the 1901 Constitution, was understood as one of the most important levers to progress, prosperity, and power. As such, it had to be jealously guarded, just like the vote. Incursions on white educational advantage, implicitly understood as a type of insurgency against white domination, engendered the most intense emotions from whites. If anything, these emotions were even more sensitive and pronounced among the poor whites than other classes. It was the poor folk, after all, who most closely felt the hot breath of black economic and social ambition and competition. Because of their proximity, plain folk felt more vulnerable than other white groups—closest in terms of economic and social leveling to blacks in the eyes of society. Their reaction was intense, emotional, and raw. " 'All coons look alike' to us, educated or uneducated," explained one Hill Country Jeffersonian. They have "the same smell whether his name is Booker Washington" or not. He is "still a negro and should understand that he should remain in his proper place." Tampering with this natural order of things—by blacks or even by white patricians who sought to gain a practical education for blacks—could only result in disaster for the white race as a whole, poor whites predicted. Sexual purity and the very future of the white race was at stake, they claimed, relying on the emotional gender theme to keep both blacks and women in their "proper" places. " '[S]lobbering' over the educated negro," the Jeffersonians warned, encouraged blacks to "believe themselves equal to the white man" and invariably, "insults and assaults upon white women follow."[74]

Many poor whites, like other white southerners of differing classes, had a distinct aversion to taxes. In their minds, taxation was forever coupled with the stigma and stench of Reconstruction. Opposition to a new constitution, for some, centered on a fear of increased taxation, especially to finance education for blacks, which might lead to all kinds of social changes. An Alabama Jeffersonian who backed constitutional ratification echoed the demagogues: "The average negro has no more idea of mathematics, grammar, [and] rhetoric . . . than a hog knows about Sunday."[75] Plain whites in the hills of Marshall, Fayette, DeKalb, and Etowah Counties, and in Piney Woods and Wiregrass counties like Crenshaw, objected strenuously to having any percentage of their taxes go to educating blacks. It "almost shatter[ed their] patriotism" to know that they "continue ruining . . . field hands." While the plain folk couched much of their complaint in terms of the futility of continuing to "help" African Americans, self-interest and self-preservation were motives easy to discern just beneath the altruistic veneer of their rhetoric. "For thirty-five years the negro has been advised, tutored, helped, financially and every otherwise . . . with the hope that he would see its good and help himself," Fayette whites lamented, "but we see them today as about as far from it as they ever were." Booker T. Washington is about "the only blackberry on the vine." A number of the anti-Democrats coupled their opposition to taxation and the whole concept of black education with full-throated exhortations to white farmers to get themselves educated.[76]

If vulgarity is an index of how deeply the poor whites were frightened by the prospect of a literate and hence reenfranchised black population, the conclusion is inescapable. The fear was intense, their anxiety palpable. But it was more than fear and worry that drove them. A definite, almost desperate type of self-conscious superiority was at work as well. Blacks were so inferior, so innately and immanently less capable, that their efforts to improve themselves were pathetic—and even a little offensive. Controlled rage mixed with abject fear, haunting worry, and even outright disdain in a witch's brew of poor-white emotion over the threat. Consider the reaction of a Hill Country Jeffersonian to the news that a black kindergarten had opened in Tuskegee: "Imagine thirty dirty-nosed, rusty-heeled, bench-legged, flat-footed, knock-kneed pickaninies bevied together around the knees of an ebon schoolmarm, lisping in Ethiopian lingo! A beautiful sight to see! Close your eyes and view the prospect o'er."[77]

Other anti-Democrats, in the Upcountry and elsewhere, recommended that blacks know their place, satisfy themselves with their station as whites defined it, and pay attention to improving their depraved moral state rather than their intellectual prospects. First, advised one Hill Country Republican who had favored the disfranchisement constitution, they should "educate the Negro on morals, teaching him self-respect, and that labor is honorable." "Above all," the Republicans advised in summoning the pat rationale for black docility and submission, "let the Negro understand that his best friend is the southern white man."[78] Integration of the sort practiced in some northern schools was infamous—and completely alien. It was perfectly "outrageous" that white and black students should be "forced together thus," wrote a Hill Country Populist editor. "Such a thing" was representative of a debauched northern culture and "would not be tolerated in the South."[79]

As it turned out, plain whites did not have much to fear from the type of educational reform pushed by Alabama's paternalists and fledgling progressives. In virtually every way, the disadvantages facing black schools were actually exacerbated by the era's "reforms." After a decade and a half of such reform, in 1909, 74 percent of Alabama's white children attended school compared to only 46 percent of black children; the average white school year ran 131 days compared to only 90 for blacks; the state had almost twenty-five hundred more schools for whites than for blacks although the populations of black and white school-age children were actually quite close in size; and black teachers made only half of what white teachers were paid.[80] Black students enjoyed access to only 8 percent of the state's $262,218 worth of educational equipment and only twenty-five of the state's almost four hundred public-school libraries.[81] Although blacks made up nearly 90 percent of Alabama's prison population in 1896, and many of these inmates were petty offenders who were quite young, Alabama did not establish a black reform school until eleven years after one had been built for whites.[82]

But patrician rhetoric to the contrary, many Alabama whites were not enthusiastic about black education. For their part, many Black Belt whites were reluctant to use their state education funds for black schools even though they received more money from the state than the white counties precisely because of their large black populations. The ruling basis of the appropriation was total population.[83] Jim Crow implied a dual system in education—as in public health, transportation, welfare, and social services—often with few dollars available to finance even one set of facilities adequately. Segregation condemned blacks to inadequate funds, subpar quality, and poor facilities—if not outright exclusion. One Black Belt school superintendent frankly explained that black education

was acceptable only as long as it could be accomplished "without too great a sacrifice on the part of the white taxpayers."[84] In some respects, disparities between
the races were only widened by the "reform," leaving for future generations the
riddle of a Jim Crow educational system of woeful inequity, lopsided facilities,
and racial imbalance.

Because of the perverting power of race and the overarching self-interest of
the various white groups competing for power, the progressive impulse achieved
similar results in myriad other areas. In public health reform, as in education,
Alabama whites were generally reluctant to see their tax dollars go for improvements that would benefit people of color. As a result, Jim Crow facilities for
blacks remained fewer, inferior, and more irregular. They were staffed by black
volunteers, maintained by meager black funds, and usually came into existence
long after parallel white facilities had already been put into place. The story was
much the same in recreation, welfare, social services, and farm extension work.
Yet when outside aid came, southern whites, so often averse to accepting advice
from northerners on racial matters, had considerably less difficulty accepting
Yankee dollars.[85]

The influence of race during the Progressive Era continued a tradition in the
Deep South in which race and racial considerations managed to twist and con-
tort the course of history. Race repeatedly exerted pressure on poor whites to ally
themselves with their privileged white "betters" against their own class interests
and potential biracial alliance, and race produced a series of reforms that largely
made life better for whites and worse or no better for blacks. During the Progressive Era, the consuming desire of Alabama whites to control race relations,
combined with an obsessive fear of revisiting Reconstruction, led to a curious
series of "reforms." The results were often distortions more extreme than mere
paradox, contradiction, or irony. Not surprisingly, confusion has reigned. Be it
Populism, Progressivism, or a host of other reform movements, historians have
disagreed endlessly, and with a resultant and concluding confusion as to the
very essence or elementary nature of these movements.[86]

In a very real way, the racism that permeated the Progressive Era in the South
also perverted the movement as a whole. Combined with the era's genuine and
unarguably beneficial reforms in a host of areas, the racism resulted in a weird,
variegated, almost contradictory movement in Alabama and the Deep South:
the elevation of the white race (including some poor and many middle-class
whites) with the simultaneous and increased solidification of repression for
blacks. Much of Alabama Progressivism, like much of southern Progressivism
generally, was played as a zero-sum game in which whites believed progress was
attainable only with a corresponding decline in black status—and the status of
any poor whites who sought to make common cause with blacks.

Consider the most self-conscious political "reform" of the Progressive Era in Alabama, the 1901 Constitution. There can be little question that its framers saw themselves as engaged in a decidedly "progressive" endeavor: removing fraud, corruption, and undesirable elements from politics; and establishing honest elections. They talked endlessly of its God-ordained qualities and endemic virtue.[87] But the ultimate product of their labors was a curiosity fit for the ages—a document that purified and reformed politics through exclusionary, undemocratic, and frankly unconstitutional means.[88] Although at least one lone voice had called for the 1901 Constitution to release the state from its seemingly endless reaction to Reconstruction, the new document did no such thing.

Disfranchisement, of course, was a direct reaction to the Reconstruction inauguration of black voting. But the obvious racial exclusion and the more hidden class-oriented exclusion of poor whites were not the only results of the constitution tied to Alabama's conservative Reconstruction legacy. The document did effect disfranchisement in clinically creating a more purely conservative electorate. But it also imposed an exceedingly conservative set of results on the state—a direct reflection of the railroad, corporation, and large landholding interests that controlled the constitutional convention.[89] For example, the 1901 Constitution did not remove the restrictive safeguards on taxation favored by in-state landholders and out-of-state absentee landlords and industrialists, setting up a tax system that would saddle Alabama with financial problems for a century as the nation's lowest taxed state. Nor did the constitution remove the retrenchment provisions that were so prominent in Alabama's 1875 Constitution.[90] It did not provide for an elective railroad commission to regulate bloated freight rates, ignored the blights of convict-lease and child labor, rejected the principal of local taxation for education, declined to reestablish a state board of education, added a debt limit for counties and municipalities, set a lower ceiling on state and county taxes, failed to provide for internal improvements that would have likely been financed by taxation, declined to set a limit on the state acreage a single corporation could hold, and furnished only a modicum of municipal reform.[91]

The period in Alabama was also colored by related attempts to memorialize the Lost Cause, disparage Reconstruction, glorify Redemption, romanticize the Reconstruction Klan, and paint a dark picture of the era as a tragic time of black rule, Yankee pillage, federal repression, corruption, and chaos. One such memorial ceremony, in April 1903, attracted a record crowd of fifty-five hundred people across north Alabama to Florence, where they heard a Confederate veteran give a speech that repudiated virtually every despised aspect of the Reconstruction syndrome: blacks, Yankees, outsiders, the federal government, taxes, and liberalism.[92]

In an Alabama that was in the midst of its greatest "whitening," the marriage of the progressive impulse with a pervasive and enduring racism and a determination to preserve white supremacy in a host of areas produced a bizarre series of reform offspring. More drastic than mere irony or contradiction, the products of these unions between reform and racism often constituted profound and stubbornly persistent distortions.[93] Some were monstrously deformed progeny that today defy conventional labels such as "conservative" or "liberal." Combining the two produced tragic and perverse legacies of contradiction with which future generations would have to wrestle. The essence of the perverting of the reform impulse lay in a determination by white Alabamians that controlling race relations and not revisiting Reconstruction should be involved in virtually every facet of their lives: education, health, welfare, recreation, criminal justice, public services, temperance, women's suffrage, public ceremonial functions, and, above all, politics.[94]

CONCLUSION

 We can wish, we can hope, we can pray that ordinary citizens, in all times and in all places, will make political decisions based on rational estimations of their political interests. But we cannot ignore the historical record.

It is clear that in turn-of-the-century Alabama, other forces were at play for plain-white people besides just rational evaluation. Emotion played a very large role in this story: decision making based on emotional, hot-button issues.

In 1901 Alabama, race and the retention of white supremacy were the most powerful emotional issues available. They were the preeminent "card" that could be played by the elite defenders of Alabama's status quo to sway the masses to their way of thinking. They played it—quite skillfully and with much experience. And to a degree that many historians have been unable or unwilling to see, it worked.

It is not the position of this study that previous scholars actually saw evidence contrary to the disfranchisement myth they eventually constructed and purposely ignored such evidence. This study maintains only that their questions, and focus, and perspectives, and energies, and perhaps even their own emotions were concentrated in another direction: discerning plain-white rationality and examples of class consciousness.

To be sure, there is plenty of evidence that such rationality and consciousness were present among the plain folk—even at the turn of the century, even in a Deep South setting such as Alabama. But while this side of the story has been given due attention—perhaps more than its due attention—the other side has not.

It is not a pretty sight to see plain people unwittingly work harm to their future prospects because of a shortsighted indulgence of emotion and, in fact, of prejudice. But to a larger extent than has been allowed, this happened as well in Alabama in 1901.

Nothing is to be gained by dismissing the darker side of this record—except perhaps a temporary and ultimately false sense of solace and contentment. But there is, potentially at least, far more to be learned from the frank engagement of those darker corners of our collective historical past; those times when and where ordinary people indulged the darker impulses of their natures only to work a lasting disservice to their own prospects, both material and political.

The turn of the century was not the first time, nor would it be the last, that significant numbers of plain whites in Alabama let themselves be distracted by a politics of emotion. In 1901, and before, during Reconstruction and even the 1880s and 1890s, *the* issue was race, with its ever-attendant fear and animus toward a "meddling" federal government and the unwanted attentions of Yankee outsiders. The political party that worked these deep-seated, ingrained, and fiercely held passions of the common folk to their advantage was the party of wealth, power, and prestige in the Solid South: the Democratic Party or, to be more precise, the Democratic and Conservative Party. After all, the privileged shared with the plain these deeply rooted antifederal and white supremacist beliefs. And race, or rather allegiance to the doctrine of white supremacy, did not stand alone, like some sacred statue suspended in a vacuum. Every major societal institution and buttress was mobilized to support it—religious, patriotic, social, civic. In such a society, adherence to this race-based notion of conformity was the telling mark of a godly person, a solid citizen, a devout patriot—in fact, the mark of a good human being. A very strong *principle of moral reflection* was at work. A vote for the right side of white supremacy was not merely a vote on some abstract political issue; it was a statement, a public proclamation to one's friends and neighbors as well as to oneself, that an individual was a solid citizen, a reliable patriot, a religious and upstanding person, and a good human being. A vote for the other side was interpreted as a statement in the opposite direction—a declaration that one was suspect, morally inferior, not completely trustworthy, a position that often led to the social ostracism and community scorn due political treason and religious heresy.

Later, during the 1920s, folk resentment of the Bourbons would again coalesce and seethe, almost reaching a boiling point. But again, to a large extent, Alabama's plain folk would get sidetracked by other issues, mainly focused on people who were in some way different from themselves: alcohol would become an obsession, immigration, traditional family values and conventional gender roles, morality, nativism, anti-Catholicism, anti-Semitism, and the ever-present racism. Plain-folk distrust of corporate concentration and planter-industrialist unresponsiveness would eventually self-destruct in an orgy of hatred and violence represented by the gigantic Ku Klux Klan. Despite several encouraging early victories over the machine, poor and middle-class folk left few lasting marks of triumph over their privileged antagonists.

Then came the unprecedented crises and storms of the Great Depression, when most people were too busy trying to feed themselves to spend energy on the largely imaginary threats posed by different races, creeds, and nationalities. Afterward, though, another war, a new wave of superpatriotism, and national civil rights initiatives would again attract plain folk to a new, but still in many ways same, old standard: the Dixiecrat standard, the Klan's fiery cross, "massive resistance," and even George Wallace's third-party politics.

Eventually, though, as the national parties slowly swapped places on the race issue, southern partisan allegiances reflected the switch. Still, white southerners themselves remained strangely transfixed in terms of political ideology even in the midst of a series of high-profile partisan shifts: still compelled by racial conservatism, tax cuts, laissez-faire economics (except when government intervention helped business), and hyperpatriotism. As the years went by, Alabama and the South became more and more Republican in outlook, instead of solidly Democratic, as they had once been. But Alabama did not change its essential political self or ideology. Only the labels of the party that would cater to Alabama's enduring predilections changed. For Alabamians, the ascendancy of the Republican Party has not meant deliverance from the weight of a politics waged principally on emotion rather than reason. On the contrary, the race issue has remained ever present—more muted, more subtle, expressed in more sophisticated ways, to be sure, but ever present and ever vital. To this has been added a morality-based notion of conformity and good citizenship that has largely displaced the less subtle and now mostly discredited overt racial appeal. In this morality-based conformity type of politics, good citizenship, patriotism, reliability, and social acceptance have been increasingly defined as an allegiance to a canon of religious and moral positions that, it is clear, has much to do with emotion. What is not as clear is if the orthodoxy has a significant relationship to the day-to-day lives and fortunes of most average Alabamians. Issues such as gun control, abortion, prayer in the schools, homosexual rights, hyperpatriotism, militarism, national loyalty, and display of the Ten Commandments and the Confederate battle flag now augment the battery of emotional politics that once stood alone on the pillar of white supremacy. Like race-based conformist politics, the morality-based variant has much to do with psychological and emotional feelings of superiority toward those who do not subscribe to the majority orthodoxy. In a sense, it is the new racism, a litmus test of southern conformity and social acceptance based on moral chauvinism in addition to just white supremacy. This kind of test of convention can give instant and easily understood results as to who is a reliable and good citizen and who is not. Yet this kind of politics, for so long controlled by the Conservative Democratic Party in the South, has, in recent decades, become increasingly dominated by the GOP. Although expressed under a different party banner in recent years, this brand of politics is no less reliant on keeping millions of average citizens so worked up about their fears, anxieties, and dislikes that they have difficulty focusing on economic, bread-and-butter, some would even say, rational, issues.

It is not enough simply to look at the events of 1901 and acknowledge that the Populists were racists and move on—as if taking some routine inventory of the many human frailties we all possess. It is not sufficient simply to blame the most powerful and wealthy in society for raising, abusing, and then exploiting the race issue—however accurate that assessment is. An equally important question is how and to what extent did such an appeal resonate with the common folk; what effect did it have; and to what degree did indulging that limitation and prejudice affect the fortunes of plain whites *and* plain blacks? Populists, independents, and anti-Democrats of all stripes in late-nineteenth- and early-twentieth-century Alabama made an attempt at mounting a biracial political challenge to entrenched, conservative, oligarchical rule. Various successes were achieved, but no lasting change was effected. It could be argued that fair elections did not take place in Alabama between 1874 and the Second Reconstruction. So, without viable federal supervision, fair adjudication at the polls regardless of the nature of the political challenge was a structural impossibility. Between 1874 and 1901, electoral fraud in Alabama and the South was rife. After 1901, the character of electoral dishonesty was different yet no less severe. Fraud and ballot-box stuffing were replaced by the statutory exclusion of hundreds of thousands of blacks and poor whites.

That fact still begs the question of the lasting effects of significant numbers of the Jeffersonians turning their backs on their erstwhile black allies to participate in their formal exclusion through the disfranchisement constitution, the all-white primary, and lily-white party politics. To what extent did poor whites buy the racial arguments of the privileged on suffrage restriction, and what effects did that white solidarity have? Some stubborn African Americans in Alabama, no matter how intense the economic appeal of the anti-Redeemers, preferred to cast their lot with that of privileged Democracy. No doubt old slave ties played a role for some, as did old and new black distrust of the plain folk. For plain whites, racial prejudice may have been understandable, if not attractive or particularly noble. It might have been only a form of human frailty. But indulging the doctrine and prejudice of white supremacy was a luxury the insurgents did not have. Unlike their privileged adversaries, the Jeffersonians depended on black comity for survival. Any independent challenge to the planter-industrialist clique did. Participation in, and even sympathy with, the cause of excluding blacks from the political process eroded the credibility of white insurgents, fed black distrust, and did nothing to help the prospects for biracial, class-based political reform in the future. Because of the nature of the political revolt, racism came at a price for the anti-Democrats—a price far higher than that paid by their privileged planter-industrialist adversaries.

As difficult as it is for southerners to engage the lessons of 1901, we would do well to try. Then perhaps we might recognize the striking parallels between the old race and Reconstruction-based politics and the newer politics of emotion; between the old reliance on race to define good citizenship in a way that served Conservative Democrats and the newer reliance on religious and moral chauvinism that has augmented race to serve the recent Republican ascendance. We might also recognize the enduring resonance of these issues with the southern white electorate. Therein lies, perhaps, the only hope of preventing a historian a century from now from setting down another sobering experience for yet another generation to read.

APPENDIX

Table 1. Alabama's Black Belt Counties* and Black Population in 1900

County	White	Black	Percent Black
Autauga	6,742	11,173	62
Barbour	12,781	22,371	64
Bullock	5,846	26,097	82
Choctaw	7,858	10,277	57
Clarke	11,952	15,829	57
Dallas	9,285	45,372	83
Greene	3,307	20,875	86
Hale	5,664	25,347	82
Lee	12,759	19,067	60
Lowndes	4,762	30,889	87
Macon	4,252	18,874	82
Marengo	8,841	29,473	77
Monroe	10,529	13,116	55
Montgomery	19,825	52,207	72
Perry	6,821	24,962	79
Pickens	10,481	13,921	57
Russell	5,930	21,152	78
Sumter	5,672	27,038	83
Wilcox	6,979	28,652	80

Sources: The 1900 population statistics are compiled from figures in the *Twelfth Census of the United States,* vol. 1: *Population,* part 1, table 19, p. 529. I also used the physiographic map located in Webb, *Two-Party Politics in the One-Party South,* xii.

* For purposes of the tables in this volume, a Black Belt county in Alabama is defined as one that is physiographically part of the Black Belt (i.e., having rich, dark, fertile soil) and in which African Americans comprised at least 55 percent of the population in the 1900 Census. If a 60 percent black majority had been used, counties with definite Black Belt characteristics such as Choctaw, Clarke, Monroe, and Pickens would not have been included.

Table 2. Alabama's White Counties* and Black Population in 1900

County	White	Black	Percent Black	Percent of Total Male Voting-Age Population Black
Baldwin	9,015	4,179	32	33
Bibb	12,285	6,213	34	34
Blount	21,338	1,781	8	32
Butler	12,514	13,246	51	48
Calhoun	24,247	10,626	30	29
Chambers	15,139	17,415	53	49
Cherokee	18,080	3,016	14	15
Chilton	13,258	3,264	20	19
Clay	15,215	1,884	11	11
Cleburne	12,325	881	7	6
Coffee	16,739	4,233	20	22
Colbert	12,795	9,546	43	39
Conecuh	9,720	7,793	44	43
Coosa	10,856	5,288	33	29
Covington	12,912	2,434	16	22
Crenshaw	14,057	5,601	28	27
Cullman	17,828	21	0	0
Dale	16,320	4,869	23	22
DeKalb	22,586	972	4	4
Elmore	14,048	12,051	46	45
Escambia	7,683	3,515	31	33
Etowah	22,995	4,366	16	16
Fayette	12,431	1,701	12	11
Franklin	14,353	2,158	13	17
Geneva	15,878	3,218	17	22
Henry	22,543	13,604	38	37
Jackson	26,860	3,642	12	10
Jefferson	83,489	56,917	41	43
Lamar	13,015	3,069	19	17
Lauderdale	19,169	7,390	28	26
Lawrence	12,967	7,156	36	22
Limestone	12,558	9,828	44	41
Madison	23,827	19,875	45	42
Marion	13,716	778	5	10
Marshall	21,789	1,500	6	6
Mobile	34,306	28,409	45	43
Morgan	21,439	7,378	26	24
Pike	16,697	12,474	43	41
Randolph	16,469	5,178	24	22
Saint Clair	15,983	3,442	18	17

continued

Table 2. *Continued*

County	White	Black	Percent Black	Percent of Total Male Voting-Age Population Black
Shelby	16,680	7,004	30	31
Talladega	17,547	18,223	51	48
Tallapoosa	18,987	10,688	36	32
Tuscaloosa	21,509	14,638	40	39
Walker	21,046	4,116	16	21
Washington	6,106	5,028	45	45
Winston	9,547	7	0	1

Sources: Black population statistics by county in 1900 from the *Twelfth Census of the United States,* vol. 1: *Population,* part 1, table 19, p. 529. Physiographic characteristics from the map located in Webb, *Two-Party Politics in the One-Party South,* xii. Percentage of blacks in total male voting age population in 1900 from the map located in appendix 1 in Hackney, *Populism to Progressivism in Alabama,* 335.

* For purposes of the tables in this volume, a white county in Alabama is defined as one that is physiographically part of the Tennessee Valley, Hill Country, Wiregrass, or Gulf Coast Plain and in which African Americans comprised less than 50 percent of the total male voting-age population in 1900 and less than 55 percent of the population in the 1900 Census.

Table 3. White Counties and Their Vote in the 1900 U.S. Senate Election

"For" Morgan	"For" Johnston
Baldwin	Jackson
Bibb	Marshall
Blount	Saint Clair
Butler	Winston
Calhoun	
Chambers	
Cherokee	
Chilton	
Clay	
Cleburne	
Coffee	
Colbert	
Conecuh	
Coosa	
Covington	
Crenshaw	
Cullman	
Dale	
DeKalb	
Elmore	
Escambia	
Etowah	
Fayette	
Franklin	
Geneva	
Henry	
Jefferson	
Lamar	
Lauderdale	
Lawrence	
Limestone	
Madison	
Marion	
Mobile	
Morgan	
Pike	
Randolph	
Shelby	
Talladega	
Tallapoosa	
Tuscaloosa	
Walker	
Washington	

Source: *Birmingham Age-Herald,* 15 Apr. 1900, 1.

Table 4. Vote in Alabama's Black Belt on April 1901 Referendum Calling the Convention

County	Votes "for" Calling	Votes "against" Calling	Percent "for" Calling
Autauga	512	63	89
Barbour	1,361	347	80
Bullock	371	149	71
Choctaw	498	349	59
Clarke	531	247	68
Dallas	5,668	200	97
Greene	1,479	19	99
Hale	2,318	66	97
Lee	1,487	547	73
Lowndes	3,226	338	91
Macon	372	299	55
Marengo	2,197	241	90
Monroe	429	166	72
Montgomery	1,137	233	83
Perry	2,295	43	98
Pickens	241	209	54
Russell	807	66	92
Sumter	1,440	69	95
Wilcox	1,689	25	99
TOTAL	28,058	3,676	88

Source: Compiled from figures in the *Alabama Official and Statistical Register*, 141–42.

Table 5. Vote in Alabama's White Counties on April 1901 Referendum Calling the Convention

County	Votes "for" Calling	Votes "against" Calling	Percent "for" Calling
Baldwin	302	553	35
Bibb	719	565	56
Blount	912	1,256	42
Butler	950	1,099	46
Calhoun	949	760	56
Chambers	3,194	498	87
Cherokee	340	1,186	22
Chilton	361	1,239	23
Clay	883	1,204	42
Cleburne	225	203	53
Coffee	311	368	46
Colbert	1,175	713	62
Conecuh	660	1,142	37
Coosa	854	1,135	43
Covington	662	446	61
Crenshaw	735	743	50
Cullman	540	1,452	27
Dale	574	1,040	36
DeKalb	785	1,357	37
Elmore	1,147	1,480	44
Escambia	357	166	68
Etowah	929	1,118	45
Fayette	427	856	33
Franklin	464	975	32
Geneva	370	820	31
Henry	1,029	786	57
Jackson	942	1,223	44
Jefferson	1,913	1,893	50
Lamar	436	243	64
Lauderdale	1,050	1,229	46
Lawrence	1,144	507	69
Limestone	1,394	1,213	53
Madison	2,551	1,521	63
Marion	627	751	46
Marshall	286	1,021	22
Mobile	696	378	65
Morgan	1,254	652	66
Pike	1,121	958	54
Randolph	740	114	87
Saint Clair	429	1,261	25

continued

Table 5. Continued

County	Votes "for" Calling	Votes "against" Calling	Percent "for" Calling
Shelby	660	1,106	37
Talladega	1,892	640	75
Tallapoosa	2,063	1,360	60
Tuscaloosa	848	569	60
Walker	1,599	1,276	56
Washington	373	80	82
Winston	375	684	35
TOTAL	42,247	41,829	50

Source: Compiled from figures in the *Alabama Official and Statistical Register,* 141–42.

Table 6. Vote in Alabama's Black Belt and White Counties on April 1901 Referendum Calling the Convention

Place	Votes "For"	Votes "Against"	Percent "For"
Black Belt (19)	28,058	3,676	88*
White Counties (47)	42,247	41,829	50†
Statewide	70,305	45,505	61
Percent of Statewide Vote "for" Coming from Black Belt	40	—	
Percent of Statewide Vote "for" Coming from White Counties	60	—	
Percent of Statewide Vote "against" Coming from Black Belt	—	8	
Percent of Statewide Vote "against" Coming from White Counties	—	92‡	

Source: Figures compiled from the *Alabama Official and Statistical Register*, 141–42.

*That almost 90 percent of the Black Belt voted "for" calling the disfranchisement convention is usually the first point of focus for scholars examining the issue.

†An often unnoticed point is that the white counties, while they did supply the bulk of opposition to calling the convention, did not do so in a consensus manner. On a percentage basis, the vote was split in half in the white counties, with an actual numerical majority voting "for" calling the disfranchisement convention. This indicates that the racial appeal of the constitution's effectiveness in disfranchising blacks won over many white voters in the white counties—virtually half of them, given the figures. In addition, the fact that blacks still voted relatively freely outside the Black Belt, and we can safely assume that most blacks voted "against" calling a convention advertised as seeking their own disfranchisement, further detracts from the split white vote in the white counties. That is, if the vote was split in the white counties among all voters, factoring out the black vote as "against" calling the convention, we see that a clear majority of white voters in the white counties voted "for" calling the disfranchisement convention.

‡That over 90 percent of the opposition to calling the convention came from the white counties is another point of focus for scholars. This fact, taken in conjunction with the first point noted here, has led to the mythical dichotomy of Black Belt support for disfranchisement and white-county resistance against it.

Table 7. Vote by Alabama Region on April 1901 Referendum Calling the Convention

	Counties "For" (Percent "For")		Counties "Against" (Percent "For")	
I. TENNESSEE VALLEY (5–2)				
	Colbert	(62)	Jackson	(44)
	Lawrence	(69)	Lauderdale	(46)
	Limestone	(53)		
	Madison	(63)		
	Morgan	(66)		
II. HILL COUNTRY (11–16)				
	Bibb	(56)	Blount	(42)
	Calhoun	(56)	Cherokee	(22)
	Chambers	(87)	Chilton	(23)
	Cleburne	(53)	Clay	(42)
	Jefferson	(50)	Coosa	(43)
	Lamar	(64)	Cullman	(27)
	Randolph	(87)	DeKalb	(37)
	Talladega	(75)	Elmore	(44)
	Tallapoosa	(60)	Etowah	(45)
	Tuscaloosa	(60)	Fayette	(33)
	Walker	(56)	Franklin	(32)
			Marion	(46)
			Marshall	(22)
			Shelby	(37)
			Saint Clair	(25)
			Winston	(35)
III. WIREGRASS (5–5)				
	Covington	(61)	Butler	(46)
	Crenshaw	(50)	Coffee	(46)
	Escambia	(68)	Conecuh	(37)
	Henry	(57)	Dale	(36)
	Pike	(54)	Geneva	(31)
IV. GULF COAST PLAIN (2–1)				
	Mobile	(65)	Baldwin	(35)
	Washington	(82)		
V. BLACK BELT (19–0)				
	Autauga	(89)		
	Barbour	(80)		
	Bullock	(71)		
	Choctaw	(59)		
	Clarke	(68)		
	Dallas	(97)		
	Greene	(99)		
	Hale	(97)		

continued

Table 7. Continued

	Counties "For" (Percent "For")	Counties "Against" (Percent "For")
Lee	(73)	
Lowndes	(91)	
Macon	(55)	
Marengo	(90)	
Monroe	(72)	
Montgomery	(83)	
Perry	(98)	
Pickens	(54)	
Russell	(92)	
Sumter	(95)	
Wilcox	(99)	

Source: Voting results from the *Alabama Official and Statistical Register,* 141–42. Physiographic regions from the map in Webb, *Two-Party Politics in the One-Party South,* xii.

Table 8. Alabama's White Counties, Black Population, and Vote on April 1901 Referendum Calling the Convention

County	Percent Black	Percent of Total Male Voting-Age Population Black	Percent "For"
Baldwin	32	33	35
Bibb	34	34	56
Blount	8	32	42
Butler	51	48	46
Calhoun	30	29	56
Chambers	53	49	87
Cherokee	14	15	22
Chilton	20	19	23
Clay	11	11	42
Cleburne	7	6	53
Coffee	20	22	46
Colbert	43	39	62
Conecuh	44	43	37
Coosa	33	29	43
Covington	16	22	61
Crenshaw	28	27	50
Cullman	0	0	27
Dale	23	22	36
DeKalb	4	4	37
Elmore	46	45	44
Escambia	31	33	68
Etowah	16	16	45
Fayette	12	11	33
Franklin	13	17	32
Geneva	17	22	31
Henry	38	37	57
Jackson	12	10	44
Jefferson	41	43	50
Lamar	19	17	64
Lauderdale	28	26	46
Lawrence	36	22	69
Limestone	44	41	53
Madison	45	42	63
Marion	5	10	46
Marshall	6	6	22
Mobile	45	43	65
Morgan	26	24	66
Pike	43	41	54
Randolph	24	22	87

continued

Table 8. Continued

County	Percent Black	Percent of Total Male Voting-Age Population Black	Percent "For"
Saint Clair	18	17	25
Shelby	30	31	37
Talladega	51	48	75
Tallapoosa	36	32	60
Tuscaloosa	40	39	60
Walker	16	21	56
Washington	45	45	82
Winston	0	1	35

Sources: Black population statistics from the *Twelfth Census of the United States*, vol. 1: *Population*, part 1, table 19, p. 529. Voting returns from the *Alabama Official and Statistical Register*, 141–42. Percentage of total male voting-age population from map located in appendix 1 in Hackney, *Populism to Progressivism in Alabama*, 335.

Table 9. Vote in Alabama's Black Belt on November 1901 Referendum on Ratification of the Constitution

County	Votes "For"	Votes "Against"	Percent "For"
Autauga	905	920	50
Barbour	2,905	1,121	72
Bullock	962	560	63
Choctaw	862	983	47
Clarke	1,448	444	77
Dallas	8,125	235	97
Greene	1,077	101	91
Hale	4,698	95	98
Lee	1,174	2,371	33
Lowndes	1,390	1,642	46
Macon	1,073	190	85
Marengo	1,958	341	85
Monroe	1,039	442	70
Montgomery	4,285	1,224	78
Perry	3,209	88	97
Pickens	869	417	58
Russell	1,865	649	74
Sumter	2,930	168	95
Wilcox	4,652	178	96
TOTAL	45,426	12,169	
AVERAGE			79

Source: Compiled from figures in the *Alabama Official and Statistical Register,* 141–42.

Table 10. Vote in Alabama's White Counties on November 1901 Referendum on Ratification of the Constitution

County	Votes "For"	Votes "Against"	Percent "For"
Baldwin	508	414	55
Bibb	1,210	1,044	54
Blount	795	1,692	32
Butler	1,058	1,705	38
Calhoun	2,546	1,929	57
Chambers	4,604	553	89
Cherokee	508	1,442	26
Chilton	394	1,664	19
Clay	683	1,709	29
Cleburne	1,459	740	66
Coffee	778	833	48
Colbert	2,011	748	73
Conecuh	834	1,174	42
Coosa	948	1,355	41
Covington	698	1,023	41
Crenshaw	1,249	835	60
Cullman	544	1,764	24
Dale	753	1,710	31
DeKalb	812	1,572	34
Elmore	1,757	543	76
Escambia	703	450	61
Etowah	1,189	2,141	36
Fayette	542	1,031	34
Franklin	528	1,245	30
Geneva	527	1,024	34
Henry	1,882	1,590	54
Jackson	633	2,893	18
Jefferson	8,088	6,160	57
Lamar	677	678	50
Lauderdale	1,125	2,046	35
Lawrence	1,229	872	58
Limestone	2,243	584	79
Madison	4,255	2,244	65
Marion	515	1,411	26
Marshall	401	2,217	15
Mobile	1,862	1,867	50
Morgan	1,066	2,249	31
Pike	1,627	1,185	58
Randolph	1,365	1,304	51
Saint Clair	387	1,572	20

continued

Table 10. Continued

County	Votes "For"	Votes "Against"	Percent "For"
Shelby	587	2,293	20
Talladega	2,693	1,371	66
Tallapoosa	1,308	2,685	33
Tuscaloosa	1,354	1,122	55
Walker	1,426	1,387	51
Washington	480	512	48
Winston	346	793	30
TOTAL	63,187	69,375	
AVERAGE			48

Source: Compiled from figures in the *Alabama Official and Statistical Register*, 141–42.

Table 11. Vote in Alabama's Black Belt and White Counties on November 1901 Referendum on Ratification of the Constitution

Place	Votes "For"	Votes "Against"	Percent "For"
Black Belt (19)	45,426	12,169	79*
White Counties (47)	63,187	69,375	48[†]
Statewide	108,613	81,734	57
Percent of Statewide Vote "for" Coming from Black Belt	42	—	
Percent of Statewide Vote "for" Coming from White Counties	58	—	
Percent of Statewide Vote "against" Coming from Black Belt	—	15	
Percent of Statewide Vote "against" Coming from White Counties	—	85[‡]	

Source: Compiled from figures in the *Alabama Official and Statistical Register,* 141–42.

* That almost 80 percent of the Black Belt voted "for" ratifying the disfranchisement constitution is usually the first point of focus for scholars examining the issue.

† An often unnoticed point is that the white counties, while they did supply the bulk of opposition to ratification, did not do so in a consensus manner. On a percentage basis, the vote was split almost in half in the white counties. This indicates that the racial appeal of the constitution's effectiveness in disfranchising blacks won over many white voters in the white counties—virtually half of them, given the figures. In addition, the fact that blacks still voted relatively freely outside the Black Belt, and we can safely assume that most blacks voted "against" ratifying a constitution advertised as seeking their own disfranchisement, further detracts from the split white vote in the white counties. That is, if the vote was split in the white counties among all voters, factoring out the black vote as "against" ratification, we see that, in fact, a clear majority of white voters in the white counties voted "for" ratification.

‡ That 85 percent of the opposition to ratification came from the white counties is another point of focus for scholars. This fact, taken in conjunction with the first point noted here, has led to the mythical dichotomy of Black Belt support for disfranchisement and white-county resistance against it.

Table 12. Comparison of Vote in Alabama's Black Belt on April 1901 and November 1901 Referenda

County	Votes "for" Calling	Votes "against" Calling	Percent "for" Calling	Votes "for" Ratification	Votes "against" Ratification	Percent "for" Ratification
Autauga	512	63	89	905	920	50
Barbour	1,361	347	80	2,905	1,121	72
Bullock	371	149	71	962	560	63
Choctaw	498	349	59	862	983	47
Clarke	531	247	68	1,448	444	77
Dallas	5,668	200	97	8,125	235	97
Greene	1,479	19	99	1,077	101	91
Hale	2,318	66	97	4,698	95	98
Lee	1,487	547	73	1,174	2,371	33
Lowndes	3,226	338	91	1,390	1,642	46
Macon	372	299	55	1,073	190	85
Marengo	2,197	241	90	1,958	341	85
Monroe	429	166	72	1,039	442	70
Montgomery	1,137	233	83	4,285	1,224	78
Perry	2,295	43	98	3,209	88	97
Pickens	241	209	54	869	417	58
Russell	807	66	92	1,627	1,185	58
Sumter	1,440	69	95	1,865	649	74
Wilcox	1,689	25	99	2,930	168	95
TOTAL	28,058	3,676	88	45,426	12,169	79

Source: Compiled from figures in the *Alabama Official and Statistical Register,* 141–42.

Table 13. Comparison of Vote in Alabama's White Counties on April 1901 and November 1901 Referenda

County	Votes "for" Calling	Votes "against" Calling	Percent "for" Calling	Votes "for" Ratification	Votes "against" Ratification	Percent "for" Ratification
Baldwin	302	553	35	508	414	55
Bibb	719	565	56	1,210	1,044	54
Blount	912	1,256	42	795	1,692	32
Butler	950	1,099	46	1,058	1,705	38
Calhoun	949	760	56	2,546	1,929	57
Chambers	3,194	498	87	4,604	553	89
Cherokee	340	1,186	22	508	1,442	26
Chilton	361	1,239	23	394	1,664	19
Clay	883	1,204	42	683	1,709	29
Cleburne	225	203	53	1,459	740	66
Coffee	311	368	46	778	833	48
Colbert	1,175	713	62	2,011	748	73
Conecuh	660	1,142	37	834	1,174	42
Coosa	854	1,135	43	948	1,355	41
Covington	662	446	61	698	1,023	41
Crenshaw	735	743	50	1,249	835	60
Cullman	540	1,452	27	544	1,764	24
Dale	574	1,040	36	753	1,710	31
DeKalb	785	1,357	37	812	1,572	34
Elmore	1,147	1,480	44	1,757	543	76
Escambia	357	166	68	703	450	61
Etowah	929	1,118	45	1,189	2,141	36
Fayette	427	856	33	542	1,031	34
Franklin	464	975	32	528	1,245	30
Geneva	370	820	31	527	1,024	34
Henry	1,029	786	57	1,882	1,590	54
Jackson	942	1,223	44	633	2,893	18
Jefferson	1,913	1,893	50	8,088	6,160	57
Lamar	436	243	64	677	678	50
Lauderdale	1,050	1,229	46	1,125	2,046	35
Lawrence	1,144	507	69	1,229	872	58
Limestone	1,394	1,213	53	2,243	584	79
Madison	2,551	1,521	63	4,255	2,244	65
Marion	627	751	46	515	1,411	26
Marshall	286	1,021	22	401	2,217	15
Mobile	696	378	65	1,862	1,867	50
Morgan	1,254	652	66	1,066	2,249	31
Pike	1,121	958	54	1,627	1,185	58
Randolph	740	114	87	1,365	1,304	51

continued

Table 13. Continued

County	Votes "for" Calling	Votes "against" Calling	Percent "for" Calling	Votes "for" Ratification	Votes "against" Ratification	Percent "for" Ratification
Saint Clair	429	1,261	25	387	1,572	20
Shelby	660	1,106	37	587	2,293	20
Talladega	1,892	640	75	2,693	1,371	66
Tallapoosa	2,063	1,360	60	1,308	2,685	33
Tuscaloosa	848	569	60	1,354	1,122	55
Walker	1,599	1,276	56	1,426	1,387	51
Washington	373	80	82	480	512	48
Winston	375	684	35	346	793	30
TOTAL	42,247	41,829	50	63,187	69,375	48

Source: Compiled from figures in the *Alabama Official and Statistical Register,* 141–42.

Table 14. Vote by Section on November 1901 Referendum on Ratification of the Constitution

	Counties "For" (Percent "For")		Counties "Against" (Percent "For")	
I. TENNESSEE VALLEY (4–3)				
	Colbert	(73)	Jackson	(18)
	Lawrence	(58)	Lauderdale	(35)
	Limestone	(79)	Morgan*	(31)
	Madison	(65)		
II. HILL COUNTRY (11–16)				
	Bibb	(54)	Blount	(32)
	Calhoun	(57)	Cherokee	(26)
	Chambers	(89)	Chilton	(19)
	Cleburne	(66)	Clay	(29)
	Elmore*	(76)	Coosa	(41)
	Jefferson	(57)	Cullman	(24)
	Lamar	(50)	DeKalb	(34)
	Randolph	(51)	Etowah	(36)
	Talladega	(66)	Fayette	(34)
	Tuscaloosa	(55)	Franklin	(30)
	Walker	(51)	Marion	(26)
			Marshall	(15)
			Shelby	(20)
			Saint Clair	(20)
			Tallapoosa*	(33)
			Winston	(30)
III. WIREGRASS (4–6)				
	Crenshaw	(60)	Butler	(38)
	Escambia	(61)	Coffee	(48)
	Henry	(54)	Conecuh	(42)
	Pike	(68)	Covington*	(41)
			Dale	(31)
			Geneva	(34)
IV. GULF COAST PLAIN (2–1)				
	Baldwin*	(55)	Washington*	(48)
	Mobile	(50)		
V. BLACK BELT (16–3)				
	Autauga	(50)	Choctaw*	(47)
	Barbour	(72)	Lee*	(33)
	Bullock	(63)	Lowndes*	(46)
	Clarke	(77)		
	Dallas	(97)		
	Greene	(91)		
	Hale	(98)		
	Macon	(85)		

continued

Table 14. Continued

	Counties "For" (Percent "For")	Counties "Against" (Percent "For")
	Marengo	(85)	
	Monroe	(70)	
	Montgomery	(78)	
	Perry	(97)	
	Pickens	(68)	
	Russell	(74)	
	Sumter	(95)	
	Wilcox	(96)	

Source: Compiled from voting results from the *Alabama Official and Statistical Register,* 141–42. Physiographic regions from the map located in Webb, *Two-Party Politics in the One-Party South,* xii.

*Denotes a county that reversed its position from the April 1901 referendum on calling the constitutional convention. Nine counties in all did so. See tables 12 and 13.

Table 15. 1892 Populist Counties and Their 1901 Votes on the Constitution

County	Votes "for" Calling	Votes "against" Calling	Percent "for" Calling	Votes "for" Ratification	Votes "against" Ratification	Percent "for" Ratification
Bibb	719	565	56	1,210	1,044	54
Blount	912	1,256	42	795	1,692	32
Butler	950	1,099	46	1,058	1,705	38
Chambers	3,194	498	87	4,604	553	89
Cherokee	340	1,186	22	508	1,442	26
Chilton	361	1,239	23	394	1,664	19
Choctaw	498	349	59	862	983	47
Clay	883	1,204	42	683	1,709	29
Cleburne	225	203	53	1,459	740	66
Coffee	311	368	46	778	833	48
Coosa	854	1,135	43	948	1,355	41
Covington	662	446	61	698	1,023	41
Crenshaw	735	743	50	1,249	835	60
Cullman	540	1,452	27	544	1,764	24
Dale	574	1,040	36	753	1,710	31
DeKalb	785	1,357	37	812	1,572	34
Elmore	1,147	1,480	44	1,757	543	76
Etowah	929	1,118	45	1,189	2,141	36
Fayette	427	856	33	542	1,031	34
Franklin	464	975	32	528	1,245	30
Geneva	370	820	31	527	1,024	34
Henry	1,029	786	57	1,882	1,590	54
Lamar	436	243	64	677	678	50
Lawrence	1,144	507	69	1,229	872	58
Lee	1,487	547	73	1,174	2,371	33
Limestone	1,394	1,213	53	2,243	584	79
Macon	372	299	55	1,073	190	85
Madison	2,551	1,521	63	4,255	2,244	65
Marshall	286	1,021	22	401	2,217	15
Pickens	241	209	54	869	417	58
Randolph	740	114	87	1,365	1,304	51
Saint Clair	429	1,261	25	387	1,572	20
Shelby	660	1,106	37	587	2,293	20
Tallapoosa	2,063	1,360	60	1,308	2,685	33
Tuscaloosa	848	569	60	1,354	1,122	55
Walker	1,599	1,276	56	1,426	1,387	51
Winston	375	684	35	346	793	30

continued

Table 15. Continued

Strong Populist Counties* in 1892

County	Kolb	Jones	Percent Vote "for" in April 1901	Percent Vote "for" in November 1901
Autauga	844 (45%)	1,027	89	50
Calhoun	2,627 (46%)	3,040	56	57
Colbert	1,670 (47%)	1,908	62	73
Escambia	908 (49%)	961	68	61
Lauderdale	1,727 (47%)	1,924	46	35
Morgan	1,953 (50%)	1,964	66	31
Pike	1,236 (49%)	1,296	54	58
Talladega	2,438 (46%)	2,826	75	66

Summary for Table 15

	"For"	"Against"
A. POPULIST COUNTIES ON REFERENDA		
Populist Counties on April 1901 Referendum	18	19
Populist Counties on November 1901 Referendum	15	22
B. POPULIST COUNTIES WITH STRONG† "FOR" VOTE ON REFERENDA		
Populist Counties with Strong "for" Vote in April 1901	25	12
Populist Counties with Strong "for" Vote in November 1901	19	18
C. EIGHT STRONG POPULIST COUNTIES* ON REFERENDA		
Strong Populist Counties on April 1901 Referendum	25	20
Strong Populist Counties on November 1901 Referendum	22	23

Source: Compiled from figures in the Secretary of State Records, Election Files (1892–1898), box SG 2481, ADAH; the *Alabama Official and Statistical Register*, 141–42; election returns in the *Birmingham Age-Herald*, 14 Aug. 1892, 1; and the 1892 election map in Rogers, *One-Gallused Rebellion*, 223.

*A strong Populist county returned at least 45 percent of the county vote "for" the 1892 Populist gubernatorial candidate.

†A Populist county with a strong "for" vote on the referenda returned at least 40 percent of the county "for" the 1901 referenda.

Table 16. 1894 Populist Counties and Their 1901 Votes on the Constitution

County	Votes "for" Calling	Votes "against" Calling	Percent "for" Calling	Votes "for" Ratification	Votes "against" Ratification	Percent "for" Ratification
Bibb	719	565	56	1,210	1,044	54
Blount	912	1,256	42	795	1,692	32
Butler	950	1,099	46	1,058	1,705	38
Chambers	3,194	498	87	4,604	553	89
Cherokee	340	1,186	22	508	1,442	26
Chilton	361	1,239	23	394	1,664	19
Choctaw	498	349	59	862	983	47
Clay	883	1,204	42	683	1,709	29
Cleburne	225	203	53	1,459	740	66
Coffee	311	368	46	778	833	48
Conecuh	660	1,142	37	834	1,174	42
Coosa	854	1,135	43	948	1,355	41
Covington	662	446	61	698	1,023	41
Crenshaw	735	743	50	1,249	835	60
Cullman	540	1,452	27	544	1,764	24
Dale	574	1,040	36	753	1,710	31
DeKalb	785	1,357	37	812	1,572	34
Elmore	1,147	1,480	44	1,757	543	76
Etowah	929	1,118	45	1,189	2,141	36
Fayette	427	856	33	542	1,031	34
Franklin	464	975	32	528	1,245	30
Geneva	370	820	31	527	1,024	34
Lawrence	1,144	507	69	1,229	872	58
Lee	1,487	547	73	1,174	2,371	33
Limestone	1,394	1,213	53	2,243	584	79
Marion	627	751	46	515	1,411	26
Marshall	286	1,021	22	401	2,217	15
Randolph	740	114	87	1,365	1,304	51
Russell	807	66	92	1,627	1,185	58
Saint Clair	429	1,261	25	387	1,572	20
Shelby	660	1,106	37	587	2,293	20
Talladega	1,892	640	75	2,693	1,371	66
Tallapoosa	2,063	1,360	60	1,308	2,685	33
Tuscaloosa	848	569	60	1,354	1,122	55
Walker	1,599	1,276	56	1,426	1,387	51
Winston	375	684	35	346	793	30

continued

Table 16. Continued

Strong Populist Counties* in 1894

County	Kolb	Oates	Percent Vote "for" in April 1901	Percent Vote "for" in November 1901
Calhoun	2,072 (45%)	2,542	56	57
Colbert	1,198 (48%)	1,297	62	73
Escambia	576 (46%)	688	68	61
Henry	1,619 (45%)	1,991	57	54
Jackson	1,684 (46%)	1,998	44	18
Jefferson	4,567 (50%)	4,589	50	57
Morgan	1,549 (48%)	1,651	66	31
Pickens	1,746 (49%)	1,802	54	58
Pike	1,400 (45%)	1,710	54	58

Summary for Table 16

	"For"	"Against"
A. POPULIST COUNTIES ON REFERENDA		
Populist Counties on April 1901 Referendum	15	21
Populist Counties on November 1901 Referendum	12	24
B. POPULIST COUNTIES WITH STRONG[†] "FOR" VOTE ON REFERENDA		
Populist Counties with Strong "for" Vote in April 1901	23	13
Populist Counties with Strong "for" Vote in November 1901	17	19
C. NINE STRONG POPULIST COUNTIES ON REFERENDA		
Strong Populist Counties on April 1901 Referendum	23	22
Strong Populist Counties on November 1901 Referendum	19	26

Source: Compiled from figures in the Secretary of State Records, Election Files (1892–1898), box SG 2481, ADAH; the *Alabama Official and Statistical Register;* 141–42; and the 1894 election map in Rogers, *One-Gallused Rebellion,* 284.

* A strong Populist county returned at least 45 percent of the county vote "for" the 1894 Populist gubernatorial candidate.

† A Populist county with a strong "for" vote on the referenda returned at least 40 percent of the county "for" the 1901 referenda.

Table 17. 1896 Populist Counties and Their Votes on the 1901 Constitution

County	Votes "for" Calling	Votes "against" Calling	Percent "for" Calling	Votes "for" Ratification	Votes "against" Ratification	Percent "for" Ratification
Bibb	719	565	56	1,210	1,044	54
Butler	950	1,099	46	1,058	1,705	38
Cherokee	340	1,186	22	508	1,442	26
Chilton	361	1,239	23	394	1,664	19
Choctaw	498	349	59	862	983	47
Cleburne	225	203	53	1,459	740	66
Coffee	311	368	46	778	833	48
Conecuh	660	1,142	37	834	1,174	42
Coosa	854	1,135	43	948	1,355	41
Covington	662	446	61	698	1,023	41
Crenshaw	735	743	50	1,249	835	60
Cullman	540	1,452	27	544	1,764	24
Dale	574	1,040	36	753	1,710	31
Elmore	1,147	1,480	44	1,757	543	76
Etowah	929	1,118	45	1,189	2,141	36
Fayette	427	856	33	542	1,031	34
Franklin	464	975	32	528	1,245	30
Geneva	370	820	31	527	1,024	34
Henry	1,029	786	57	1,882	1,590	54
Lawrence	1,144	507	69	1,229	872	58
Marshall	286	1,021	22	401	2,217	15
Pike	1,121	958	54	1,627	1,185	58
Saint Clair	429	1,261	25	387	1,572	20
Shelby	660	1,106	37	587	2,293	20
Talladega	1,892	640	75	2,693	1,371	66
Tallapoosa	2,063	1,360	60	1,308	2,685	33

Strong Populist Counties* in 1896

County	Goodwyn	Johnston	Percent Vote "for" in April 1901	Percent Vote "for" in November 1901
Blount	1,757 (48%)	1,930	42	32
Calhoun	2,299 (48%)	2,536	56	57
Clay	1,286 (49%)	1,351	42	29
Colbert	1,688 (47%)	1,885	62	73
DeKalb	1,360 (47%)	1,506	37	34

continued

Table 17. Continued

Strong Populist Counties* in 1896

County	Goodwyn	Johnston	Percent Vote "for" in April 1901	Percent Vote "for" in November 1901
Jackson	2,076 (45%)	2,496	44	18
Jefferson	5,619 (45%)	6,946	50	57
Limestone	1,654 (47%)	1,850	53	79
Morgan	1,914 (49%)	2,031	66	31
Pickens	1,717 (45%)	2,108	54	58
Randolph	1,358 (49%)	1,428	87	51
Tuscaloosa	1,950 (45%)	2,402	60	55

Summary for Table 17

	"For"	"Against"
A. POPULIST COUNTIES ON REFERENDA		
Populist Counties on April 1901 Referendum	10	16
Populist Counties on November 1901 Referendum	8	18
B. POPULIST COUNTIES WITH STRONG[†] "FOR" VOTE ON REFERENDA		
Populist Counties with Strong "for" Vote in April 1901	15	11
Populist Counties with Strong "for" Vote in November 1901	13	13
C. TWELVE STRONG POPULIST COUNTIES ON REFERENDA		
Strong Populist Counties on April 1901 Referendum	18	20
Strong Populist Counties on November 1901 Referendum	15	23

Source: Compiled from figures in the Secretary of State Records, Election Files (1892–1898), box SG 2481, ADAH; the *Alabama Official and Statistical Register*, 141–42; and the 1896 election map in Rogers, *One-Gallused Rebellion*, 315.

[*] A strong Populist county returned at least 45 percent of the county vote "for" the 1896 Populist gubernatorial candidate.

[†] A Populist county with a strong "for" vote on the referenda returned at least 40 percent of the county "for" the 1901 referenda.

Table 18. Populist Counties in 1892 or 1894 and Their Votes on the 1901 Constitution

A. Counties That Went Populist in Both 1892 and 1894 but Not in 1896

County	Votes "for" Calling	Votes "against" Calling	Percent "for" Calling	Votes "for" Ratification	Votes "against" Ratification	Percent "for" Ratification
Blount	912	1,256	42	795	1,692	32
Chambers	3,194	498	87	4,604	553	89
Clay	883	1,204	42	683	1,709	29
DeKalb	785	1,357	37	812	1,572	34
Lee	1,487	547	73	1,174	2,371	33
Limestone	1,394	1,213	53	2,243	584	79
Randolph	740	114	87	1,365	1,304	51
Tuscaloosa	848	569	60	1,354	1,122	55
Walker	1,599	1,276	56	1,426	1,387	51
Winston	375	684	35	346	793	30

B. Counties That Went Populist in Either 1892 or 1894 but Not in 1896

County	Votes "for" Calling	Votes "against" Calling	Percent "for" Calling	Votes "for" Ratification	Votes "against" Ratification	Percent "for" Ratification
Conecuh*	660	1,142	37	834	1,174	42
Lamar[†]	436	243	64	677	678	50
Macon[†]	372	299	55	1,073	190	85
Madison[†]	2,551	1,521	63	4,255	2,244	65
Marion*	627	751	46	515	1,411	26
Pickens[†]	241	209	54	869	417	58
Russell*	807	66	92	1,627	1,185	58

Summary for Table 18

	"For"	"Against"
A. POPULIST COUNTIES ON REFERENDA		
Populist Counties on April 1901 Referendum	11	6
Populist Counties on November 1901 Referendum	10	7
B. POPULIST COUNTIES WITH STRONG[‡] "FOR" VOTE ON REFERENDA		
Populist Counties with Strong "for" Vote in April 1901	14	3
Populist Counties with Strong "for" Vote in November	11	6

Source: Compiled from figures in the Secretary of State Records, Election Files (1892–1898), box SG 2481, ADAH; the *Alabama Official and Statistical Register,* 141–42; and the election maps in Rogers, *One-Galloused Rebellion,* 223, 284, and 315.

*County went Populist in 1894.

[†]County went Populist in 1892.

[‡]A strong "for" vote is 40 percent or higher.

Table 19. Vote by County in SDEC on All-White, Direct Primary, 1902

"For" the Primary (16)	*"Against" the Primary (13)*
Emmett O'Neal, Lauderdale	Robert J. Lowe, Jefferson
Alfred M. Tunstall, Hale	Thomas McCorvey Stevens, Mobile
J. Thomas Heflin, Chambers	Stephen Smith*
William Dickson Dunn, Clarke[†]	Tipton Mullins*
Bibb Graves, Montgomery	Benjamin Meek Miller, Wilcox
William H. Samford, Pike	Hugh S. D. Mallory, Dallas
Thomas Sydney Frazer (Frasier), Bullock[†]	A. H. Merrill, Barbour
Richard Henry Arrington, Coffee	A. P. Smith, Greene
Charles C. Whitson, Talladega	R. J. Seale, Sumter
Brightman*	Thomas Goode Jones, Montgomery
Charles E. Mitchell, Marion	William T. Sanders, Limestone
William Wallace Haralson, DeKalb[†]	Judge Kumpe, Lawrence[†]
W. A. Givhan, Madison	(John V. Smith), Russell[‡]
Robert F. Hall, Henry[†]	
C. B. Smith, Sumter	
(Gorman)[‡]	

Sources: Compiled from material in the *Minutes of the State Democratic Executive Committee* (SDEC), Montgomery, Alabama, 10 July 1902, 1, and 40–41, box 3, folder 1, SDEC Records, Alabama Department of Archives and History, Montgomery, Alabama. Also from Owen, *History of Alabama and Dictionary of Alabama Biography*, 3:59, 523, 613, 728 and 4:742, 1,148, 1,212, 1,499, 1,574, 1,576, 1,584, 1,621, and 1,760–61; and J. C. DuBose, *Notable Men of Alabama*, 1:45–47.

[*] First name and/or county not known.

[†] Probable first name and county as far as could be determined from available biographical information.

[‡] John V. Smith clearly indicated his desire to vote against the primary and Gorman's desire to vote for it, yet abstained from formally voting, in an act of honor, because Gorman had to leave the SDEC proceedings just before the vote to attend the funeral of his brother. Before leaving, Gorman had communicated his belief to Smith that his vote and Smith's would cancel each other's out. J. V. Smith came from a long line of planters and slaveholders. By 1904, he had moved to Montgomery County, which he represented in the state legislature.

Table 20. Vote in the Black Belt on 1902 Democratic Gubernatorial Primary

County	Jelks	Johnston	Percent "for" Jelks
Autauga	652	315	67
Barbour	1,080	846	56
Bullock	576	402	59
Choctaw	587	173	77
Clarke	1,102	415	73
Dallas	1,209	365	77
Greene	316	189	63
Hale	594	390	60
Lee	1,148	503	70
Lowndes	539	334	68
Macon	393	320	55
Marengo	893	382	70
Monroe	652	153	81
Montgomery	1,735	1,142	60
Perry	504	475	51
Pickens	943	176	84
Russell	499	172	74
Sumter	764	70	92
Wilcox	766	439	64
TOTAL	14,952	7,552	66

Source: Compiled from returns in the *Minutes of the State Democratic Executive Committee* (SDEC), 3 Sept. 1902, p. 21, box 3, folder 6, SDEC Records, ADAH.

Table 21. Vote in White Counties on 1902 Democratic Gubernatorial Primary

County	Jelks	Johnston	Percent "for" Jelks
Baldwin	418	152	73
Bibb	771	492	61
Blount	824	498	62
Butler	1,006	415	71
Calhoun	1,171	759	61
Chambers	1,239	562	69
Cherokee	729	131	85
Chilton	335	73	82
Clay	812	319	72
Cleburne	524	129	80
Coffee	712	276	72
Colbert	579	407	59
Conecuh	530	53	91
Coosa	825	166	83
Covington	554	530	51
Crenshaw*	775	802	49
Cullman	796	224	78
Dale	702	309	69
DeKalb	750	163	82
Elmore*	928	1,023	48
Escambia	482	172	74
Etowah	674	198	77
Fayette	365	28	92
Franklin	410	53	89
Geneva	529	165	76
Henry	2,213	1,659	57
Jackson	1,321	666	66
Jefferson	3,833	2,946	57
Lamar	1,015	292	78
Lauderdale	1,056	652	62
Lawrence	660	55	92
Limestone	905	327	73
Madison	1,807	1,088	62
Marion	570	295	66
Marshall*	417	502	45
Mobile	2,059	2,038	50
Morgan	1,184	1,071	52
Pike	1,108	1,101	50
Randolph	1,064	244	81
Saint Clair	255	241	51
Shelby	645	178	78
Talladega	1,228	539	69

continued

Table 21. Continued

County	Jelks	Johnston	Percent "for" Jelks
Tallapoosa*	1,235	1,404	47
Tuscaloosa	1,033	473	69
Walker	888	552	62
Washington	493	110	82
Winston	309	55	85
TOTAL	42,738	24,587	63

Source: Compiled from returns in the *Minutes of the State Democratic Executive Committee* (SDEC), 3 Sept. 1902, p. 21, box 3, folder 6, SDEC Records, ADAH.

*County that went "for" Johnston.

Table 22. Lynching by Decade, Region, and Race, 1889–1919

	1889–1899	*1900–1909*	*1910–1919*
Lynchings in Alabama	177	67	58*
Lynchings in the South	1,365	783	712
Lynchings in the United States	1,722	904	802
Percent Black Lynched in Alabama	70.1	100.0	95.2
Percent Black Lynched in the United States	70.3	88.2	89.4[†]
Percent U.S. Victims Lynched in the South	78.9	86.7	88.8

Sources: Compiled from statistics in NAACP, *Thirty Years of Lynching in the United States,* 29; and the Tuskegee Institute News Clipping Files, "Lynching File," TU.

Statistics for the years 1911–1917 reflect additional incidents of lynching that were omitted from the original statistics. The source for these data is the Papers of the NAACP, part 7, series A, reel 3, at the Ralph Brown Draughon Library, AU. Also available in hard copy and film from the LC.

Statistics for 1919 are also from the Papers of the NAACP, reel 21.

* Alabama's record for 1918 reflects the lynchings of four blacks that occurred in Shubuta, Mississippi, but after a chase that originated in Mobile, Alabama. The lynchings were probably the work primarily of citizens from Mobile. Therefore, responsibility for them has been assigned to Alabama, not Mississippi, for the year 1918 in this and the following table.

[†] In 1915, Texas mobs lynched forty-three Mexicans. If this minority is classified as "non-Anglo white," along with the black victims, the percentage of nonwhites lynched in the United States in the period 1910–19 would rise to 94.7 percent.

Table 23. Lynchings in Alabama, the South, and the United States by Race and Year, 1900–1921

Year	Alabama	(Percent)	The South	(Percent)	United States	(Percent)
1900	4	(100.0)	88	(94.3)	101	(88.1)
1901	16	(100.0)	112	(85.7)	135	(80.0)
1902	5	(100.0)	73	(95.9)	94	(89.3)
1903	5	(100.0)	85	(92.9)	104	(83.6)
1904	6	(100.0)	79	(93.7)	86	(91.8)
1905	3	(100.0)	61	(93.4)	65	(92.3)
1906	6	(100.0)	60	(95.0)	68	(94.1)
1907	11	(100.0)	55	(98.2)	62	(95.2)
1908	3	(100.0)	94	(90.4)	100	(92.0)
1909	8	(100.0)	76	(88.2)	89	(84.3)
1910	7	(100.0)	68	(89.7)	90	(88.9)
1911	5	(80.0)	64	(92.2)	77	(89.6)
1912	9	(88.9)	74	(98.6)	79	(96.2)
1913	6	(100.0)	71	(98.6)	79	(98.7)
1914	5	(100.0)	63	(100.0)	72	(93.1)
1915	9	(100.0)	125	(68.9)	132	(67.4)
1916	2	(100.0)	62	(93.5)	69	(89.9)
1917	5	(100.0)	48	(95.8)	54	(96.3)
1918	7	(100.0)	63	(96.8)	67	(94.0)
1919	8	(87.5)	74	(98.6)	83	(92.8)
1920	6	(83.3)	51	(96.1)	65	(87.7)
1921	2	(50.0)	63	(90.1)	65	(92.2)
TOTAL	138		1,609		1,856	
BLACK	133	(96.4)	1,477	(91.8)	1,626	(88.6)
YEARLY AVERAGE LYNCHED	6.3		73.1		83.5	

Sources: Compiled from statistics in NAACP, *Thirty Years of Lynching in the United States,* 29; and the Tuskegee Institute News Clipping Files, "Lynching File," TU.

Statistics for 1919–21 are also from the Papers of the NAACP, reel 21.

Statistics for the years 1911–17 reflect additional incidents of lynching that were omitted from the original statistics. The source for that is the Papers of the NAACP, part 7, series A, reel 3, at the Ralph Brown Draughon Library, AU. Also available in hard copy and film from the LC.

NOTES

AAMA   Alabama A and M University Archives, Normal, Alabama

ADAH   Alabama Department of Archives and History, Montgomery, Alabama

ALA   Alabama Labor Archives, Alabama State AFL-CIO, Montgomery, Alabama

ASU   National Center for the Study of Civil Rights and African-American Culture, Department of Special Collections, Alabama State University, Montgomery, Alabama

AWHC   Archives of Wiregrass History and Culture, Troy State University, Dothan, Alabama

AU   Auburn University Archives, Ralph Brown Draughon Library, Auburn, Alabama

BCRI   Birmingham Civil Rights Institute, Birmingham, Alabama

BPLA   Department of Archives, Birmingham Public Library, Linn-Henley Research Library, Birmingham, Alabama

DTS   Documenting the South, or The Southern Experience in Nineteenth-Century America (URL: http://docsouth.unc.edu/washington/about.html), University of North Carolina at Chapel Hill Libraries, Chapel Hill, North Carolina

LC   Library of Congress, Washington, D.C.

MCM   Museum of the City of Mobile, Mobile, Alabama

MILES   Mattie Mashaw Jackson African American Center, Miles College Archives, W. A. Bell Library, Ensley, Alabama

OCA   Oakwood College Archives, Huntsville, Alabama

SHC   Southern Historical Collection, University of North Carolina, Chapel Hill, North Carolina

SLOSS   Sloss Furnaces National Historic Landmark Archives, Museum of History and Industry, Birmingham, Alabama

SU   Department of Special Collections, Harwell Goodwin Davis Library, Samford University, Homewood, Alabama

TCSH   Tutwiler Collection of Southern History, Linn-Henley Research Library, Birmingham Public Library, Birmingham, Alabama

TU   Tuskegee University Archives, Hollis Burke Frissell Library, Tuskegee, Alabama

UA   W. Stanley Hoole Special Collections Library, University of Alabama, Tuscaloosa, Alabama

UAB   University Archives, Mervyn H. Sterne Library, University of Alabama at Birmingham, Birmingham, Alabama

INTRODUCTION

1. On Woodward's romanticization of poor southern whites, especially the Populists, see O'Brien, "From a Chase to a View," 239, 242–43, 247; Williamson, "C. Vann Woodward and the Origins of a New Wisdom," 207; and Rabinowitz, "More Than the Woodward Thesis," 190. See also Shaw, *Wool Hat Boys;* Gaither, *Blacks and the Populist Revolt,* 77–78; Crowe, "Tom Watson, Populists, and Blacks Reconsidered," 99–116; and Saunders, "Southern Populists and the Negro," 240–61.

2. Kousser, *Shaping of Southern Politics,* 6.

3. Woodward, *Origins of the New South,* 342. Of course, as recent scholars have shown, "white" and "black" were socially constructed terms, and "whiteness," to some extent, was as much the creation of particular societies, a living term subject to changing definitions, as anything based in "real" and pure differences. See, in particular, the interesting work of Roediger, *Wages of Whiteness;* and Hale, *Making Whiteness.* See also a pioneering work on the subject: Fields, "Ideology and Race in American History," 143–77. For an overview of this developing literature, see Kolchin, "Whiteness Studies," 154–73. Still, in the human experience, which is the basis for historical study, perception is often greater than reality. In fact, quite often perception *is* reality, that is, many people are governed by their perceptions of events just as, or more strongly than, they are influenced by any objective reality. The present study, without denying the social and spatial nature of race construction, treats "white" and "black" and "race" as useful categorical terms in the way the subjects themselves understood them to exist in the turn-of-the-century South. Granted, race was, to some extent, a socially constructed idea and absolutely pure white and black bloodlines seldom, if ever, existed. But for the subjects of this study, the idea of race and their perception of its accuracy in reality were very real and very powerful.

4. Kousser explicitly mentioned Alabama's ratification example in *Shaping of Southern Politics,* 166. See Key, *Southern Politics in State and Nation,* 533–35; and Woodward, *Origins of the New South,* 343–44. Key's fait accompli thesis, up until Woodward's assault on it, had been accepted by a number of Southern historians. See, for example, Simkins and Roland, *History of the South,* 351–52.

5. Woodward, *Strange Career of Jim Crow,* 82; O'Brien, "From a Chase to a View," 239; Williamson, "C. Vann Woodward and the Origins of a New Wisdom," 206; Perman, *Struggle for Mastery,* 3.

6. Perman, *Struggle for Mastery,* 4–5, 8.

7. Kousser, *Shaping of Southern Politics,* 3, 167, 168.

8. Woodward, *Origins of the New South,* 337, 328–29.

9. See Kousser's "Note on Regression Estimation of Voting Behavior" in *Shaping of Southern Politics,* xi–xii, and also note 11 (and related text) of this chapter.

10. Kousser, *Shaping of Southern Politics,* 165–71; quoted terms from 167 and 168. For the negative percentages, see the note at the bottom of table 6.8 on p. 168. For the 81 percent figure, see table 6.8, section A, on p. 168.

11. Lichtman in "Correlation, Regression, and the Ecological Fallacy," 417–33; quotations on 417, 420, 421, 422, 432, and 433. Lichtman also advises historians to employ multi-

variate analysis to better target relationships and provide for a number of variables that affect voting behavior over time: age, mobility, social status, economic status, and the like. Kousser's analysis employed only the single independent variable of voting behavior in a prior election in looking at the dependent variable of voting behavior on the referendum questions. For the other articles in the series, see E. T. Jones, "Ecological Inference and Electoral Analysis," 249–62; E. T. Jones, "Using Ecological Regression," 593–96; and the related piece by Hanushek, Jackson, and Kain, "Model Specification, Use of Aggregate Data, and the Ecological Correlation Fallacy," 87–106. Perhaps the most dubious part of the methodological controversy, apart from its absence of mention in Kousser's book, is his willingness to substitute "impressionistic" evidence to explain things when illogical statistical results are reached. Of all the southern states and elections covered in his book, in his journal article in the series Kousser chose the subject of Alabama Populists' voting behavior on disfranchisement to illustrate what to do when linear regression analysis gives "unreliable or logically impossible results." To cope with these "imperfections of statistical methodology," such as the "illogical estimate" of negative Populist support for disfranchisement, what should the researcher do? Rely on "impressionistic evidence," Kousser answers, evidence supplied by "memoirs, congressional debates, newspapers, etc." And since "contemporaries believed that the Populists overwhelmingly opposed disfranchisement in Alabama," Kousser alleged the "illogical estimate" involved in his regression "should be interpreted to mean: 'Only a very few Populists voted for disfranchisement in Alabama.'" See Kousser, "Ecological Regression and the Analysis of Past Politics," 237–62, esp. 250–52.

12. This tendency is apparent throughout the book and appears in the book's subtitle, but see especially Kousser, *Shaping of Southern Politics*, 167, 168, and 284 (when commenting on the Joseph H. Taylor article).

13. Quotations from Perman, *Struggle for Mastery*, 325, 324, and 328; see also p. 8. Perman might have done better to take some stock of the broader context of the era as a number of studies in the last few decades have done. Several recent studies are excellent, such as Simon, *Fabric of Defeat*, 7–9, 222–23, which provides a nuanced interpretation of the shifting importance that plain-white textile workers placed on race, class, and gender concerns during various epochs. Other excellent studies are Gilmore, *Gender and Jim Crow;* Dailey, *Before Jim Crow;* Kantrowitz, *Ben Tillman and the Reconstruction of White Supremacy;* Williamson, *Crucible of Race;* J. D. Hall, *Revolt against Chivalry;* and Fredrickson, *Black Image in the White Mind.*

14. Key, *Southern Politics in State and Nation*, 540–41, 548; and Perman, *Struggle for Mastery*, 2.

15. Key, *Southern Politics in State and Nation*, 550; Perman, *Struggle for Mastery*, 2–3. Key could have added the partial example of Alabama to South Carolina and Georgia, for in Alabama the Populists led by Reuben Kolb pushed the disfranchisement idea hard in 1894. See Rogers and Ward, part 2, of the first-rate history by Rogers et al., *Alabama*, 312–14; and Letwin, *Challenge of Interracial Unionism*, 111.

16. Perhaps the only exception to this statement, and the only exception consistently found in Alabama, was the conduct of N. B. Spears at the 1901 constitutional convention.

Spears, alternatively identified by historians as Napoleon Bonaparte Spears and Newton B. Spears, was an exotic anomaly in his eloquent and passionate defense of black voting rights in their essence. Spears's fellow Populists and even the Republicans at the Alabama convention spoke in favor of various mechanisms that would disfranchise blacks and even some poor whites, including a character clause and the poll tax restriction. A very few who spoke out early in favor of universal manhood suffrage invariably reversed themselves on the issue, a point that will be discussed in detail later. The overwhelming majority expressed outright approval for the notion of blacks losing the vote. See chapter 3 for a discussion of Spears. His contemporaries are discussed in various chapters of this book. Spears's certain identity is a matter of some confusion. There was another Saint Clair County Populist, Napoleon Bonaparte Spradley, a justice of the peace and the county school superintendent. See J. C. DuBose, *Notable Men of Alabama*, 2:281–82. But at least one Populist newspaper closely acquainted with Spears identified him as Col. Napoleon Bonaparte Spears. See *Gadsden-Etowah County People's Voice*, 25 Oct. 1900, 4; see also 11 Oct. 1900, 4.

17. See, for example, the *Carrollton, Alabama Alliance News*, 31 July 1900, 2; and 7 Aug. 1900, 2, which explained its Hill Country Populist opposition to the calling of a disfranchisement convention by darkly referring to "negro rule and domination" and "negro supremacy" as a "hateful sight" in comparing the "[eighteen] seventies . . . the latter sixties and the early seventies" and the Reconstruction political situation in 1874 to 1900. Populist gubernatorial candidate Gilbert B. Deans, from Shelby County in the Upcountry, explained his opposition to a disfranchising convention in similar terms by denouncing "electoral fraud and negro rule" and making the clarion call for "white supremacy" (quoted in the Hill Country Populist newspaper *Cullman People's Protest*, 1 July 1898, 1). A Wiregrass Populist newspaper, the *Geneva Reaper*, self-described as "an index to . . . liberal and progressive" thought in Geneva County, opposed ratification of the 1901 Constitution because its editorial staff thought the document would disfranchise poor whites but allow blacks to vote, thus perpetuating "nigger domination," which had been "obnoxious to whites . . . [f]or thirty-five years" (16 Oct. 1901, 2; and 6 Nov. 1901, 2). A lily-white Republican newspaper in north Alabama opposed ratification on racial grounds, "because many white men will be disfranchised," a position that "shows clearly which side ha[s] the endorsement of the white people of Alabama" (*Huntsville Republican*, 9 Nov. 1901, 2; and 16 Nov. 1901, 2).

18. First set of quotations from Webb, *Two-Party Politics in the One-Party South*, 9. Webb defined "anti-Democrats" as that group of whites who opposed the Bourbon Democrats or Redeemers from 1874 to 1920, including the Greenbackers, Independents, Populists, and Republicans (275). Quotations from Webb's essay in "From Independents to Populists to Progressive Republicans," 726 and 736.

19. In fact, in *Southern Politics in State and Nation*, Key supplied ample evidence and reasoning that could be used to bolster differing versions of disfranchisement. On pp. 540–41 and 548, Key placed blame for the disfranchisement movement on the Black Belt. He also stressed that "by no means were all whites united on the issue" (535) and that

"southern whites were bitter in division rather than united on the disfranchisement question" (542). His specific discussion of Alabama divided things neatly into white-county resistance against and Black Belt advocacy for disfranchisement (544). See also pp. 5, 43–44. Yet, Key's fait accompli thesis implied that disfranchisement was a done deal by the time the movement was legally codified (533). Key's emphasis on fait accompli, the white primary, and the extralegal character of disfranchisement (539, 618), and his mentioning of the "disillusionment" of the defeated Populists (534) all seemed to suggest a broader white consensus on disfranchisement than mere Black Belt guilt. See also p. 45. "[I]n the disillusionment brought about by the Populist defeat, the black belts were able to recruit enough upcountry support to adopt poll taxes, literacy tests, and other instruments to disfranchise the Negro," Key told us, even though "[w]hile the upcountryman had no love for the Negro he suspected, at times rightly, that the black belt was trying to disfranchise him as well as the black man" (8). So, too, did Key's acknowledgment that, in the final analysis of southern politics, racial solidarity overrode all other factors: "In its grand outlines the politics of the South revolves around the position of the Negro. . . . [I]n the last analysis the major peculiarities of the southern political process go back to the Negro" (5). "The overshadowing race question, in which the big farmers [of the Black Belt] have the most immediate stake," according to Key, "blots up a latent radicalism [of the white counties] by converting [economic] discontent into aggression against the Negro" (44). White solidarity, white unity, was absolutely "essential in order that the largest possible block could be mobilized to resist any national move toward interference with southern authority to deal with the race question as was desired locally. And the threat of Federal intervention remained. . . . On the fundamental issue . . . of national intervention to protect Negro rights . . . only the Federal Government was to be feared" (9). "[T]he fundamental explanation of southern politics is that the black-belt whites succeeded in imposing their will on their states and thereby presented a solid regional front in national politics on the race issue," Key tells us (11). "By yielding to their black belts in their desire for solidarity in national politics" on the race issue, the whites of the South "condemned themselves internally" (11–12).

Finally, after noting the Populist-led character of disfranchisement in South Carolina and Georgia and likely frustrated with the contradictory nature of the evidence, Key concluded that "[p]erhaps the sounder generalization is that the groups on top at the moment, whatever their political orientation" pushed disfranchisement (550).

20. Webb, *Two-Party Politics in the One-Party South*, 1–4, 169–73, 253–55.

21. Kousser, *Shaping of Southern Politics*, 170. The Alabama example was, indeed, critical for Kousser. He observed that the apparent clear-cut sociopolitical nature of the state—north Alabama vs. south Alabama, planters and industrialists vs. poor whites— and good primary sources "have led students to base too many generalizations for the region as a whole primarily on the Alabama experience" (283). Given Kousser's black-and-white interpretation of Alabama and his overall thesis for the South, it is fair to ask if he himself might have fallen prey to the same tendency that he noted in others.

22. See notes 9–11 as well as the corresponding earlier text.

23. Kousser, *Shaping of Southern Politics,* 170. J. Thomas Heflin's representation of plain whites and the rarity of N. B. Spears's racial beliefs are discussed in detail in later chapters.

24. Webb, *Two-Party Politics in the One-Party South,* 9 and 123; and Webb, "Jacksonian Democrat in Postbellum Alabama," 259 and 273. This type of rigid dichotomy, leading toward a distorted understanding, is found in Webb's various writings on the subject. For example: "Many hill country voters who supported . . . Roosevelt in the 1930s . . . and Stevenson in the 1950s came from families whose roots had not been in the party of white supremacy" (Webb, "From Independents to Populists to Progressive Republicans," 736). Michael W. Fitzgerald specifically objected to Webb's assertions about the insignificance of race for poor, anti-Democratic whites in his "Review of Samuel L. Webb," 424–25.

25. The term "God and country issues" was introduced and first discussed in relation to these ideas in Feldman, "Introduction," 4 and 6.

26. See text associated with note 18.

27. Key, *Southern Politics in State and Nation,* 5–6.

28. Webb, *Two-Party Politics in the One-Party South,* 169–73. Ayers, in his sweeping synthesis of the New South, succinctly restates the myth; see *Promise of the New South,* 304.

29. D. A. Harris, "Racists and Reformers," 150, 154–55, 181, and 185; Sparks, "Alabama Negro Reaction to Disfranchisement," 15, 19, and 49; Sledge, "Alabama Republican Party," 75–77. Taylor, in "Populism and Disfranchisement in Alabama," 410–27, also echoed the myth. Ironically, Kousser dismissed Taylor's article as having "argued incorrectly that the Populists favored disfranchisement" (*Shaping of Southern Politics,* 284). But, in fact, Taylor's article did no such thing.

30. Gross, "Alabama Politics and the Negro." On plain-white complicity, see pp. 229–31, 234, 236, 246–47, 251, 253–54, 264, 268–69. Still, Gross concludes by adhering to the myth's sharp dichotomy of blame for disfranchisement assigned to the Black Belt; see pp. 261, 272–73, 277. In a similar vein, Rodabaugh ("Fusion, Confusion, Defeat, and Disfranchisement," 131–53) documents Populist complicity in disfranchisement (147, 149, and 150), but then concludes with equivocation, a restatement of the myth, and even the suggestion that perhaps there might be no relationship between Populism and disfranchisement at all except a temporal coincidence (145 and 151–52).

31. Samuel L. Webb makes the rather extreme argument that race was basically irrelevant for southern politics a virtual centerpiece of his book, *Two-Party Politics in the One-Party South.* Prior to 1954, Alabama politics was allegedly "rarely a simple morality play in which race played the pivotal role" (2). In 1946, Alabama was supposedly a "liberal oasis"; observers were struck by the "contrast between the state's liberal political heritage and the reactionary racist climate that surfaced after *Brown*" (1). "If one believes, like W. J. Cash, that southerners had no minds or were culturally encased or so obsessed with race that nothing else mattered, then one may conveniently avoid an analysis of ideology" (123). "Anyone who left the Democratic party to vote for the Populists or Jeffersonians said, in effect, that white unity was less important than other issues," Webb argued simplistically. "[T]he overall stance of the Populists on racial questions

was more tolerant than the Democrats" (128, 129). Webb's discussion on disfranchise-ment is a study in sanitizing race from the issue of denying blacks the vote (169–73). In general, "race was rarely the dominant force in [the] . . . political decision making" of his Hill Country protagonists. The result of the 1901 referenda "was an extraordinary demonstration of white sentiment against suffrage restrictions" (123). Webb has even gone to the length of pinning the blame for Alabama's racism on the Black Belt to the exclusion of the state's white counties: "Racial tension has been a driving and polarizing force across the state, and the Black Belt has been its source," according to the assessment attributed to Webb; "Race has been the constant obsession of the Black Belt" (Webb, quoted in the *Birmingham News*, 13 Oct. 2002, 18A). This view erects a simplistic wall between supposedly racially "enlightened" white counties and the "racist" Black Belt. It also artificially compartmentalizes racism and white supremacy in the Black Belt while, ultimately, misleadingly exonerating and romanticizing Alabama's white counties.

32. "Populists were racists," Webb apologized, "but that charge could have been made about every white-dominated political party in the United States in 1892" (*Two-Party Politics in the One-Party South*, 128–29).

33. Graves's lamentable record on civil liberties and dealing with the vigilante violence of the Klan and other groups extended to the 1930s as well, including the infamous case of the assault on Jewish communist Joseph Gelders. See, for example, Bibb Graves to Lee, 21 Oct. 1936; Joseph Gelders to Bibb Graves, 5 Jan. 1937; and Bibb Graves to Chappell, 22 Jan. 1937, all in box SG 12179, folder "Joseph Gelders." Also see Arthur Garfield Hays to Bibb Graves, 31 July 1935, and related correspondence in box SG 12165, folder "Communism," all in the Alabama Governors Papers, Bibb Graves Papers, ADAH.

34. Street was a consistent fiscal conservative and a virulent anti–New Dealer who proposed that Franklin Roosevelt be impeached and denounced him as a Socialist, a Communist, and a thief, and for "dishonest[y] . . . on a stupendous scale . . . as . . . the robber [who] . . . at the point of a gun . . . strips the traveler of his money. . . . [The New Deal] took from the industrious and thrifty element . . . their savings against old age or misfortune and distributed them among the lazy, trifling, shiftless, indolent hobos and vagrants who will never hit another lick of work as long as the government will continue to rob its people to feed and bed and clothe them" (Oliver Day Street to editor, *Birmingham Age-Herald*, 29 July 1935, 4). For Street's long record of illiberalism and bigotry, see chapter 3, notes 15–17.

35. Quotation from McMillan, *Constitutional Development in Alabama*, 358. See also Key, *Southern Politics in State and Nation*; notes 15 and 19 of this chapter; and Brittain, "Negro Suffrage and Politics in Alabama since 1870," 128, 138, 144–48.

36. Quotations from part 2 by Rogers and Ward in Rogers et al., *Alabama*, 353. Other older historians, in assessing the South as a region, agreed with this assessment. For example, Ezell, *South since 1865*, 177; Current, Williams, and Friedel, *American History*, 470–71; and Clark and Kirwan, *South since Appomattox*, 74.

37. Three quotations from, respectively, Webb, *Two-Party Politics in the One-Party South*, 9; Woodward, *Origins of the New South*, 342; and Kousser, *Shaping of Southern Politics*, 170.

CHAPTER ONE Prelude to Disfranchisement

1. For instance, in 1901 the *Brooklyn Eagle* advocated repeal of the Fifteenth Amendment, which provided for black suffrage. "Human nature is a higher constitution than the Federal compact," its editor argued, sounding much like the delegates to southern disfranchisement conventions. "White control is a better preservative of government and civilization than Constitutional amendments which threaten to ignore or cross it" (*Brooklyn Eagle*, quoted in the *Mobile Register*, 26 July 1901, cited prominently in the *Official Proceedings of the Constitutional Convention of the State of Alabama, May 21, 1901 to Sept. 3, 1901*, 3:3,003, hereafter referred to as *Official Proceedings, 1901*).

2. *Williams v. Mississippi*, 170 US 213 (1898). Five southern states accomplished disfranchisement using new state constitutions: Mississippi (1890), South Carolina (1895), Louisiana (1898), Alabama (1901), and Virginia (1902). North Carolina (1900), Georgia (1908), and Oklahoma (1910) used constitutional amendments. Four others opted for a poll-tax law: Florida (1889), Tennessee (1890), Arkansas (1891), and Texas (1902). See Hackney's excellent book, *Populism to Progressivism in Alabama*, 147. See also Key, *Southern Politics in State and Nation*, 550.

3. McMillan, *Constitutional Development in Alabama*, 306, 358–59. Alabama's 1901 Constitution was extreme, not only in the variety and number of its disfranchising mechanisms but also in its length; eventually, with amendments, it became the longest constitution in the world (Whitmire, "Constitution Conundrum," 6).

4. Hackney, *Populism to Progressivism in Alabama*, 177.

5. Papers of the NAACP, part 7, series A, reels 3 and 21, AU and LC; NAACP, *Thirty Years of Lynching in the United States;* Brundage, *Lynching in the New South;* and Tolnay and Beck, *Festival of Violence.*

6. Papers of the NAACP, part 7, series A, reels 3 and 21, AU and LC; NAACP, *Thirty Years of Lynching in the United States.*

7. Henry Cabot Lodge's "force bill" to provide for federal supervision of southern elections was defeated in the Senate in 1890 and posed no threat by 1894. The U.S. Supreme Court, in a series of "civil rights" decisions very narrowly interpreted the Fourteenth and Fifteenth Amendments, making circumvention of the spirit of these laws quite possible. See McMillan, *Constitutional Development in Alabama*, 230–32.

8. Bailey, *Liberalism in the New South*, 51–52. Other examples abound.

9. Northern sympathy and the absence of fear of intrusion from the federal government were a marked part of Alabama's 1901 deliberations on black suffrage. See note 1 for this chapter. See also the *Official Proceedings, 1901*, 2:2,247. U.S. congressman, and future senator, Oscar W. Underwood asked for northern and federal latitude for Alabama to work out its own solutions to its race-relations problems and, typically, tied the racial and the economic together in a chamber-of-commerce type of racism. He asked for laissez-faire on race, especially "if you are in favor of upholding the Negro race . . . of honest governments in the Southern states . . . yes, and the investments that you have brought there among us." See the *Congressional Record* 34, 56th Cong., 2d sess., 557 (Jan. 1901), quoted in McMillan, *Constitutional Development in Alabama*, 291 n. 41.

10. Many social workers, psychologists, and statisticians, some of them from the Ivy League, concurred. One journalist put it this way: "To reform his character is an almost hopeless task. . . . The Negro is a Negro. We must deal with him as he is." Quotations from Oshinsky, *"Worse Than Slavery,"* 94–96. See also Osofsky, *Burden of Race,* 184–87, 201–5; and Newby, *Jim Crow's Defense,* 7. On the Alabama estimation of the North's "full sympathy" for their racial situation, see, e.g., T. G. Jones, quoted in *Official Proceedings, 1901,* 3:2,885–86.

11. Villard quoted in Bailey, *Liberalism in the New South,* 51–52; Johnson quoted in Tindall, *Ethnic Southerners,* 60; *New York Age,* 9 Nov. 1911 clipping; *New York World,* n.d. clipping; and miscellaneous, 26 Aug. 1911, clipping in MLD's Donor Scrapbook, OCA.

12. *Proceedings of the Race Conference Held by the Southern Society for the Promotion of the Study of Race Conditions and Problems in the South, in Montgomery, Alabama, 1900,* p. 31. Hereafter cited as the *1900 Montgomery Race Conference Proceedings.* See also Singal, "Ulrich B. Phillips," 881; and Hackney, *Populism to Progressivism in Alabama,* 188–89. The "race problem" for Murphy was "the problem of taking . . . [Democratic] institutions . . . which are the flowering of the political consciousness of the most politically efficient of all the races of mankind . . . and securing the just coordination under them . . . with a race which with all its virtues, is socially and politically almost the least efficient of the families of men"; in *The Basis of Ascendancy* Murphy wrote: "Where two social or racial groups—a stronger and a weaker—find themselves in inevitable contact upon the same soil, what elementary principles shall ultimately determine the policies of the state? . . . Shall [they be] . . . repressive or constructive?" (quoted in H. H. Hall, "Montgomery Race Conference," 18–19). As paternalist Thomas Nelson Page expressed it: "What of value to the human race has the Negro mind as yet produced?" (*Negro,* 249). On the Tuskegee model of vocational and trade education, see Cooper, "Booker T. Washington and William J. Edwards of Snow Hill Institute," 111, 126–27; and W. A. Link, *Paradox of Southern Progressivism,* 76–77, 129, 244, 246. On vocational education at Tuskegee, see the reminiscences from the Harriette Booth interview by Alfonso Smith, 2 May 1974, Tuskegee, Alabama, 5:3–4, interview no. 78, ACHE no. T.I. 78; the Ophelia Coyer interview by Alfonso T. Smith, 28 May 1974, Tuskegee, Alabama, 7:8, interview no. 092; and the Frederick D. Patterson interview by Alfonso T. Smith, 26 Aug. 1974, Tuskegee, Alabama, 8:6, interview no. 101, all in Statewide Oral History Project: Transcriptions of Interviews, Alabama Center for Higher Education, MILES.

13. Murphy quotation in Grantham, *Southern Progressivism,* 233.

14. Grantham wrote that "even the minority of whites that criticized repressive measures against the Negroes were often motivated by a concern for whites rather than blacks" (*Southern Progressivism,* 231). See also Kirby, *Darkness at the Dawning,* 59–63. The historian of the race conference ultimately damned it for its failure "to distinguish between the principles of the highest and best traditions of their society and the social and political expedients to which they had become accustomed. . . . [Granted, they were] expedients which would have tended to eliminate the most flagrant abuses of the Negro but which were nonetheless intended to uphold the doctrine of white supremacy" (H. H. Hall, "Montgomery Race Conference," v and 107–8).

15. Murphy quoted in Kirby, *Darkness at the Dawning*, 71–72; see also 63–64.

16. H. H. Hall, "Montgomery Race Conference," 107–8. On firsthand recollections of Booker T. Washington's philosophy and influence, see Lillie Wilson interview by Helen Dibble and Jessie Guzman, 25 Jan. 1973, Tuskegee, Alabama, 4:10–17, interview no. 061, ACHE no. T.I. 61; B. H. Crutcher interview by James Underwood, 8 Oct. 1972, Tuskegee, Alabama, 4:1–6, interview no. 065, ACHE no. T.I. 65, Statewide Oral History Project: Transcriptions of Interviews, Alabama Center for Higher Education, MILES.

17. Booker T. Washington, "The Montgomery Race Conference," *Century* 61:641, quoted in H. H. Hall, "Montgomery Race Conference," 29. See also Shapiro, *White Violence and Black Response*, 135–36.

18. Murphy to Johnston, 19 Mar. 1900, Alabama Governors Papers, Joseph F. Johnston Papers, ADAH, and the *Montgomery Advertiser*, 11 Feb. 1900, both quoted in H. H. Hall, "Montgomery Race Conference," 29–33; see also 15, 17, 20, 27–29, 84, 119. Also Hammett, "Reconstruction History before Dunning," 185–96, esp. 186.

19. Hart, *Southern South*, 91.

20. Bailey, *Liberalism in the New South*, 66; and Hackney, *Populism to Progressivism in Alabama*, 189 n. 25.

21. *1900 Montgomery Race Conference Proceedings*, 37; and Hilary A. Herbert, "The Race Problem in the South," *Annals of the American Academy of Political and Social Science* 18 (1901): 100, both quoted in H. H. Hall, "Montgomery Race Conference," 93–94; Edgar Gardner Murphy, "Open Letter to Chairman Smith" (1901), quoted in H. H. Hall, 94, 100; Oscar W. Underwood, "The Negro Problem in the South," *Forum* 30 (July 1900): 215–19, quoted in H. H. Hall, 98; Alfred Bushnell Hart, "Conditions of the Southern Problem," *Independent* 58 (23 Mar. 1905): 646, 649; and Hart, *Southern South*, 59, quoted in W. A. Link, *Paradox of Southern Progressivism*, 8–9. See also Bailey, *Edgar Gardner Murphy*.

22. Harvey to W. D. Jelks, 8 Mar. 1906, Alabama Governors Papers, W. D. Jelks Papers, ADAH; *1900 Montgomery Race Conference Proceedings*, 88, 205–10, 212–14, 216, quoted in H. H. Hall, "Montgomery Race Conference," 57–61; Cochran quotation from a T. G. Jones quote in *Official Proceedings, 1901*, 4:4,303. Throughout the period, local politicians raised the taxes on northern labor agents to discourage the exodus of black labor; see C. V. Harris, *Political Power in Birmingham*, 226–27. In an excellent study, Ward and Rogers described Jones as "a paragon of antilabor, probusiness Bourbonism" (*Convicts, Coal, and the Banner Mine Tragedy*, 39). Of course, a staple of this kind of paternalism was antiunionism. For a discussion of how Birmingham mine owners preached antiunionism as a part of their corporate welfare efforts toward blacks, see Kelly, "Policing the 'Negro Eden,'" 168–69; and Kelly, *Race, Class, and Power in the Alabama Coalfields*.

23. B. F. Riley, president of Howard University, published *The White Man's Burden* in 1910, which advocated education for blacks; see Williamson, *Crucible of Race*, 282. Wayne Flynt estimated that most Birmingham Protestants were paternalistic toward blacks ("Religion in the Urban South," 132). Paternalists such as W. C. Oates and T. G. Jones favored trade education for blacks; see McMillan, *Constitutional Development in Alabama*, 264, 275, 304; H. H. Hall, "Montgomery Race Conference," 17, 37–39, 57; and Bailey, *Liberalism in the New South*, 145–51. In fact, Bailey somewhat sanguinely described

the "educational renaissance . . . conceived and executed by Southern social reformers [as] . . . the[ir] most positive program" (153).

24. Quotation in McKiven, *Iron and Steel,* 119–20.

25. *Birmingham News,* 2 Jan. 1902; 3, 10, 15 Feb. 1902; and 20 Sept. 1902, quoted in McKiven, *Iron and Steel,* 118, 120.

26. *Birmingham Age-Herald,* cited in McWilliams, "New Day Coming," 183–84; C. V. Harris, *Political Power in Birmingham,* 173.

27. Quotations from Rogers et al., *Alabama,* 335. See also A. O. Harwell and A. T. Goodwyn to ———, 4 Apr. 1893, box 2, folder 62; Reuben F. Kolb to Cabot Lull, 9 Nov. 1894, box 2, folder 63; and W. H. Skaggs to Cabot Lull, 2 Jan. 1895, box 2, folder 64, all in the Cabot Lull Collection, UA.

28. John V. Smith quoted in *Minutes of the State Democratic Executive Committee* (SDEC), 3 Apr. 1901, p. 3, box 3, folder 1, SDEC Records, ADAH.

29. Thomas H. Watts quoted in *Official Proceedings, 1901,* 3:2,982.

30. Charles H. Greer of Perry County quoted in *Official Proceedings, 1901,* 3:3,079, also quoted in McMillan, *Constitutional Development in Alabama,* 284 n. 6; *Mobile Register,* 14 Jan. 1893, also cited in McMillan, 230; see also 229, 283–84. Some patricians expressed fear that north Alabama whites were learning how to manipulate ethnic votes through force and fraud. "I told them to go to it, boys, count them out," admitted patrician former governor William C. Oates, "[b]ut we have gone on from bad to worse until it has become such a great evil. White men have gotten to cheating each other" (quoted in *Official Proceedings, 1901,* 3:2,788–89). See also Woodward, *Origins of the New South,* 326. Some also expressed concern that the federal government might intervene in southern elections if they continued to be so blatantly controlled by force and fraud, a privileged concern that would also fuel opposition to lynching and the Ku Klux Klan in later years. Others simply objected that the practice of buying votes was becoming too expensive monetarily. "I want cheaper votes," bluntly explained William A. Handley, wealthy Randolph County delegate to the 1901 constitutional convention (quoted in *Official Proceedings, 1901,* 3:2,877). See also Rogers et al., *Alabama,* 351; and "Defense of the Negro Race— Charges Answered," Speech of Hon. George H. White of North Carolina in the House of Representatives, 29 Jan. 1901, electronic edition, pp. 6–7, DTS.

31. William C. Oates, inaugural address, quoted in the *Montgomery Advertiser,* 2 Dec. 1894, cited in McMillan, *Constitutional Development in Alabama,* 226.

32. *Birmingham Age-Herald* 1901, cited in McMillan, *Constitutional Development in Alabama,* 225–26.

33. *Selma Times,* 6 Dec. 1895. For an excellent study of Reconstruction politics, see Fitzgerald, *Union League Movement in the Deep South.*

34. John Tyler Morgan to John Hollis Bankhead, in the *Mobile Register,* 28 Feb. 1900.

35. Suffrage would, therefore, be restricted to only those with "virtue and intelligence"; it would be denied to the "ignorant and vicious." Quotations from McMillan, *Constitutional Development in Alabama,* 230 and 269 n. 41. See, for example, the *Montgomery Advertiser,* 8 June 1892; *Official Proceedings, 1901,* 3:2,914, 2,926, 2,929, 3,024, 3,028, 3,056, 3,194; Murphy, *Problems of the Present South,* 199; and Horton, "Testing the Limits of

Class Politics in Postbellum Alabama," 63–84. Some "reform-wing" whites also favored the calling of a constitutional convention because they saw it as an opportunity to increase state educational expenditures by constitutional mechanism; see D. A. Harris, "Racists and Reformers," 126, 185.

36. On the transitory, ephemeral, and pragmatic nature of Populist biracialism, see Flynt, *Poor but Proud*, 253 and 254; Flynt, *Dixie's Forgotten People*, 52; and Fredrickson, *Arrogance of Race*, 157. On poor whites generally, see also Newby, *Plain Folk in the New South*.

37. Quotations from Gaither, *Blacks and the Populist Revolt*, 28–29. See also DeVine, "Free Silver and Alabama Politics," 71–72.

38. Quotations from *Birmingham State Herald*, 12 May 1896, and the *Covington Times*, 15 Oct. 1897, both cited in Gross, "Alabama Politics and the Negro," 205–6; see also 210–11. The *Birmingham State Herald*, a newspaper owned by Joseph F. Johnston, gloated in 1896 that "an overdose of bichloride of Negro" had killed the Populist Party (quoted in Gross, "Alabama Politics and the Negro," 212).

39. Quotation from Gaither, *Blacks and the Populist Revolt*, 28–29. This expression of community displeasure and ostracism had a long history in Europe, where the ritual was known as "charivari." See N. Z. Davis, *Society and Culture in Early Modern France*. The tactic of disparaging political independence via personal and moral character assassination had been used by the Redeemers against the political precursors to the Populists. For example, Jourd White, editor of the Redeemer newspaper in Lawrence County, had castigated his opposite number at the *Alabama State Wheel*, also published in Lawrence, as "destitute to all amenities . . . required to make up a gentleman. Destitute of truth— festering with filth and rotten with communism—he has sunk too low to be reached as a decent gentleman" by publishing the *Wheel*, "a disgrace to journalism." See the *Moulton Advertiser*, 9 Aug. 1888, quoted in Horton, "Testing the Limits of Class Politics in Postbellum Alabama," 78.

40. A number of studies comment on the variances in economic status and occupation of the Populists and other anti-Redeemers. See, for example, Hyman, *Anti-Redeemers*, 11–13 and 177–81; Hahn, *Roots of Southern Populism*; Hair, *Bourbonism and Agrarian Protest*; and Woodman, "Economic Reconstruction and the New South," 279–81, cited in Boles and Nolen, *Interpreting Southern History*.

41. Gaither, *Blacks and the Populist Revolt*, 21.

42. The instances occurred in 1892 and 1896. See Hackney, *Populism to Progressivism in Alabama*, 149; DeVine, "Free Silver and Alabama Politics," 82–83, 230; and Kousser, *Shaping of Southern Politics*, 132.

43. Flynt, *Poor but Proud*, 253.

44. Quotation from Rodabaugh, "Fusion, Confusion, Defeat, and Disfranchisement," 140. Kolb eventually came out for a disfranchising constitutional convention along with prominent Alabama Populists Joseph Manning, William H. Skaggs, and others. See Gaither, *Blacks and the Populist Revolt*, 105 and 110.

45. Woodward conjectured that some poor whites blamed blacks for causing the

Populist defeat because some blacks had voluntarily voted with the Democrats. See *Origins of the New South*, 323. Shaw gives credence to this view in *Wool Hat Boys*.

46. *Montgomery Alliance Herald* quoted in the *Anniston Weekly Times*, 25 May 1893, cited in Rogers et al., *Alabama*, 312. For examples of Kolb's involvement at this time, see the documents in Griffith, *Alabama*, 515–19. On the Populist advocacy of an all-white direct primary, see Gaither, *Blacks and the Populist Revolt*, 108; and Atkins, "Populism in Alabama," 179–80.

47. *Tallapoosa New Era*, Hill Country newspaper quoted in the *Birmingham People's Weekly Tribune*, 3 Dec. 1896. Also see the *Birmingham People's Weekly Tribune*, 26 Nov. and 10 Dec. 1896 and 14 Jan. 1897 (fifth quotation), all cited in Gaither, *Blacks and the Populist Revolt*, 108–10 (first set of quotations).

48. Rodabaugh, "Fusion, Confusion, Defeat, and Disfranchisement," 145; Rogers and Ward in the excellent state history by Rogers et al., *Alabama*, 312–14; and Letwin, *Challenge of Interracial Unionism*, 111.

49. *Tuscaloosa American* quoted in another Populist newspaper, the *Cullman People's Protest*, 1 Apr. 1898, 4. Also see McMillan, *Constitutional Development in Alabama*, 230, 232.

50. Denson, in the *Proceedings of the Democratic State Convention* (DSC), SDEC records, ADAH, 29 Mar. 1899, 23, 25–27. Denson's ardor cooled as it became increasingly apparent that patrician promises to protect poor-white voting in a constitutional convention were empty. For T. A. Street's support of Denson, see Webb, *Two-Party Politics in the One-Party South*, 108. Also on Denson, see Hackney, *Populism to Progressivism in Alabama*, 54, 165, 235; and DeVine, "Free Silver and Alabama Politics," 82, 87, 108, and 113. For a sample of the pledges, see Hackney, *Populism to Progressivism in Alabama*, 159, 164–66, 168, 175; and Rogers et al., *Alabama*, 346. Hackney has written that "Progressives and Populists too for that matter, were no less racist or prejudiced than their fellow Alabamians" (326). Wayne Flynt concurred that "[i]n some respects poor whites were harsher racists than yeomen or planters" (*Dixie's Forgotten People*, 11).

51. I. L. Brock to O. D. Street, 13 Sept. 1902, Oliver Day Street Papers, UA, quoted in Hackney, *Populism to Progressivism in Alabama*, 203. For more on Brock, see the *Cullman People's Protest*, 22 July 1898, 4. The *Cherokee Sentinel* was published at Centre in Cherokee County. Also see DeVine, "Free Silver and Alabama Politics," 315. For the *Sentinel's* Populist politics, see Hackney, *Populism to Progressivism in Alabama*, 119 and 154. On Denson, see also Hackney, 54, 165, and 235.

52. *Clanton Banner*, 17 Oct. 1901, 4.

53. *Cullman People's Protest*, 9 Sept. 1898, 2.

54. *Cullman People's Protest*, 9 Sept. 1898, 2.

55. Quotations from *Huntsville Republican*, 26 Mar. 1901, quoted in McMillan, *Constitutional Development in Alabama*, 261; see also 232, as well as Lamis, *Two-Party South*. *Huntsville Tribune* quoted in the *Choctaw Alliance*, 10 Apr. 1901, 1. Also see Taylor, "Populism and Disfranchisement in Alabama," 417 n. 16; Gaither, *Blacks and the Populist Revolt*, 108; and Moore, *History of Alabama*, 635. On the Populist and "black-and-tan"

Republican enmity, see Hackney, *Populism and Progressivism in Alabama*, 34–35; and DeVine, "Free Silver and Alabama Politics," 109, 112, and 334. Republicans William F. Aldrich and Truman H. Aldrich won in the fourth and the ninth congressional district, respectively, both after contested elections.

56. Deans was from Calera in the Upcountry county of Shelby. See the *Randolph Toiler*, 15 July 1898, 2; and also Hackney, *Populism to Progressivism in Alabama*, 155. See also McMillan, *Constitutional Development in Alabama*, 250. Among those plain-white leaders apprehensive about the disfranchisement of their constituents were Governor Joseph F. Johnston, future governor Bibb Graves, Sam Will John, Rufus W. Cobb, John W. A. Sanford, Congressman William H. Denson, and *Montgomery Southern Argus* editor Robert McKee. See John W. A. Sanford to McKee, 20 Mar. 1899, Robert McKee Papers, ADAH, cited in D. A. Harris, "Racists and Reformers," 132–33, 181. See also material in box 5, folder 7, John W. A. Sanford Papers, ADAH. And see Joseph F. Johnston to Chappell Cory, n.d.; J. V. van Der veer to Chappell Cory, 8 Sept. 1897; and W. H. Raymond to Chappell Cory, 20 Sept. 1897, in box 1, folder 5, Chappell Cory Papers, ADAH. Later Sanford would protest the new constitution's property and educational qualifications as so restrictive that "Christ and his Disciples might be here [and] . . . they could not vote" (quoted in *Official Proceedings, 1901*, 3:3,197).

57. Quoted in *Cullman People's Protest*, 1 July 1898, 1.

58. Quoted in *Randolph Toiler*, 22 July 1898, 5. The newspaper was published in Wedowee.

59. Black identification with patrician whites had, of course, been present to some extent since slavery. The term "poor-white trash" can be found in Katherine "Ma" Eppes interview by Susie R. O'Brien, Uniontown, Alabama, 25 May 1937, in the Federal Writers' Project, *Slave Narratives*, 120. See also Cash, *Mind of the South*, 317–18; and Woodward, *Origins of the New South*, 323.

60. Williams Parker quoted in the *Tuskaloosa Chronicle*, 11 Feb. 1899, 2.

61. Deans quotation from *Randolph Toiler*, 22 July 1898, 5. DuBose quotations from "Forty Years in Alabama," chap. 32, 1,018 and 1,020, in box 3, folder 22, John Witherspoon DuBose Papers, ADAH. The strategy and power of appealing to plain-white emotions over white supremacy and solidarity to stimulate support for a disfranchising constitutional convention were much discussed by regular Democrats. See, e.g., *Minutes of the* SDEC, 3 Apr. 1901, 4, 5, 6–7, and 8. Perhaps the most dramatic of these Reconstruction appeals was that of the *Montgomery Advertiser*, leading platform for Bourbon interests: "South Alabama raises her manacled hands in mute appeal to the mountain counties. The chains on the wrists of her sons, and the midnight shrieks of her women, sound continually in their ears. She lifts up her eyes, being tormented, and begs piteously for relief from the bondage. Is there a white man in North Alabama so lost to all his finer feelings of human nature as to slight her appeal?" (1 Nov. 1874).

62. Former Populists should be included as anti-Democrats for the purposes of exploring this issue. By 1901, many of the former Populists were in transit to either the Democratic or the Republican Party, yet it would be a mistake to expel them from the "anti-Democratic" pool for analytical reasons. Many of the old Populists—even though

they had decided to bury old squabbles and reunite with the Democratic Party on the basis of white unity, the promise of black disfranchisement, and despair with the electoral possibilities of a third party—retained their Jeffersonian approach to politics, especially economics, and only a marginal and nominal attachment to Democracy understood as the old Democratic and Conservative Party. The Jeffersonian journal the *Marshall Banner,* for example, termed A. McHan's Populist *Boaz Signal* "the defunct organ of the defunct party" in its 17 Aug. 1899 issue (p. 2), yet the *Banner* and its editor were themselves considered by some contemporaries to be Populists and were, at the very least, Jeffersonian. See the *Marshall Banner,* 14 Sept. 1899, 2. For the Democratic Party understood as the Democratic and Conservative Party of Alabama, see Henry De Lamar Clayton, quoted in the *Proceedings of the* DSC, 25 Apr. 1900, 12; and J. Thomas Heflin, quoted in the *Minutes of the* SDEC, 15 Jan. 1901, 12. See also DeVine, "Free Silver and Alabama Politics," 319. For Populist reentry into the Democratic Party on the basis of white unity and black disfranchisement, see the *Proceedings of the* DSC, 25 Apr. 1900, 12 (Henry De Lamar Clayton) and 15 (Frank S. White), box 2, folder 2; *State Democratic Executive Committee* (SDEC) *Minutes,* 15 Jan. 1901, 12 (J. Thomas Heflin) and 18 (A. P. Smith and Edmund L. Pettus), box 2, folder 4; and the *Minutes of the* SDEC, 3 Apr. 1901, 12 (T. G. Jones and Whitson), box 3, folder 1, all documents in the SDEC Records, ADAH. See also the *Carrollton, Alabama Alliance News,* 24 and 31 July 1900, 2 in both. For Populist disillusionment and temporary apathy in Alabama, see the *Carrollton, Alabama Alliance News,* 7 Aug. 1900, 2; and in other southern states, Dailey, *Before Jim Crow,* 162.

63. *Tuscaloosa American,* 28 July 1898, cited in McMillan, *Constitutional Development in Alabama,* 254. See also the *Randolph Toiler,* 24 June 1898, 2; and the *Centre Cherokee Sentinel* editorial reprinted with approval by the *Carrollton, Alabama Alliance News,* 23 May 1899, 2. For the private admission of the *Cherokee Sentinel*'s editor, see I. L. Brock to O. D. Street, 13 Sept. 1902, in Street Papers, UA, quoted in Hackney, *Populism to Progressivism in Alabama,* 203.

64. See both the *Sheffield Reaper* and the *Murfreesboro (Tennessee) Banner,* cited in the *Randolph Toiler,* 24 June 1898, 2.

65. Party platform quoted in the *Randolph Toiler,* 13 May 1898, 2.

66. Apportionment on the basis of a county's total population, of course, favored the Black Belt counties, which were able to dominate the state legislature by counting their heavy black populations for purposes of representation. See also Rogers et al., *Alabama,* 343; Hackney, *Populism to Progressivism in Alabama,* 150–51; and McWilliams, "New Day Coming," 178 and 179.

67. *Tuscaloosa American,* 28 July 1898, quoted in Gross, "Alabama Politics and the Negro," 226.

68. Hyman, *Anti-Redeemers,* 167–91.

69. Ibid., 175 (both quotations).

70. First quotation from Hyman, *Anti-Redeemers,* 190, 191; quotations regarding Lawrence County example from Horton, "Testing the Limits of Class Politics in Postbellum Alabama," 77, 78, and 81; see also 63–84. Subsistence farmers and dirt farmers in Lawrence sometimes tried to make ends meet as well by hiring on part-time as artisans.

71. First quotation from *Marshall Banner,* 6 and 20 Apr. 1899; second quotation from Hackney, *Populism to Progressivism in Alabama,* 66. See also Gross, "Alabama Politics and the Negro," 221, 234, 236, 246–47; and DeVine, "Free Silver and Alabama Politics," 229. "Palmer and Buckner" referred to the 1896 national gold Democratic ticket, the conservative monetary policy ticket.

72. *Carrollton, Alabama Alliance News,* 10 July 1900, 2, and 7 Aug. 1900, 2.

73. *Carrollton, Alabama Alliance News,* 31 July 1900, 2.

74. *Montgomery Advertiser,* 8 June 1892, quoted in McMillan, *Constitutional Development in Alabama,* 252 n. 26; Hackney, *Populism to Progressivism in Alabama,* 149, 151; and Kousser, *Shaping of Southern Politics,* 132. Under the Sayre measure, which took effect after the 1892 elections, Democratic election officers could deny people the vote or vote them the "right way" (McMillan, *Constitutional Development in Alabama,* 224). Sayre, though, was a mild restriction in comparison to the 1901 provisions. See Taylor, "Populism and Disfranchisement in Alabama," 410–27, esp. 414 and 418. The law's author, Anthony Dickinson Sayre, had an impeccable pedigree as the nephew of John Tyler Morgan and the son-in-law of U.S. senator Simon Bolivar Bruckner of Kentucky, a former Confederate general and gold Democratic candidate for vice president (Kousser, *Shaping of Southern Politics,* 133). Answering one of Sayre's queries to southern secretaries of state, Arkansas's officeholder replied that their Sayre-like law "works smoothly, quietly, satisfactorily, beautifully, and I pray to God every Southern State may soon have one like it. It neutralizes . . . the Fifteenth Amendment, the blackest curse of the nineteenth century" (quoted in Perman, *Struggle for Mastery,* 20).

75. Rodabaugh, "Fusion, Confusion, Defeat, and Disfranchisement," 132–35, 140, 143, 144, and 146; D. A. Harris, "Racists and Reformers," 39–42, 137.

76. First, second, and third quotations from Rodabaugh, "Fusion, Confusion, Defeat, and Disfranchisement," 139; fourth quotation from D. A. Harris, "Racists and Reformers," 47, also 44–48, 76, and 83. See also Bagwell, " 'Magical Process,' " 83–104.

77. Moore, *History of Alabama,* 632. For examples of Populist support of Johnston, see the *Ozark Free Press,* 4 May 1899, 5; and 15 Mar. 1900, 5; and the *Gadsden Tribune,* 3 Aug. 1899, 4. Johnston used appointments such as I. L. Brock to the Cherokee County probate judgeship to shore up his Populist base of support through patronage; see DeVine, "Free Silver and Alabama Politics," 224–25 and 103, 105, 166–67, 181, 232, 237, and 243. On the "halfway" Populist quote, see Gross, "Alabama Politics and the Negro," 225.

78. Quotation from *Randolph Toiler,* 2 Dec. 1898, 2; see also Hackney, *Populism to Progressivism in Alabama,* 157.

79. See text associated with note 90 in this chapter. Willis Brewer, George P. Harrison, Richard Henry Clark, G. L. Comer, W. D. Jelks, John B. Knox, Sydney J. Bowie, John V. Smith, and Wiley and Alfred M. Tunstall were other gold Democrats gaining control of the momentum for a constitutional convention. See also Hackney, *Populism to Progressivism in Alabama,* 166, 175, and 178.

80. The quotation is from the *Atlanta Constitution.* See also McMillan, *Constitutional Development in Alabama,* 251–52, 255–56.

81. *Selma Times* quoted in the *Montgomery Advertiser,* 18 Apr. 1899; and the *Wilcox*

Progress quoted in the *Montgomery Advertiser,* 13 May 1899. Also see McMillan, *Constitutional Development in Alabama,* 257–58.

82. The pledge not to harm poor white suffrage was made repeatedly by the likes of W. C. Oates, William D. Jelks, G. L. Comer, Alfred M. Tunstall, U.S. senators John Tyler Morgan and Edmund L. Pettus, and congressman John H. Bankhead. See Hackney, *Populism to Progressivism in Alabama,* 159, 164–65, 166, 168, 175; D. A. Harris, "Racists and Reformers," 146–47; and Rogers et al., *Alabama,* 336, 345. The 1901 constitutional convention delegates voted 87 to 27 to keep total population as the basis of apportionment but called for a reapportionment after each new census, the next one in 1910; the state legislature, though, refused to reapportion itself until the 1960s. See also McMillan, *Constitutional Development in Alabama,* 308 n. 158; and the *Shelby Sentinel,* 14 July and 24 Nov. 1898, p. 2 in both.

83. The 1898 conditions also included the promise to keep the state capital in Montgomery and to include a "fighting grandfather clause" to protect the vote of former sailors and soldiers. See also *Proceedings of the* DSC, 19 Mar. 1901, quoted in McMillan, *Constitutional Development in Alabama,* 259 n. 76, and also see 251, 259–60, 271; and Rogers et al., *Alabama,* 336, 345.

84. Quoted in *Proceedings of the* DSC, 3 Apr. 1901, 3. See also the *Birmingham Age-Herald,* 22 Mar. 1901.

85. Perman, *Struggle for Mastery,* 177.

86. Rufus W. Cobb to Robert McKee, 20 July 1899, Robert McKee Papers, ADAH, cited in D. A. Harris, "Racists and Reformers," 139. To a lesser extent, the election concerned the issue of a direct primary. Johnston favored such a primary as a democratizing reform over the customary party nominating convention and a vehicle that would favor him with his plain-white constituency. Morgan, of course, opposed it. See D. A. Harris, "Racists and Reformers," 146–47. See also the *Carrollton, Alabama Alliance News,* 28 Nov. 1899, 2. On the important concept of "honor," see Wyatt-Brown, *Shaping of Southern Culture, Honor and Violence in the Old South,* and *Southern Honor.*

87. The term "New Men" refers to one of Woodward's best-known theses from *Origins of the New South.* There is, of course, an extensive literature associated with this term and debate. For a sample, see Lewis, *Sloss Furnaces and the Rise of the Birmingham District;* Doyle, *New Men, New Cities, New South;* Cobb, "Beyond Planters and Industrialists," 45–68; and Wiener, *Social Origins of the New South.* For more on Johnston, see D. A. Harris, "Racists and Reformers," 21, 23.

88. Fry, "Governor Johnston's Attempt to Unseat Senator Morgan," 243–44, 247, 279. For more on the lives of Birmingham District workers at Sloss, black and white, see the U. S. Anderson oral history; the George Brown oral history by Cliff Kuhn and Brenda McCallum, 25 Apr. 1983, 3, and 12–15; the Clarence Dean oral history by Brenda McCallum, 7 May 1983, 13; the Charles Harrell oral history, 3; and others among the seventy-odd interviews in the Oral History Project, SLOSS.

89. Quotation from Fry, "Governor Johnston's Attempt to Unseat Senator Morgan," 250–51. See also Frank S. White to Joseph F. Johnston, 19 Feb. 1900, and William W. Brandon to Joseph F. Johnston, 20 Apr. 1900, in folder "Correspondence Political, Jan.–

June 1900," administrative files, Alabama Governors' Papers, Joseph F. Johnston Papers, ADAH. References to repairing the damage of Reconstruction "carpetbaggers" and "scalawags" were a ubiquitous part of the 1901 constitutional convention. See, e.g., the *Official Proceedings, 1901,* 3:2,779, 2,855, 2,885, and 3,002.

90. Hackney, *Populism to Progressivism in Alabama,* 170–72, 234; Gross, "Alabama Politics and the Negro," 228; and Fry, "Governor Johnston's Attempt to Unseat Senator Morgan," 252, 255. Johnston infuriated Morgan on a personal level when he criticized the proposed cutting of a canal through Nicaragua, the senator's pet project, by mocking the senator: "We want a canal full of water, not wind."

91. Quotations from Fry, "Governor Johnston's Attempt to Unseat Senator Morgan," 257–59, 273.

92. The Reconstruction syndrome was introduced and first discussed in Feldman, *Politics, Society, and the Klan in Alabama,* 75, 187, 327, 375 n. 41, and 391 n. 44. It is also discussed in Feldman, "Introduction," 5–6, in *Reading Southern History.* The Second Reconstruction cemented and personalized these beliefs in the minds of a new generation of white southerners and their children. To a large extent, the unfortunate propensities characteristic of this syndrome still persist at, or just under, the surface of the present-day South—shaping and coloring the region's approach to politics, economics, and social mores. Often, these predilections appear in softer, sanitized, and more euphemistic forms. Yet appear they still do as an almost manic concern for states' rights, local autonomy, individual freedom, political conservatism, sectional pride, and traditional values, religion, and gender roles—in fact, reverence for all things traditional, including pride in the white race's leadership and achievements and disdain for hyphenated Americanism in favor of ethnic, racial, and cultural homogeneity, in sum, for all the things that "made this country great." See also chapter 5, note 52.

93. Robert McKee was denied a Democratic patronage position because of his 1892 support of Populist Reuben Kolb. See DeVine, "Free Silver and Alabama Politics," 89–90, also 319; and D. A. Harris, "Racists and Reformers," 44. John Witherspoon DuBose's support of Reuben Kolb and the Populist ticket in 1894 is discussed in J. C. DuBose, *Notable Men of Alabama,* 1:81; see also 80–82. On John Witherspoon DuBose, his Populism, and his editorship of the Populist newspaper, see DeVine, "Free Silver and Alabama Politics," 226; Hackney, *Populism to Progressivism in Alabama,* 119, 120; Owen, *History of Alabama and Dictionary of Alabama Biography,* 3:511; and the introduction to J. W. DuBose, *Tragic Decade.*

94. Quoted material in paragraph and block quote from chap. 32, 1,008, 1,011–20; chap. 25, 854; chap. 26, 883; introduction, 23, 25, 136; chap. 1, 257, 262, 266–68; chap. 3, 292; chap. 4, 338, 340–42; chap. 5, 349, 350, 353, 357–59; chap. 6, 391, 397, in John Witherspoon DuBose, "Forty Years in Alabama," in box 3, folders 15, 17, 18, and 22, and box 4, folder 30, in John Witherspoon DuBose Papers, ADAH. The subject of allegedly debased black morals and its relation to black suffrage was a recurring theme at the 1901 constitutional convention. See, e.g., *Official Proceedings, 1901,* 3:2,816–17 and 3,092. The Dunning School conception of Reconstruction and like matters persisted into the twentieth century. A particularly good example of the genre was supplied by Thomas Chalmers McCorvey, a

student of Dunning's at the University of Chicago and for fifty years a professor of history at the University of Alabama. McCorvey's son, Gessner, served four terms as State Democratic Executive Committee chair before helping to lead the Dixiecrat revolt in Alabama and eventually joining the ranks of the Republican Party. See McCorvey, *Alabama,* esp. chap. 10 on the Reconstruction KKK. Also see Houghton and Houghton, *Two Boys in the Civil War and After,* electronic edition in DTS. The sentiment was common to both plain and patrician whites in Alabama. State senator John T. Milner, one of the founding industrial fathers of the Birmingham District, furnished a representative sample in arguing passionately against any federal role in southern elections by explaining that the African American was "unfitted by nature to govern himself, much less other races of men." After a "partial civilization, and . . . a quasi-incorporation into the family of nations," the black, "left to himself," would gravitate "slowly but surely backwards toward his original barbarism," replete with "unthrift, idleness, vice, immorality, voodooism, and even cannibalism." Reconstruction and federal involvement in southern affairs had been a "more devilish system" than had ever "been known in the history of civilized nations . . . a Saturnalia of evil" distinguished by the "abject misery of the white man." It would be far "better . . . that Alabama with her freighted cargo should sink beneath the waves and be forever lost" than to continue the mistake of black voting (speech of John T. Milner, "White Men of Alabama Stand Together, 1860 and 1890," [1890], 3, 9, 74–75, 79, box 5, folder 32, Alabama Pamphlet Collection, ADAH).

95. John Tyler Morgan to Thomas Goode Jones, 2 Dec. 1899, in Robert McKee Papers, ADAH, quoted in Fry, "Governor Johnston's Attempt to Unseat Senator Morgan," 263, 265; and *Birmingham Age-Herald,* 17 Dec. 1899, cited in Fry, 272. Also Gross, "Alabama Politics and the Negro," 228.

96. *Montgomery Advertiser,* 19 Nov. 1899, cited in Fry, "Governor Johnston's Attempt to Unseat Senator Morgan," 258; *Montgomery Journal* 8 Feb., 17 Mar., 2 Apr. 1900, cited in Fry, 272. Chappell Cory, the private secretary to Governor Joseph F. Johnston, bought into Horace Hood's *Montgomery Journal* in October 1899. See the *Anniston Republican,* 12 Feb. 1898, 4; and the *Marshall Banner,* 12 Oct. 1899, 2, and 8 Sept. 1901, 4.

97. Alabama politics was so contentious that it split families during this era. John Tyler Morgan was a silver Democrat for over two decades, converted to gold Democracy in 1896, and functioned the whole time as Alabama's senior U.S. senator. Brother Philander was a Populist newspaper publisher who briefly rejoined silver Democracy from 1896 to 1898 before returning to Populism until after 1902 and, finally, wound up on the right wing of Alabama Democracy. G. L. Comer was a Barbour County planter, lawyer, and gold Democrat. Brother B. B. Comer was a silver Democrat and, later, progressive governor. See DeVine, "Free Silver and Alabama Politics," 197–98, 226, 239, 317, and 327; and Hackney, *Populism to Progressivism in Alabama,* 118–20.

98. Fry, "Governor Johnston's Attempt to Unseat Senator Morgan," 266–68, 270–74. Morgan's 1900 victory was reinforced by Bourbon William J. Samford's gubernatorial win. In 1902, Morgan gained additional revenge by helping William D. Jelks defeat Johnston in their gubernatorial race. Morgan again fatally wounded Johnston with charges of racial treason and of backing a Reconstruction-like plot to restore "the negro to the

ballot"; see W. D. Jelks to John Tyler Morgan, 20 June 1902, John Tyler Morgan Papers, LC, quoted in Fry, "Governor Johnston's Attempt to Unseat Senator Morgan," 278.

99. DeVine, "Free Silver and Alabama Politics," 243–44.

CHAPTER TWO *Toward Disfranchisement*

1. The opinion of J. Thomas Heflin quoted in *Proceedings of the Democratic State Convention* (DSC), 25 Apr. 1900, 6. These proceedings are found in box 2, folder 2, State Democratic Executive Committee (SDEC) Records, ADAH.

2. For a discussion of these developments and the rise of *the new racism*, see chapter 3, note 113. The politics of emotion was introduced and discussed in Feldman, *Reading Southern History,* 6 and 364.

3. Frank S. White quoted in *Proceedings of the* DSC, 25 Apr. 1900, 4–5.

4. Heflin quoted in *Proceedings of the* DSC, 25 Apr. 1900, 6. For more of Heflin's activities during this period, see the J. Thomas Heflin Scrapbooks, SU.

5. The delegates considered it a great responsibility to decide what to do with the victory the people of Alabama had given them. See, for example, *Proceedings of the* DSC, 25 Apr. 1900, 9 (Russell M. Cunningham speaking) and 15 (Frank S. White speaking). Unity over the end of black disfranchisement was apparent and accepted by virtually every Alabama white. The dispute to come was largely over means. "We all want, perhaps, the same thing," a patrician Democrat would say, "but we must get at it in the proper manner" (W. C. Oates, quoted in *Minutes of the State Democratic Executive Committee* [SDEC], 3 Apr. 1901, 16, SDEC Records, ADAH). "God never made whiter men than these Black Belt Democrats," a plain-white 1901 delegate who differed on methods would answer. "They have suffered long [and] . . . they turned to the hill counties and raised a Macedonian cry, 'Come help us.' I . . . tell you, hold forth, we are coming" (J. T. Martin, quoted in *Official Proceedings, 1901,* 3:3,011).

6. Johnston quotation from Hackney, *Populism to Progressivism in Alabama,* 120. See also Jackson, "White Supremacy Triumphant," in Thomson, *Century of Controversy,* 19; DeVine, "Free Silver and Alabama Politics," 181, 197–98, and 219–20; and Rodabaugh, "Fusion, Confusion, Defeat, and Disfranchisement," 137.

7. Hackney, *Populism to Progressivism in Alabama,* 115–19; and DeVine, "Free Silver and Alabama Politics," 313–15, 319–20, 323–27, and 333.

8. *Huntsville Journal,* 10 Nov. 1899, quoted in Hackney, *Populism to Progressivism in Alabama,* 186.

9. Robert J. Lowe (first quotation) and J. B. Graham (second quotation), both in *Proceedings of the* DSC, 25 Apr. 1900, 3.

10. Clayton quoted in *Proceedings of the* DSC, 25 Apr. 1900, 10–11. See also members of the SDEC speaking about "populites" and "Republicans" who had been "converted to Democracy" and "come in" (F. L. Pettus, quoted in *Minutes of the* SDEC, 15 Jan. 1901, 17, box 2, folder 4, SDEC Records, ADAH). A leading planter-industrialist newspaper rejoiced that "Peace Now Reigns Throughout the Ranks of Alabama Democracy . . . Perfect Harmony," as the state convention "Declares Unequivocally for a Constitutional Conven-

tion" (*Birmingham Age-Herald*, 27 Apr. 1900, 1). On Clayton, see DeVine, "Free Silver and Alabama Politics," 316.

11. Cunningham quoted in *Proceedings of the* DSC, 25 Apr. 1900, 10. On Cunningham, see DeVine, "Free Silver and Alabama Politics," 169–70, 242, and 318.

12. Heflin quoted in *Proceedings of the* DSC, 25 Apr. 1900, 6–7.

13. See comments of F. L. Pettus in *Minutes of the* SDEC, 15 Jan. 1901, 5 and 18. Tennent Lomax connected states' rights and black disfranchisement with the "protect[ion] [of] your homes and civilization." See Address of Tennent Lomax, Esq. to State Democratic Convention, ca. 1900, box 1077, folder 7, Tennent Lomax Collection, UA.

14. White quoted in *Proceedings of the* DSC, 25 Apr. 1900, 5.

15. Knox quoted in *Proceedings of the* DSC, 25 Apr. 1900, 14. For years Knox continued to make the same argument about the new constitution having "established white supremacy" for "your children and to succeeding generations" (Address of Hon. John B. Knox, Jones's Chapel in Cullman County, Alabama, 4 July 1906, 14, TCSH).

16. Clayton quoted in *Proceedings of the* DSC, 25 Apr. 1900, 11.

17. White quoted in *Proceedings of the* DSC, 25 Apr. 1900, 15–16. Populists who favored a disfranchisement constitution were also not averse to casting their advocacy as an emotional appeal to duty to posterity. See e.g., the *Choctaw Alliance*, 10 Apr. 1901, 1.

18. Knox quoted in *Proceedings of the* DSC, 25 Apr. 1900, 14, and *Official Proceedings, 1901*, 1:8, 9, and 10. Also in *Journal of the Proceedings of the Constitutional Convention of the State of Alabama*, 8–11.

19. Clayton quoted in *Proceedings of the* DSC, 25 Apr. 1900, 12.

20. Knox quoted in *Proceedings of the* DSC, 25 Apr. 1900, 14.

21. Cunningham quoted in *Proceedings of the* DSC, 25 Apr. 1900, 9.

22. Knox quoted in *Proceedings of the* DSC, 25 Apr. 1900, 13.

23. Knox quoted in *Proceedings of the* DSC, 25 Apr. 1900, 13. See also H. C. Bullock to Cabot Lull, 9 Aug. 1894, box 2, folder 65, Cabot Lull Collection, UA.

24. Alabama's Democratic Party, reflecting its basic conservative nature during this period, was officially known during the late nineteenth and early twentieth centuries as the Democratic and Conservative Party and was commonly referred to as such. See, for example, Frank S. White, chmn., and R. E. L. Wiel, sec. to Robert P. McDavid, Secretary of State, 13 June 1900, box SG 2482, folder 8, Secretary of State Papers, ADAH; *Roanoke Herald*, 9 and 23 Sept. 1898, 2; *Proceedings of the* DSC, 25 Apr. 1900, 12; and *Minutes of the* SDEC, 15 Jan. 1901, 12, and 10 July 1902, 30 and 31, box 3, folder 1, SDEC Records, ADAH. Seale was from Livingston in Sumter County in the Black Belt. Givhan was from Gurley in the Tennessee Valley county of Madison.

25. F. L. Pettus quoted in *Minutes of the* SDEC, 15 Jan. 1901, 4–6 and 18. On Pettus, see Hackney, *Populism to Progressivism in Alabama*, 149, 178; and DeVine, "Free Silver and Alabama Politics," 329.

26. John V. Smith quoted in *Minutes of the* SDEC, 15 Jan. 1901, 9–10.

27. Quotations from *Minutes of the* SDEC, 15 Jan. 1901, 10–11 (Lowe), and 12 (A. P. Smith, second quotation).

28. Quotations from *Minutes of the* SDEC, 15 Jan. 1901, 13 (Bowie), 12 (Heflin), and 16

(John V. Smith). On Lowe's election as SDEC chair, see the *Proceedings of the* DSC, 25 Apr. 1900, 3. For more on the independent culture of poor whites in the Wiregrass, see the various collections at the AWHC.

29. Quotations from *Minutes of the* SDEC, 15 Jan. 1901, 11 (Lowe), and 17–19 (F. L. Pettus).

30. Bowie quoted in *Minutes of the* SDEC, 15 Jan. 1901, 13.

31. John V. Smith quoted in *Minutes of the* SDEC, 15 Jan. 1901, 16 and 19.

32. Pettus quoted in *Minutes of the* SDEC, 15 Jan. 1901, 5 and 18. For the 15–14 vote in the SDEC, see p. 20.

33. *Proceedings of the* DSC, 26 Apr. 1900, 31. Poor whites generally understood the pledge to be that no white man would be disfranchised. See the *Pickens County Alliance*, 7 July 1900, cited in Brittain, "Negro Suffrage and Politics in Alabama since 1870," 128; and Gross, "Alabama Politics and the Negro," 237, 270.

34. Webb, *Two-Party Politics in the One-Party South*, especially 168–76. Former Populist Frank Crichton edited the *Clanton Banner*, still the mouthpiece of Chilton Populism and Independent Democrats. See also the text corresponding to note 24 in the introduction.

35. See *Official Proceedings, 1901*, 3:3,281 (Reynolds's support for the character clause) and 3:3,284.

36. By the time the ratification vote came around, Frank Crichton, the former-Populist editor of the *Clanton Banner*, along with other Populist readers, was in favor of constitutional ratification—warts and all. See *Clanton Banner*, 17 Oct. 1901, 4; Civis to ed., *Clanton Banner*, 24 Oct. 1901, 1; and 7 Nov. 1901, 1; and editor's comment, 24 Oct. 1901, 4; 31 Oct. 1901, 4; and 7 Nov. 1901, 4.

37. L. H. Reynolds to ed., *Clanton Banner*, 18 Apr. 1901, 1.

38. L. B. Pounds to ed., *Clanton Banner*, 11 Apr. 1901, 1.

39. L. T. Vickers to ed., *Clanton Banner*, 18 Apr. 1901, 1.

40. Rex, from Thorsby, to ed., *Clanton Banner*, 11 Apr. 1901, 1.

41. S. R. Letcher to ed., *Clanton Banner*, 18 Apr. 1901, 1.

42. R. A. Aldridge to ed., *Clanton Banner*, 23 May 1901, 1. Racism and religious orthodoxy were closely tied together for many Jeffersonians. See, e.g., the *Collinsville Clipper*, 27 Dec. 1900, 4. Orthodox religion and attitudes on gender and industrial/business relations were tied to racial conservatism and maintaining the southern status quo for many whites. See Hackney, *Populism to Progressivism in Alabama*, 42, 177.

43. *Cherokee Sentinel*, reprinted in Carrollton, *Alabama Alliance News*, 23 May 1899, 2.

44. Quotations from Carrollton, *Alabama Alliance News*, 16 May 1899, 2. For a sample of the newspaper's politics, see 28 Nov. 1899, 2.

45. Quotation from Carrollton, *Alabama Alliance News*, 23 May 1899, 2; see also 9 May 1899, 2, and 24 July 1900, 2. Pickens County is classified as a Black Belt county for statistical purposes in this study and thus appears as such in the tables. See table 1 in the appendix. Still, Pickens had substantial Hill Country characteristics, including physiography. Gaston was a Populist judge and journalist in Butler County. See Hackney, *Pop-

ulism to Progressivism in Alabama, 169; and DeVine, "Free Silver and Alabama Politics," 320.

46. Carrollton, *Alabama Alliance News,* 30 May 1899, 2. L. H. Reynolds of Chilton County also subscribed to this conspiracy theory "to get in the negro in the black belt" in order to benefit the planters (Reynolds to ed., *Clanton Banner,* 19 Sept. 1901, 1 and 4).

47. Quotations from Webb, "Jacksonian Democrat in Postbellum Alabama," 239–74. See especially 244, 249, 273, and 274. Webb repeated the simplistic dichotomy of the disfranchisement myth: "Democrats emphasized racial issues," while the politics of Jacksonian Democrats such as McKee allegedly "transcended race"(259 and 273). Jerry W. DeVine described McKee, accurately, as an "archetypal Jeffersonian" ("Free Silver and Alabama Politics," 326; also see 89–90 and 319). See also Harris, "Racists and Reformers," 44.

48. *Montgomery Southern Argus,* reprinted in the *Alabama Alliance News,* 12 Sept. 1899, 2. McKee, who had previously published and edited the *Selma Southern Argus,* published the first issue of the Montgomery version of his newspaper on 5 May 1899. It ran for about six months. See "Robert McKee Biographical Sketch," in the Finding Aid to Personal Papers, ADAH. McKee, for all intents and purposes, equated Populism with free-silver Democracy. See his editorial, "A Bugbear," from the *Southern Argus,* reprinted in Captain A. McHan's *Gadsden Tribune,* 17 Aug. 1899, 1. For samples of McKee's extensive influence, see Sam Will John to McKee, 1 June 1898, box 3, folder 11; and J. W. Hughes to McKee, 4 May 1899; Frank P. O'Brien to McKee, 17 May 1899; and John C. Pugh to McKee, 17 July 1899, all in box 3, folder 12, Robert McKee Papers, ADAH. McKee's editorial reputation was considered "second to none in Alabama." He had previously edited the *Maysville (Ky.) Express* and the *Louisville Courier.* During the Civil War, McKee fought with the Kentucky Brigade and was wounded at Shiloh (Owen, *History of Alabama and Dictionary of Alabama Biography,* 4:1,120).

49. For the Populist cast of the *Marshall Banner,* see the issues of 10 Aug. 1899, 2; 31 Aug. 1899, 2; and 14 Sept. 1899, 2. For the *Marshall Banner*'s "half-Populist" politics, see 15 June 1899, 1–3; 13 and 20 July 1899, 2 in both. For bragging that the Populist *Cherokee Sentinel* received only three "Democratic" newspapers in its offices, all three the half-Populist variety—the *Marshall Banner,* Robert McKee's *Montgomery Southern Argus,* and Horace Hood and Chappell Cory's *Montgomery Journal*—see the *Marshall Banner,* 6 July 1899, 2. For the denunciation of former Populists who were allegedly Populists "only skin deep," see the *Marshall Banner,* 30 June 1899, 2 (quoted here); 27 July 1899, 2; 17 Aug. 1899, 2; 30 Nov. 1899, 2; and 7 Dec. 1899, 1. For the *Marshall Banner*'s early antipathy to calling a disfranchising convention, see 23 and 30 Nov. 1899, 2. For its later support of ratification, see the *Marshall Banner,* 24 Oct. 1901, 4, and 21 Nov. 1901, 4. The editor and owner of the *Marshall Banner* was James H. Meigs of Albertville, who had a running personal feud with another Jeffersonian, Captain A. McHan, the Populist editor of the *Gadsden Tribune.* See the *Marshall Banner,* 30 June, 27 July, and 10 Aug. 1899, 2 in all three; the *Gadsden Tribune* 27 July 1899, 2; and 3 Aug. 1899, 4. Despite Meigs's charges that McHan had left the Populist Party and was some kind of Jeffersonian who was a Populist

only "skin deep," McHan emphatically defended himself as a Populist and the *Gadsden Tribune* as a Populist journal. See the *Marshall Banner*, 30 June 1899, 2 (Meigs quotation); and the *Gadsden Tribune*, 31 Aug. 1899, 4. See also Ellison, *History and Bibliography of Alabama Newspapers in the Nineteenth Century*, 2; and Duncan and Smith, *History of Marshall County, Alabama*, 90.

50. Letter from an Etowah white in the *Marshall Banner*, 4 Apr. 1901, 4.

51. *Gadsden Tribune*, 25 May 1899, 4.

52. *Marshall Banner*, 13 July 1899, 2.

53. W. H. Bartlett to ed., *Marshall Banner*, 4 Apr. 1901, 1; see also 25 Apr. 1901, 4. Regarding the newspaper's opposition to a disfranchising convention, see *Marshall Banner*, 28 Sept. 1899, 2. For Populists supporting the Republican Bartlett, see Webb, *Two-Party Politics in the One-Party South*, 170.

54. *Choctaw Alliance* discussed in McMillan, *Constitutional Development in Alabama*, 348–49. For the Clarke County feud, see Jackson, "Mitcham War," 33–43, especially 35 and 38; Jackson's exemplary article, "Middle-Class Democracy Victorious," 453–78; and Jackson's first-rate monograph, in collaboration with Burrage and Cox, *Mitcham War of Clarke County, Alabama*.

55. Ed M. Johnson and his brothers published the paper on behalf of Geneva County's Jeffersonians and made it a self-consciously Populist organ. See, for example, the issues of 24 July 1901, 2; and 23 October 1901, 2. "The Reaper is distinctly the Reaper," its editorial page explained. "There are no other papers like it, in that it stands flatfooted and opposes the new constitution alone" (*Geneva Reaper*, 16 Oct. 1901, 2).

56. *Geneva Reaper*, 16 Oct. 1901, 2.

57. *Gadsden Tribune*, 25 May 1899, 4; and 18 Apr. 1901, 4. On Captain A. McHan and his Populist and Confederate background, see the *Gadsden Tribune*, 31 Aug. 1899, 2 and 4; and 10 Jan. 1901, 4; the *Marshall Banner*, 30 June 1899, 2; 27 July 1899, 2; and 10 Aug. 1899, 2; and the *Cullman People's Protest*, 1 July 1898, 2. On McHan's *Boaz Signal* being a Populist newspaper, see the *Marshall Banner*, 17 Aug. 1899, 2.

58. *Marshall Banner*, 21 Oct. 1901, 4; and 21 Nov. 1901, 4. This kind of thing occurred in other sections apart from the Hill Country. See *Ozark Free Press*, 6 Apr. 1899, 4; 3 May 1900, 2 and 4; and 9, 16, 23, and 30 Aug. 1900, 4 in all issues.

59. By the time the ratification vote came around, the editor of the Populist *Clanton Banner*, along with other Populist readers, favored ratification of the constitution, despite any shortcomings in it. See the *Clanton Banner*, 17 Oct. 1901, 4; Civis to ed., *Clanton Banner*, 24 Oct. 1901, 1; 7 Nov. 1901, 1; editor's comment, 24 Oct. 1901, 4; 31 Oct. 1901, 4; and 7 Nov. 1901, 4. Webb, while restating the disfranchisement myth, described Chilton's strong Independentism in "From Independents to Populists to Progressive Republicans," 707–36.

60. Quotations from *Attalla Mirror*, 3 Jan. 1901, 2; and 28 Mar. 1901, 2. The *Attalla Mirror* was owned and operated by Captain Joe C. Williams, an Etowah County railroad conductor who also owned and published, sometimes in tandem with George M. Holder of Attalla, the Populist newspapers the *Cherokee Sentinel* and its successor, the *Cherokee Harmonizer*, and the *Collinsville Clipper*, which had a former Hill Country Republican as

its editor and was considered a Republican newspaper by some of its peers. For example, Sheldon Hackney identified the *Cherokee Sentinel* as a Populist newspaper in *Populism to Progressivism in Alabama*, 119 and 154. Lawson A. Fields, editor of the *Attalla Mirror* for Williams, also managed the *Mirror*, the *Cherokee Harmonizer*, and the *Collinsville Clipper* until October 1901, when he resigned in favor of James L. Tucker, editor of the *Harmonizer*. See *Marshall Banner*, 31 Aug. 1899, 2; and 14 Sept. 1899, 2; *Attalla Mirror*, 14 Feb. 1901, 2; and 10 October 1901, 2; and *Collinsville Clipper*, 17 Jan. 1900, 2; and 15 Mar. 1900, 2. Jeffersonian newspapers such as the *Marshall Banner* and the *Attalla Mirror* frequently reprinted similar editorial copy from one another, sometimes accompanying the pieces with extra, supporting commentary. See, for example, the *Marshall Banner* editorial in the *Attalla Mirror*, 2 May 1901, 2; and the *Attalla Mirror* editorials in the *Marshall Banner*, 31 Aug. 1899, 2; and 14 Sept. 1899, 2. See also Ellison, *History and Bibliography of Alabama Newspapers in the Nineteenth Century*, 7.

61. *Attalla Mirror*, 7 Mar. 1901, 2.

62. Quotations from *Cullman People's Protest*, 15 Apr. 1898, 4; and 2 Sept. 1898, 2. William M. Wood, a Populist probate judge, edited this newspaper as a Populist organ with Emil Ahlrichs. See *Cullman People's Protest*, 8 and 29 Apr. 1898, 2 in both.

63. *Carrollton, Alabama Alliance News*, 10 July 1900, 2.

64. *Marshall Banner*, 11 Apr. 1901, 4.

65. *Coosa River News*, reprinted in the *Attalla Mirror*, 17 Oct. 1901, 2. See also the *Marshall Banner*, 14 Sept. 1899, 2, for the *Coosa River News*'s Republican politics. Also see the *Jacksonville Republican*, 2 Aug. 1902, 2; and the *Anniston Republican*, 1 Jan.; 26 Feb.; 5, 12, and 19 Mar.; and 2 Apr. 1898, 4 in all issues. See also Hackney, *Populism to Progressivism in Alabama*, 367, for the *Anniston Republican*'s lily-white GOP politics.

66. *Huntsville Tribune*, mentioned in the *Anniston Republican*, 15 Jan. 1898, 4; and quoted in the *Choctaw Alliance*, 10 Apr. 1901, 1. See also the *Huntsville Republican*, 26 Mar. 1901, quoted in McMillan, *Constitutional Development in Alabama*, 261; see also 232 in McMillan as well as Lamis, *Two-Party South*. General white Republican sentiment "in favor of ratification" mentioned in General Charles M. Shelley to Oscar W. Underwood, letter, printed in the Populist *Newton-Dale County Harmonizer*, 17 Oct. 1901, 1.

67. Franklin O. Deese, Park, Ala., to ed., *Newton-Dale County Harmonizer*, 25 May 1901, 2. The *Newton Harmonizer* was designed and published as the "Populists' or People's Party organ of Dale County and Southeast Alabama." It stood opposed to the calling of a convention but emphasized that the issue was not a partisan one: "Party lines were ignored on this question." See 30 Mar. 1901, 2 (first quotation in note); and 27 Apr. 1901, 2 (second quotation in note).

68. *Ozark Free Press*, 9 and 23 Aug. 1900, 2 in both issues.

69. Quotations from *Minutes of the* SDEC, 3 Apr. 1901, 2–3 (John V. Smith); 10 (Williams); and 16 (Knox). See also p. 8 (Ferguson of Jefferson County speaking).

70. Coleman quoted in *Minutes of the* SDEC, 3 Apr. 1901, 17–18. Another leading Democrat, Judge Howse, echoed Coleman in this sentiment; see p. 18.

71. *Minutes of the* SDEC, 3 Apr. 1901, 5 (Ward of Blount and J. L. Long of Butler reporting); 5–6 (Caffee of Chilton reporting); and 6 (R. H. Smith of Dale reporting).

72. H. T. Davis quoted in *Minutes of the* SDEC, 3 Apr. 1901, 6–7.

73. Ray quoted in *Minutes of the* SDEC, 3 Apr. 1901, 7.

74. Beddow quoted in *Minutes of the* SDEC, 3 Apr. 1901, 7.

75. Appraisals of county leanings from *Minutes of the* SDEC, 3 Apr. 1901, 5 (Sidney J. Bowie of Calhoun); 8 (N. Smith of Lamar); 10 (J. C. Eyster of Morgan, first quotation); 12 (Jones of Saint Clair, second quotation); 12 (C. C. Whitson of Talladega, third quotation); and 13 (Thomas L. Bulger of Tallapoosa, fourth quotation).

76. Reports of county support in *Minutes of the* SDEC, 3 Apr. 1901, 8 (J. B. Weakley of Lauderdale and Judge Kumpe of Lawrence); and 9 (J. W. Grayson of Madison, quotation in text).

77. Quotations from *Minutes of the* SDEC, 3 Apr. 1901, 8 (John V. Smith); 9–10 (Williams); 11 (Watts of Montgomery); and 11 (Taylor of Perry). Out-of-state absentee landlords and factory owners exerted pressure on regular Democrats to resist increased taxation, a continuing request in Alabama politics. W. H. Rowe Jr. of New York City, the proprietor of eight knitting companies, including one in Huntsville, Alabama, requested that Alabama lawmakers "exempt all corporations in that State from taxation for a period of 10 years." See W. H. Rowe Jr. to Judge J. J. Willett (whose brother Ed served as a constitutional delegate from Pickens County), 7 Mar. 1901, folder "Correspondence, 1 Oct. 1900–18 May 1901," O–S, Joseph J. Willett Papers, SU. See also *Birmingham Age-Herald,* 20 Apr. 1900, 1.

78. DuBose quoted in Bond, *Negro Education in Alabama,* 145.

79. Heflin quoted in *Minutes of the* SDEC, 3 Apr. 1901, 19. On Heflin's appeal to the rural white masses, especially the textile workers and small farmers of north Alabama, see Thornton, "Alabama Politics, J. Thomas Heflin, and the Expulsion Movement of 1929," 83–112, esp. 95, 97–100, 104, 107, and 108; Roper, *C. Vann Woodward,* 2; and Tanner, "Wonderful World of Tom Heflin," 163–84. Heflin's enduring appeal to plain rural whites was also commented on by veteran Alabama political observer Atticus Mullin in the *Montgomery Advertiser,* 18 Aug. 1927. For examples of Populist support for Heflin, see the *Randolph Toiler,* 19 Aug. 1898, 2; and 4 Nov. 1898, 2. It is also significant that Heflin did not view himself as of the Black Belt or representing it. He referred to the representatives of the Black Belt interests as "they" and "him" but referred to the white-county forces as "we" (quoted in *Minutes of the* SDEC, 10 July 1902, 34).

80. D. H. S. Moseley and Frank Arrico, Legislative Committee, Birmingham Trades Council to Delegates to the Constitutional Convention, 3 Apr. 1901, in *Minutes of the* SDEC, 3 Apr. 1901, 19–20. For more general information on organized labor in the district during this period, see the Phillip H. Taft Research Notes at the BPLA.

81. *Birmingham Labor Advocate,* 19 Oct. 1901, quoted in Letwin, *Challenge of Interracial Unionism,* 136; see other examples on 240 n. 43.

82. Quoted in *Brewton Laborers' Banner,* 2 Nov. 1901, 2. See also Letwin, *Challenge of Interracial Unionism,* 240 n. 43. This note also supplies other instances of white unionist support for the disfranchising schemes.

83. Ray quoted in *Minutes of the* SDEC, 3 Apr. 1901, 7.

84. Caffee quoted in *Minutes of the* SDEC, 3 Apr. 1901, 5.

85. *Minutes of the* SDEC, 3 Apr. 1901. On apathy and the time-consuming demands of the planting season preventing the plain folk from voting, see p. 8 (C. C. NeSmith of Lamar speaking); p. 12 (W. H. Taylor of Perry speaking); p. 13 (T. L. Bulger of Tallapoosa speaking); and p. 15 (W. C. Oates, at-large, speaking). On the fear that a new constitution might mean increased taxation, see pp. 9–10 (G. Williams of Marengo speaking); p. 12 (Taylor of Perry speaking); pp. 12–13 (C. C. Whitson of Talladega speaking); and p. 13 (Bulger of Tallapoosa speaking). For Populist suspicion of a new constitution because of aversion to increased taxation, see *Ozark Free Press,* 3 May 1900, 4, 6; and Gross, "Alabama Politics and the Negro," 233.

86. Thomas L. Long (first sentence) and O'Rear of Walker County quoted in *Minutes of the* SDEC, 3 Apr. 1901, 14–15.

87. Oates quoted in *Minutes of the* SDEC, 3 Apr. 1901, 15.

88. Coleman quoted in *Minutes of the* SDEC, 3 Apr. 1901, 17.

89. Knox quoted in *Minutes of the* SDEC, 3 Apr. 1901, 16–17.

90. O'Neal quoted in *Minutes of the* SDEC, 3 Apr. 1901, 18–19. George Houston had hailed from Limestone County. Antipathy toward Yankees and the North, intermingled with resentment of the federal government and the Republican Party, would figure prominently in the inflammatory rhetoric of the 1901 convention. See, e.g., references to the "South haters" imposing the black vote on the South, a vote that is "harder to bear than the lash of the cruel task-master," a vote that made the white South "slaves to the slaves of our own fathers" (*Official Proceedings, 1901,* 3:2,817 [first quotation], 3:2,836 [second and third quotations]).

91. See chapter 3, note 113, for a discussion of the new racism.

92. Rogers et al., *Alabama,* 345; McMillan, *Constitutional Development in Alabama,* 261–62.

93. L. H. Reynolds to ed., *Clanton Banner,* 9 May 1901, 1. Samuel L. Webb repeats the same faulty claim as "a credible argument" in *Two-Party Politics in the One-Party South* (173).

94. *Geneva Reaper,* 23 Oct. 1901, 2.

95. Quotations from L. H. Reynolds to ed., *Clanton Banner,* 9 May 1901, 1. Webb portrayed the results of the 1901 referenda as "an extraordinary demonstration" of poor-white "sentiment against suffrage restrictions" (*Two-Party Politics in the One-Party South,* 173).

96. Woodward, *Origins of the New South,* 342.

CHAPTER THREE *Disfranchisement*

1. For background and reunion material concerning the 1901 convention, see "The Constitutional Convention, 1901" in Public Information Subject Files, ALAV89–A39, box SG 006951, folder 9, ADAH. For the list of the fourteen anti-Democratic delegates at the 1901 convention, see the *Birmingham News,* 22 May 1901, 1. See also Black and Black, *Politics and Society in the South,* 11; and Key, *Southern Politics in State and Nation,* 6.

2. William C. Oates to J. J. Willett, 19 Feb. 1901, folder "Correspondence, 1 Oct. 1900–18

May 1901," O–S, Joseph J. Willett Papers, su. Also McMillan, *Constitutional Development in Alabama*, viii, 263–65.

3. *Official Proceedings, 1901*, 1:10. Also D. A. Harris, "Racists and Reformers," 152–54; and McMillan, *Constitutional Development in Alabama*, 265–69.

4. *Official Proceedings, 1901*, 1:9 (first and second quotations), 12 (third and fourth quotations), and 15–16 (fifth quotation).

5. White quoted in *Proceedings of the Democratic State Convention* (DSC), 25 Apr. 1900, 5, ADAH. Regarding O'Neal's position, see *Official Proceedings, 1901*, 3:2,783. See also D. A. Harris, "Racists and Reformers," 148–49; the outstanding study by Rogers et al., *Alabama*, 345; and *Official Proceedings, 1901*, 1:8, 3:3,003, 3,087.

6. Flynt, *Poor but Proud*, 256; see also notes 14–17 of this chapter.

7. Oates quoted in the *Montgomery Advertiser*, 15 May 1901, and the *Mobile Register*, 25 May 1901, both cited in McMillan, *Constitutional Development in Alabama*, 264, 273.

8. McMillan, *Constitutional Development in Alabama*, 275. Speaking about representatives of the plain whites refers as much to the targets of demagoguery as to the actual backgrounds of the politicians employing such. James K. Vardaman married into wealth and subsequently bought newspapers and attained a law degree. Thomas Watson's family owned considerable land and slaves. "Little Jeff" Davis was the son of a judge and local elite and an attorney himself. And Ben Tillman did not possess unquestionable poor-white credentials. Yet Watson, Davis, and Vardaman all experienced familial bouts of poverty and had firsthand knowledge of living among and being themselves, at least for a time, poor whites. These experiences must have furnished some insight into the lives and culture of poor whites even if the politicians themselves eventually achieved affluence. See Woodward, *Tom Watson*, 10–13; Arsenault, *Wild Ass of the Ozarks*, 25–31; Holmes, *White Chief*, 3–7; and Kantrowitz, *Ben Tillman and the Reconstruction of White Supremacy*, 273–80 and 307–8. In the Alabama case, J. Thomas Heflin appealed to poor whites but was himself the member of a relatively prosperous family that included doctors, lawyers, and ministers. Joseph F. Johnston also manipulated poor-white fears but himself possessed impeccable credentials of privilege.

9. *Official Proceedings, 1901*, 3:2,836 (first quotation), 2,837 (second quotation).

10. Heflin quoted in *Official Proceedings, 1901*, 3:2,841; see also p. 2,846. Both J. Morgan Kousser and Michael Perman identify Heflin as of the Black Belt, although Chambers County was physiographically mostly in the Hill Country and had a much closer identification with poor-white textile workers. See Kousser, *Shaping of Southern Politics*, 170; and Perman, *Struggle for Mastery*, 179 and 308. For examples of Populist support for Heflin, see the *Randolph Toiler*, 19 Aug. 1898, 2; and 4 Nov. 1898, 2. See also note 79 of chapter 2.

11. Quotations from *Official Proceedings, 1901*, 3:2,840 (Williams) and 4:4,302–3 (Heflin).

12. *Official Proceedings, 1901*, 3:2,812 (for Newman H. Freeman's position), 2:2,719 (Thomas Long quotation).

13. Woodward, *Origins of the New South*, 340.

14. *Official Proceedings, 1901*, 1:8–15 on Heflin's conception of himself as a friend of the

"negro . . . in his place," see 3:2,846. Frank Crichton was the former-Populist editor of the *Clanton Banner.* Captain A. McHan was the Populist editor of the *Sand Mountain Signal,* the *Boaz Signal,* and the *Gadsden Tribune.* See also D. A. Harris, "Racists and Reformers," 157; Hackney's impressive work, *Populism to Progressivism in Alabama,* 204–5; Williamson's thorough and detailed work, *Crucible of Race,* 234; and Webb, *Two-Party Politics in the One-Party South,* 170. On Cole Blease, see Bryant Simon's excellent book, *A Fabric of Defeat.* Watson, of course, had once famously uttered the warning to black and white Populists: "You are kept apart that you may separately be fleeced of your earnings." But Watson and Hoke Smith enthusiastically pushed for black disfranchisement to strengthen their poor-white movement in Georgia. "Everybody knew that the Disfranchisement issue was the cause of our success," Watson said. After 1900, Watson made a stellar career of damning the "HIDEOUS, OMINOUS, NATIONAL MENACE of negro domination" and answered his own question: "What does Civilization owe the Negro? Nothing! *Nothing!* NOTHING!" (quotations from Kennedy, *Southern Exposure,* 41, 45, and 46).

15. Oliver Day Street to Chauncey Sparks, 6 May 1943, in box SG 12398, folder 19, Alabama Governors Papers, Chauncey Sparks Papers, ADAH. Also Street to ed., *Birmingham News,* 10 Feb. 1944, box 31, folder "Political Scrap," Oliver Day Street Papers, ADAH.

16. Oliver Day Street to ed., *Birmingham Age-Herald,* 29 July 1935, 4. See also John Temple Graves II's "Morning" column in *Birmingham Age-Herald,* 17 Sept. 1935, 1. Graves, a proponent of the New Deal, contrasted Street's version of economically conservative Republicanism unfavorably with the progressive Republicanism of Theodore Roosevelt. O. D. Street was a confirmed bigot—anti-Semitic, anti-Catholic, xenophobic, and racist. For Street's bigotry in 1928, which was so raw it earned him the censure of the chairman of the national Republican Party, see O. D. Street to Marshall, 10 Oct. 1928; Ransom to O. D. Street, 20 Sept. 1928; and the flyer "Governor Smith's Membership in the Roman Catholic Church and Its Proper Place as an Issue in This Campaign," all in box 26, folder "Intolerance," Oliver Day Street Papers, ADAH; and the *Chicago Tribune,* 20 Oct. 1928.

17. First quotation from Oliver Day Street to Chauncey Sparks, 6 May 1943, box SG 12398, folder 19, Chauncey Sparks Papers, ADAH. Second quotation from O. D. Street to Thomas H. Lawson, Alabama Attorney General, 14 Mar. 1941, box 10, folder "1941 Republican Political Correspondence"; third quotation from Street to Frank M. Dixon, 15 Aug. 1942, box 10, folder "1942 Political Republican Correspondence," both in the Oliver Day Street Papers, ADAH. The Street to Dixon, 15 Aug. 1942 letter also appears in box SG 12276, folder 10, Alabama Governors Papers, Frank M. Dixon, ADAH. Fourth quotation from Street to ed., *Birmingham News,* 10 Feb. 1944, box 31, folder "Political Scrap," Oliver Day Street Papers, ADAH. Much of Street's aversion to Franklin Roosevelt and the New Deal was tied to his considerable anti-Semitism and racism. For instance, Street urged people to "wake up the Roosevelt worshippers of the South to what the New Deal, including President and Mrs. Roosevelt, is doing to torpedo the Southern doctrine of white supremacy, . . . deliberately sacrificing the white people of the South for the Negro votes of the North" (Street to Thomas Lawson, Ala. Attorney General, 14 Mar. 1941, box 10, folder "1941 Republican Political Correspondence," Oliver Day Street Papers, ADAH). See also Street to ed., *Birmingham News,* ca. 18 May 1935 and 10 Jan. 1936, draft in box 31,

folder "Political Scrap," and Street to Joseph Martin, 9 Aug. 1940, box 10, folder "1940 Republican Political Correspondence"; Street to B. L. Noonjin, 25 Mar. 1944, box 10, folder "1941 Republican Political Correspondence"; and Street to Frank M. Dixon, 15 Aug. 1942, box 10, folder "1942 Political Republican Correspondence," all in the Oliver Day Street Papers, ADAH. The Street to Dixon, 15 August 1942, letter, as noted, also appears in the Frank Dixon Papers.

18. *Attalla Mirror,* 14 Nov. 1901, 2.

19. Quotations from *Marshall Banner,* 9 May 1901, 4. For more on the role of native white southerners in the Civil Rights movement, see Chappell, *Inside Agitators.*

20. Washington, of course, had become the leading black spokesman in America after his 1895 "Atlanta Compromise" speech, promising black industry, civic obedience, and a relinquishment of the goal of civil and political rights in return for practical and industrial education and economic opportunity. William H. Councill was probably Alabama's second leading accommodationist voice. See Rogers et al., *Alabama,* 329–30. For additional Councill speeches and sermons during this period, see the William H. Councill Papers, AAMA.

21. Quotation from Washington et al. to Convention, *Official Proceedings, 1901,* 1:191.

22. Booker T. Washington to Thomas W. Coleman, 4 June and 22 July 1901; and Washington to Thomas G. Jones, 23 Sept. 1901, all in Harlan and Smock, *Booker T. Washington Papers,* 6:143, 179–80, and 215–16.

23. Quotation from Willis E. Steers, M.D., Decatur, to Convention, 18 June 1901, in the *Journal of the Proceedings of the Constitutional Convention of the State of Alabama,* 309–10. C. Vann Woodward intimated that the meekness of the black position actually encouraged and hastened the process of disfranchisement, a position echoed by Malcolm Cook McMillan and W. E. B. Du Bois. See Woodward, *Origins of the New South,* 323; McMillan, *Constitutional Development in Alabama,* 302–5; and Du Bois, *New Negro,* 226. William Warren Rogers and Robert David Ward, though, reacted strongly to this assertion: "Blacks were not disfranchised in Alabama because they promised to work hard or 'know their place' and not cause trouble. They were disfranchised because the white majority took the vote away from them. That decision would only have been more firmly and violently enforced if the blacks had sharply protested. The first decade of the twentieth century was not the sixth . . . and reading racial strategies backward leads to distortion and historical injustice. . . . It is always easier to shed the blood of others in the past, and bloodshed would have been the result had blacks followed the implied advice of some historians a half century later" (Rogers et al., *Alabama,* 351–52).

24. Addison Wimbs to Booker T. Washington, 6 July 1901, in Harlan and Smock, *Booker T. Washington Papers,* 6:167–68.

25. *Official Proceedings, 1901,* 2:1,348 and 4:4,294–97. See also A. W. Jones, "Political Reforms of the Progressive Era," 176; and McMillan, *Constitutional Development in Alabama,* 322–24.

26. *Marshall Banner,* 9 May 1901, 4.

27. *Geneva Reaper,* 23 Oct. 1901, 2.

28. *Official Proceedings, 1901,* 1:228 (Ordinance 152 proposing that "no negro, black

man, or person of African descent" be allowed to vote) and 1:648 (Ordinance 382 on antimiscegenation). Section 102, Article 4 of the 1901 Alabama State Constitution, still in effect, was repealed by a 60–40 popular vote in conjunction with the 7 Nov. 2000 presidential election. By doing so, Alabama became the last state in the union to repeal a statute barring miscegenation, although a political scientist demonstrated that actually a majority of whites in Alabama had voted to retain the statute (Natalie M. Davis, "Pine Tree Reveals Much about State," *Birmingham News*, 26 Nov. 2000, C1. See also Simmons, "Black and White and Married in Alabama."

29. *Official Proceedings, 1901*, 1:191.

30. Councill quotation from Gross, "Alabama Politics and the Negro," 266–67; second quotation from the *Huntsville Journal*, 1 Feb. 1901, in Hackney, *Populism to Progressivism in Alabama*, 186.

31. Holtzalaw quoted in *Official Proceedings, 1901*, 2:2,071.

32. Jones quoted in *Official Proceedings, 1901*, 4:4,303. See also the *Montgomery Advertiser*, 15 May 1901. For more on Jones and race, see Aucoin, "Thomas Goode Jones and African-American Civil Rights in the New South," 257–72.

33. *Mobile Southern Watchman*, 1 and 8 June 1901, quoted in Hackney, *Populism to Progressivism in Alabama*, 197; *Mobile Weekly Press* quoted in the *Montgomery Advertiser*, 26 Sept. 1901; Jones's quotation in Alsobrook, "Mobile's Forgotten Progressive," 191. See also *Montgomery Advertiser*, 27 June 1901, and *Birmingham News*, n.d., quoted in *Advertiser*, 1 Sept. 1901. Booker T. Washington did surreptitiously work to overturn the 1901 Constitution by backing two lawsuits. See Bulah E. Cooper interview by Alfonso T. Smith, 20 May 1974, Tuskegee, Alabama, 8:17, interview no. 103, ACHE no. T.I. 102, Statewide Oral History Project: Transcription of Interviews, MILES. Black newspapers such as Anniston's *Baptist Leader* and *Union Leader*, Tuscumbia's *American Star*, and the *Mobile Southern Watchman* questioned the Christianity of the white religious papers that endorsed black disfranchisement, such as the *Anniston Hot Blast* and the *Alabama Baptist*. See Sparks, "Alabama Negro Reaction to Disfranchisement," 55–58, 60–61, and 70.

34. Quotations from the *Cherokee Harmonizer*, 6 June 1901, 4. See *Giles v. Harris*, 189 US 475 (1903); and *Atlanta Journal*, 3 June 1901, 1, cited in Harlan and Smock, *Booker T. Washington Papers*, 6:144–45. The "grandfather clause" was not declared unconstitutional until an Oklahoma case reached the Supreme Court in 1915. See *Guinn v. U.S.*, 238 US 347 (1915); and also McMillan, *Constitutional Development in Alabama*, 303, 357.

35. *Official Proceedings, 1901*, 3:2,971 (first quotation), 2,973 (second quotation), and 2,979 (third quotation); see also 3:2,967–81, 3,018–19, and 3,285. See also Hackney, *Populism to Progressivism in Alabama*, 204; McMillan, *Constitutional Development in Alabama*, 292; and Kousser, *Shaping of Southern Politics*, 170.

36. *Attalla Mirror*, 2 May 1901, 2.

37. Quotation from *Geneva Reaper*, 24 July 1901, 2; see also 16 Oct. 1901, 2.

38. J. W. DuBose, "Forty Years in Alabama," boxes 3 and 4, John Witherspoon DuBose Papers, ADAH. DuBose edited Reuben Kolb's newspaper, the *People's Weekly Tribune*, after Kolb sold it to fellow Populist, Philander Morgan. See Hackney, *Populism to Progressivism in Alabama*, 118–19, 120; and DeVine, "Free Silver and Alabama Politics," 226. See also the

Birmingham People's Weekly Tribune, 2 Sept. 1897, 4. Also see the works of the Dunning School of historiography, specifically Fleming, *Civil War and Reconstruction in Alabama*; and Moore, *History of Alabama*. For an example of the complaint of black ignorance as justification for disfranchisement, see *Official Proceedings*, 1901, 3:2,779.

39. Oshinsky, *"Worse Than Slavery"*, 89, 183, and 301. The prohibitions against black education went back, of course, to slavery. A Sumter County, Alabama, slave remembered that if whites caught slaves learning how to read and write, "dey cut us han' off" (George Young interview by Ruby Pickens Tartt, Livingston, Alabama, 3 June 1937, 433, in the Federal Writers' Project, *Slave Narratives*).

40. In 1890, 41 percent of all Alabamians over ten years of age were illiterate. This figure included 18 percent of the whites and 57 percent of the blacks. Only South Carolina, Louisiana, Mississippi, and New Mexico had higher rates of illiteracy. See D. A. Harris, "Racists and Reformers," 85.

41. In 1901 Alabama, 31,681, or 14 percent, of the 232,476 white males of voting age were illiterate; 73,399, or 41 percent, of the 181,345 black males of voting age were illiterate. See McMillan, *Constitutional Development in Alabama*, 239 n. 43, 271. The 1901 delegates had no problem acknowledging that "education is never the test of intelligence"—when it came to poor-white voters—and also were not averse to excusing poor-white illiteracy because small farmers could not "stay away from the farm next year long enough to learn how to read and write." See, e.g., *Official Proceedings*, 1901, 3:3,137 (second quotation) and 3,221 (first quotation).

42. Of course, regular Democrats did not worry much about the black vote in the Black Belt counties where force and fraud were rampant and effective, in spite of the efforts of blacks such as Frank True of Marengo County, who worked hard to "roll up the vote against" a convention. In Perry and Russell, two Black Belt counties, there is evidence that a number of blacks favored the convention or at least conveyed that impression to regular Democrats in order to differentiate themselves from the "worst element" of whites and other blacks (quotations from *Minutes of the* SDEC, 3 Apr. 1901, 5, 7, 10 and 11; see also 12). At times, the inconsistency existed within the same work by the same author. J. L. M. Curry, Alabama education reformer, defended the humanity of slavery but condemned it as "wrong"; admitted that both black and white illiteracy were rampant yet insisted on white suffrage; praised the "impoverished white people" of the South for footing the tax burden to educate African Americans after the Civil War and denounced black voting as "an indescribable blunder" yet recognized that it did not follow that the illiterate were politically uninformed; deplored raw racism and mob violence but insisted that northern racism was just as bad and that southern lynching was attributable to a few bad apples (Curry, *South in the Olden Time*, 7, 8, 13 [first quotation], 14 [second and third quotations], and 15, DTS).

43. The constitutionality question was often discussed in 1901. See, for example, Optimist to ed., *Montgomery Advertiser*, 12 June 1901, in box 5, folder 7, John W. A. Sanford Papers, ADAH. Also see cases, for example, *Williams v. Mississippi*, 170 US 213 (1898); and *Giles v. Harris*, 189 US 475 (1903). The series of late-nineteenth-century cases, including *Plessy v. Ferguson*, 163 US 537 (1896), that were collectively known as "the Civil Rights

cases" are relevant here. Coosa County Republican delegate John H. Porter advocated the adoption of a poll tax restriction as an acceptable method but warned the constitutional convention that direct flouting of the Fifteenth Amendment would risk incurring federal intervention in southern elections. "Are we willing to risk the chances of reconstruction again?" Porter asked in explaining his qualified opposition to more direct methods of disfranchisement. "I hope not" (quoted in *Official Proceedings, 1901,* 3:3,018, 3,020).

44. Knox quoted in *Official Proceedings, 1901,* 1:12.

45. See notes 40, 41, and 72 for this chapter.

46. *Marshall Banner,* 25 Apr. 1901, 4.

47. The *Attalla Mirror* reprinted the *Marshall Banner* editorial approvingly; see 2 May 1901, 2.

48. See, for example, *Official Proceedings, 1901,* 3:2,887.

49. C. Vann Woodward emphasized the generational aspects of the split and the youth of this faction. He cast the white counties as "flatly" opposed to the disfranchisement work of 1901. See *Origins of the New South,* 339–40, 342. Francis L. Pettus of the Black Belt would have almost certainly been a leading voice for the minority faction, but he died shortly before the convention. See *Minutes of the* SDEC, 3 Apr. 1901, 3. He was replaced on the SDEC as a state-at-large member by Alfred M. Tunstall of Hale County, another scion of Black Belt privilege.

50. Gessner Williams, a rarity as a Black Belt member of the majority on this question, pointed to the widespread desire of whites to see black disfranchisement as the thing that "has made us here . . . of one mind. . . . It is simply because . . . we have over us taskmasters to control the votes of this country, had he but the brains to control it with," he explained. "It is to get rid of this particular class of people— . . . a race subservient for hundreds of years to a superior race turned loose upon us by force and . . . the bayonet [for] thirty-six years"—that they met there with "one idea." The delegate expressed his majority-plan desire for the "absolute disfranchisement of the negro as a negro" and "not . . . disfranchising a single white vote" (quoted in *Official Proceedings, 1901,* 3:2,837).

51. For uses of the phrase "race, color, and previous condition of servitude" during the deliberations, see, e.g., the *Official Proceedings, 1901,* 3:2,778, 3,069, and 3,095. The problem of navigating the Fifteenth Amendment and disfranchisement was ever present at the convention. See, e.g., 3:2,771 and 3,044.

52. McMillan, *Constitutional Development in Alabama,* 306, 358–59; Gross, "Alabama Politics and the Negro," 261.

53. McMillan, *Constitutional Development in Alabama,* 296–97, 306; Hackney, *Populism to Progressivism in Alabama,* 192–96.

54. See, for example, the *Alabama Alliance News,* 16 May 1899, 2.

55. *Official Proceedings, 1901,* 3:3,099–101. See also Hackney, *Populism to Progressivism in Alabama,* 192–96. Another clue that hinted that the Black Belt was not yet through with fraud, if the occasion demanded it, was the admission by a Sumter County member of the SDEC, just prior to the April 1901 referendum, called ostensibly to "reform" elections, that "[a]ll we want is a small vote and a large count" (C. B. Smith, quoted in *Minutes of the* SDEC, 3 Apr. 1901, 12). J. L. M. Curry was an eloquent exponent of the Reconstruction

syndrome and the politics of emotion and used their power both to praise the South's poor whites and then to recommend their disfranchisement through the abolition of constitutional safeguards. His Southern History Association publication, *The South in the Olden Time* (1901), skillfully welded together virtually every tenet of the conservative orthodoxy that had its seeds in Old South romance and the Reconstruction trauma: self-reliance; independence; self-government; honor; hostility to taxation, especially for the purpose of educating blacks; resentment over the "ill-advised and revengeful reconstruction legislation"; rhetorical praise for poor whites; white solidarity; white supremacy and the validity of "exclusion" as a cure for the "least taint of inferior racial blood"; neighborliness; kinship; courtesy; the family unit as the core of "decency and honesty"; the threat of "alien immigration" and "assertive labor"; and the connection of all these tenets to patriotism, "prosperity and happiness," and a "religion . . . of the accepted orthodox character" wherein "[i]nfidelity or skepticism . . . was regarded with horror and not infrequently made synonymous with untrustworthiness" (quotations on pp. 5, 6, 7, 8, 9, 10, 14, 15, and 16, DTS).

56. *Official Proceedings, 1901*, 3:2,789 (first quotation, Oates), 2:2,720 (second quotation), and 3:3,434 (third quotation). Fourth quotation from the *Birmingham Ledger* quoted in the *Montgomery Advertiser*, 31 July 1901, cited in McMillan, *Constitutional Development in Alabama*, 293–95, and 297 n. 85; see also Woodward, *Origins of the New South*, 330.

57. Oates quoted in *Official Proceedings, 1901*, 3:2,793 and 2,795.

58. Oates quoted in *Official Proceedings, 1901*, 3:2,792–94.

59. "[T]here were but two ways to correct . . . [the] evils almost untold [of] . . . the carpet-baggers and scalawags," Oates rationalized. "One of these was to take shot guns and go to the polls. . . . The other way was to cheat them. I was an advocate of the latter because it didn't take life" (quoted in *Official Proceedings, 1901*, 3:2,788).

60. Lomax quoted in *Official Proceedings, 1901*, 3:3,089; see also 3,088.

61. Oates quoted in *Official Proceedings, 1901*, 3:2,792 and 3,106–7. The former governor admonished the delegates behind the majority report: "Gentlemen, you may . . . turn us down, but, like truth crushed to earth, we will rise again." There was no question that the memory of the war was highly charged. It had cost the South "a river of blood and tears" (William H. Banks, quoted in *Official Proceedings, 1901*, 3:2,813). This type of hyperpatriotism was a marked part of the powerful politics of emotion. See note 113 of this chapter for a fuller explanation.

62. White quoted in *Official Proceedings, 1901*, 3:2,857. This language about the "black heel upon the white throat" was common when speaking about Reconstruction, as was the desire for it never to happen again: "[B]y the blood of our Caucasian ancestors who fought [for] and secured this land . . . we will rule it by the shotgun or by fraud" (T. Lomax, quoted in 3:3,088–89).

63. *Official Proceedings, 1901*, 3:2,789–92.

64. Harrison quoted in *Official Proceedings, 1901*, 3:2,854–56.

65. William H. Banks of Russell County quoted in *Official Proceedings, 1901*, 3:2,813.

66. Jones quoted in *Official Proceedings, 1901,* 3:2,886. See also, e.g., 3:2,884 and 4:4,303.

67. Oates quoted in *Official Proceedings, 1901,* 3:2,789.

68. William H. Banks quoted in *Official Proceedings, 1901,* 3:2,816. In this passage Banks also maintained that "[e]very state in the United States [was] waiting to hear Alabama's answer." See also 3:3,099–101. Solemnity and graveness were not limited to the Black Belt patricians on this matter. The majority-report adherents were united on this score. "[A]ll other questions . . . fade into mere minor matters compared with the great question of suffrage and election," a Piney Woods delegate remarked. "We were . . . sent here almost solely for the purpose of settling this one great question" (J. O. Sentell, quoted in 3:3,069). "We are here for one purpose. . . . The eyes of the people of the world are upon us," another said (J. T. Heflin, quoted in 3:2,819 and 2,821). Suffrage is the "all-absorbing question," a Hill Country Republican held (J. H. Porter, quoted in 3:3,015). A Wiregrass delegate went even further: "When Napoleon lectured his army near the pyramids in Egypt, he told them that forty centuries looked down upon them. . . . [T]he attention of a greater people and government than Napoleon knew is fixed upon us" (Mike Sollie, quoted in 3:3,043).

69. Oates quoted in *Official Proceedings, 1901,* 3:2,792.

70. Lowe quoted in *Official Proceedings, 1901,* 3:2,827.

71. See note 10 of this chapter; and also Gross, "Alabama Politics and the Negro," 251.

72. Sentell quoted in *Official Proceedings, 1901,* 3:3,069–70 and 3,072. See also J. O. Sentell to Thomas G. Jones, 6 Apr. 1901, box 2, folder 15, Thomas Goode Jones Personal Papers, ADAH. "This is a white man's country and it is the duty of the Convention to save it to white men," Sentell also noted in the "Stenographic Report of Constitutional Convention," *Montgomery Advertiser,* 31 July 1901 (cited in Taylor, "Populism and Disfranchisement in Alabama," 424). Despite his passionate expression of innate white superiority and immutable distinctions, at some level this Piney Woods delegate, like other representatives of the plain whites in their opposition to increased black education and literacy, realized that ultimately the question was one of power. "I represent my people" of the Piney Woods, Sentell said, "when I say . . . that the negro has not the capacity for exercising any control in the government . . . because the power to vote is the power to control . . . one of the greatest and most sacred powers exercised by any citizen" (quoted in *Official Proceedings, 1901,* 3:3,071). Thomas L. Long of the coal-mining county of Walker stood against the employment clause because he thought it unnecessary and feared it would reduce the numbers of working-class white voters: "We have quite enough traps [already] to catch all the Negroes in Africa" (quoted in 3:3,170). See also Gross, "Alabama Politics and the Negro," 253–54.

73. Sollie quoted in *Official Proceedings, 1901,* 3:3,045.

74. Martin quoted in *Official Proceedings, 1901,* 3:3,009–10. On some occasions, both camps of regular Democrats utilized the vagueness strategy outlined in chapter 2. During the debate in the suffrage committee, SDEC chairman Robert Lowe revealed his frustration at the patrician's pet ploy being used against them. "You tell me it [the grandfather clause] means white supremacy! . . . the greatness of our race. That I believe in," Lowe

244 · Notes to Chapter Three

said. But "not one of them who has spoken has defended the proposition . . . not one of them," he complained. "They have spoken in generalities . . . but they have been very silent" as to the particulars of their plan (quoted in 3:2,827).

75. Heflin quoted in *Official Proceedings, 1901,* 3:2,824–25.

76. Regarding Kousser's and Perman's misidentification of Heflin with the Black Belt, see note 10 of this chapter. Both Kousser and Perman identify Heflin as of the Black Belt, although Chambers County was physiographically mostly in the Hill Country and had a much closer identification with poor-white textile workers. See Kousser, *Shaping of Southern Politics,* 170; and Perman, *Struggle for Mastery,* 179 and 308. For examples of Populist support for Heflin, see the *Randolph Toiler,* 19 Aug. 1898, 2; and 4 Nov. 1898, 2. See also note 79 of chapter 2.

77. Heflin quoted in *Official Proceedings, 1901,* 3:2,825. See also 3:2,844.

78. Heflin quoted in *Official Proceedings, 1901,* 3:2,820–22, 2,825, 2,841–42, 2,844, and 2,846–48. Heflin, who remained undefeated in state politics for three and a half decades, had also dramatically vowed, "I believe as truly as I believe I am standing here, that God Almighty intended the negro to be the servant of the white man" (quoted in 3:2,841). Other delegates also made the potent religious connection. "Would to God" that the new constitution set up a "permanent, hereditary, governing class" of "white men in permanent supremacy in Alabama," a delegate arguing for adoption of the majority report stated. "[L]et us have the inheritance, and let us send it down to our children unspotted and as pure as the Caucasian blood." White supremacy was a fait accompli dictated by a higher being. "[W]e do not place that difference . . . on the white man," he explained. "God Almighty Himself put the seal on the white man and He put it upon the negro. He has made the distinction" (Gessner Williams, quoted in 3:2,839). A Perry County planter, for instance, had defended Black Belt vote fraud as "Christianity, but not orthodox. . . . It is wrong but right" (Charles Greer, quoted in 3:3,079). Jeffersonian newspapers also used religious examples to buttress their white supremacist arguments against "nigger lovers"; see, e.g., *Collinsville Clipper,* 27 Dec. 1900, 4. And most religious groups around the state favored the constitution. See D. A. Harris, "Racists and Reformers," 185. On the connection between race, religion, and a sense of patriotism in Alabama politics, see notes 55, 61, 74, 92, 93, 99, and especially 113 of this chapter.

79. Sentell quoted in *Official Proceedings, 1901,* 3:3,071–72.

80. J. T. Martin of Calhoun County quoted in *Official Proceedings, 1901,* 3:3,008–9.

81. Sollie quoted in *Official Proceedings, 1901,* 3:3,044–45.

82. Porter quoted in *Official Proceedings, 1901,* 3:3,016 and 3,020.

83. Bulger quoted in *Official Proceedings, 1901,* 3:3,082.

84. J. T. Martin of Calhoun County quoted in *Official Proceedings, 1901,* 3:3,010.

85. Heflin quoted in *Official Proceedings, 1901,* 3:2,824, 2,841, and 2,843–45; also see 2,822–23. "I am opposed to the disfranchisement of any white man, I care not whether he is learned or unlearned, whether he wears the purple robes of good fortune, or the tattered garments of poverty and want . . . [or] whether he is in a little hut on the hillside," Heflin declared. "He is a descendant of those who fought for our freedom . . . that we love so well, and will die to maintain" (quoted in 3:2,848).

86. Martin quoted in *Official Proceedings, 1901,* 3:3,011.

87. Freeman quoted in *Official Proceedings, 1901,* 3:2,809–12.

88. Reynolds quoted in *Official Proceedings, 1901,* 3:3,280 and 3,285. Reynolds said: "Yes, sir. . . . I am in favor of disfranchising every negro in Alabama that is vicious, that will sell his vote or barter his vote. . . . I am not in favor of disfranchising Booker Washington" (quoted in 3:3,285). Samuel L. Webb simply and sanguinely maintained that Reynolds "demonstrated his continuing commitment to reform at the 1901 constitutional convention. Reynolds . . . opposed disfranchisement measures" ("From Independents to Populists to Progressive Republicans," 724).

89. *Huntsville Journal* quoted in Hackney, *Populism to Progressivism in Alabama,* 179. Other blacks realized the same thing. The editor of a black newspaper in the Hill Country was even more despondent as he surveyed the situation. Writing about the prospect of black disfranchisement in the new constitution, he noted: "Now what about recognition? You can't get it answered by the white man. Why? You are a negro. Is that all? That is all. I tried to get round telling you, but you have forced me to" (*Calhoun County Union Leader,* 24 Oct. 1901, 1).

90. Quotations from *Official Proceedings, 1901,* 3:2,839 (Williams) and 3:3,205 and 3,207 (Smith). See also Gross, "Alabama Politics and the Negro," 248–49, 251.

91. DeVine, "Free Silver and Alabama Politics," 169–70, 242, and 318. Cunningham knew the plain whites of north Alabama, although he was not one of them. He had spent his early life in the anti-Redeemer hotbed of Lawrence County and represented Franklin County in the general assembly before moving to Jefferson. See J. C. DuBose, *Notable Men of Alabama,* 2:17–18.

92. Many examples abound in these pages of anti-Democrats who hewed to the traditional Reconstruction syndrome credo of white supremacy, states' rights, antifederalism, anti-Yankeeism, and illiberalism on taxation and other issues. The example of John Witherspoon DuBose is only one. The patrician roots in constructing a race-based conformist citizenship is clear in the life and work of Hilary A. Herbert, former U.S. congressman, navy secretary, and editor of the widely read *Why the Solid South?* (1890). The relationship between conservatism and white supremacy as a central part of the status quo being perpetuated is also apparent. For more on the relationship between political conservatism and racism, see chapter 5, note 35, and the text associated with this note. Herbert dedicated his book to "the businessmen of the North" and what "ought not to be done by the federal government" (*Why the Solid South?,* iii and xvii). As a founder and moving force of the Southern Society for the Study of Race Conditions, and in various books, speeches, and articles over a long career, Herbert passionately articulated this doctrine based on an endemic notion of southern "conservatism"; states' rights; divine authorship; social Darwinism; antipathy to "Negroism" and federal government "Centralism"; the use of "[e]ducation, morality and religion" as " 'conservative forces' through which whites elevated and controlled the Negro, preserved civilization, and maintained a classified society"; the "natural inferiority of the Negro"; black political exclusion as a form of "patriotism"; and an unshakable faith in laissez-faire economics. "The Constitution of Alabama declares . . . that the sole end of government is to pro-

tect property," Herbert wrote. "These words ought to be written in letters of gold above every hearthstone in the land." The southern people, predominantly Anglo-Saxon, were the "most conservative people in America. . . . I was always a conservative and day by day am becoming more so." See H. C. Davis, "Hilary A. Herbert," 216–25, quotations on 217, 220, 222, 224, and 225; and Hammett, "Reconstruction History before Dunning," 185–96, especially 190 (quoting Herbert, *Why the Solid South?*, 17–18, 37–38 regarding "patriotism"). See also notes 55, 61, 74, 78, 93, 99, and 113 in this chapter.

93. Cunningham indulged in race-based conformist citizenship, connecting "patriotism" and national fealty to the supremacy of the "Anglo-Saxon" and both to the "laws of nature . . . [sanctioned] by God himself" and asserted that the United States had been reserved as the "home of the greatest natural inheritance" of white supremacy. The "negro" could not be blamed too harshly for his failure "to develop," Cunningham reasoned, because "he is intrinsically and essentially and naturally inferior to the white race, and will always be." Thomas Heflin had indulged in clearly connecting race with patriotism as well. See *Official Proceedings, 1901*, 3:2,841 and the text related to notes 55, 74, 78, 92, 99, and 113. Connecting white supremacy or "Caucasian Democracy" to a notion of patriotism or fealty to the "Southern country" was common among Alabama whites. See, e.g., the Address of Tennent Lomax, Esq. to State Democratic Convention, ca. 1900 and the 1898 address to the same body, both in box 1077, folder 7, Tennent Lomax Collection, UA. Further, Cunningham opined that southern youth could be taught that the Civil War was really about noble purposes such as states' rights, "State sovereignty," and precious constitutional liberties instead of more distasteful subjects such as race and slavery. Guilt was an obvious part of this historical revision. Cunningham realized that slavery was "contrary to the laws of nature" and offensive to the "supreme intelligence that rules the world" (Cunningham, quoted in *Official Proceedings, 1901*, 3:2,996–99, 3,000, and 3,001). See also 3:2,996, 2,997, 2,998–99, and 3,002. A more candid assessment that race and slavery were at the core of the conflict seeped through the debates. "The negroes knew what that war was for," a patrician notable admitted. "They knew that their freedom was involved" (W. C. Oates, quoted in 3:2,794). Other delegates also felt guilt over slavery. A Wiregrass delegate rebuked the "national sin" of slavery, which had been driven by "our sinful love of power and gain," yet favored black disfranchisement and did not see any parallel with slavery (Mike Sollie, quoted in 3:3,043). For more on the causes of the Civil War, see one of the most recent salvoes in the debate: Dew, *Apostles of Disunion*. On the fortification of white supremacy ideology with the concept of patriotism and religion, see notes 61, 78, 92, 99, and 113 in this chapter and note 58 in chapter 4.

94. Cunningham quoted in *Official Proceedings, 1901*, 3:2,996, 2,999–3,001. "No man if he . . . did not hate somebody . . . would ever commit such a crime" as enfranchising the black race, Cunningham declared. "Vengeance was in the air. The evil genius of mankind was at the throttle. He . . . dethroned judgment and punctured the . . . human heart [to] . . . set in operation these engines of destruction" (quoted in 3:3,001). See also the "Speech of R. M. Cunningham in support of the majority report of the Committee on Suffrage and Elections in the Constitutional Convention of Alabama, July 27, 1901," UAB.

95. O'Neal quoted in *Official Proceedings, 1901,* 3:2,771, 2,778, and 2,781–82. For more on O'Neal, see J. C. DuBose, *Notable Men of Alabama,* 2:377–79.

96. O'Neal quoted in *Official Proceedings, 1901,* 3:2,781 and 2,783. Delegates from both the white and the black counties argued that disfranchisement was actually in the best interest of African Americans. "Let him go on, and it won't be two years until he [is] . . . happier by far . . . with his condition . . . than he is today. Why, as soon as you elevate him, you ruin him. . . . [I]t is best for the negro race" (J. T. Heflin, quoted in 3:2,848). See also 3:3,041 (Charles H. Miller of Marengo); 3:3,071 (J. O. Sentell of Crenshaw); 4:4,303 (T. G. Jones of Montgomery); and the *Minutes of the* SDEC, 3 Apr. 1901, 14. Also see R. B. Dow to ed., *Choctaw Alliance,* 26 June 1901, 1.

97. O'Neal quoted in *Official Proceedings, 1901,* 3:2,779–80. O'Neal also enumerated the "moral and financial ruin" caused by this "unwise experiment" and denounced the "giant confiscation of [slave] property" forced by the power of "the Federal compact, . . . the prejudices and ignorance of the blacks, organized . . . into a compact political party . . . by the aid of federal power . . . compelled by military authority . . . at the point of . . . Federal bayonets," a clear "violation of the original compact between the States [that] changed the nature of our government" simply to "perpetuate the rule of the Republican party." The suddenness of the whole thing was also an issue: "The shackles were scarcely stricken from [the freedman's] limbs before the ballot was placed in his hands" (quoted in 3:2,779–82).

98. O'Neal quoted in *Official Proceedings, 1901,* 3:2,780 and 2,782. O'Neal's account of Redemption, like that of Reconstruction, was suitably maudlin and marked by sexual imagery and roles: "Impoverished though she was, crushed by defeat, exhausted by the protracted struggle in which she had lost the flower of her manhood, rallying her sons from the ashes of their homes and the graves of her dead as she closed her decimated ranks, determined at any cost to preserve her social purity and maintain her civilization. She braved federal bayonets and federal power and her brave sons stood with unyielding ranks around the inner temple of her social system" (quoted in 3:2,780).

99. O'Neal quotations in *Official Proceedings, 1901,* 3:2,783 and 2,785. O'Neal's argument was a classic in its use of the politics of emotion. O'Neal insisted that these deserving poor whites were "educated not in books but in the traditions and principles of free government" (quoted in 3:2,785). He also claimed that Alabama's whites had tried to do their best with the unfair burden of the Reconstruction amendments pinned to their breasts. Alabama had for "a third of a century . . . tried in humiliation" and "in patience, the experiment of unlimited suffrage, which heedless animosity and hate put upon us." But the state had "tasted its bitterness, drained the cup of hatred . . . to its dregs, inhaled its poison until [Alabama] . . . reels from its effects" (quoted in 3:2,781). On social Darwinism, see the still-classic Hofstadter, *Social Darwinism in American Thought.* Another North Alabama representative of regular Democracy, convention president John Knox of Anniston, also invoked the sword of religion to compel orthodox thinking on the race issue and disfranchisement in a Fourth of July patriotic speech, given in a church and published throughout the state by the Democratic and Conservative Party. Five years after the passage and ratification of the 1901 Alabama Constitution, Knox praised his

role in effecting the "one great reform" of disfranchisement "whereby the negro vote was eliminated and control of this State placed where it ought to be and ought always to have been—in the hands of the white people. . . . The movement . . . for a new constitution," Knox revealed, "was not only a movement [of] . . . political reform . . . but it" was also "a great moral reform as well." "Most of our people are church people," Knox explained. "You cannot go into the most . . . thinly-settled district in this State without finding a church and close by a man of God" who shapes "from Sunday to Sunday [the] . . . moral and spiritual needs of the people" through the "great moral and restraining influence of the church. . . ." "[T]he demand for a new constitution in this State was . . . a demand for better moral conditions" according to Knox, a demand for "what is right, what is honorable and what is best for the people" in "ridding ourselves of negro rule and carpet-bag government," the "shackles [of] . . . negro suffrage" and "negro supremacy . . . fastened . . . on the people of the South . . . by old Thad Stevens and his fellow conspirators . . . the most bitter and implacable enemy of the South" during Reconstruction. " . . . [T]his is a white man's country, and . . . the white man ought to control it," Knox declared. "[L]argely increasing the negro vote . . . is the great danger which we sought to escape . . . by the adoption of the New Constitution," Knox admitted. "Is that man a patriot, does he really love his country, who would seek to prejudice you against . . . the New Constitution and lead you in such a path as would restore the negro to political power in this State? I think not." "Patriotism," the "high standard of patriotism . . . the highest," is that of the "brave men who stood for the defense of the Southern Confederacy." Address of Hon. John B. Knox, at Jones' Chapel, Cullman County, Alabama, 4 July 1906, 7–11, 13, and 21–24 (quoted), Tutwiler Collection of Southern History (TCSH), Birmingham Public Library, Birmingham, Alabama. For the connections between white supremacy, religious orthodoxy, and a southern sense of patriotism *(race-based conformist citizenship)*, see also notes 61, 78, 92, 93, and especially 113.

100. See discussion in the introduction to this book.

101. Billy the Kid to ed., *Clanton Banner,* 20 June 1901, 1.

102. F. M. Langston to ed., *Clanton Banner,* 19 Sept. 1901, 1. This concern over poor whites losing the vote was ubiquitous in the Hill Country among the political dissenters. See, for example, the *Cherokee Sentinel* editorial reprinted with approval by the *Alabama Alliance News,* 23 May 1899, 2.

103. L. H. Reynolds to ed., *Clanton Banner,* 19 Sept. 1901, 1 and 4.

104. Bulger quoted in *Official Proceedings, 1901,* 3:3,083. Second quotation from *Attalla Mirror* quoted in the *Montgomery Advertiser,* 10 Aug. 1901, cited in McMillan, *Constitutional Development in Alabama,* 288–90, 294; see also 318. Third quotation: Mike Sollie of Dale County, in Wiregrass, quoted in *Official Proceedings, 1901,* 3:3,052–53. Also see *Official Proceedings, 1901,* 3:3,377.

105. *Marshall Banner,* 9 May 1901, 4.

106. Quotations from *Official Proceedings, 1901,* 3:2,785–86 (O'Neal); and 1:8–11, 12 (Knox); see also 1:15. Many historians have written on the racism of poor whites. For a sample, see Ayers, *Promise of the New South,* 431–32; Flynt, *Poor but Proud,* x–xii, 22, 212, 213, 215–17, 257, 260; Flynt, *Dixie's Forgotten People,* 11; Rogers et al., *Alabama,* 335, 353;

Grantham, *Southern Progressivism,* 125–26; Kirby, *Darkness at the Dawning,* 62, 65, and 68; McMillan, *Constitutional Development in Alabama,* 318; D. A. Harris, "Racists and Reformers," 255; and H. H. Hall, "Montgomery Race Conference," 54, 66–72, 92, 100, 102, and 107–8. Wayne Flynt writes of white farmers in Pike and Crenshaw Counties, two Populist strongholds, going on whipping sprees as "whitecaps" during the Panic of 1893 over fear that local white hiring of black laborers would reduce their own status to tenancy (*Poor but Proud,* 213).

107. Woodward, *Origins of the New South,* 348 n. 102; Webb, *Two-Party Politics in the One-Party South,* 9, 171–73. See also notes 87 and 88 of this chapter.

108. *Official Proceedings, 1901,* 3:2,811 (Freeman on poll tax); 3:3,017–18 (Porter on poll tax). On the extent of the damaging nature of the poll tax to poor-white suffrage, see Key, *Southern Politics in State and Nation,* 618.

109. Reynolds quoted in *Official Proceedings, 1901,* 3:3,284. Regarding Reynolds's position on the character clause, see 3:3,281.

110. Freeman quoted in *Official Proceedings, 1901,* 3:2,812.

111. Porter quoted in *Official Proceedings, 1901,* 3:3,017–19.

112. Reynolds quoted in the *Official Proceedings, 1901,* 3:3,279, 3,281, and 3,285.

113. The concept of a politics of emotion was introduced and discussed in Feldman, "Introduction," 6, 364. The new racism refers to the recent and effective GOP strategy of substituting for the now-discredited overt racial appeal (and adding to the still-usable subtle racial appeal) other emotional issues of religion, character, morality, patriotism, conventional sexuality, and traditional family values. The effect of using this new type of "racism," especially in the South, has been very similar to the old race-baiting that the Conservative Democratic Party used so successfully—thus the term; the new racism is used to disparage political opponents, discredit progressive politics as something "immoral" or decidedly inferior in the way racial liberals were once considered culturally decadent and inferior, and to convince poor whites to submerge class concerns to vote for actual economic conservatives who also run as social conservatives. It capitalizes on the distracting power of vagueness (discussed in chapter 2) that eschews a detailed, specific, issue-oriented approach for broad, sweeping generalizations that often produce distorted understandings of complex and content-rich issues. The politics of emotion uses the distracting power of vagueness to both stimulate the electorate's emotions and provide calming generalizations so that voters' impulses to reason about detailed issues are clouded by emotional considerations, but simultaneously pacified and suppressed by reassuring and vague generalities. The method has proven stubbornly persistent and extremely successful in Alabama. While it is not the province of just one party, it has traditionally been most frequently used by ideologically conservative groups and candidates as a method of winning over large numbers of poor, working-class, and plain-white votes to support a more elite-oriented program. The Democratic and Conservative Party mastered it, but in recent decades, this strategy has been a Republican, not a Democratic, province. To a large extent, the result has been the recent replacement of the old, discredited *race-based conformist citizenship* with a newer, respectable *morality-based conformist citizenship.* In his classic work, V. O. Key alluded to such a phenomenon: "[T]hose of the

South, and those who love the South are left with the cold, hard fact that the South as a whole has developed no system or practice of political organization and leadership adequate to cope with its problems." Although in certain moments, "Alabama voters divide along lines that parallel" rational, realistic concerns, "this type of division is exceptional." The political organization and leadership "necessary for a consistent politics of issues" is not present (*Southern Politics in State and Nation*, 4 and 46). See also notes 61, 78, 92, 93, and 99 of this chapter; note 58 of chapter 4; and chapter 5, note 52.

114. Quotations from *Official Proceedings, 1901*, 3:3,198 (Coleman); 3,381 (second quotation, O. R. Hood); 3,333 (third quotation, H. F. Reese). See also *Birmingham Age-Herald*, 19 May 1901, quoted in McMillan, *Constitutional Development in Alabama*, 298–302. The *Ashville Southern Argus* saw the poll tax as a measure that would also help guarantee black disfranchisement because the "Negro nine times out of ten votes because it is a free right. . . . If he has to pay $2 . . . the free part will drop out and so will the Negro" (quoted in the *Birmingham Age-Herald*, 11 May 1901). In Bullock, Lowndes, Macon, Perry, Wilcox, Dallas, and Greene Counties the aggregate number of literate black residents exceeded the number of literate whites. For example, Dallas County had 3,184 literate blacks compared to only 2,288 literate whites; Greene's totals were 1,264 literate blacks to 807 literate whites. See McMillan, *Constitutional Development in Alabama*, 301–2 n. 118.

115. The reasoning was that of William H. Banks of Russell County, who ended up voting against adoption of the convention's majority suffrage restrictions because he objected to methods, not the end of black disfranchisement (quoted in *Official Proceedings, 1901*, 3:2,813–17, 3,134–35, and 2,815). Banks firmly believed that blacks were inferior to whites and regarded it an inexorable law of nature that "in every sphere inferiority must yield to the control of the superior." Still, for Banks, the question was about methods: "Methods have a great deal to do with it. . . . Methods are important . . . as important as the ends that you desire" (quoted in 3:2813–15). On sympathetic national opinion for the race issue, see *Official Proceedings, 1901*, 1:8; 2:2,247; and 3:2,783, 3,003, and 3,087. See also chapter 1, notes 8–11.

116. R. B. Dow to ed., *Choctaw Alliance*, 26 June 1901, 1. See also *Official Proceedings, 1901*, 3:3,017–19. Such views were longstanding among whites of different classes. See the Speech of John T. Milner (an industrialist), "White Men of Alabama Stand Together, 1860 and 1890," (1890), pp. 74–75, box 5, folder 32, Alabama Pamphlet Collection, ADAH. See also T. Lomax, quoted in *Official Proceedings, 1901*, 3:3,088.

117. *Official Proceedings, 1901*, 3:3,099–101, 3,134–35, and 4:4,919–20.

118. Ibid., 4:4,984.

119. Ibid., 3:3,100 and 3,135.

CHAPTER FOUR *Ratification*

1. Alabama's was the only southern disfranchising constitution to be submitted to a popular vote. Jelks had became governor after Thomas D. Samford died on 1 June 1901. Business-progressive support for the constitution coalesced around the *Birming-*

ham Age-Herald and the Alabama Commercial and Industrial Association, which had produced the 1896 pamphlet titled "The State Must Not Stop Its Progress—Business Men Declare in Favor of a Constitutional Convention." Education advocates also supported ratification. See D. A. Harris, "Racists and Reformers," 181, 185; Hackney, *Populism to Progressivism in Alabama,* 167–68; McMillan, *Constitutional Development in Alabama,* 234–35, 340–48; and *Birmingham Age-Herald,* 20 Jan. and 18 Sept. 1901.

2. *Shelby County People's Advocate,* reprinted in *Geneva Reaper,* 23 Oct. 1901, 3. See also McMillan, *Constitutional Development in Alabama,* 342–43; D. A. Harris, "Racists and Reformers," 181–85. For an example of Jesse F. Stallings, referred to as "Piney Woods Jess," see quotation in *Marshall Banner,* 27 July 1899, 2. For Populist support of Stallings, see, e.g., *Ozark Free Press,* 8 Mar. 1900, 4; 15 Mar. 1900, 5; and also DeVine, "Free Silver and Alabama Politics," 87, 113.

3. *Marshall Banner,* 27 July 1899, 2; Webb, *Two-Party Politics in the One-Party South,* 108.

4. Denson quotation from *Birmingham Age-Herald,* 27 July 1890, quoted in Hackney, *Populism to Progressivism in Alabama,* 41–42. See chapter 3, notes 61, 78, 92, 93, 99, and 113, and, in this chapter, note 58.

5. *Birmingham News* and *Montgomery Advertiser,* 26 Sept. 1901. A recent study that makes clear just how naive that belief was is Phillips, *AlabamaNorth.*

6. DeVine, "Free Silver and Alabama Politics," 167. On the black mistrust of poor whites, see Flynt, *Poor but Proud,* 212, 215–16.

7. Thomas G. Jones to Booker T. Washington, 20 Sept. 1901, quoted in Harlan and Smock, *Booker T. Washington Papers,* 6:213–14; see also Woodward, *Origins of the New South,* 323.

8. Brittain, "Negro Suffrage and Politics in Alabama since 1870," 138 (quotation) and 139; see also *Giles v. Harris,* 189 US 475 (1903); Hackney, *Populism to Progressivism in Alabama,* 227–28; Gross, "Alabama Politics and the Negro," 269.

9. *Official Proceedings, 1901,* 3:3,377; Hackney, *Populism to Progressivism in Alabama,* 157, 180, 186, 191, 203, 326; and the *Huntsville Journal,* 10 Nov. 1899, quoted in Hackney, 186. One Populist reminded a former Populist who was in the process of converting to the lily-white Republican faction that the Populists had always been in favor of disfranchising blacks if it could be done without losing white votes (Brock to Street, 13 Sept. 1902, O. D. Street Papers, UA, cited in Hackney, 203). See also Rogers et al., *Alabama,* 335.

10. See discussion in the introduction.

11. Johnston quoted in *Montgomery Advertiser,* 15 Oct. and 10 Nov. 1901, cited in Gross, "Alabama Politics and the Negro," 268. Stallings appeared all over the state, especially in old Populist strongholds in the Hill Country such as Chilton County. See *Clanton Banner,* 3 Oct. 1901, 1. For Stallings's involvement in this movement, see folders 1–10, Jesse Francis Stallings Papers, no. 2405, SHC.

12. Denson quoted in *Proceedings of the Democratic State Convention* (DSC), 29 Mar. 1899, 23, 25–27. See also quotations from Johnston in *Montgomery Advertiser,* 15 Oct. and 10 Nov. 1901, cited in McMillan, *Constitutional Development in Alabama,* 343, and D. A. Harris, "Racists and Reformers," 133–34, 182.

13. *Clanton Banner* editorial, 24 Oct. 1901, 4.

14. *Attalla Mirror,* 7 Nov. 1901, 2.

15. *Geneva Reaper,* 27 Nov. 1901, 2.

16. On Kolb and the others, see Rodabaugh, "Farmers' Revolt in Alabama," 85–87. For the *Choctaw Alliance*'s position, see McMillan, *Constitutional Development in Alabama,* 348–49. See the *Clanton Banner* citations in notes 19, 34, 36, 43, and 44. See the *Attalla Mirror,* 17 and 24 Oct. 1901; and 7 Nov. 1901, 2 in all three; and the *Coosa River News* editorial reprinted on the same page. See also the *Cherokee Harmonizer,* 9 May 1901, 4; and *Ozark Free Press,* 9, 16, 23, and 30 Aug. 1900. For the *Coosa River News*'s Republican politics, see the *Marshall Banner,* 14 Sept. 1899, 2. Also see *Huntsville Republican,* reprinted in *Montgomery Advertiser,* 11 Sept. 1901, cited in McMillan, *Constitutional Development in Alabama,* 349; and *Marshall Banner,* 24 Oct. 1901, 4. On Kolb, Skaggs, and Manning, see Hackney, *Populism to Progressivism in Alabama,* 115 n. 15 and 176. For more on Kolb, see J. C. DuBose, *Notable Men of Alabama,* 1:78–79.

17. Erle Pettus represented Limestone County, and Tom Heflin represented the Hill Country whites of Chambers County in the state legislature and at the convention. See *Official Proceedings, 1901,* 2:1,348; 4:4,294–97; A. W. Jones, "Political Reforms of the Progressive Era," 176; and McMillan, *Constitutional Development in Alabama,* 322–24.

18. T. L. Bulger quoted in *Official Proceedings, 1901,* 3:3,377.

19. *Clanton Banner* editorial, 24 Oct. 1901, 4.

20. *Attalla Mirror,* 7 Nov. 1901, 2.

21. *Marshall Banner,* 24 Oct. 1901, 4.

22. For the newspaper's early antipathy to calling a constitutional convention, see *Marshall Banner,* 23 and 30 Nov. 1899, 2 in both. For its reversal, see 24 Oct. 1901; and 21 Nov. 1901, 4 in both. The race-gender connection was, of course, common to the paternalists as well. See, e.g., Address of Tennent Lomax to the State Democratic Convention, ca. 1898, box 1077, folder 7, Tennent Lomax Collection, UA.

23. The final part of the last sentence reads "as far as the South is concerned," which makes very clear the regional nature of the slight in the eyes of the anti-Democrats (*Geneva Reaper,* 23 Oct. 1901, 3).

24. *Lafayette Sun,* reprinted in the *Montgomery Advertiser,* 25 Oct. 1901, in McMillan, *Constitutional Development in Alabama,* 344 n. 26. Also see *Randolph Toiler,* 1 July 1898, 2.

25. *Attalla Mirror,* 17 and 24 Oct. 1901, 2 in both; and 7 and 21 Nov. 1901, 2 in both. The language and reasoning about the sacrosanct nature of the White House used to denounce Theodore Roosevelt was remarkably similar to that used a century later in the impeachment controversy against President Bill Clinton.

26. *Huntsville Republican,* reprinted in *Montgomery Advertiser,* 11 Sept. 1901, cited in McMillan, *Constitutional Development in Alabama,* 349; see also Hackney, *Populism to Progressivism in Alabama,* 176, 228. On Lane, see DeVine, "Free Silver and Alabama Politics," 325; Gross, "Alabama Politics and the Negro," 231; and Rodabaugh, "Farmers' Revolt in Alabama," 85. The *Birmingham Times* perpetuated the myth by insisting that Alabama's Republicans, "almost to a man," opposed the constitution (11 Oct. 1901, 4; also see 15 Nov. 1901, 4).

27. *Montgomery Advertiser,* 15 Mar. 1901, quoted in Hackney, *Populism to Progressivism in Alabama* , 175.

28. *Birmingham Age-Herald,* 18 Oct. 1901; *Montgomery Advertiser,* 8, 12 Oct. 1901; *New Decatur Advertiser* quoted in the *Montgomery Advertiser,* 11 Sept. 1901, cited in McMillan, *Constitutional Development in Alabama,* 346.

29. *Birmingham Age-Herald,* 29 Sept. 1901; *Montgomery Advertiser,* 27 Sept. and 16 Oct. 1901; McMillan, *Constitutional Development in Alabama,* 345 n. 36 and 346; D. A. Harris, "Racists and Reformers," 184, 187; and Gross, "Alabama Politics and the Negro," 270.

30. Gessner Williams quoted in *Official Proceedings, 1901,* 3:2,838.

31. *Birmingham Age-Herald,* 18 Oct. 1901; *Montgomery Advertiser,* 29 Sept. 1901; 8 and 11–12 Oct. 1901.

32. These claims about the virtual irrelevance and unimportance of race are discussed in the introduction.

33. Taxpayer and Voter to ed., *Clanton Banner,* 17 Oct. 1901, 1. For almost identical reasoning, see the Republican *Birmingham Times,* 11 Oct. 1901, 4.

34. *Clanton Banner* editorial, 17 Oct. 1901, 4.

35. Civis to ed., *Clanton Banner,* 24 Oct. 1901, 1.

36. *Clanton Banner* editorial, 31 Oct. 1901, 4.

37. *Birmingham-Age Herald,* reprinted in the *Clanton Banner,* 31 Oct. 1901, 4.

38. Civis to ed., *Clanton Banner,* 31 Oct. 1901, 1.

39. Bowie's remarks appeared in the *Clanton Banner,* 17 Oct. 1901, 4. Bowie was a leading railroad attorney and John Knox's law partner (DeVine, "Free Silver and Alabama Politics," 231). For examples of resentment over taxation used for black education, see *Official Proceedings, 1901,* 3:3,092; and Gross, "Alabama Politics and the Negro," 233.

40. Taxpayer and Voter to ed., *Clanton Banner,* 17 Oct. 1901, 1.

41. Rex, from Thorsby, to ed., *Clanton Banner,* 11 Apr. 1901, 1. On the role of patriotism as part of the emotion in politics, see chapter 3, note 61, and the text associated with it.

42. Civis to ed., *Clanton Banner,* 24 and 31 Oct. 1901, 1 in both. For Populist suspicion of the new constitution because of aversion to taxation, see *Ozark Free Press,* 3 May 1900, 4, 6.

43. *Clanton Banner* editorial, 7 Nov. 1901, 4.

44. *Clanton Banner* editorial, 31 Oct. 1901, 4. This conviction that the North was in sympathy with the South in the disfranchisement question was common to both Democrat and anti-Democrat and was not tied purely to U.S. military involvement in the Caribbean, the Philippines, and Asia. Tennent Lomax had expressed confidence that if Alabama passed the 1901 Constitution, it would not again be "reconstructed"; see its government destroyed, its bonds valueless, its industries, furnaces, and factories closed up; and again be reduced to the status of "a conquered province" because northern investors on "Wall Street," who had put money into southern economic development, would cry " 'Murderers, stay thy hand!' and it will be stayed" (quoted in *Official Proceedings, 1901,* 3:3,087).

45. Observer to ed., *Clanton Banner,* 3 Oct. 1901, 1.

46. Both quotations from *Marshall Banner,* 5 Sept. 1901, 4. The *Huntsville Republican* echoed this view, 20 Apr. 1901, 1.

47. *Clanton Banner* editorial, 7 Nov. 1901, 4 (first quotation); *Choctaw Alliance,* 10 Apr. 1901, 1 (second quotation; the *Alliance* also portrayed the question as "the most important ballot ever cast in the history of the present generation"); *Gadsden-Etowah People's Voice,* 19 July 1900, 2 (third quotation); the *Greenville Living Truth,* 12 Apr. 1901, 4 (fourth quotation). See also *Gadsden-Etowah People's Voice,* 1 Feb. 1900, 4; 15 Mar. 1900, 4; 29 Mar. 1900, 5; and 19 Apr. 1900, 2.

48. *Marshall Banner,* 24 Oct. 1901, 4.

49. Quotation from *Attalla Mirror,* 17 Oct. 1901, 1; also see p. 2; and *Ozark Free Press,* 3 May 1900, 4, 6. The year 1861 could also probably be added to this list because the Civil War, as many have noted, was to a large extent a rich man's war and poor man's fight.

50. *Attalla Mirror,* 7 Nov. 1901, 2 (first quotation); *Gadsden Tribune,* 3 Aug. 1899, 4 (second quotation). On the constitution, see the *Gadsden Tribune,* 25 May 1899, 4; and 18 April 1901, 4. On Captain A. McHan and his Populist and Confederate background, see the *Gadsden Tribune,* 31 Aug. 1899, 2 and 4; and 10 Jan. 1901, 4; the *Marshall Banner,* 30 June 1899, 2; 27 July 1899, 2; and 10 Aug. 1899, 2; and the *Cullman People's Protest,* 1 July 1898, 2. On McHan's *Boaz Signal* being a Populist newspaper, see the *Marshall Banner,* 17 Aug. 1899, 2.

51. *Attalla Mirror,* 26 Sept. 1901, 2.

52. *Attalla Mirror,* 7 Nov. 1901, 2.

53. *Newton-Dale County Harmonizer,* 17 Oct. 1901, 1; see also 10 Oct. 1901, 1.

54. *Geneva Reaper,* 23 Oct. 1901, 2. This issue as well as that of 27 Nov. 1901, 2, made plain the newspaper's "unalterable" opposition to ratification.

55. *Geneva Reaper,* 6 Nov. 1901, 2 (first quotation); *Gadsden-Etowah County People's Voice,* 23 Aug. 1900, 2 (second quotation); *Collinsville Clipper,* 27 Dec. 1900, 4 (third quotation). The *People's Voice* was closely linked to like-minded newspapers such as the *Marshall Banner* and the *Coosa River News.* It was edited by P. A. W. Keel and, later, W. S. Griffith, both Populists, and commonly ran headlines on the "Negro Brute." See *People's Voice,* 1 Feb. 1900, 4; 1 Mar. 1900, 4 and 8; 15 Mar. 1900, 4; and 29 Mar. 1900, 5. Also see the *Collinsville Clipper,* 15 Mar. 1900, 2, and 19 July 1900, 4.

56. McMillan, *Constitutional Development in Alabama,* 338, 350–51; D. A. Harris, "Racists and Reformers," 184–87; Hackney, *Populism to Progressivism in Alabama,* 228–29, 325; Rogers et al., *Alabama,* 333–34.

57. *Minutes of the State Democratic Executive Committee,* 15 Jan. 1901, 11 (Robert Lowe speaking); and 17–19 (F. L. Pettus speaking), box 2, folder, 4, SDEC Records, ADAH. On maps 3 and 4, the few white counties that registered 50 percent "for" calling or ratifying—Crenshaw in April and Lamar and Mobile in November—were shaded as "for."

58. Racial conformity, in other words, fealty to white supremacy and solidarity with other whites, was fortified in this period by being tied very closely to the concept of patriotism or a type of national southern loyalty. The patriotism connection provided an even more powerful motivator for plain whites to put racial solidarity ahead of other competing interests. References to this type of race-based conformist citizenship were a

marked theme during this era and beyond. "A patriotism such as that," Tennent Lomax preached, "must live forever and keep free government alive so long as people are true to . . . their country and the traditions of their race." Lomax compared this patriotism to that of George Washington and the Continental Army at Valley Forge and the Battle of Yorktown; American valor during the War of 1812; Zachary Taylor, Jeff Davis, and Winfield Scott at Buena Vista and in the halls of Montezuma; Pickett at Missionary Ridge; and Hancock at Gettysburg (quoted in *Official Proceedings, 1901*, 3:3,089; see also 3,093). For other examples of this phenomenon, a creed adhered to by poor, plain, and privileged Alabama whites, see the instances in the *Official Proceedings, 1901*, 3:2,886, 3,002, 3,009, and 3,011; and the *Minutes of the* SDEC, 3 Apr. 1901, 16. See also chapter 2, note 86 (block quote); chapter 3, notes 46, 61, 78, 92, 93, 99, and 113; and chapter 4, note 41.

59. McMillan, *Constitutional Development in Alabama*, 338, 350–51; D. A. Harris, "Racists and Reformers," 184–87; Hackney, *Populism to Progressivism in Alabama*, 228–29, 325; Rogers et al., *Alabama*, 333–34.

60. *Huntsville-Madison Republican*, 16 Nov. 1901, 2 (first and third quotations); *Geneva Reaper*, 27 Nov. 1901, 2 (second quotation); 23 Oct. 1901, 3 (fourth quotation); and 27 Nov. 1901, 2 (fifth quotation). Charles Shelley, Joe Johnston, and the Republican *Birmingham Times* also claimed a 25,000–50,000 vote white majority and every white county "except possibly . . . two" as going "against" (*Birmingham Times*, 15 Nov. 1901, 4).

61. McMillan, *Constitutional Development*, 338, 350–51; D. A. Harris, "Racists and Reformers," 184–87; Hackney, *Populism to Progressivism in Alabama*, 228–29, 325; Rogers et al., *Alabama*, 333–34.

62. D. A. Harris, "Racists and Reformers," 255–56.

63. Reuben Davis interview by Horace Huntley, part 1, p. 2; Reuben Davis interview by Horace Huntley, part 2, p. 1; and Francis Foster White interview by Horace Huntley, all three conducted at Miles College and held at the BCRI Oral History Project. See also Emory O. Jackson interview no. 30, pp. 2, 5–6, and 12, box 92, folder 30, Hardy T. Frye Oral History Collection, AU; the "Voter Registration" Scrapbook in the Alabama AFL-CIO Scrapbooks, ALA; and William L. Andrews, "The Spirit of Friday Jones," 4 and 6, DTS.

64. Quotations from Address of Hon. John B. Knox, Jones's Chapel in Cullman County, Alabama, 4 July 1906, 11–13, TCSH. Regarding Page's estimate, see his *Negro*, 149, quoted in McMillan, *Constitutional Development in Alabama*, 353 n. 88; see also 352–54. Still, the percentage of whites allowed to vote was far higher than that of blacks. In 1906, 83 percent of white males of voting age were registered, compared with only 2 percent of blacks; see Hackney, *Populism to Progressivism in Alabama*, 206. For the 1941 figures, see McMillan, *Constitutional Development in Alabama*, 354, 358. This trend did not necessarily follow in other states. Poor textile-mill whites in South Carolina did not generally lose the vote in that state's disfranchisement process. See Bryant Simon's outstanding study, *Fabric of Defeat*, 4, 16.

65. Grantham, "American Politics for the South," 149–50. Historians are in general agreement that Alabama's privileged whites used the issue of race to disfranchise many poor whites as well as keep themselves in an elevated position. See D. A. Harris, "Racists and Reformers," 160; Gross, "Alabama Politics and the Negro," 22–25, 127, 152, 228;

McMillan, *Constitutional Development in Alabama*, 225–26, 228, 308–9, 338, 358, viii of the preface to the 1955 edition, and vi in the introduction to the 1988 edition; and Rogers et al., *Alabama*, 344, 353.

66. See, for example, Carter, *From George Wallace to Newt Gingrich;* and Greenhaw, *Elephants in the Cottonfields.* Political scientists Earl Black and Merle Black wrote that "[b]lack belt political influence rested not only on the widespread commitment to white supremacy of non–black belt whites, but also on alliances . . . with large-scale industry and finance, forces that were not indifferent to or unconcerned about race relations" (*Politics and Society in the South,* 11). Also see Black and Black, *Rise of Southern Republicans.* On earlier related events, see Lichtenstein, *Twice the Work of Free Labor,* 87; Gaither, *Blacks and the Populist Revolt,* 104; Kousser, *Shaping of Southern Politics,* 130; and Kirby, *Darkness at the Dawning,* 68–73.

67. For examples of patricians putting forth the Great Lie, see the *Proceedings of the* DSC, 26 Apr. 1900, 28, ADAH, cited in D. A. Harris, "Racists and Reformers," 147; McMillan, *Constitutional Development in Alabama,* 357–59; and Rogers et al., *Alabama,* 344, 346.

68. For example, the *Selma Times* defended the 1893 Sayre Law as a rule that placed "authority in the hands of those best qualified to serve the people and promote their interests" (quoted in McMillan, *Constitutional Development in Alabama,* 224 n. 44). Democratic election officers could deny people the vote or vote them the "right way" (quoted in McMillan, 224). See also McMillan (357) for the promise of a return to two-party politics so that white men could divide on issues freely without fear of black voter manipulation. In 1901, Gessner Williams, a Marengo County delegate to the 1901 constitutional convention, maintained that even if the Black Belt registered and voted blacks under the "registration plan" provisions of the new constitution, it would "still be in the best interest of the State. . . . [Plain] White men have nothing to fear from the black belt," Williams continued. "We said . . . that we would not disfranchise a single white man. We should not go back upon the pledge of the party to the people. . . . [T]he Democratic party pledged itself to this plank . . . [and] I believe we should put ourselves in the position" during ratification of reminding plain whites of this (quoted in *Official Proceedings,* 1901, 3:2,838–39).

69. The desire was not new. Bruce Palmer wrote that the Populists had "wanted black support without relinquishing white dominance" (*"Man over Money,"* xvii, 217). See also Hackney, *Populism to Progressivism in Alabama,* 39, 47.

70. Quoted in *Official Proceedings,* 1901, 3:3,039.

71. *Official Proceedings,* 1901, 3:3,116–17, 3,569, and 3,916.

72. Coleman quoted in *Official Proceedings,* 1901, 3:3,052 and 3,097.

73. Quoted in *Official Proceedings,* 1901, 2:2,691; see also 3:2,990 and 4:4,708; Rogers et al., *Alabama,* 346; McMillan, *Constitutional Development in Alabama,* 279–80, 285; and Kousser, *Shaping of Southern Politics,* 169. Among the nineteen papers that voted to forget the "no-disfranchisement" pledge were the *Greenville Advocate, Clarke County Democrat, Mobile Register, Alabama Baptist, Tuskegee News, Pratt City Herald, Montgomery Advertiser, Montevallo Sentinel,* and *Wetumpka Herald.*

74. John B. Knox, "Reduction of Representation in the South," *Outlook* 79 (1905): 171. On the breaking of the patrician pledge, see Murphy, *Problems of the Present South*, 193, quoted in Woodward, *Origins of the New South*, 330.

75. *Cherokee Harmonizer*, 9 May 1901, 4 (first quotation); 6 June 1901, 4 (second quotation); and 7 Nov. 1901, 4 (third quotation); also see 14 Nov. 1901, 4. The newspaper favored the disfranchisement of blacks by various schemes and referred to blacks derisively as "dear Cuffie" (9 May 1901, 4); see also 6 and 20 June 1901, 4. For the *Harmonizer*'s editorial policies and ownership and management, see chapter 2, note 60.

76. *Choctaw Alliance*, 17 Apr. 1901, 1 (first quotation); 14 Aug. 1901, 1 (second quotation); also see 19 July 1898, 1; 7 Feb. 1900, 1; 27 Mar. 1901, 1; 3 and 10 Apr. 1901, 1; and 3 July 1901, 1. See also McMillan, *Constitutional Development in Alabama*, 348–49.

77. The *Collinsville Clipper*, published in DeKalb County by Captain Joe C. Williams and George M. Holder, tied to Populist editor Lawson A. Fields, and edited by C. H. Davis, a former Hill Country Republican, feared a constitution that would disfranchise poor whites and placed its faith in the insurance policy of popular ratification and the patrician pledge that "[n]o white man will ever be disfranchised in Alabama" (19 July 1900, 2, 4). See also *Collinsville Clipper*, 17 Jan. 1900, 2; 31 Jan. 1900, 1; 15 Mar. 1900, 2 (also quotations from *DeKalb Times* and *Ft. Payne Journal* in this issue); 26 Apr. 1900, 1; and 12 July 1900, 2. The Populist newspaper the *People's Voice*, for example, published in Gadsden in Etowah County, focused exclusively on the disfranchisement peril facing "thousands of poor and illiterate . . . [and] uneducated white men" (21 June 1900, 2; and 2 Aug. 1900, 2). Also see *Greenville Living Truth*, 15 Nov. 1901, 4, a Populist paper in transit back to the Democratic Party.

78. *Ozark Free Press*, 6 Apr. 1899, 4; see also 20 Apr. 1899, 4.

79. *Ozark Free Press*, 29 Mar. 1900, 2; see also 17 May 1900, 4.

80. *Ozark Free Press*, 3 May 1900, 2 and 4. For Populist editorial support of Stallings, see 8 Mar. 1900, 4.

81. *Ozark Free Press*, 9 and 16 Aug. 1900, 2. In the 9 Aug. 1900 issue, the paper admitted, "[t]o recapitulate, we have in stock one dead party."

82. Quotation from *Ozark Free Press*, 23 Aug. 1900, 2. Regarding the newspaper's advocacy of a white primary, see 9 Aug. 1900, 2; see also 30 Aug. 1900, 2.

CHAPTER FIVE *Disfranchisement Cemented*

1. All quotations from *Attalla Mirror*, 21 Nov. 1901, 2.

2. A. W. Jones, "Political Reforms of the Progressive Era," 175–76, 178–79, 206. See also A. W. Jones, "Political Reform and Party Factionalism in the Deep South," 3–4, 32; McMillan, *Constitutional Development in Alabama*, 316–17; Rogers et al., *Alabama*, 355–56; Grantham, *Southern Progressivism*, 48; and D. A. Harris, "Racists and Reformers," 258.

3. Key, *Southern Politics in State and Nation*, 539, 618.

4. Charles M. Shelley to John W. A. Sanford, 19 Nov. 1901, in John W. A. Sanford Papers, ADAH, cited in D. A. Harris, "Racists and Reformers," 223–24. Also see *Geneva*

Reaper, 23 Oct. 1901, 3. For Stallings's involvement in this movement, see folders 1–10, Jesse Francis Stallings Papers, no. 2405, SHC.

5. Johnston quoted in Perman, *Struggle for Mastery,* 307.

6. Joseph F. Johnston to John Witherspoon DuBose, 1 Apr. 1902, box 2, folder 6, John Witherspoon DuBose Papers, ADAH. DuBose and a circle of influential tribunes of Alabama's plain folk backed the movement for the white primary, thinking (incorrectly) that it would lead to Johnston's victory over W. D. Jelks in the 1902 gubernatorial election. See Johnston to DuBose, 1 Apr. 1902; and A. E. Caffee to DuBose, 12 and 26 Mar., 10 and 20 May, and 4 and 9 June 1902, all in box 2, folder 6, DuBose Papers, ADAH. Andrew E. Caffee was a Lowndes County state senator and free-silver Democrat. See DeVine, "Free Silver and Alabama Politics," 233.

7. *Minutes of the State Democratic Executive Committee* (SDEC), 23 Mar. 1900 and 10 July 1902, box 3, folder 1, SDEC Records, ADAH. Also see *Birmingham Age-Herald* 9, 11 May 1901; *Mobile Register* 23 and 25 Mar. 1902, cited in A. W. Jones, "Political Reforms of the Progressive Era," 176–78; Flynt, *Poor but Proud,* 257; D. A. Harris, "Racists and Reformers," 123–24; and McMillan, *Constitutional Development in Alabama,* 357–58.

8. Oates quoted in the *Birmingham Alabamian,* 21 Feb. 1902, quoted in A. W. Jones, "History of the Direct Primary in Alabama," 138.

9. *Birmingham Age-Herald,* 20 Jan. 1901, quoted in McMillan, *Constitutional Development in Alabama,* 245.

10. Rogers et al., *Alabama,* 355–56; Hackney, *Populism to Progressivism in Alabama,* 241; and A. W. Jones, "Political Reforms of the Progressive Era," 179.

11. *Jacksonville Republican,* 30 Aug. 1901, 2. Also see Brittain, "Negro Suffrage and Politics in Alabama since 1870," 143.

12. A. W. Jones, "Political Reforms of the Progressive Era," 173–94. Rogers and Ward wisely realized that "in retrospect it has been possible to affix the progressive label to all but the most cynical reactionaries. . . . [H]istorians have bestowed the sobriquet [too] liberally" (Rogers et al., *Alabama,* 362, 375).

13. McMillan, *Constitutional Development in Alabama,* 244–45.

14. A. W. Jones, "Political Reforms of the Progressive Era," 186. In a bizarre primary, termed the "pall-bearers" or "dead-shoes" primary, Alabamians nominated two alternates to take over as U.S. senator in the case of the death of either of the state's two ancient senators, John Tyler Morgan and Edmund L. Pettus. John H. Bankhead Sr. became a U. S. senator in 1907 upon Morgan's death; Joseph Johnston finally joined him the next month when Pettus died. See A. W. Jones, "Political Reform and Party Factionalism in the Deep South," 3–32; and Republican Hand-Book, North Carolina, Republican State Executive Committee, 1906, p. 4, DTS.

15. Flynt, *Dixie's Forgotten People,* 54–55.

16. This reality was common to much of the era's political "reform." In 1911, reform governor Emmett O'Neal successfully pushed a reform of dubious nature to the primary law: the provision that no party could hold a primary at public expense unless it had garnered at least 25 percent of the popular vote in the previous general election. The law was designed to prevent the more progressive Republican Party and others from

holding their own primaries. See A. W. Jones, "Political Reforms of the Progressive Era," 180–81, 186. In Birmingham, Mayor George Ward's adoption of the commission form of government grew out of a dispute with city council president John L. Parker, was backed by Tennessee Coal and Iron, and was geared toward lessening the influence of "undesirable elements" in politics and restricting power to a "few men of intelligence, business experience, industry and character" (McKiven, *Iron and Steel,* 158).

17. L. H. Reynolds to ed., *Clanton Banner,* 19 Sept. 1901, 1 and 4.

18. Quotations from *Marshall Banner,* 5 Aug. 1899, 2; and *Clanton Banner,* 10 Oct. 1901, 4. See also *Marshall Banner,* 28 Sept. 1899, 2.

19. See, for example, *Geneva Reaper,* 23 Oct. 1901, 2.

20. Ibid., 16 Oct. 1901, 2.

21. *Gadsden Tribune,* 17 and 24 Aug. 1899, 4 in both; *Carrollton, Alabama Alliance News,* 23 May 1899, 2; and *Ozark Free Press,* 9 Aug. 1900, 2.

22. *Jacksonville Republican,* 14 June 1902 and 19 July 1902, 2 in both; *Anniston Republican,* 12 and 26 Feb. 1898, 4 in both; and the *Anniston Republican* editorial reprinted in the *Gadsden Tribune,* 17 Aug. 1899, 4. See also the "Defense of the Negro Race—Charges Answered," Speech of Hon. George H. White of North Carolina in the House of Representatives, 29 Jan. 1901, electronic ed., pp. 7–8, DTS.

23. *Minutes of the* SDEC, 10 July 1902, 1, 32, and 40, box 3, folder 1, SDEC Records, ADAH.

24. C. C. Whitson quoted in *Minutes of the* SDEC, 10 July 1902, 6. Whitson further argued that the proprimary majority was not simply made up of the plain folk but was, in addition, coming "almost unanimously" from the regular Democrats of the white counties who had "borne the brunt of battle" and "everstood on the front line" in trying to keep their county's plain whites from bolting the Democratic Party (21). William J. Samford, of Pike County, facetiously suggested that privileged committee members from Dallas and Mobile Counties who opposed the all-white, direct Democratic primary be "deputized" by the SDEC to march into the hill counties of Jackson and Marshall to "answer" their "argument for" the white-county delegates who had to deal with potential insurgency back home (32).

25. On the "grave" nature of the question stressed, see *Minutes of the* SDEC, 10 July 1902, 5 and 15.

26. C. C. Whitson made the motion; see *Minutes of the* SDEC, 10 July 1902, 3.

27. C. C. Whitson quoted in *Minutes of the* SDEC, 10 July 1902, 6. See also 2, 4, 6, 7, 17, 61.

28. Quotations from *Minutes of the* SDEC, 10 July 1902, 32 (Samford) and 60 (Graves). Whitson of Talladega used almost the exact wording as Samford, stipulating his opposition to "every man with a white skin" voting in a primary. He wanted only those who had come back into the Democratic Party and "shown their faith by their works" (6).

29. Quotations from *Minutes of the* SDEC, 10 July 1902, 15 (Emmett O'Neal); 6 (Whitson); and 15 (O'Neal); see also pp. 5, 17, 20, and 35.

30. Ibid., 5, 6, 15, 16, 20, 31–32.

31. First quotations from Samford quoted in *Minutes of the* SDEC, 10 July 1902, 32; see also 34–35, box 3, folder 1. Second quotation from J. F. Proctor quoted in *Minutes of the*

SDEC, 22 Oct. 1902, 20, box 3, folder 6, all in SDEC Records, ADAH. For other references to the vast majority of white Alabama favoring a direct primary, see *Minutes of the* SDEC, 10 July 1902, 5, 15, 16, 21, 31, 34, 64.

32. Quotations from *Minutes of the* SDEC, 10 July 1902, 28 (R. J. Lowe, first quotation), 18 (O'Neal), 21 (C. C. Whitson, third quotation), 35 (Heflin), and 31 and 33 (Samford). For other references to threats of disunity, see 6, 20, and 32.

33. SDEC chair Robert J. Lowe represented the parliamentary strategy. See the *Minutes of the* SDEC, 10 July 1902, 2, 4, 29, and 30. Hugh S. D. Mallory of Dallas County and Judge Smith of Greene chose the usurpation arguments; see 3–4, and 18. For the comparison with South Carolina's white primary and Tillman, see R. J. Lowe, quoted on pp. 28 and 29.

34. R. L. Seale quoted in *Minutes of the* SDEC, 10 July 1902, 55.

35. Lowe quoted in *Minutes of the* SDEC, 10 July 1902, 27, 28, and 30. Another representative of the Black Belt also invoked the religious propriety of white supremacy. The "democrats of the black belt have voted for the right as God gave them the power to see it," T. S. Frasier contended, defending his section (quoted on p. 54). Lowe also made the connection between the critical epoch of Reconstruction and the "epoch-making period" of the turn of the century (quoted on p. 29). At a later party council, Lowe made the point clearly that the "great work" in "[this] period of service marks an epoch in the State . . . more remarkable . . . than any . . . that has passed since the time of Reconstruction" (quoted in *Minutes of the* SDEC, 3 Sept. 1902, 38–39, box 3, folder 6, SDEC Records, ADAH). White supremacy and religious duty were tied closely together for the Jeffersonian whites as well, as in the *Collinsville Clipper*, 27 Dec. 1900, 4. For Conservative Democrats of the Bourbon variety, conservatism meant white supremacy above anything else. Montgomery County delegate to the 1901 convention, University of Alabama Trustee, and son of a Confederate veteran, Tennent Lomax eulogized what he called "Caucasian Democracy." "If there be one thing that I love better than another," Lomax said, "it is the Grand Old Democratic party . . . which has stood between my native state and negro domination. . . . [The Conservative Democratic Party is the] rock that stands between us and the black waves of negro domination" (Address of Tennent Lomax, Esq. to State Democratic Convention, ca. 1900, box 1077, folder 7, Tennent Lomax Collection, UA). For a discussion of the relationship between race, religion, patriotism, and family loyalty in southern politics, see chapter 3, notes 61, 78, 92, 93, 99, and 113, and chapter 4, note 58. For more on the relationship between political conservatism and racism in southern politics, see chapter 3, note 92.

36. Quotation from *Minutes of the* SDEC, 10 July 1902, 61. See also 41 and 54–55. Miller was another future Alabama governor.

37. *Minutes of the* SDEC, 10 July 1902, committee vote on 40–41.

38. Quotation from Flynt, *Poor but Proud*, 257. See also *Minutes of the* SDEC, 22 October 1902, 18 (Mallory speaking). Black Belt dominance in the legislature, through malapportionment based on total, including black, population, was the price the planters and their industrialist allies had ostensibly paid for the 1901 disfranchisement. Every ten years, though, the malapportioned legislature resisted the renewed call for reapportionment based on a new census. See Gross, "Alabama Politics and the Negro," 263.

39. Gilmore, *Gender and Jim Crow*, 129 (first quotation); Dailey, *Before Jim Crow*, 161 (second quotation). See also Gilmore, 119–20, 123, and 130.

40. State GOP head William J. Vaughn had, for instance, endorsed the 1898 state Populist ticket. See *Cullman People's Protest*, 8 July 1898, 4. For more on the independent culture of poor whites in the Wiregrass, see the various collections at the AWHC.

41. Quotation from *Jacksonville Republican*, 19 July 1902, 1 (quoted); see also Rodabaugh, "Farmers' Revolt in Alabama," 88. Some common ground between regular Democracy and Republicanism did exist, e.g., at times on matters of local patronage. See J. W. Hughes, postmaster, Birmingham Post Office, to J. J. Willett, 19 Feb. 1901, folder "Correspondence, 1 October 1900–18 May 1901," H–L, Joseph J. Willett Papers, SU.

42. *Cullman People's Protest*, 8 July 1898, 4. See also Emory O. Jackson interview, no. 30, p. 6, box 92, folder 30, Hardy T. Frye Oral History Collection, AU. For Republican rifts in this period, even intraparty violence, see the *Birmingham Age-Herald*, 20 Apr. 1900, 1. Black Republicans were not monolithic or always united either. An excellent new book, *Urban Emancipation*, by historian Michael W. Fitzgerald demonstrates considerable cleavages and tensions between longtime, relatively prosperous, and often freeborn black Mobilians and recently freed, poorer, rural blacks.

43. *Attalla Mirror*, 21 Nov. 1901, 2.

44. Sledge, "Alabama Republican Party," 82–83; Gross, "Alabama Politics and the Negro," 209.

45. Quotation in Brittain, "Negro Suffrage and Politics in Alabama since 1870," 144; see also 145–47; and Sledge, "Alabama Republican Party," 84–85.

46. Booker T. Washington to James Sullivan Clarkson, 16 Sept. 1902; Clarkson to Washington, 17 Sept. 1902; and William J. Stevens to Booker T. Washington, 24 Oct. 1902. Clarkson "understands the Alabama situation well," Washington told the President, "that is, as well as any one can, for no human being can understand the Southern situation thoroughly" (Booker T. Washington to Theodore Roosevelt, 27 Sept. 1902). All letters in Harlan and Smock, *Booker T. Washington Papers*, 6:515, 522–23, 527, and 558–59. Also see Gilmore, *Gender and Jim Crow*, 129.

47. *Huntsville Republican*, 15 Nov. 1902, cited in Brittain, "Negro Suffrage and Politics in Alabama since 1870," 147 (first quotation); Norrell, *James Bowron*, 174 (second quotation) and also 173, 175–76; and Sledge, "Alabama Republican Party," 86–93.

48. James Sullivan Clarkson to Booker T. Washington, 16 Oct. 1902, in Harlan and Smock, *Booker T. Washington Papers*, 6:550–52; Brittain, "Negro Suffrage and Politics in Alabama since 1870," 147; and Sledge, "Alabama Republican Party," 91.

49. This subject is addressed in several works. Probably the best known is Woodward, *Strange Career of Jim Crow*. For a discussion of the controversy that arose after the book, see Rabinowitz, "More than the Woodward Thesis," 183–202. On Jim Crow in Alabama, see the Erline Priscilla Hutto interview by Georgeann Guthrie, 1980, and the Lucille T. Summers interview by Clifton Depreast, 1980, both in the UAB.

50. Papers of the NAACP, part 7, series A, reels 3 and 21, AU and LC; and NAACP, *Thirty Years of Lynching in the United States*.

51. The observation that Progressivism was "for whites only" first appeared in A. S.

Link, "What Happened to the Progressive Movement in the 1920s?" 833–51, but it is probably more closely associated with the title of one of Woodward's chapters in *Origins of the New South*. See also Blondheim, "William Dorsey Jelks and His Crusade against Lynching."

52. See also chapter 1, note 92. On the formative importance of the Civil War experience in leaving a "far higher degree of southern unity against the rest of the world than had prevailed before," see V. O. Key's classic work. "Unity on the national scene was essential in order that the largest possible bloc could be mobilized to resist any national move toward interference with southern authority to deal with the race question as was desired locally . . . [and to protect against] national intervention to protect Negro rights." On this "fundamental issue, only the Federal Government was to be feared" (*Southern Politics in State and Nation*, 7 and 9; see also 11–12 and 44–45).

53. Segregation has given rise to much vigorous scholarly debate. C. Vann Woodward's *The Strange Career of Jim Crow* made the argument that race relations generally hardened after 1900, leading to a de jure segregation that, in many cases, replaced more fluid relations between the races. David M. Potter gently chided Woodward for his "presentism" in trying to solve mid-1950s racial problems with history. See Potter's essay, "C. Vann Woodward," 395–99, and 407. Joel R. Williamson criticized Woodward for laying too much emphasis on the appearance of Jim Crow laws around 1900 as prima facie evidence of the hardening of social customs. He pointed out that statutes historically lagged behind and served to codify established practices; see *Crucible of Race*. In *Race Relations in the Urban South*, Howard N. Rabinowitz pointed out that segregation may have ironically provided a kind of improvement for blacks who had been largely excluded before Jim Crow. Richard C. Wade documented antebellum Jim Crow in the South's urban settings in *Slavery in the Cities*, as did Ira Berlin in *Slaves without Masters*.

54. On Chilton County's Samuel M. Adams and segregation, see Hackney, *Populism to Progressivism in Alabama*, 45–46. Also on Adams, see DeVine, "Free Silver and Alabama Politics," 312.

55. *Attalla Mirror*, 7 Nov. 1901, 2.

56. Key, *Southern Politics in State and Nation*, 539, 618.

57. Flynt, *Poor but Proud*, 213. On the connection between white supremacy and gender, see also Painter, *Southern History across the Color Line*; Dailey, *Before Jim Crow*; Gilmore, *Gender and Jim Crow*; MacLean, *Behind the Mask of Chivalry*; Blee, *Women and the Klan*; Williamson, *Crucible of Race*; J. D. Hall, " 'The Mind That Burns in Each Body,' " 328–46; and J. D. Hall, *Revolt against Chivalry*.

58. This cognizance of the social aspect of race's construction is, of course, a hallmark of the recent "whiteness" studies. See, for example, Hale, *Making Whiteness*, and Roediger, *Wages of Whiteness*. Peter Kolchin gives a thorough overview of this literature in "Whiteness Studies," 154–73.

59. *Marshall Banner*, reprinted in *Attalla Mirror*, 5 Sept. 1901, 2. Of course, for the elites, the stakes in white supremacy were also very real. It served as, perhaps, the most effective emotional political issue. The privileged also had a vested interest in preserving

a cheap and docile black laboring class on the plantations and in the mills, as well as short-circuiting the possibility of biracial labor insurgency.

60. *Attalla Mirror*, 10 and 17 Oct. 1901, 2 in both.

61. Ibid., 24 Oct. 1901, 2 (first quotation). Second quotation from *Greenville Living Truth*, 18 May 1900, 3, and 31 Aug. 1900, 4.

62. J. B. Sellers, *Prohibition Movement in Alabama*, 101 (first quotation); Rogers et al., *Alabama*, 372 (second quotation). See also Howington, "John Barley Corn Subdued," 212–25. Rogers and Ward viewed prohibition as an unimpressive reform. "In a poverty-stricken land . . . based on inequality, with a less than responsive government, prohibition took up a disproportionate amount of money, time, energy, and moral outrage. . . . The use of grape juice in the observance of the Lord's Supper was not a major social reform" (Rogers et al., *Alabama*, 372). Regarding the 1907 legislation, see Rogers et al., 373.

63. *Alabama Christian Advocate*, 4 Jan. 1906. J. B. Sellers essentially agreed with these sentiments; see *Prohibition Movement in Alabama*, 101, 290. Black accommodationist William H. Councill of Huntsville favored prohibition as a measure to save the black race. White Baptist preacher B. F. Riley helped blacks establish the Negro Anti-Saloon League in 1909; see Flynt, "Religion in the Urban South," 133.

64. Thomas, *New Woman in Alabama*, 173 and 202. Thomas perceptively observed that the cause of women's suffrage in Alabama was "doomed" by the antisuffragists' use of the race issue because "almost no argument could be effective in the face of perceived danger to white supremacy" (173). As noted in the text, the discussion around white supremacy and women's suffrage has been vigorous and varied. In *Ideas of the Woman Suffrage Movement*, 163–218, Aileen S. Kraditor interpreted white supremacy as a corner-stone of the southern women's suffrage movement. Anne Firor Scott, Suzanne Lebsock, Glenda Elizabeth Gilmore, and Elna C. Green have disputed this claim. See Scott, *Southern Lady*, 182–83; Lebsock, "Woman Suffrage and White Supremacy," 62–100; Gilmore, *Gender and Jim Crow*, 203–11; and Green, *Southern Strategies*, 91–98. Marjorie Spruill Wheeler's and Drew Gilpin Faust's work has tended to reinforce Kraditor's thesis, with some qualifications and advancements, yet still taking the suffragists to task for divorcing themselves from disfranchised black men and not denouncing white supremacy. See Wheeler, *New Women of the New South*, 100–132; and Faust, *Mothers of Invention*, 253. I am grateful to Anastatia Sims for aid on this subject. Also see Sims's *Power of Femininity in the New South*, 155–88.

65. Keeler, "Alva Belmont," 142; W. A. Link, *Paradox of Southern Progressivism*, 73. Thomas, in *New Woman in Alabama*, 173, 202, argued that Alabama's suffragists did not appeal to the race issue in their 1915 campaign for passage of a state suffrage law. This interpretation is too charitable to the prosuffrage forces, which repeatedly pointed out that white women could be enfranchised without risking black voting of any kind because the constitutional safeguards of 1901, crafted for black men, would still work; see Rogers et al., *Alabama*, 381.

66. Quoted in A. W. Jones, "Political Reforms of the Progressive Era," 193–94.

67. Quotation from Thomas, *New Woman in Alabama,* 194–96. The group also de-scribed the proposed law as "a wolf gnawing at the vitals" of government (196). See also Baker and Roberts to Whole Alabama Congressional Delegation, 12 Dec. 1917, box 24, folder 2, John Hollis Bankhead Sr. Papers, ADAH.

68. Judge J. R. Thomas quoted in Thomas, *New Woman in Alabama,* 197; state senator J. B. Evins quoted in Thomas, 201; see also 197–98, 200–201; the *Montgomery Advertiser,* 7, 25 June 1919; and the *Huntsville Daily News,* 25 July 1919. M. C. Calhoun, a grand-nephew of John C. Calhoun, said that ratifying the Nineteenth Amendment in Alabama would erase principles for which Confederate soldiers shed blood and dismantle every monument erected to their "heroic memory" (quoted in Thomas, 198).

69. T. L. Bulger quoted in *Official Proceedings, 1901,* 3:3,377. See also C. V. Harris, *Political Power in Birmingham,* 207. For labor's record on race, see Kelly, *Race, Class, and Power in the Alabama Coalfields;* and Letwin, *Challenge of Interracial Unionism.*

70. *Birmingham Labor Advocate,* 17 and 31 Mar. 1917, cited in C. V. Harris, *Political Power in Birmingham,* 173.

71. *Official Proceedings, 1901,* 2:1,348, 4:4,294–97; A. W. Jones, "Political Reforms of the Progressive Era," 176; McMillan, *Constitutional Development in Alabama,* 322–24, 339, and ix of introduction to 1978 edition; D. A. Harris, "Racists and Reformers," 87. The sponsors of the idea represented the white counties: Erle Pettus of Limestone County in north Alabama and Tom Heflin, a delegate from Chambers County, a textile county. For material on the enduring effects of educational segregation, see the Papers of James U. Blacksher and the Rep. John F. Knight Collection at ASU.

72. Alabama's ancient senator John Tyler Morgan argued for repatriation of the black race to Africa, in part, because "'schooling' the negro . . . only [made] his condition worse . . . [by] unfitting him for menial . . . work and he [became] a loafer or criminal" (quoted in Baylen, "Senator John Tyler Morgan, E. D. Morel, and the Congo Reform Association," 125–26). Before the Populist movement, an industrialist newspaper had argued that black education would cause increased conflict between white employers and black employees; see the *Birmingham Age-Herald,* 31 Mar. 1890, cited in McKiven, *Iron and Steel,* 119.

73. West quoted in *Birmingham Labor Advocate,* 18 Apr. 1906, cited in McWilliams, "New Day Coming," 183. First vice-president quoted in *Birmingham Labor Advocate,* 17 and 31 Mar. 1917; see also 25 Sept. 1897, all cited in C. V. Harris, *Political Power in Birmingham,* 172–73. Vardaman quoted in Oshinsky, *"Worse Than Slavery,"* 89; see also 87 and 183. Also see Kirby, *Darkness at the Dawning,* 173; and C. V. Harris, *Political Power in Birmingham,* 173. Percy Clark, in his inaugural issue of the Birmingham weekly, praised the Old South, lamented the "evil days" of Reconstruction, and declared: "[W]hen the educated . . . negro finds his surroundings in the South uncongenial by reason of social or political ambition on his part . . . he may be encouraged to seek the benign soil of the Indies . . . or the frozen North, for warm hospitality and social recognition" (*Birmingham Anglo-Saxon of Alabama,* Aug. 1905, copy in possession of the author).

74. *Marshall Banner,* 25 Apr. 1901, 4. This editorial was also approvingly reprinted in

the *Attalla Mirror*, 2 May 1901, 2. George M. Fredrickson discusses the roots of poor-white racism, discounting a Marxian "false consciousness" while opting for a Weberian explanation of "status" competition; see *Arrogance of Race*, 157–60.

75. *Marshall Banner*, 9 May 1901, 4.

76. Quotation from *Fayette Banner*, reprinted in *Attalla Mirror*, 18 Apr. 1901, 2. The Populist newspaper the *People's Voice* approvingly printed the objections of fellow anti-Democratic newspapers such as the *Fort Payne Journal* to the notion of taxation and black education in general, while urging poor-white farmers to get themselves educated. See, e.g., *Fort Payne Journal*, quoted in *Gadsden-Etowah People's Voice*, 10 May 1900, 2; the issue of 4 Jan. 1900, 2, for the *Journal*'s editorial bent; and 30 Aug. 1900, 2, for exhortations to white farmers. On the Populist aversion to increased taxation, see *Ozark Free Press*, 3 May 1900, 4, 6. Also see the *Official Proceedings, 1901*, 3:3,070 (J. O. Sentell speaking).

77. *Attalla Mirror*, 21 Nov. 1901, 2. Tuskegee was located in the Black Belt county of Macon and was, of course, home also to Booker T. Washington's famous institute.

78. *Jacksonville Republican*, 6 Sept. 1902, 2.

79. *Carrollton, Alabama Alliance News*, 10 July 1900, 2.

80. The percentage of black children in school held almost constant over the decade near the 44 percent level of 1895–96, while white attendance jumped almost twenty percentage points. See D. A. Harris, "Racists and Reformers," 86–89, 357–61.

81. Rogers et al., *Alabama*, 325.

82. D. A. Harris, "Racists and Reformers," 81–82.

83. Ibid., 100, 359; McMillan, *Constitutional Development in Alabama*, 318. Black Belt resentment of paying for African American education had cropped up at the 1901 convention. See, e.g., *Official Proceedings, 1901*, 3:3,092.

84. Montgomery County school superintendent J. A. Thompson quoted in D. A. Harris, "Racists and Reformers," 100. See also Harris, 358–39; Bond, *Negro Education in Alabama*, 142, 246; Murphy, *Problems of the Present South*, 34, both cited in D. A. Harris, "Racists and Reformers," 359, 361; LaMonte, *Politics and Welfare in Birmingham*, 13; and Rogers et al., *Alabama*, 363.

85. C. V. Harris, *Political Power in Birmingham*, 167; LaMonte, *Politics and Welfare in Birmingham*, 12–13. This schizophrenic tendency of hypersensitivity toward outside criticism coupled with an eagerness to seek federal monies has been remarkably enduring in Alabama. For example, U.S. congressman Bob Riley's (R-Ala.) successful 2002 campaign for governor made a point of emphasizing the availability of more federal dollars than ever as a reason to vote for him. Yet Riley's campaign simultaneously stressed the Republican congressman's laissez-faire approach to business and economic development and his antipathy to governmental regulation—a distinct paradox still not recognized as such by much of Alabama's mainstream media or electorate (*Bob Riley for Governor Television Infomercial*, 2002).

86. Confusion over the Progressive movement is so extensive that historians have even considered abolishing the name "Progressive Era" altogether. See Watson, "From Populism through the New Deal," 329.

87. There are many examples of the disfranchisement effort being portrayed as a God-ordained effort, with the disfranchisers claiming the moral high ground for their "great reform." See *Official Proceedings, 1901*, 3:3,092 (M. Smith of Autauga speaking).

88. "Unconstitutional" in the sense of being in conflict with the spirit, if not the letter, of the Fourteenth and Fifteenth Amendments to the U.S. Constitution. This dilemma was confronted in other states as well. See Kantrowitz, *Ben Tillman and the Reconstruction of White Supremacy*, 199 and 219; and Dailey, *Before Jim Crow*, 163.

89. D. A. Harris, "Racists and Reformers," 161–75 and 186–87; Kousser, *Shaping of Southern Politics*, 169. As of this writing, Alabama's 1901 Constitution is still in effect.

90. A recent work that nicely illustrates the myriad problems saddled on Alabama by its 1901 Constitution is Thomson, *Century of Controversy.* See also Whitmire, "Who Would Want the Job Anyway?" 8. Conservative prerequisites were protected by a variety of means—some direct, some not so. John W. A. Sanford initiated a resolution to limit the maximum landholdings of one corporation to a thousand acres, asking that it be referred to the Committee on Amendment of the Constitution. Instead, John B. Knox referred it to the packed Committee on Corporations, eliciting a protest from Sanford to the effect that that committee had "not been heard from any more than the searchers for the North Pole" and predicting (correctly) that his resolution would not be heard from "any more than we do the Chariots of the Pharaoh" (*Official Proceedings, 1901*, 3:2,086, cited in Hackney, *Populism to Progressivism in Alabama*, 211).

91. Samuel D. Weakley in the pamphlet, "The State Must Not Stop Its Progress—Business Men Declare in Favor of a Constitutional Convention," 12, quoted in McMillan, *Constitutional Development in Alabama* 234–35; see also vi, 319, and 339. Also see Jackson, "White Supremacy Triumphant," 29. For an example of the pressure applied on regular Democrats to resist increased taxation, see W. H. Rowe Jr. (New York owner of the W. H. Rowe Knitting Co., of Huntsville, Alabama) to Judge J. J. Willett (whose brother Ed served as a constitutional delegate from Pickens County), 7 Mar. 1901, folder "Correspondence, 1 October 1900–18 May 1901," O–S, Joseph J. Willett Papers, su.

92. On the mystery associated with the Reconstruction order, see, e.g., No. 3 K + K + K, Klu [*sic*] Klux Klan file, Record no. 5717–4, MCM. A vivid contrast to the romantic memories of the Reconstruction KKK were provided in the memories of slaves in Alabama. See Mingo White interview by Levi D. Shelby Jr., 413–22; Aunt Nicey Pugh interview by Ila B. Prine and John Morgan Smith, 323–24; and Aunt Hannah Irwin interview by Gertha Couric and John Morgan Smith, 219, all three in the Federal Writers' Project, *Slave Narratives; The Glomerata: Alabama Polytechnic University Yearbook* 9 (1906), AU. Popular sheet music celebrating the original KKK also appeared during this period; see "The Bright Fiery Cross," (1913), Wade Hall Collection of Southern History and Culture, UA. Princeton University president and future United States president Woodrow Wilson was an admirer of the Reconstruction Klan and sympathized with the Dunning School depiction of Reconstruction. See Woodrow Wilson to Harper, 8 Jan. 1903, in A. S. Link, *Papers of Woodrow Wilson*, 43:540; *Florence Times*, 1 May 1903, quoted in Nelson, "Memorializing the Lost Cause in Florence, Alabama," 190–91.

93. William A. Link has described these developments as "contradiction[s]" or a

"paradox," which they were. But they were far more. They were actual perversions of the progressive impulse. See W. A. Link, *Paradox of Southern Progressivism,* 8, 239. For use of the word *irony,* see Flynt, *Poor but Proud,* 215; and Rogers et al., *Alabama,* 353. Race even entered into railroad regulation. Older Democrats opposed B. B. Comer's program of railroad regulation, as a rule, because they feared any program that might cause dissension within the ranks of whites, especially class issues. See D. A. Harris, "Racists and Reformers," 305–6.

94. See, for example, Hart, *Southern South,* 91, quoted in W. A. Link, *Paradox of Southern Progressivism,* 8, 239. For the references to the "Democratic and Conservative Party of Alabama" made throughout this book, see Henry De Lamar Clayton, quoted in *Proceedings of the Democratic State Convention* (DSC), 25 Apr. 1900, 12, box 2, folder 2, and J. Thomas Heflin, quoted in the *Minutes of the State Democratic Executive Committee* (SDEC), 15 Jan. 1901, 12, box 2, folder 4, both in the SDEC Records, ADAH.

BIBLIOGRAPHY

PRIMARY SOURCES

Manuscript Collections and Records

Alabama A and M University Archives (AAMA), Normal, Alabama. William H. Councill Papers.

Alabama Department of Archives and History (ADAH), Montgomery, Alabama. Alabama Governors Papers: Frank M. Dixon, David Bibb Graves, W. D. Jelks, Joseph F. Johnston, Thomas Goode Jones, and Chauncey Sparks. Alabama Pamphlet Collection. John Hollis Bankhead Sr. Personal Papers. Chappell Cory Personal Papers. John Witherspoon DuBose Personal Papers. Thomas Goode Jones Personal Papers. Robert McKee Personal Papers. Public Information Subject Files. John W. A. Sanford Personal Papers. Secretary of State Records. State Democratic Executive Committee Records. Oliver Day Street Personal Papers.

Alabama Labor Archives (ALA), Alabama AFL-CIO State Headquarters, Montgomery, Alabama. Voter Registration "Scrapbook."

Archives of Wiregrass History and Culture (AWHC), Troy State University, Dothan, Alabama. General Files.

Auburn University Archives (AU), Ralph Brown Draughon Library, Auburn, Alabama. Hardy T. Frye Oral History Collection. The Glomerata Collection. Papers of the NAACP.

Birmingham Civil Rights Institute (BCRI), Birmingham, Alabama. Oral History Project.

Birmingham Public Library Archives (BPLA), Linn-Henley Research Library, Birmingham, Alabama. Phillip H. Taft Research Notes.

Documenting the South, or The Southern Experience in Nineteenth-Century America (DTS). URL: http://docsouth.unc.edu/washington/about.html. University of North Carolina Libraries. Chapel Hill, North Carolina. Speech of Hon. George H. White in the House of Representatives. Curry, J. L. M. *The South in the Olden Time.* "The Spirit of Friday Jones." Houghton, W. R., and M. B. Houghton, *Two Boys in the Civil War and After.* Republican Handbook, 1906. North Carolina Republican Executive Committee.

Library of Congress (LC), Washington, D.C. John Tyler Morgan Papers. Papers of the National Association for the Advancement of Colored People.

Mattie Mashaw Jackson African American Center (MILES), Miles College Archives, W. A. Bell Library, Ensley, Alabama. Statewide Oral History Project.

Museum of the City of Mobile (MCM), Mobile, Alabama. Ku Klux Klan File.

National Center for the Study of Civil Rights and African-American Culture (ASU),

Department of Special Collections, Alabama State University, Montgomery, Alabama. Rep. John F. Knight Collection. Papers of James U. Blacksher.

Oakwood College Archives (OCA), Huntsville, Alabama. MLD's Donor Scrapbook.

Samford University Department of Special Collections (SU), Harwell Goodwin Davis Library, Homewood, Alabama. J. Thomas Heflin Scrapbooks. Joseph J. Willett Papers.

Sloss Furnaces National Historic Landmark Archives (SLOSS), Museum of History and Industry, Birmingham, Alabama. Oral History Project.

Southern Historical Collection (SHC), University of North Carolina at Chapel Hill, Chapel Hill, North Carolina. Jesse Francis Stallings Papers.

Tuskegee University Archives (TU), Hollis Burke Frissell Library, Tuskegee, Alabama. Lynching File. Tuskegee Institute News Clipping Files.

Tutwiler Collection of Southern History (TCSH), Linn-Henley Research Library, Birmingham Public Library, Birmingham, Alabama. Rucker Agee Map Collection. John B. Knox Address.

University of Alabama at Birmingham Archives (UAB), Mervyn H. Sterne Library, Birmingham, Alabama. Oral History Project.

W. Stanley Hoole Special Collections Library (UA), University of Alabama, Tuscaloosa, Alabama. Martha B. Blondheim Collection. Wade Hall Collection of Southern History and Culture. Tennent Lomax Collection. Cabot Lull Collection. Oliver Day Street Papers.

Published Primary Sources

Alabama Official and Statistical Register. Montgomery: Alabama Department of Archives and History, 1903.

Congressional Record, Washington, D.C., 1873–.

Federal Writers' Project. *Slave Narratives: A Folk History of Slavery in the United States, from Interviews with Former Slaves.* Vol. 5, *Alabama and Indiana Narratives.* Saint Clair Shores, Mich.: Scholarly Press, 1976.

Griffith, Lucille. *Alabama: A Documentary History to 1900.* 1968. Reprint, Tuscaloosa: University of Alabama Press, 1972.

Harlan, Louis R., and Raymond W. Smock, eds. *The Booker T. Washington Papers.* Vol. 6, *1901–2.* Urbana: University of Illinois Press, 1977.

Journal of the Proceedings of the Constitutional Convention of the State of Alabama, Held in the City of Montgomery, Commencing May 21, 1901. Montgomery: Brown Printing Co., 1901.

Link, Arthur S., ed. *The Papers of Woodrow Wilson.* Vol. 43. Princeton, N.J.: Princeton University Press, 1983.

Norrell, Robert J. *James Bowron: The Autobiography of a New South Industrialist.* Chapel Hill: University of North Carolina Press, 1991.

Official Proceedings of the Constitutional Convention of the State of Alabama, May 21, 1901 to Sept. 3, 1901. 4 Vols. Wetumpka, Ala.: Wetumpka Printing Co., 1940.

Proceedings of the Race Conference Held by the Southern Society for the Promotion of the Study of Race Conditions and Problems in the South, in Montgomery, Alabama, May 8, 9, 10 A.D. *1900.* Richmond, Va.: B. F. Johnson Publishing, 1900.
Twelfth Census of the United States. Vol. 1, *Population,* part 1. Washington: U.S. Census Office, 1901.

Court Records and Documents

Giles v. Harris, 189 US 475 (1903).
Guinn v. United States, 238 US 347 (1915).
Plessy v. Ferguson, 163 US 537 (1896).
Williams v. Mississippi, 170 US 213 (1898).

Newspapers

Alabama Baptist, 1901.
Alabama Christian Advocate, 1906.
Albertville Marshall Banner, 1899–1901.
Anniston Republican, 1898.
Anniston Weekly Times, 1893.
Ashville Southern Argus, 1901.
Atlanta Constitution, 1898.
Atlanta Journal, 1901.
Attalla Mirror, 1901.
Birmingham Age-Herald, 1890, 1899–1901, 1935.
Birmingham Alabamian, 1902.
Birmingham Anglo-Saxon of Alabama, 1905.
Birmingham Labor Advocate, 1897, 1901, 1906, 1917.
Birmingham Ledger, 1901.
Birmingham News, 1901–2, 1935, 1944, 2000, 2002.
Birmingham People's Weekly Tribune, 1896–97.
Birmingham State Herald, 1896.
Birmingham Times, 1901.
Brewton Laborers' Banner, 1901.
Brooklyn (N.Y.) Eagle, 1901.
Calhoun County Union Leader, 1901.
Carrollton, Alabama Alliance News, 1899–1900.
Centre Cherokee Sentinel, 1899.
Cherokee Harmonizer, 1901.
Chicago Tribune, 1928.
Choctaw Alliance, 1898, 1901.
Clanton Banner, 1901.
Collinsville Clipper, 1900.

Coosa River News, 1899, 1901.
Covington Times, 1897.
Cullman People's Protest, 1898.
DeKalb Times, 1900.
Fayette Banner, 1901.
Florence Times, 1903.
Fort Payne Journal, 1900.
Gadsden-Etowah County People's Voice, 1900.
Gadsden Tribune, 1899.
Geneva Reaper, 1901.
Greenville Living Truth, 1900–1901.
Huntsville Daily News, 1919.
Huntsville Journal, 1899, 1901.
Huntsville Republican, 1901.
Huntsville Tribune, 1898, 1901.
Jacksonville Republican, 1901–2.
Lafayette Sun, 1901.
Lawrence County, Alabama State Wheel, 1888.
Marshall Banner (see Albertville above), 1899–1901.
Mobile Press, 1901.
Mobile Register, 1893, 1900–2.
Mobile Southern Watchman, 1901.
Mobile Weekly Press, 1901.
Montgomery Advertiser, 1874, 1892, 1894, 1899–1901, 1919, 1927.
Montgomery Alliance Herald, 1893.
Montgomery Journal, 1899.
Montgomery Southern Argus, 1899.
Moulton Advertiser, 1888.
Murfreesboro (Tenn.) Banner, 1898.
New Decatur Advertiser, 1901.
New York Age, 1911.
New York World, 1911.
Newton-Dale County Harmonizer, 1901.
Ozark Free Press, 1899–1900.
Pickens County Alliance, 1900.
Randolph Toiler, 1898.
Roanoke Herald, 1898.
Selma Times, 1895, 1899.
Sheffield Reaper, 1898.
Shelby County People's Advocate, 1901.
Shelby Sentinel, 1898.
Tallapoosa New Era, 1896.
Tuscaloosa American, 1898.

Tuskaloosa Chronicle, 1899.
Wilcox Progress, 1899.

Oral Histories and Interviews

Anderson, U. S. Oral history. n.d. SLOSS
Booth, Harriett. Interview by Alfonso T. Smith. Tuskegee, Ala., 2 May 1974. MILES.
Brown, George. Oral history by Cliff Kuhn and Brenda McCallum. 25 Apr. 1983. SLOSS.
Cooper, Bulah. Interview by Alfonso T. Smith. Tuskegee, Ala., 20 May 1974. MILES.
Coyer, Ophelia. Interview by Alfonso T. Smith. Tuskegee, Ala., 28 May 1974. MILES.
Crutcher, B. H. Interview by James Underwood. Tuskegee, Ala., 8 Oct. 1972. MILES.
Davis, Reuben. Interview by Horace Huntley, part 1. Birmingham, Ala., 20 Mar. 1996.
    Vol. 13, section 4, BCRI.
Davis, Reuben. Interview by Horace Huntley, part 2. Birmingham, Ala., 3 Apr. 1996.
    Vol. 13, section 5, BCRI.
Dean, Clarence. Oral history by Brenda McCallum. 7 May 1983. SLOSS.
Eppes, Katherine "Ma." Interview by Susie R. O'Brien. Uniontown, Ala., 25 May 1937.
    In *Slave Narratives*, by the Federal Writer's Project.
Harrell, Charles. Oral history. n.d. SLOSS.
Hutto, Erline Priscilla. Interview by Georgeann Guthrie. Birmingham, Ala., 1980. UAB.
Irwin, Aunt Hannah. Interview by Gertha Couric and John Morgan Smith. Louisville,
    Ala., 25 May 1937. In *Slave Narratives*, by the Federal Writer's Project.
Jackson, Emory O. Interview no. 30 by Hardy T. Frye. Birmingham, Ala. AU.
Patterson, Frederick D. Interview by Alfonso T. Smith. Tuskegee, Ala., 26 Aug. 1974.
    MILES.
Pugh, Aunt Nicey. Interview by Ila B. Prine and John Morgan Smith. Prichard, Ala., 25
    June 1937. In *Slave Narratives*, by the Federal Writer's Project.
Summers, Lucille T. Interview by Clifton Depreast. Birmingham, Ala., 1980. UAB.
White, Francis Foster. Interview by Horace Huntley. Birmingham, Ala., 28 Feb. 1996.
    Vol. 12, section 6, BCRI.
White, Mingo. Interview by Levy D. Shelby Jr. Tuscumbia, Ala., 18 June 1937. In *Slave
    Narratives*, by the Federal Writers' Project.
Wilson, Lillie. Interview by Helen Dibble and Jessie Guzman. Tuskegee, Ala., 25 Jan.
    1973. MILES.
Young, George. Interview by Ruby Pickens Tartt. Livingston, Ala., 3 June 1937. In *Slave
    Narratives*, by the Federal Writers' Project.

SECONDARY SOURCES

Books, Articles, Theses, and Dissertations

Alsobrook, David E. "Mobile's Forgotten Progressive: A. N. Johnson, Editor and
    Entrepreneur." *Alabama Review* 32 (July 1979): 188–202.

Arsenault, Raymond. *The Wild Ass of the Ozarks: Jeff Davis and the Social Bases of Southern Politics.* 1984. Reprint, Knoxville: University of Tennessee Press, 1988.

Atkins, Leah Rawls. "Populism in Alabama: Reuben F. Kolb and the Appeals to Minority Groups." *Alabama Historical Quarterly* 32 (fall–winter 1970): 167–80.

Aucoin, Brent J. "Thomas Goode Jones and African-American Civil Rights in the New South." *The Historian* 60 (winter 1998): 257–72.

Ayers, Edward L. *The Promise of the New South: Life after Reconstruction.* New York: Oxford University Press, 1992.

Bagwell, David Ashley. "The 'Magical Process': The Sayre Election Law of 1893." *Alabama Review* 25 (Apr. 1972): 83–104.

Bailey, Hugh C. *Edgar Gardner Murphy: Gentle Progressive.* Coral Gables, Fla.: University of Miami Press, 1968.

———. *Liberalism in the New South: Southern Social Reformers and the Progressive Movement.* Coral Gables, Fla.: University of Miami Press, 1969.

Baylen, Joseph O. "Senator John Tyler Morgan, E. D. Morel, and the Congo Reform Association." *Alabama Review* 15 (Apr. 1962): 117–32.

Berlin, Ira. *Slaves without Masters: The Free Negro in the Antebellum South.* New York: Pantheon Books, 1974.

Black, Earl, and Merle Black. *Politics and Society in the South.* Cambridge: Harvard University Press, 1987.

———. *The Rise of Southern Republicans.* Cambridge, Mass.: Belknap Press of Harvard University Press, 2002.

Blee, Kathleen M. *Women and the Klan: Racism and Gender in the 1920s.* Berkeley: University of California Press, 1994.

Blondheim, Martha B. "William Dorsey Jelks and His Crusade against Lynching." Unpublished paper, 1954. Martha B. Blondheim Collection. UA.

Boles, John B., and Evelyn Thomas Nolen, eds. *Interpreting Southern History: Historiographical Essays in Honor of Sanford W. Higginbotham.* Baton Rouge: Louisiana State University Press, 1987.

Bond, Horace Mann. *Negro Education in Alabama: A Study in Cotton and Steel.* 1939. Reprint, Tuscaloosa: University of Alabama Press, 1994.

Brittain, Joseph Matt. "Negro Suffrage and Politics in Alabama since 1870." Ph.D. diss., Indiana University, 1958.

Brundage, W. Fitzhugh. *Lynching in the New South, 1880–1930: Georgia and Virginia.* Urbana: University of Illinois Press, 1993.

Canfield, Rosemary, ed. *Perspectives: The Alabama Heritage.* Troy, Ala.: Troy State University Press, 1978.

Carter, Dan T. *From George Wallace to Newt Gingrich: Race in the Conservative Counterrevolution, 1963–1994.* Baton Rouge: Louisiana State University Press, 1996.

Cash, W. J. *The Mind of the South.* New York: Alfred A. Knopf, 1941.

Chappell, David L. *Inside Agitators: White Southerners in the Civil Rights Movement.* Baltimore: Johns Hopkins University Press, 1994.

Clark, Thomas B., and Albert D. Kirwan, *The South since Appomattox: A Century of Regional Change*. New York: Oxford University Press, 1967.

Clayton, Bruce. *The Savage Ideal: Intolerance and Intellectual Leadership in the South, 1890–1914*. Baltimore: Johns Hopkins University Press, 1972.

Cobb, James C. "Beyond Planters and Industrialists: A New Perspective on the South." *Journal of Southern History* 54 (Feb. 1988): 45–68.

Cooper, Arnold. "Booker T. Washington and William J. Edwards of Snow Hill Institute, 1893–1915." *Alabama Review* 40 (Apr. 1987): 111–32.

Crowe, Charles R. "Tom Watson, Populists, and Blacks Reconsidered." *Journal of Negro History* 55 (Apr. 1970): 99–116.

Cunliffe, Marcus, and Robin W. Winks, eds. *Pastmasters: Some Essays on American Historians*. New York: Harper and Row, 1969.

Current, Richard M., T. Harry Williams, and Frank Friedel. *American History: A Survey*. Rev. ed. New York: Alfred A. Knopf, 1966.

Curry, J. L. M. *The South in the Olden Time*. Harrisburg, Pa.: Harrisburg Publishing, 1901.

Dailey, Jane. *Before Jim Crow: The Politics of Race in Postemancipation Virginia*. Chapel Hill: University of North Carolina Press, 2000.

Davis, Hugh C. "Hilary A. Herbert: Bourbon Apologist." *Alabama Review* 20 (July 1967): 216–25.

Davis, Natalie M. "Pine Tree Reveals Much about State." *Birmingham News*, 26 Nov. 2000, C1.

Davis, Natalie Zemon. *Society and Culture in Early Modern France: Eight Essays*. Stanford, Calif.: Stanford University Press, 1975.

DeLand, T. A., and A. Davis Smith. *Northern Alabama: Historical and Biographical*. Chicago: Donohue and Henneberry, 1888.

DeVine, Jerry W. "Free Silver and Alabama Politics, 1890–1896." Ph.D. diss., Auburn University, 1980.

Dew, Charles B. *Apostles of Disunion: Southern Secession Commissioners and the Causes of the Civil War*. Charlottesville: University Press of Virginia, 2001.

Doster, James F. *Railroads in Alabama Politics, 1875–1914*. Tuscaloosa: University of Alabama Press, 1957.

Doyle, Don H. *New Men, New Cities, New South: Atlanta, Nashville, Charleston, and Mobile, 1860–1910*. Chapel Hill: University of North Carolina Press, 1990.

Du Bois, W. E. B. *The New Negro*. New York: Hertzog and Holt, 1915.

DuBose, Joel C., ed. *Notable Men of Alabama: Personal and Genealogical with Portraits*. 2 vols. Spartanburg, S.C.: Reprint Company, 1976.

DuBose, John Witherspoon. "Forty Years in Alabama: A History of the Lapse and Recovery of Civil Government." Unpublished book manuscript. 1904. ADAH.

———. *The Tragic Decade: Ten Years of Alabama, 1865–1874*. Edited by James K. Greer. Birmingham: Webb Book Company, 1940.

Duncan, Katherine McKinstry, and Larry Joe Smith. *The History of Marshall County, Alabama*. Vol. 1, *Prehistory to 1939*. Albertville, Ala.: Thompson Printing, 1969.

Ellison, Rhoda Coleman. *History and Bibliography of Alabama Newspapers in the Nineteenth Century.* Tuscaloosa: University of Alabama Press, 1954.

Ezell, John Samuel. *The South since 1865.* New York: Macmillan, 1963.

Faust, Drew Gilpin. *Mothers of Invention: Women of the Slaveholding South in the American Civil War.* Chapel Hill: University of North Carolina Press, 1996.

Feldman, Glenn. "Introduction: The Pursuit of Southern History." In *Reading Southern History: Essays on Interpreters and Interpretations,* edited by Glenn Feldman, 1–13. Tuscaloosa: University of Alabama Press, 2001.

———. *Politics, Society, and the Klan in Alabama, 1915–1949.* Tuscaloosa: University of Alabama Press, 1999.

———, ed. *Reading Southern History: Essays on Interpreters and Interpretations.* Tuscaloosa: University of Alabama Press, 2001.

Fields, Barbara J. "Ideology and Race in American History." In *Race, Region, and Reconstruction: Essays in Honor of C. Vann Woodward,* edited by J. Morgan Kousser and James M. McPherson, 143–77. New York: Oxford University Press, 1982.

Fitzgerald, Michael W. "Review of Samuel L. Webb, *Two-Party Politics in the One-Party South: Alabama's Hill Country, 1874–1920.*" *Journal of Southern History* 65 (May 1999): 424–25.

———. *The Union League Movement in the Deep South: Politics and Agricultural Change during Reconstruction.* Baton Rouge: Louisiana State University Press, 1989.

———. *Urban Emancipation: Popular Politics in Reconstruction Mobile, 1860–1890.* Baton Rouge: Louisiana State University Press, 2002.

Fleming, Walter Lynwood. *Civil War and Reconstruction in Alabama.* New York: Columbia University Press, 1905.

Flynt, Wayne. *Dixie's Forgotten People: The South's Poor Whites.* Bloomington: Indiana University Press, 1979.

———. *Poor but Proud: Alabama's Poor Whites.* Tuscaloosa: University of Alabama Press, 1989.

———. "Religion in the Urban South: The Divided Mind of Birmingham, 1900–1930." *Alabama Review* 30 (Apr. 1977): 108–34.

Fredrickson, George M. *The Arrogance of Race: Historical Perspectives on Slavery, Racism, and Social Inequality.* Middletown, Conn.: Wesleyan University Press, 1988.

———. *The Black Image in the White Mind: The Debate on Afro-American Character and Destiny.* New York: Harper and Row, 1971.

Fry, Joseph A. "Governor Johnston's Attempt to Unseat Senator Morgan, 1899–1900." *Alabama Review* 38 (Oct. 1985): 243–79.

Gadd, Mike. "Alabama Vote." (2002). Http//:www.youthradio.org.

Gaither, Gerald H. *Blacks and the Populist Revolt: Ballots and Bigotry in the "New South."* Tuscaloosa: University of Alabama Press, 1977.

Gilmore, Glenda Elizabeth. *Gender and Jim Crow: Women and the Politics of White Supremacy in North Carolina, 1896–1920.* Chapel Hill: University of North Carolina Press, 1996.

Going, Allen Johnston. *Bourbon Democracy in Alabama, 1874–1890*. 1951. Reprint, Tuscaloosa: University of Alabama Press, 1992.

Grantham, Dewey W. "An American Politics for the South." In *The Southerner as American*, edited by Charles G. Sellers Jr., 148–79. Chapel Hill: University of North Carolina Press, 1960.

———. *Southern Progressivism: The Reconciliation of Progress and Tradition*. Knoxville: University of Tennessee Press, 1983.

Green, Elna C. *Southern Strategies: Southern Women and the Woman Suffrage Question*. Chapel Hill: University of North Carolina Press, 1997.

Greenhaw, Wayne. *Elephants in the Cotton Fields: Ronald Reagan and the New Republican South*. New York: Macmillan, 1982.

Greer, James K., ed. *The Tragic Decade: Ten Years of Alabama, 1865–1874*, by John Witherspoon DuBose. Birmingham: Webb Book Company, 1940.

Gross, Jimmie Frank. "Alabama Politics and the Negro, 1874–1901." Ph.D. diss., University of Georgia, 1969.

Hackney, Sheldon. *Populism to Progressivism in Alabama*. Princeton, N.J.: Princeton University Press, 1969.

Hahn, Steven. *The Roots of Southern Populism: Yeoman Farmers and the Transformation of the Georgia Upcountry, 1850–1890*. New York: Oxford University Press, 1983.

Hair, William Ivy. *Bourbonism and Agrarian Protest: Louisiana Politics, 1877–1900*. Baton Rouge: Louisiana State University Press, 1969.

Hale, Grace Elizabeth. *Making Whiteness: The Culture of Segregation in the South, 1890–1940*. New York: Pantheon Books, 1998.

Hall, Hines Holt, III. "The Montgomery Race Conference: Focal Point of Racial Attitudes at the Turn of the Century." Master's thesis, Auburn University, 1965.

Hall, Jacquelyn Dowd. *Revolt against Chivalry: Jesse Daniel Ames and the Women's Campaign against Lynching*. New York: Columbia University Press, 1979.

———. " 'The Mind That Burns in Each Body': Women, Rape, and Racial Violence." In *Powers of Desire: The Politics of Sexuality*, edited by Elizabeth Ann Snitow, Christine Stansell, and Sharon Thompson, 328–46. New York: Monthly Review Press, 1983.

Hamilton, Virginia Van der Veer. *Lister Hill: Statesman of the South*. Chapel Hill: University of North Carolina Press, 1987.

Hammett, Hugh B. "Reconstruction History before Dunning: Hilary Herbert and the South's Victory of the Books." *Alabama Review* 27 (July 1974): 185–96.

Hanushek, Eric A., John E. Jackson, and John F. Kain. "Model Specification, Use of Aggregate Data, and the Ecological Correlation Fallacy." *Political Methodology* 1 (winter 1974): 87–106.

Harris, Carl V. *Political Power in Birmingham, 1871–1921*. Knoxville: University of Tennessee Press, 1977.

Harris, David Alan. "Racists and Reformers: A Study of Progressivism in Alabama, 1896–1911." Ph.D. diss., University of North Carolina at Chapel Hill, 1967.

Hart, Alfred Bushnell. *The Southern South*. New York: D. Appleton, 1910.

Herbert, Hilary Abner. *Why the Solid South? Or Reconstruction and Its Results.* Baltimore: R. H. Woodward and Company, 1890.

Hewitt, Nancy A., and Suzanne Lebsock, eds. *Visible Women: New Essays on American Activism.* Urbana: University of Illinois Press, 1993.

Hofstadter, Richard. *Social Darwinism in American Thought.* Boston: Beacon Press, 1955.

Holmes, William F. *The White Chief: James Kimble Vardaman.* Baton Rouge: Louisiana State University Press, 1970.

Horton, Paul. "Testing the Limits of Class Politics in Postbellum Alabama: Agrarian Radicalism in Lawrence County." *Journal of Southern History* 57 (Feb. 1991): 63–84.

Houghton, W. R., and M. B. Houghton. *Two Boys in the Civil War and After.* Montgomery: Paragon Press, 1912.

Howington, Arthur F. "John Barley Corn Subdued: The Enforcement of Prohibition in Alabama." *Alabama Review* 23 (July 1970): 212–25.

Hyman, Michael R. *The Anti-Redeemers: Hill-Country Political Dissenters in the Lower South from Redemption to Populism.* Baton Rouge: Louisiana State University Press, 1990.

Jackson, Harvey H., III. "The Middle-Class Democracy Victorious: The Mitcham War of Clarke County, Alabama, 1893." *Journal of Southern History* 57 (Aug. 1991): 453–78.

———. "The Mitcham War." *Alabama Heritage* 25 (summer 1992): 33–43.

———. "White Supremacy Triumphant: Democracy Undone." In *A Century of Controversy: Constitutional Reform in Alabama,* edited by Bailey Thomson, 17–33. Tuscaloosa: University of Alabama Press, 2002.

Jackson, Harvey H., III, in collaboration with Joyce White Burrage and James A. Cox. *The Mitcham War of Clarke County, Alabama.* Grove Hill, Ala.: Clarke County Democrat, 1988.

Jones, Allen W. "A History of the Direct Primary in Alabama, 1840–1903." Ph.D. diss., University of Alabama, 1964.

———. "Political Reform and Party Factionalism in the Deep South: Alabama's 'Dead Shoes' Primary of 1906." *Alabama Review* 26 (Jan. 1973): 3–32.

———. "Political Reforms of the Progressive Era." *Alabama Review* 21 (July 1968): 173–94.

Jones, E. Terrence. "Ecological Inference and Electoral Analysis." *Journal of Interdisciplinary History* 2 (winter 1973): 249–62.

———. "Using Ecological Regression." *Journal of Interdisciplinary History* 4 (spring 1974): 593–96.

Jones, Terry Lawrence. "Attitudes of Alabama Baptists toward Negroes, 1890–1914." Master's thesis, Samford University, 1968.

Kantrowitz, Stephen. *Ben Tillman and the Reconstruction of White Supremacy.* Chapel Hill: University of North Carolina Press, 2000.

Keeler, Rebecca T. "Alva Belmont: Exacting Benefactor for Women's Suffrage." *Alabama Review* 41 (Apr. 1988): 132–45.

Kelley, Robin D. G. *Race Rebels: Culture, Politics, and the Black Working Class.* New York: Free Press, 1994.

Kelly, Brian. "Policing the 'Negro Eden': Racial Paternalism in the Alabama Coalfields, 1908–1921, Part One." *Alabama Review* 51 (July 1998): 163–83.

———. *Race, Class, and Power in the Alabama Coalfields, 1908–21.* Urbana: University of Illinois Press, 2001.

Kennedy, Stetson. *Southern Exposure.* 1946. Reprint, Boca Raton: Florida Atlantic Universities Press, 1991.

Key, V. O., Jr. *Southern Politics in State and Nation.* 1949. Reprint, Knoxville: University of Tennessee Press, 1984.

Kirby, Jack Temple. *Darkness at the Dawning: Race and Reform in the Progressive South.* Philadelphia: J. B. Lippincott, 1972.

Knox, John B. "Reduction of Representation in the South." *Outlook* 79 (1905): 171.

Kolchin, Peter. "Whiteness Studies: The New History of Race in America." *Journal of American History* 89 (June 2002): 154–73.

Kousser, J. Morgan. "Ecological Regression and the Analysis of Past Politics." *Journal of Interdisciplinary History* 4 (autumn 1973): 237–62.

———. *The Shaping of Southern Politics: Suffrage Restriction and the Establishment of the One-Party South, 1880–1910.* New Haven, Conn.: Yale University Press, 1974.

Kousser, J. Morgan, and James M. McPherson, eds. *Region, Race, and Reconstruction: Essays in Honor of C. Vann Woodward.* New York: Oxford University Press, 1982.

Kraditor, Aileen S. *The Ideas of the Woman Suffrage Movement, 1890–1920.* New York: Columbia University Press, 1965.

Lamis, Alexander P. *The Two-Party South.* New York: Oxford University Press, 1984.

LaMonte, Edward Shannon. *Politics and Welfare in Birmingham, 1900–1975.* Tuscaloosa: University of Alabama Press, 1995.

Lebsock, Suzanne. "Woman Suffrage and White Supremacy: A Virginia Case Study." In *Visible Women: New Essays on American Activism,* edited by Nancy A. Hewitt and Suzanne Lebsock, 62–100. Urbana: University of Illinois Press, 1993.

Letwin, Daniel. *The Challenge of Interracial Unionism: Alabama Coal Miners, 1878–1921.* Chapel Hill: University of North Carolina Press, 1998.

Lewis, W. David. *Sloss Furnaces and the Rise of the Birmingham District: An Industrial Epic.* Tuscaloosa: University of Alabama Press, 1994.

Lichtenstein, Alex. *Twice the Work of Free Labor: The Political Economy of Convict Labor in the New South.* New York: Verso, 1996.

Lichtman, Allan J. "Correlation, Regression, and the Ecological Fallacy: A Critique." *Journal of Interdisciplinary History* 4 (winter 1974): 417–33.

Link, Arthur S. "What Happened to the Progressive Movement in the 1920s?" *American Historical Review* 64 (July 1959): 833–51.

Link, William A. *The Paradox of Southern Progressivism, 1880–1930.* Chapel Hill: University of North Carolina Press, 1992.

MacLean, Nancy. *Behind the Mask of Chivalry: The Making of the Second Ku Klux Klan.* New York: Oxford University Press, 1994.

McCorvey, T. C. *Alabama: Historical Sketches.* Charlottesville: University Press of Virginia, 1960.

McKiven, Henry M., Jr. *Iron and Steel: Class, Race, and Community in Birmingham, Alabama, 1875–1920.* Chapel Hill: University of North Carolina Press, 1995.

McMillan, Malcolm Cook. *Constitutional Development in Alabama, 1798–1901: A Study in Politics, Sectionalism, and the Negro.* 1955. Reprint, Spartanburg, S.C.: Reprint Company, 1978.

McMillen, Neil R. *Dark Journey: Black Mississippians in the Age of Jim Crow.* Urbana: University of Illinois Press, 1989.

McWilliams, Tennant S. "A New Day Coming: Alabama and the Problem of Change, 1877–1920." In *Perspectives: The Alabama Heritage,* edited by Rosemary Canfield, 178–85. Troy, Ala.: Troy State University Press, 1978.

Moore, Albert Burton. *History of Alabama.* 1934. Reprint, Tuscaloosa: Alabama Book Store, 1951.

Murphy, Edgar Gardner. *Problems of the Present South: A Discussion of Certain of the Educational, Industrial, and Political Issues in the Southern States.* New York: Grosset and Dunlap, 1904.

NAACP. *Thirty Years of Lynching in the United States.* New York: Negro Universities Press, 1969.

Nelson, Lawrence J. "Memorializing the Lost Cause in Florence, Alabama, 1866–1903." *Alabama Review* 41 (July 1988): 179–92.

Newby, I. A. *Jim Crow's Defense: Anti-Negro Thought in America, 1900–1930.* Baton Rouge: Louisiana State University Press, 1965.

———. *Plain Folk in the New South: Social Change and Cultural Persistence, 1880–1915.* Baton Rouge: Louisiana State University Press, 1989.

Norrell, Robert J. *James Bowron: The Autobiography of a New South Industrialist.* Chapel Hill: University of North Carolina Press, 1991.

O'Brien, Michael. "From a Chase to a View: The Arkansan." In *C. Vann Woodward: A Southern Historian and His Critics,* edited by John Herbert Roper, 234–52. Athens: University of Georgia Press, 1997.

Oshinsky, David M. *"Worse Than Slavery": Parchman Farm and the Ordeal of Jim Crow Justice.* New York: Free Press, 1996.

Osofsky, Gilbert. *The Burden of Race: A Documentary History of Negro-White Relations in America.* New York: Harper and Row, 1967.

Owen, Thomas McAdory. *Alabama Newspapers and Periodicals.* Montgomery: Brown Printing Company, 1915.

———. *History of Alabama and Dictionary of Alabama Biography.* 4 vols. 1921. Reprint, Spartanburg: Reprint Company, 1978.

Page, Thomas Nelson. *The Negro: The Southerner's Problem.* New York: Charles Scribner's Sons, 1901.

Painter, Nell Irvin. *Southern History across the Color Line.* Chapel Hill: University of North Carolina Press, 2002.

Palmer, Bruce. *"Man over Money": The Southern Populist Critique of American Capitalism*. Chapel Hill: University of North Carolina Press, 1980.

Perman, Michael. *Struggle for Mastery: Disfranchisement in the South, 1888–1908*. Chapel Hill: University of North Carolina Press, 2001.

Phillips, Kimberley L. *AlabamaNorth: African-American Migrants, Community, and Working-Class Activism in Cleveland, 1915–45*. Urbana: University of Illinois Press, 1999.

Potter, David M. "C. Vann Woodward." In *Pastmasters: Some Essays on American Historians*, edited by Marcus Cunliffe and Robin W. Winks, 395–407. New York: Harper and Row, 1969.

Rabinowitz, Howard N. "More than the Woodward Thesis: Assessing the Strange Career of Jim Crow." In *C. Vann Woodward: A Southern Historian and His Critics*, edited by John Herbert Roper, 183–202. Athens: University of Georgia Press, 1997.

———. *Race Relations in the Urban South, 1865–1890*. New York: Oxford University Press, 1978.

Rodabaugh, Karl Louis. "The Farmers' Revolt in Alabama, 1890–1896." Ph.D. diss., East Carolina University, 1977.

———. "Fusion, Confusion, Defeat, and Disfranchisement: The 'Fadeout' of Populism in Alabama." *Alabama Historical Quarterly* 34 (summer 1972): 131–53.

Roediger, David R. *The Wages of Whiteness: Race and the Making of the American Working Class*. New York: Verso, 1991.

Rogers, William Warren, Sr. *The One-Gallused Rebellion: Agrarianism in Alabama, 1865–1896*. Baton Rouge: Louisiana State University Press, 1970.

Rogers, William Warren, Sr., Robert David Ward, Leah Rawls Atkins, and Wayne Flynt. *Alabama: The History of a Deep South State*. Tuscaloosa: University of Alabama Press, 1994.

Roper, John Herbert, ed. *C. Vann Woodward: A Southern Historian and His Critics*. Athens: University of Georgia Press, 1997.

Saunders, Robert. "Southern Populists and the Negro, 1893–1895." *Journal of Negro History* 54 (July 1969): 240–61.

Scott, Anne Firor. *The Southern Lady: From Pedestal to Politics, 1830–1930*. Chicago: University of Chicago Press, 1970.

Sellers, Charles G., Jr., ed. *The Southerner as American*. Chapel Hill: University of North Carolina Press, 1960.

Sellers, James B. *The Prohibition Movement in Alabama, 1702–1943*. Chapel Hill: University of North Carolina Press, 1943.

Shapiro, Herbert M. *White Violence and Black Response: From Reconstruction to Montgomery*. Amherst: University of Massachusetts Press, 1988.

Shaw, Barton C. *The Wool Hat Boys: Georgia's Populist Party*. Baton Rouge: Louisiana State University Press, 1984.

Simkins, Francis Butler. *Pitchfork Ben Tillman, South Carolinian*. Baton Rouge: Louisiana State University, 1967.

Simkins, Francis Butler, and Charles Pierce Roland. *A History of the South*. New York: Alfred A. Knopf, 1972.

Simmons, Judy Dothard. "Black and White and Married in Alabama." (22 Feb. 2001). Http://www.africana.com.

Simon, Bryant. *A Fabric of Defeat: The Politics of South Carolina Millhands, 1910–1948*. Chapel Hill: University of North Carolina Press, 1998.

Sims, Anastatia. *The Power of Femininity in the New South: Women's Organizations and Politics in North Carolina, 1880–1930*. Columbia: University of South Carolina Press, 1997.

Singal, Daniel Joseph. "Ulrich B. Phillips: The Old South and the New." *Journal of American History* 63 (Mar. 1977): 871–91.

Sledge, James Lamar, III. "The Alabama Republican Party, 1865–1978." Ph.D. diss., Auburn University, 1998.

Snitow, Elizabeth Ann, Christine Stansell, and Sharon Thompson, eds. *Powers of Desire: The Politics of Sexuality*. New York: Monthly Review Press, 1983.

Sparks, John. "Alabama Negro Reaction to Disfranchisement, 1901–1904." Master's thesis, Samford University, 1973.

Tanner, Ralph M. "The Wonderful World of Tom Heflin." *Alabama Review* 36 (July 1983): 163–84.

Taylor, Joseph H. "Populism and Disfranchisement in Alabama." *Journal of Negro History* 34 (Oct. 1949): 410–27.

Thomas, Mary Martha. *The New Woman in Alabama: Social Reforms and Suffrage, 1890–1920*. Tuscaloosa: University of Alabama Press, 1992.

Thomson, Bailey, ed. *A Century of Controversy: Constitutional Reform in Alabama*. Tuscaloosa: University of Alabama Press, 2002.

Thornton, J. Mills, III. "Alabama Politics, J. Thomas Heflin, and the Expulsion Movement of 1929." *Alabama Review* 21 (Apr. 1968): 83–112.

Tindall, George Brown. *The Ethnic Southerners*. Baton Rouge: Louisiana State University Press, 1976.

Tolnay, Stuart M., and E. M. Beck. *A Festival of Violence: An Analysis of Southern Lynchings, 1882–1930*. Urbana: University of Illinois Press, 1995.

Wade, Richard C. *Slavery in the Cities: The South, 1800–1860*. New York: Oxford University Press, 1964.

Ward, Robert David, and William Warren Rogers Sr. *Convicts, Coal, and the Banner Mine Tragedy*. Tuscaloosa: University of Alabama Press, 1987.

Watson, Richard L. "From Populism through the New Deal." In *Interpreting Southern History: Historiographical Essays in Honor of Sanford W. Higginbotham*, edited by John B. Boles and Evelyn Thomas Nolen, 308–89. Baton Rouge: Louisiana State University Press, 1987.

Webb, Samuel L. "From Independents to Populists to Progressive Republicans: The Case of Chilton County, Alabama, 1880–1920." *Journal of Southern History* 59 (Nov. 1993): 707–36.

————. "A Jacksonian Democrat in Postbellum Alabama: The Ideology and Influence of Journalist Robert McKee." *Journal of Southern History* 62 (May 1996): 239–74.

————. *Two-Party Politics in the One-Party South: Alabama's Hill Country, 1874–1920*. Tuscaloosa: University of Alabama Press, 1997.

Wheeler, Marjorie Spruill. *New Women of the New South: The Leaders of the Woman Suffrage Movement in the Southern States*. New York: Oxford University Press, 1993.

Whitmire, Kyle. "Constitution Conundrum." *Birmingham Weekly*, 7–14 Nov. 2002, p. 6.

————. "Who Would Want the Job Anyway?" *Birmingham Weekly*, 14–21 Nov. 2002, p. 8.

Wiener, Jonathan. *Social Origins of the New South: Alabama, 1860–1885*. Baton Rouge: Louisiana State University Press, 1978.

Wiggins, Sarah Woolfolk, comp. *From Civil War to Civil Rights in Alabama, 1860–1960*. Tuscaloosa: University of Alabama Press, 1987.

Williamson, Joel R. *The Crucible of Race: Black/White Relations in the American South since Emancipation*. New York: Oxford University Press, 1984.

————. "C. Vann Woodward and the Origins of a New Wisdom." In *C. Vann Woodward: A Southern Historian and His Critics*, edited by John Herbert Roper, 203–24. Athens: University of Georgia Press, 1997.

Woodman, Harold D. "Economic Reconstruction and the Rise of the New South, 1865–1900." In *Interpreting Southern History: Historiographical Essays in Honor of Sanford W. Higginbotham*, edited by John B. Boles and Evelyn Thomas Nolen, 254–307. Baton Rouge: Louisiana State University Press, 1987.

Woodward, C. Vann. *Origins of the New South, 1877–1913*. 1951. Reprint, Baton Rouge: Louisiana State University Press, 1971.

————. *The Strange Career of Jim Crow*. 3rd ed. New York: Oxford University Press, 1974.

————. *Tom Watson: Agrarian Rebel*. 1938. Reprint, New York: Oxford University Press, 1969.

Wyatt-Brown, Bertram. *Honor and Violence in the Old South*. New York: Oxford University Press, 1986.

————. *The Shaping of Southern Culture: Honor, Grace, and War, 1760s–1890s*. Chapel Hill: University of North Carolina Press, 2001.

————. *Southern Honor: Ethics and Behavior in the Old South*. New York: Oxford University Press, 1982.

INDEX

Abolition, 16, 36, 123–24, 160

Abortion, 9, 114, 169

Accommodationism, black, and disfranchisement, 79–83, 238 (n. 23); views against, 113. *See also* Councill, William H.; Paternalism; Rogers, William Warren, Sr.; Ward, Robert David; Washington, Booker T.; Woodward, C. Vann

Adams, Henry, 16

Adams, Samuel M., 45, 156–57

Africa, 56, 103, 104, 243 (n. 72), 264 (n. 72)

African American. *See* Blacks

Afro-American Exodus Union, 82

Agricultural Wheel, 31

Agriculture, 19, 20; effect of, on politics, 24, 31, 66, 235 (n. 85); planting season depresses white literacy, 240 (n. 41); poverty related to, 38, 223 (n. 70). *See also* Black Belt; Farmer's Alliance; Free silver; Gold Democrats; Populists; Slavery

Ahlrichs, Emil, 233 (n. 62)

Alabama, 15, 211 (n. 15), 213 (n. 21); map of physiographical regions, 40

Alabama Alliance News. See Carrollton, Alabama Alliance News

Alabama Association Opposed to Woman Suffrage, 160

Alabama Baptist, 256 (n. 73)

Alabama Commercial and Industrial Association, 250 (n. 1)

Alabama constitution of 1875, 165

Alabama constitution of 1901, 4, 5, 9, 10, 12, 13, 16; amendments to, 216 (n. 3); antimiscegenation statute in, 238 (n. 28); conservative results of, 165–66, 266 (n. 90); constitutional convention for, 74–110; as critical moment, 123, 137; as culmination of Redemption, 37, 105, 112–13, 118, 165–66, 260 (n. 35); duration of, 266 (nn. 89–90); effect of, on voter rolls, 136; extreme nature of, 15, 216 (n. 3); as a "reform," 17; solidified by all-white direct Democratic primary, 143–51;

submitted to popular referendum, 250 (n. 1). *See also* Constitutional convention of 1901; Disfranchisement; Ratification; Referendum

Alabama Press Association, 138

Alabama Railroad Commission, 34, 146

Alabama State Bank, 35

Alabama State Wheel, 220 (n. 39)

Alabamians, personality of, 15

Albertville, 231 (n. 49)

Albertville Banner. See Marshall Banner

Alcohol, and blacks, 38. *See also* Prohibition

Aldrich, Truman, 27, 155, 221 (n. 55). See also *Birmingham Times*

Aldrich, William H., 27, 155, 221 (n. 55)

Alliance. *See* Farmer's Alliance

All-white direct Democratic primary, 9, 212 (n. 19), 225 (n. 86); origins of, 145; poor white support for, 143–51; Populist support for, 25, 221 (n. 46); relationship of, to the lily-white purge movement, 151–55; as solidification of disfranchisement, 17–18, 25, 143–51; threats of revolt and, 148–49; vote within State Democratic Executive Committee on, 151; white supremacy in, 144–46; white unity theme and, 146–49. *See also* Jelks, William D.; Johnston, Joseph F.

Altman, John J., 45

American Federation of Labor, 161

American Journal of Psychiatry, 16

Anniston, 48, 74. *See also* Bowie, Sydney J.; Knox, John B.

Anniston Republican, 62, 146, 233 (n. 65)

Anti-Democrats, 5, 9, 11, 39, 42, 170, 252 (n. 23); definition of, 222 (n. 62); and disfranchisement, 8, 10, 12, 13, 23–32, 62, 211 (n. 16); importance of race to, 119–25, 170, 214 (n. 24), 253 (n. 32). *See also* Alabama constitution of 1901; Anti-Redeemers; Constitutional convention of 1901; Greenbackers; "Half Populists"; Independent Democrats; Jeffersonian Democrats; Poor

relations, 15, 216 (nn. 7, 9), 240 (n. 43); schizophrenic southern attitude toward, 265 (n. 85); and Second Reconstruction, 170, 226 (n. 92); southern antipathy to, 37–39, 79, 121–22, 150, 165, 213 (n. 19), 219 (n. 30), 227 (n. 94), 245 (n. 92), 247 (nn. 97, 98), 260 (n. 35), 262 (n. 52); —, as emotional appeal, 156, 168; —, among Populists, 24, 28–29. *See also* Dixiecrats; Outsiders; Politics of emotion; Reconstruction; Reconstruction syndrome; Republican Party, modern-day; Wallace, George C.; Washington, D.C.; Xenophobia; Yankees

Fields, Barbara J., 210 (n. 3)

Fields, Lawson A., 232 (n. 60), 257 (n. 77). See also *Attalla Mirror; Cherokee Harmonizer; Cherokee Sentinel; Collinsville Clipper*

Fifteenth Amendment, 216 (n. 7); concern about, used by minority-report adherents, 89, 91, 97; criticized for creating black voting, 69, 98, 104, 216 (n. 1), 224 (n. 74); as disastrous for blacks, 104; as form of federal tyranny, 67; grouped with the Nineteenth Amendment, 160; as impediment to blanket black disfranchisement, 85, 93, 240 (n. 43), 241 (n. 51), 266 (n. 88); one disfranchisement plan as a direct challenge to, 80–81. *See also* Reconstruction

Fighting grandfather clause. *See* Grandfather clause

Fiscal retrenchment. *See* Taxation

Fiske, John, 16

Fitzgerald, Michael W., 214 (n. 24), 219 (n. 33); *Urban Emancipation,* 261 (n. 42)

Florida, disfranchisement in, 24, 216 (n. 2)

Flynt, Wayne: on all-white primary, 145; and paternalism of Birmingham Protestants, 218 (n. 23); on poor-white racism, 221 (n. 50), 248 (n. 106); on Populists and race, 220 (n. 36)

"Force Bill," 24, 216 (n. 7)

Forrest, Nathan Bedford, 93

Fort Payne Journal, 265 (n. 76)

Fort Sumter, 99

Forty Years of Alabama, 37

Fourteenth Amendment, 39, 67, 160, 216 (n. 7), 266 (n. 88)

Franklin County, 245 (n. 91)

Frasier, Thomas Sydney, 151, 260 (n. 35)

Fraud, 43, 76, 80, 108–9, 122, 170; attacked, 21–22, 27, 219 (n. 30); and blacks, 48–49; defended, 21–22, 48–49, 219 (n. 30); effects of, 30; and federal government, 48–49, 219 (n. 30); and poor whites, 50, 133, 135, 219 (n. 30); possible persistence of, 94, 241 (n. 55), 242 (n. 62); and relationship to the "best whites," 22, 94, 240 (n. 42), 241 (n. 55), 242 (n. 62); variability of, 127

Frazer, Thomas Sydney. *See* Frasier, Thomas Sydney

Fredrickson, George M., 211 (n. 13), 220 (n. 36), 264 (n. 74)

Freedom, 36–37, 226 (n. 92), 244 (n. 85). *See also* Conservatism; Patriotism; Reconstruction syndrome; States' rights

Free labor, 31

Freeman, Newman H., 77, 100, 107

Free silver, 28, 32–33, 46, 227 (n. 97), 258 (n. 6); and Bryan, William Jennings, 5, 36, 43, 45, 59

Freight rates. *See* Railroads

Fusion, of Populism and Republicanism, 33

Gadsden-Etowah County People's Voice, 125, 254 (n. 55), 257 (n. 77), 265 (n. 76)

Gadsden Tribune, 236 (n. 14); politics of, 231 (n. 49); relationship of, with *Montgomery Southern Argus,* 231 (n. 48); support of, for all-white primary, 146; —, for constitutional convention, 61

Garrison, Lloyd McKim, 16

Garrison, William Lloyd, 16, 83

Gaston, Zell, 58, 230 (n. 45)

Gelders, Joseph S., 215 (n. 33)

Gender, 12, 112, 116–17, 156, 162, 230 (n. 42); and alleged sexual promiscuity of blacks, 16–17; and chivalry, 28; and emotional appeal during Redemption, 222 (n. 61); and race, 59, 86–87, 158, 252 (n. 22); and women's suffrage, 159–60, 263 (nn. 64, 65). *See also* Politics of emotion; Sexuality; Traditional family values

Geneva County, 212 (n. 17), 232 (n. 55)

Geneva Reaper: as index of Wiregrass Populist thought, 61, 232 (n. 55); opposition of, to constitution, 61, 84, 125; —, to ratification, 125, 254 (n. 54); and probable origins of disfranchisement myth, 70; revulsion of, at Washington-Roosevelt dinner, 116

Industrialism, 76. *See also* Big Mules
Inflation. *See* Free silver; Gold Democrats
Intelligence. *See* Education; "Scientific racism"
Iscariot, Judas, 34
Ivy League, 217 (n. 10)

Jackson, Andrew, 140
Jackson, Harvey H., III, 232 (n. 54)
Jackson, Thomas "Stonewall," 99
Jackson County, 36, 149, 259 (n. 24); vote of, in
   April 1901, 71; —, in November 1901, 129
Jacksonian Democrats (Jacksonians), 9, 10, 55
Jacksonville, 99
Jacksonville Republican, 62, 146
Jacobs, Patti Ruffner, 159
James, Henry, 16
Jasper Land Company, 35
Jefferson County, 45, 64, 245 (n. 91); as
   headquarters for antiratification, 112; as
   headquarters for proratification, 111; vote of,
   in April 1901, 73; —, in November 1901, 129.
   See also Johnston, Joseph F.; Lowe, Robert J.
Jeffersonian Democrats (Jeffersonians), 31, 33,
   45, 46, 124, 170, 222 (n. 62), 230 (n. 42),
   244 (n. 78); and alleged transcendence
   of race, 9, 55; and all-white primary, 25,
   143–51; and disfranchisement, 10, 13, 23–32,
   55–63, 211 (n. 16); God and religion invoked
   for white supremacy by, 260 (n. 35); and
   meaning of 1900 election, 43–55; opposition
   of, to ratification, 111–15, 119–25; and
   Reconstruction memories, 32; support of,
   for ratification, 115–25. *See also* Alabama
   constitution of 1901; Anti-Democrats;
   Constitutional convention of 1901; "Half
   Populists"; Independent Democrats;
   Populists; Ratification; Referendum
Jelks, William D., 224 (n. 79); becomes
   governor, 250 (n. 1); on committee for
   ratification, 111; and election of 1900, 227
   (n. 98); and election of 1902, 145, 151, 258
   (n. 6); pledges to protect poor-white vote,
   225 (n. 82)
Jesus Christ (name invoked), 22, 104, 141; in
   opposition to constitution, 222 (n. 56). *See
   also* God
Jews, 12, 21, 168, 215 (n. 33), 237 (n. 17)
Jim Crow. *See* Segregation
John, Sam Will, 222 (n. 56)

Johnson, A. N., 82, 113
Johnson, Ed. M., 232 (n. 55)
Johnson, James Weldon, 17
Johnston, Joseph F., 20, 45, 59, 60, 222 (n. 56);
   and all-white primary, 144, 145, 151, 225
   (n. 86), 227 (n. 98), 258 (n. 6); black
   suspicion of, 113; early gubernatorial
   elections of, 32–33, 113, 131, 133; friendship
   of, with Denson, William H., 26; —, with
   DuBose, John Witherspoon, 37, 85; as "half
   Populist," 33, 114, 224 (n. 77); as owner of
   newspaper, 220 (n. 38); Populist support
   for, 33, 59, 224 (n. 77); position of, on
   constitutional convention, 32–42; —, on
   ratification, 111, 113, 114; and possible origins
   of disfranchisement myth, 255 (n. 60); and
   repeal of Enabling Act, 33–34; and senate
   election, 35–55, 226 (n. 90), 228 (n. 5), 258
   (n. 14); socioeconomic background of, 236
   (n. 8); use of patronage by, 224 (n. 77); white
   supremacy of, 36, 42. *See also* Democratic
   Party
Jones, Thomas Goode, 33; and calling of
   constitutional convention, 34; chairs
   executive committee at convention, 75;
   invokes children and posterity argument,
   94; as model Bourbon, 218 (n. 22); positions
   of, on race, 82, 113, 218 (n. 23); supports
   minority report, 91; vote of, on all-white
   primary, 151
Judas Iscariot, 34
Judge Lynch, 158. *See also* Lynching

Kantrowitz, Stephen, 211 (n. 13)
Keel, P. A. W., 254 (n. 55). See also *Gadsden-
   Etowah County People's Voice*
Kentucky, 224 (n. 74), 231 (n. 48)
Kentucky Brigade, 231 (n. 48)
Key, V. O., Jr.: on all-white primary, 144; and
   disfranchisement myth, 3, 13, 211 (n. 15), 212
   (n. 19); on emotion in southern politics,
   249 (n. 113); and "fait accompli" thesis, 3, 4,
   6–7, 210 (n. 4), 212 (n. 19); and formative
   influence of Civil War, 262 (n. 52); and
   Kousser, J. Morgan, 4; and Perman, Michael,
   6–7; and political skill of Black Belt, 10; on
   South and federal government, 262 (n. 52);
   and Webb, Samuel L., 8; and Woodward, C.
   Vann, 3, 210 (n. 4)

Property qualification, 24, 79, 81, 90, 108, 119,
   222 (n. 56). *See also* Alabama constitution of
   1901; Constitutional convention of 1901
Prostitution, 159
Protestants and paternalism, 218 (n. 23)
Psychology. *See* Politics of emotion
Purge movement, lily-white, 143–56. *See also*
   Republican Party, lily-white faction of, and
   disfranchisement

Rabinowitz, Howard N., 262 (n. 53)
Race, 10, 150, 156, 166, 167–71; and campaign
   to call convention, 63–70; and disfranchisement, 2, 4, 7, 9, 255 (n. 65); importance
   of, in thinking of poor whites, 60–63; as
   issue in 1896 gubernatorial election, 32–33;
   as issue in 1900 election, 45–46; as issue in
   1902 gubernatorial election, 227 (n. 98); as
   issue in railroad regulation, 266 (n. 93);
   as issue in women's suffrage, 263 (nn. 64,
   65); relationship of, to class and politics,
   8, 9–10, 11, 74, 87, 119–25, 137, 138–42, 156,
   214 (nn. 24, 31); —, to Reconstruction and
   the perversion of Alabama Progressivism,
   164–66; study of, 18–21, 245 (n. 92); and
   white man as the Negro's "best friend,"
   163; and "whiteness," 210 (n. 3). *See also*
   Blacks; Class; Constitutional convention
   of 1901; Disfranchisement; Education,
   spending of tax revenue for black; Politics
   of emotion; Poor whites; Privileged whites;
   Reconstruction syndrome
Race-based conformist citizenship, 150, 169,
   171, 241–42 (n. 55), 242 (n. 61), 243–44
   (n. 74), 245 (n. 92), 246 (n. 93), 247 (n. 99),
   254–55 (n. 58), 260 (n. 35); at constitutional
   convention, 101–5, 109–10, 244 (n. 78);
   defined, 101–2; modern-day, 226 (n. 92),
   249–50 (n. 113). *See also* Cultural conformity
   and conservatism; Morality; Morality-based
   conformist citizenship; Patriotism; Politics
   of emotion; Principle of moral reflection;
   Reconstruction syndrome
Racial accommodation. *See* Councill, William
   H.; Washington, Booker T.
Racism, 13, 19, 79, 137, 143, 167, 212 (n. 19),
   217 (n. 10); and alleged Northern purity,
   17, 264 (n. 73); and alleged odor of blacks,
   106, 117, 161; among antidisfranchisers, 7–8;

chamber-of-commerce type, 160, 216 (n. 9);
   emanating from the Black Belt, 214 (n. 31);
   as issue in 1900 senatorial election, 36; as
   issue related to Enabling Act of 1898, 34–35;
   and labor needs, 18; in the North, 15–17, 216
   (nn. 1, 9), 240 (n. 42), 250 (n. 115), 251 (n. 5),
   264 (n. 73); and paternalism not a form of
   civil rights, 94; of poor whites, 62, 105–6,
   109–10, 221 (n. 50), 248 (n. 106); price of,
   for whites, 170; and racial stereotypes, 38,
   56–57, 109–10, 120–21, 125, 163, 226 (n. 94),
   264 (n. 72); versus reason, 2; turn-of-the-
   century, 15–17; use of, in politics, 10, 11,
   12, 28–29, 96, 119–25. *See also* Alabama
   constitution of 1901; Anti-Democrats;
   Black Belt; Bourbons; Conservatism, and
   relationship to racism; Constitutional
   convention of 1901; Democratic Party;
   Disfranchisement; Fraud; Hill Country;
   Jeffersonian Democrats; Ku Klux Klan;
   Politics of emotion; Poor whites; Populists;
   Race; Reconstruction syndrome; Religion,
   invoked to justify racism; Republican Party;
   Segregation
Radicals. *See* Republican Party, during
   Reconstruction
Railroads, 29, 34, 74–75, 146, 165, 266 (n. 93)
Randolph County, 219 (n. 30); goes for
   Johnston, Joseph F., in 1896, 133; vote of, in
   April 1901, 73; —, in November 1901, 129
Randolph Toiler, 29, 33, 222 (n. 58)
Rape. *See* Lynching; Sexuality
Ratification, 111–42; black suspicions about
   antiratificationists, 113–14; children and
   posterity argument for, 122–23; God and
   country invoked for, 122–23; morality and
   sexuality as issue in, 120–21; and myth,
   133–42; partisan versus racial nature of, 122,
   125; and poor-white insistence on white
   supremacy, 114–15; poor-white opposition
   to, 111–15, 119–25; poor-white support
   for, 115–18, 119–25; Progressive support
   for, 250 (n. 1); race as issue in, 119–25;
   referendum vote and analysis of, 125–34.
   See also Referendum, November 1901, for
   ratification
Reason, 108. *See also* Politics of emotion
Reconstruction, 10, 34, 36, 66, 121, 165–66,
   171, 212 (n. 17), 219 (n. 33), 266 (n. 92);